T0325003

Innovative Machine Learning Applications for Cryptography

J. Anitha Ruth
SRM Institute of Science and Technology, India

G.V. Vijayalakshmi
BMS Institute of Technology and Management, India

P. Visalakshi
SRM Institute of Science and Technology, India

R. Uma
Sai Ram Engineering College, India

A. Meenakshi
SRM Institute of Science and Technology, India

A volume in the Advances in Computational
Intelligence and Robotics (ACIR) Book Series

Published in the United States of America by
   IGI Global
   Engineering Science Reference (an imprint of IGI Global)
   701 E. Chocolate Avenue
   Hershey PA, USA 17033
   Tel: 717-533-8845
   Fax: 717-533-8661
   E-mail: cust@igi-global.com
   Web site: http://www.igi-global.com

                  Library of Congress Cataloging-in-Publication Data

CIP Pending
ISBN: 979-8-3693-1642-9
EISBN: 979-8-3693-1643-6

This book is published in the IGI Global book series Advances in Computational Intelligence and Robotics (ACIR) (ISSN: 2327-0411; eISSN: 2327-042X)

British Cataloguing in Publication Data
A Cataloguing in Publication record for this book is available from the British Library.

For electronic access to this publication, please contact: eresources@igi-global.com.

Advances in Computational Intelligence and Robotics (ACIR) Book Series

Ivan Giannoccaro
University of Salento, Italy

ISSN:2327-0411
EISSN:2327-042X

MISSION

While intelligence is traditionally a term applied to humans and human cognition, technology has progressed in such a way to allow for the development of intelligent systems able to simulate many human traits. With this new era of simulated and artificial intelligence, much research is needed in order to continue to advance the field and also to evaluate the ethical and societal concerns of the existence of artificial life and machine learning.

The **Advances in Computational Intelligence and Robotics (ACIR) Book Series** encourages scholarly discourse on all topics pertaining to evolutionary computing, artificial life, computational intelligence, machine learning, and robotics. ACIR presents the latest research being conducted on diverse topics in intelligence technologies with the goal of advancing knowledge and applications in this rapidly evolving field.

COVERAGE

- Machine Learning
- Brain Simulation
- Computational Intelligence
- Algorithmic Learning
- Heuristics
- Computational Logic
- Pattern Recognition
- Adaptive and Complex Systems
- Cyborgs
- Artificial Life

IGI Global is currently accepting manuscripts for publication within this series. To submit a proposal for a volume in this series, please contact our Acquisition Editors at Acquisitions@igi-global.com or visit: http://www.igi-global.com/publish/.

Titles in this Series

For a list of additional titles in this series, please visit:
http://www.igi-global.com/book-series/advances-computational-intelligence-robotics/73674

Artificial Intelligence of Things (AIoT) for Productivity and Organizational Transition
Sajad Rezaei (University of Worcester, UK) and Amin Ansary (University of the Witwatersrand, South Africa)
Business Science Reference • © 2024 • 320pp • H/C (ISBN: 9798369309933) • US $275.00

Bio-inspired Swarm Robotics and Control Algorithms, Mechanisms, and Strategies
Parijat Bhowmick (Indian Institute of Technology, Guwahati, India) Sima Das (Bengal College of Engineering and Technology, India) and Farshad Arvin (Durham University, UK)
Engineering Science Reference • © 2024 • 300pp • H/C (ISBN: 9798369312773) • US $315.00

Deep Learning, Reinforcement Learning, and the Rise of Intelligent Systems
M. Irfan Uddin (Kohat University of Science and Technology, Pakistan) and Wali Khan Mashwani (Kohat University of Science and Technology, Pakistan)
Engineering Science Reference • © 2024 • 320pp • H/C (ISBN: 9798369317389) • US $300.00

Predicting Natural Disasters With AI and Machine Learning
D. Satishkumar (Nehru Institute of Technology, India) and M. Sivaraja (Nehru Institute of Technology, India)
Engineering Science Reference • © 2024 • 340pp • H/C (ISBN: 9798369322802) • US $315.00

Impact of AI on Advancing Women's Safety
Sivaram Ponnusamy (Sandip University, Nashik, India) Vibha Bora (G.H. Raisoni College of Engineering, Nagpur, India) Prema M. Daigavane (G.H. Raisoni College of Engineering, Nagpur, India) and Sampada S. Wazalwar (G.H. Raisoni College of Engineering, Nagpur, India)
Engineering Science Reference • © 2024 • 315pp • H/C (ISBN: 9798369326794) • US $315.00

Empowering Low-Resource Languages With NLP Solutions
Partha Pakray (National Institute of Technology, Silchar, India) Pankaj Dadure (University of Petroleum and Energy Studies, India) and Sivaji Bandyopadhyay (Jadavpur University, India)
Engineering Science Reference • © 2024 • 330pp • H/C (ISBN: 9798369307281) • US $300.00

AIoT and Smart Sensing Technologies for Smart Devices
Fadi Al-Turjman (AI and Robotics Institute, Near East University, Nicosia, Turkey & Faculty of Engineering, University of Kyrenia, Kyrenia, Turkey)
Engineering Science Reference • © 2024 • 250pp • H/C (ISBN: 9798369307861) • US $300.00

701 East Chocolate Avenue, Hershey, PA 17033, USA
Tel: 717-533-8845 x100 • Fax: 717-533-8661
E-Mail: cust@igi-global.com • www.igi-global.com

Table of Contents

Detailed Table of Contents

Preeti Mariam Mathews, MIT Mahaguru Institute of Technology, India
Anjali Sandeep Gaikwad, Bharati Vidyapeeth, India
Mathu Uthaman, Mahaguru Institute of Technology, India
B. Sreelekshmi, Mahaguru Institute of Technology, India
V. Dankan Gowda, BMS Institute of Technology and Management, India

Cryptography and machine learning are part of mega-tech today. The whole of this chapter is about digital currencies. This is what will happen in the encryption world. First, the authors show how to use PMBeast-1 for something and then later on with bitcoin cryptography where information privacy is concerned. The objective of cryptography is to make data impossible for a human eye by encryption so that only someone in possession of the secret key can determine their length. Yet cryptography is ancient. But actually, it's only within the last few hundred years that their methods and purpose have completely changed. Later parts of this chapter review some recent advances in areas such as symmetric and asymmetric encryption, public-key infrastructure (PKI), and cryptographic hashes. In this way, information becomes one's tutor—machine-like learning. The only difference is that we want these next-generation machines to understand the process of machine learning so as to enhance encryption systems.

Dankan Gowda V., BMS Institute of Technology and Management, India
Joohi Garg, Mody University of Science and Technology, India
Shaifali Garg, Amity Business School, Amity University, Gwalior, India
K. D. V. Prasad, Symbiosis Institute of Business Management, Symbiosis International
    University, India
Sampathirao Suneetha, Andhra University College of Engineering, Andhra University, India

Artificial intelligence (AI) and cryptography have recently made rapid progress respectively, forming a surprising mutual relationship. With the development of AI, it is now evolving to a point where an AI can study and even design cryptography systems. Cryptographic researchers are continually bringing out new ways to protect AI infrastructures from the ever-changing nature of attack, however. So, in this area, the authors examine the future topography and consider various possible ways these two breaking fields of study could meet up. Meanwhile, quantum computing and neuromorphic technology could push advanced

AI further than any computer has been able to go before. On the one hand, cryptographic methods also help keep AI models open, safe, and within legal privacy regulations even facing attack. In a nutshell, cutting-edge AI and cryptography research are together reinventing the frontier of internet security within artificial intelligence. What lies ahead? This chapter lays out the problems and prospects of this exciting intersection.

Cryptography is a technological term to protect a secret message or information. The practices of converting the normal text into unreadable form are called encryption. It is possible through key management. Artificial intelligence is a technology that supports all domain in decision making. Bio-inspired cryptography is bio-cryptography that can identify the human unique features and covert as a key and incorporate in the encryption process through artificial intelligence multiple bio-cryptographic keys that can be linked into a single key module with artificial intelligence decision-making support in the decryption part. Through decision-making support, exact and accurate authentication can be made possible.

Security functions which are present now, such as the SHA series of hash functions, other brute force prevention protocols, and much more, are keeping our cyber fields safe from any script-kiddies and professional hackers. But the recent study shows that penetration tools are optimised in numerous ways, enabling the hackers to take in a big advantage over our key logging and brute forcing prevention tactics, allowing them to make a clean hit over the fragile databases. Many of the existing domains now are optimised with the added benefit of artificial intelligence support. Specifically, the OpenAI API market has grown plentiful of their uses, and the password hash automation now has a time to get upgraded.

Machine learning is a powerful tool in both cryptosystem and cryptanalysis. Intrusion detection is a significant part of cyber defence plans where improvements are needed to deal with the challenges such as detection of false alarms, everyday new threats, and enhancing performance and accuracy. In this chapter, an optimized deep learning model is proposed to detect intrusion using whale optimization algorithm (WOA) with light gradient boosting machine (LightGBM) algorithm. To increase the performance of the model, the collected network data from the KDD dataset are pre-processed with feature selection and dimensionality reduction methods. The WOA-LightGBM algorithm processes the pre-processed data for training. The outcomes of these experiments are compared with the performance of benchmarking algorithms to prove that this intrusion detection model provides better performance and accuracy. The proposed model detects the intrusion with high accuracy in short period of time.

M. Indira, P.K.R. Arts College for Women (Autonomous), Gobichettipalayam, India
K. S. Mohanasundaram, P.K.R. Arts College for Women (Autonomous), Gobichettipalayam, India
M. Saranya, P.K.R. Arts College for Women (Autonomous), Gobichettipalayam, India

The intersection of machine learning and encryption has emerged as a key area in technology. A model shift in technology and data security has brought the combination of machine learning and encryption. In order to provide insight on the underlying algorithms and techniques, this survey was taken between the domains. It presents an overview of machine learning and cryptography algorithms. A wide variety of algorithms are examined in the field of machine learning. This survey also clarifies the interaction between machine learning and cryptography, demonstrating how these two fields work together to produce privacy-preserving ML, secure authentication, anomaly detection, and other benefits. A new era of data privacy and security has methods like secure multi-party computation (SMPC) and homomorphic encryption, which allow calculations on encrypted data. An updated overview of machine learning techniques used in cryptography is presented in this survey. The report offers recommendations for future study initiatives and summarizes the work.

R. Thenmozhi, SRM Institute of Science and Technology, India
D. Vetriselvi, SRM Institute of Science and Technology, India
A. Arokiaraj Jovith, SRM Institute of Science and Technology, India

Cryptography is the process of encrypting data or transforming plain text to ciphertext so that it can be deciphered only by appropriate key. Quantum cryptography employs quantum physics principles to encrypt and transport data in an unpackable manner. Quantum key distribution (QKD) is a technique for creating and exchanging private keys over quantum channels between two parties. Then, using standard cryptography, the keys can be used to encrypt and decrypt messages. Unbreakable encryption is something we really must have. The integrity of encrypted data is now in danger due to the impending development of quantum computers. Fortunately, quantum cryptography, via QKD, provides the answer we require to protect our information for a very long time to come. This is all based on the intricate principles of quantum mechanics. This chapter is discussing the various algorithms used and the applications of quantum cryptography.

Abirami M. S., SRM Institute of Science and Technology, India
Manoj Kushwaha, SRM Institute of Science and Technology, India

Rear-end collisions are a threat to road safety, so reliable collision avoidance technologies are essential. Traditional systems present several issues due to data loss and privacy concerns. The authors introduce an encrypted artificial neural network (ANN) method to prevent front-vehicle rear-end collisions. This system uses encryption techniques and ANN algorithm to recognize the front vehicle brake light in real time. Information can't be deciphered without the appropriate key using encryption. Intercepting data during transmission prevents reading. The system works day and night. ANN outperforms LR, SVM, DT, RF, and KNN in accuracy. An encrypted ANN-based ML model distinguishes between brake and normal signals. ANN accuracy was 93.7%. Driver receives further alerts to avoid rear-end collisions. This work proposes a lightweight, secure ANN-based brake light picture encryption method. The proposed approach may be applied to other collision circumstances, including side and frontal strikes. The technique would be more adaptable and applicable to many road safety circumstances.

Chapter 9

M. Sivasakthi, SRM Institute of Science and Technology, India
A. Meenakshi, SRM Institute of Science and Technology, India

Applying machine learning algorithms for encryption problems is reasonable in today's research connecting with cryptography. Using an encryption standard such as DES can give insight into how machine learning can help in breaking the encryption standards. The inspiration for this chapter is to use machine learning to reverse engineer hash functions. Hash functions are supposed to be tough to reverse one-way functions. The hash function will be learned by machine learning algorithm with a probability of more than 50%, which means the can develop their guesstimate of the reverse. This is concluded by executing the DES symmetric encryption function to generate N numerous values of DES with a set key and the machine learning algorithm is trained on a neural network to identify the first bit of the input based on the value of the function's output. Testing has ended through a new table, which was created similarly but with different inputs. The SVM runs on the new table, and it compares to the other table, and a confusion matrix is used to measure the excellence of the guesstimates.

Chapter 10

Neethu Krishna, SCMS School of Engineering and Technology, Karukutty, India
Kommisetti Murthy Raju, Shri Vishnu Engineering College For Women, India
V. Dankan Gowda, BMS Institute of Technology and Management, India
G. Arun, Erode Sengunthar Engineering College, India
Sampathirao Suneetha, Andhra University College of Engineering, Andhra University, India

In cryptography, performing computations on encrypted material without first decrypting it has long been an aspiration. This is exactly what homomorphic encryption (HE) accomplishes. By allowing computation on encrypted data, the associated privacy and security of sensitive information are beyond imagination to date. This chapter delves into the vast and intricate realm of HE, its fundamental theories, and far-reaching implications for machine learning. As a result of the sensitive nature of the data on which machine learning is based, privacy and security issues often arise. In this vein, homomorphic encryption, which allows algorithms to learn from and predict encrypted data, emerges as a possible panacea. The authors thus set out in this chapter to prepare the ground for a deeper understanding of that synergy, showing how it is there but also what lies ahead.

Chapter 11

Vijayalakshmi G. V. Mahesh, BMS Institute of Technology and Management, India

Authentication based on biometric technology is largely preferred in providing access control to the systems. This technology has gained wider attention due to the rise in data generation and the need of data security. The authentication depends upon the physiological traits of human such as face, fingerprint, hand geometry, iris scan, retinal scan, and voice. Depending upon the level of security required, a single trait or multiple traits could be utilized. The key features or patterns extracted from the biometric data play a significant role during authentication process that involves pattern recognition. That is, the patterns that exist in the database are matched with the patterns provided during log on. The access is provided based on complete match. Though biometry-based authentication systems provide an effective way of accessing the system, still it is affected by attacks that try to get unauthorized entry into the system. Thus, this chapter focuses on working with the methodologies that provide additional security to the biometric authentication system by utilizing encryption algorithm.

Chapter 12

S. Metilda Florence, SRM Institute of Science and Technology, India
Akshay Raghava, SRM Institute of Science and Technology, India
M. J. Yadhu Krishna, SRM Institute of Science and Technology, India
Shreya Sinha, SRM Institute of Science and Technology, India
Kavya Pasagada, SRM Institute of Science and Technology, India
Tanuja Kharol, SRM Institute of Science and Technology, India

Crypto ransomware presents an ever-growing menace as it encrypts victim data and demands a ransom for decryption. The increasing frequency of ransomware attacks underscores the need for advanced detection techniques. A machine learning classification model is proposed to identify ransomware families. These models utilize specific network traffic features, with a particular emphasis on analyzing the user datagram protocol (UDP) and internet control message protocol (ICMP). Importantly, this approach incorporates feature selection to enhance efficiency without compromising accuracy, resulting in reduced memory usage and faster processing times. The proposed experiment utilizes various machine learning algorithms, including decision trees and random forest, to create highly accurate models for classifying ransomware families. Furthermore, the experiment combined network traffic analysis with other sophisticated methods such as behavioral analysis and honeypot deployment to effectively scale crypto ransomware detection.

Chapter 13

M. Saranya, School of Computing, SRM Institute of Science and Technology, Kattankulathur, Chennai, India
B. Amutha, Computing, SRM Institute of Science and Technology, Kattankulathur, Chennai, India

Smart cities are emerging as a response to the growing need for urban housing, with the goal of improving residents' quality of life through the integration of innovative machine learning technology. For these "smart cities" to work, massive amounts of data need to be collected and analyzed for insights. However, due to the various and noisy nature of the data generated, only a small portion of the enormous smart city data that is collected is actually used. The capacity to process massive amounts of noisy, inaccurate data is a hallmark of artificial intelligence and state-of-the-art machine learning. There are numerous significant everyday uses for it, including healthcare, pollution prevention, efficient transportation, improved energy management, and security. Plus, this chapter presents the ideas and evaluations of numerous innovative machine learning algorithms for their particular applications.

    B. Prakash, Computing Technologies, School of Computing, SRM Institute of Science and Technology, India
    P. Saravanan, Computing Technologies, School of Computing, SRM Institute of Science and Technology, India
    V. Bibin Christopher, Computing Technologies, School of Computing, SRM Institute of Science and Technology, India
    A. Saranya, School of Computing, SRM Institute of Science and Technology, India
    P. Kirubanantham, Computing Technologies, School of Computing, SRM Institute of Science and Technology, India

Smart environments (SE) aim to improve daily comfort in the form of the internet of things (IoT). It starts many everyday services due to its stable and easy-to-use operations. Any real-world SE based on IoT architecture prioritises privacy and security. Internet of things systems are vulnerable to security flaws, affecting SE applications. To identify attacks on IoT smart cities, an IDS based on an iterative layered neuro-fuzzy inference network (ILNFIN) is presented. Initially the TON-IoT dataset was preprocessed, and the sparse wrapper head selection approach isolates attack-related features. The Iterative stacking neuro-fuzzy inference network classifies attacked data from the normal data. The asymmetric prime chaotic Rivest Shamir Adleman technique ensures the secure transmission of non-attacked data. To show the effectiveness of the suggested secure data transfer techniques, the authors compare their experimental results to existing approaches.

Preface

Machine learning stands at the forefront of technological advancements, offering unparalleled capabilities to analyze data trends and fortify the security of encryption and decryption systems. This reference book delves into the symbiotic relationship between machine learning, data analysis, and the intricate domain of cryptography.

Machine learning's prowess in constructing analytical models, automating processes, and adapting to vast datasets transforms the landscape of encryption and decryption. The association of machine learning approaches, such as boosting and mutual learning, with cryptosystems enables the generation of private cryptographic keys over public and potentially vulnerable channels. The inherent characteristics of machine learning approaches pave the way for the development of safer and more effective encryption and decryption methods, potentially mitigating the impact of human errors that could compromise organizational security.

The primary objective of this comprehensive reference book is to provide an extensive overview of recent theoretical and empirical work at the intersection of machine learning and cryptography. Readers will find relevant theoretical frameworks and the latest empirical research findings, shedding light on how machine learning can bolster encryption and decryption procedures by identifying and addressing data patterns that may expose vulnerabilities.

Addressing a diverse audience of students, professors, engineers, and scientists involved in cryptography and machine learning, this book offers valuable insights into the cross-pollination of ideas between these domains. The content explores realized concepts and untapped potentials, providing a rich resource for specialists, academics, and students working in cryptography, machine learning, and network security.

The thematic exploration spans various crucial topics within the field, including Encryption, Algorithm, Security, Elliptic Curve Cryptography, Cryptanalysis, Pairing-based Cryptography, Artificial Intelligence, Machine Learning, Authentication, Stream Cipher, Message Authentication, Homomorphism Encryption, Digital Signature Algorithm, Network Security, Quantum Cryptography, Biological Cryptography, and Neural Cryptography.

This reference book aspires to be a cornerstone for advancing knowledge in the intricate intersection of machine learning and cryptography, fostering innovation and understanding among professionals and enthusiasts alike.

ORGANIZATION OF THE BOOK

Chapter 1: Introduction to Modern Cryptography and Machine Learning

Authored by Preeti Mariam Mathews, Anjali Sandeep Gaikwad, Mathu Uthaman, Sreelekshmi B, and Dankan Gowda V, this chapter navigates the dynamic landscape of digital currencies within the realms of cryptography and machine learning. The exploration begins with the practical application of PM-Beast-1 and extends to the intricacies of Bitcoin Cryptography, emphasizing the pivotal role of information privacy. The chapter spans the historical evolution of cryptography, highlighting recent advances in symmetric and asymmetric encryption, public-key infrastructure (PKI), and cryptographic hashes. The authors draw connections between the age-old practice of cryptography and modern machine-like learning, envisioning next-generation machines adept at understanding the nuances of machine learning to fortify encryption systems.

Chapter 2: Future Outlook Synergies Between Advanced AI and Cryptographic Research

Dankan Gowda V, Joohi Garg, Shaifali Garg, KDV Prasad, and Sampathirao Suneetha delve into the rapidly progressing domains of artificial intelligence (AI) and cryptography. This chapter explores the surprising symbiosis between AI and cryptographic research, envisioning a future where AI not only studies but also designs cryptographic systems. The narrative probes into the challenges and possibilities at the intersection of these fields, contemplating the impact of quantum computing and neuromorphic technology. The authors shed light on how cryptographic methods contribute to maintaining the openness, safety, and legal privacy regulations of AI models, ultimately reshaping the frontier of internet security within the realm of artificial intelligence.

Chapter 3: Artificial Intelligence Supported Bio Cryptography Protection

Authored by Sriprasadh K, this chapter introduces the convergence of cryptography, artificial intelligence, and bio-inspired approaches. Focusing on the protection of secret messages or information, the chapter explores the integration of artificial intelligence to support decision-making in various domains. The innovative concept of bio-cryptography, utilizing human unique features as cryptographic keys, is discussed. The author highlights the role of artificial intelligence in linking multiple bio-cryptographic keys and enhancing security services through accurate authentication. This chapter presents a forward-looking perspective on leveraging artificial intelligence to fortify bio-inspired cryptographic methods.

Chapter 4: An Adaptive Cryptography Using OpenAI API: Dynamic Key Management Using Self-Learning AI

Valarmathi R, R. Uma, P. Ramkumar, and Srivatsan Venkatesh contribute a chapter that focuses on the integration of adaptive cryptography with the OpenAI API. Addressing the evolving landscape of security functions, the chapter highlights the vulnerabilities introduced by optimized penetration tools. The authors advocate for the adoption of Artificial Intelligence Support, particularly leveraging the OpenAI API, to upgrade password hash automation and enhance dynamic key management. The chapter underscores the need for adapting cryptographic techniques to counter evolving cyber threats and explores the potential of self-learning AI in key management processes.

Chapter 5: Optimized Deep Learning-Based Intrusion Detection Using WOA With LightGBM

Authored by Jayashree R and Venkata J, this chapter presents an optimized deep learning model for intrusion detection, utilizing the Whale Optimization Algorithm (WOA) with Light Gradient Boosting Machine (LightGBM) algorithm. Focusing on the challenges in cyber defense, the authors propose a model that preprocesses network data with feature selection and dimensionality reduction methods. The WOA-LightGBM algorithm is then employed for training, demonstrating superior performance compared to benchmarking algorithms. This chapter provides a comprehensive approach to enhancing intrusion detection through the integration of deep learning and optimization techniques, promising improved accuracy and efficiency.

Chapter 6: A Survey of Machine Learning and Cryptography Algorithms

INDIRA M, Mohanasundaram K S, and SARANYA M present a survey chapter that delves into the intersection of machine learning and encryption, shedding light on various algorithms and techniques. The authors provide an overview of machine learning algorithms and their applications in cryptography, emphasizing privacy-preserving machine learning, secure authentication, and anomaly detection. The survey captures the essence of the paradigm shift in data privacy and security, showcasing advancements such as Secure Multi-Party Computation (SMPC) and Homomorphic Encryption. The chapter serves as a valuable resource for understanding the contemporary landscape of machine learning techniques in cryptography.

Chapter 7: Quantum Cryptography: Algorithms and Applications

In this chapter, R Thenmozhi, Vetriselvi D and A Arokiaraj Jovith explore the fascinating realm of Quantum Cryptography. The authors delve into the foundational principles of quantum physics employed in encrypting and transporting data in an unpackable manner. The chapter particularly focuses on Quantum Key Distribution (QKD), a technique for creating and exchanging private keys over quantum channels. The authors emphasize the critical role of quantum cryptography in safeguarding encrypted data against potential threats from quantum computers. The chapter provides insights into various algorithms and applications within the context of quantum cryptography.

Chapter 8: Minimizing Data Loss by Encrypting Brake-Light Images and Avoiding Rear-End Collisions Using Artificial Neural Network

Authored by Abirami MS and Manoj Kushwaha, this chapter addresses road safety concerns related to rear-end collisions. The authors propose an encrypted artificial neural network (ANN) method to prevent such collisions, utilizing encryption techniques and ANN algorithms to recognize brake lights in real-time. The chapter emphasizes the security aspects of encryption, ensuring that information cannot be deciphered without the appropriate key. The proposed ANN-based model outperforms other algorithms in accuracy, providing further alerts to drivers and presenting a secure approach to collision avoidance. The work introduces a novel method for applying encryption in road safety scenarios.

Chapter 9: Machine Learning Techniques to Predict the Inputs in Symmetric Encryption Algorithm

Sivasakthi M and Meenakshi A contribute a chapter that explores the application of machine learning algorithms to predict inputs in symmetric encryption algorithms. Focusing on the challenge of reverse engineering hash functions, the authors use machine learning to learn and predict hash function outputs. The chapter details experiments involving the DES symmetric encryption function and a neural network trained to identify the first bit of the input based on the output value. The proposed approach presents an innovative perspective on leveraging machine learning for understanding and predicting inputs in encryption algorithms.

Chapter 10: Homomorphic Encryption and Machine Learning in the Encrypted Domain

Neethu Krishna, Kommisetti Murthy Raju, Dankan Gowda V, G. Arun, and Sampathirao Suneetha delve into the intricate world of homomorphic encryption (HE) and its synergies with machine learning. The chapter provides an in-depth exploration of HE, its fundamental theories, and implications for machine learning in the encrypted domain. With a focus on enhancing privacy and security in machine learning applications, the authors discuss the potential of HE to allow computation on encrypted data. The chapter aims to pave the way for a deeper understanding of the synergy between homomorphic encryption and machine learning, laying the groundwork for future advancements in this domain.

Chapter 11: An Effective Combination of Pattern Recognition and Encryption Scheme for Biometric Authentication System

Authored by Vijayalakshmi G V Mahesh, this chapter emphasizes the integration of pattern recognition and encryption in the realm of biometric authentication systems. The chapter underscores the significance of physiological traits for authentication and explores patterns extracted from biometric data during the authentication process. Recognizing the vulnerabilities of biometric systems to unauthorized access, the authors propose methodologies that enhance security through encryption algorithms. The chapter provides insights into achieving additional security in biometric authentication systems through the effective combination of pattern recognition and encryption schemes.

Chapter 12: Enhancing Crypto Ransomware Detection Through Network Analysis and Machine Learning

Metilda S, Akshay Raghava, Yadhu Krishna M J, Shreya Sinha, Kavya Pasagada, and Tanuja Kharol address the rising threat of crypto ransomware in this chapter. The authors propose a machine learning classification model for identifying ransomware families, focusing on specific network traffic features, especially within the User Datagram Protocol (UDP) and Internet Control Message Protocol (ICMP). The chapter incorporates feature selection to optimize efficiency without compromising accuracy. By combining network traffic analysis with behavioral analysis and honeypot deployment, the authors present a comprehensive approach to scale crypto ransomware detection. The work contributes to advanced techniques for detecting and mitigating the impact of crypto ransomware through network analysis and machine learning.

Chapter 13: A Survey of Innovative Machine Learning Approaches in Smart City Applications

Saranya M and Amutha B present a survey chapter that explores the application of innovative machine learning approaches in the context of smart cities. Recognizing smart cities as a response to urban housing needs, the chapter highlights the role of massive data collection and analysis for improving residents' quality of life. The authors delve into various machine learning algorithms and their applications across domains such as healthcare, pollution prevention, transportation, energy management, and security within smart cities. The chapter serves as a valuable resource for understanding the potential applications of innovative machine learning approaches in shaping the future of smart cities.

Chapter 14: Securing the IoT System of Smart Cities by Iterative Layered Neuro-Fussy Inference Network Classifier With Asymmetric Cryptography

Authored by Prakash B, Saravanan P, Bibin Christopher V, Saranya A, and Kirubanantham P, this chapter addresses the security challenges in Internet of Things (IoT) systems within smart cities. The authors present an Intrusion Detection System (IDS) based on an Iterative Layered Neuro-Fuzzy Inference Network (ILNFIN) to identify attacks on IoT smart cities. The chapter employs the asymmetric prime chaotic Rivest Shamir Adleman technique for secure data transmission. Through preprocessing the TON-IoT dataset and feature selection, the authors showcase the effectiveness of their proposed approach in securing IoT systems within smart cities. The chapter contributes to the growing body of knowledge on enhancing the security of IoT systems through the integration of neuro-fuzzy inference networks and asymmetric cryptography.

IN CONCLUSION

As editors of this comprehensive reference book, we find ourselves both delighted and invigorated by the rich tapestry of insights, innovations, and collaborations presented across its diverse chapters. The amalgamation of cryptography and machine learning, explored by esteemed authors in each section, has illuminated the evolving landscape where the security of information meets the dynamism of intelligent data analysis.

From the foundational chapters unraveling the historical context of cryptography to the cutting-edge applications like quantum cryptography and encrypted artificial neural networks, this compilation serves as a beacon for scholars, practitioners, and enthusiasts navigating the intricate intersection of machine learning and cryptography.

The varied perspectives showcased within these chapters underscore the symbiotic relationship between these two fields. We witness the transformation of traditional cryptographic practices through the lens of modern machine learning algorithms, offering novel approaches to encryption, authentication, and intrusion detection. The future outlook, as envisioned by our authors, unveils promising synergies between advanced AI, bio-inspired cryptography, and the fascinating realm of homomorphic encryption.

Each chapter serves as a testament to the dynamic nature of this interdisciplinary domain. The survey chapters provide invaluable summaries of the state-of-the-art, while the applied chapters showcase real-world implications, from securing IoT systems in smart cities to enhancing cybersecurity against crypto ransomware.

As editors, we extend our heartfelt gratitude to the esteemed authors who have contributed their expertise and insights to make this reference book a comprehensive and forward-looking resource. We hope this compilation sparks further exploration, research, and collaboration in the ever-evolving realms of machine learning and cryptography.

In the spirit of continuous learning and innovation, we invite readers to delve into the depths of this book, embracing the opportunities presented by the cross-pollination of ideas, and contributing to the ongoing narrative of progress in the fascinating confluence of machine learning and cryptography.

May this reference book inspire future generations of researchers, academics, and practitioners to unravel new dimensions in securing information and advancing the frontiers of technology.

J. Anitha Ruth
SRM Institute of Science and Technology, India

Vijayalakshmi G.V. Mahesh
BMS Institute of Technology and Management, India

P. Visalakshi
SRM Institute of Science and Technology, India

R. Uma
Sri Sai Ram Engineering College, India

A. Meenakshi
SRM Institute of Science and Technology, India

Chapter 1
Introduction to Modern Cryptography and Machine Learning

Preeti Mariam Mathews
MIT Mahaguru Institute of Technology, India

Anjali Sandeep Gaikwad
Bharati Vidyapeeth, India

Mathu Uthaman
Mahaguru Institute of Technology, India

B. Sreelekshmi
Mahaguru Institute of Technology, India

V. Dankan Gowda
ⓘ https://orcid.org/0000-0003-0724-0333
BMS Institute of Technology and Management, India

ABSTRACT

Cryptography and machine learning are part of mega-tech today. The whole of this chapter is about digital currencies. This is what will happen in the encryption world. First, the authors show how to use PMBeast-1 for something and then later on with bitcoin cryptography where information privacy is concerned. The objective of cryptography is to make data impossible for a human eye by encryption so that only someone in possession of the secret key can determine their length. Yet cryptography is ancient. But actually, it's only within the last few hundred years that their methods and purpose have completely changed. Later parts of this chapter review some recent advances in areas such as symmetric and asymmetric encryption, public-key infrastructure (PKI), and cryptographic hashes. In this way, information becomes one's tutor—machine-like learning. The only difference is that we want these next-generation machines to understand the process of machine learning so as to enhance encryption systems.

DOI: 10.4018/979-8-3693-1642-9.ch001

1. INTRODUCTION

In an era of technology so advancing by the nano-second that it is known as cutting edge only if you have a single letter hanging off it somewhere--the age itself seems to be mutating into a technical one. But among all this change two fields enjoy ascendancy over everything else; each field wields its power and potential according to its own particularity. The twin foundations that are transforming our digital world, machine learning (a technical subfield of artificial intelligence in which a computer does discoveries and creates new facts) lets the Internet learn from itself; cryptography is an age-old discipline for encrypting information. Their convergence represents a nexus of innovation and transformation, with profound implications for the realm of cybersecurity and beyond. In this chapter, we will explore the vast landscape of machine learning and the complex web of contemporary encryption. Our mission is twofold: to unravel the essential concepts and techniques that underlie these fields and to illuminate the extraordinary synergy that emerges at their intersection.

Cryptography and Cryptanalysis are two subfields of cryptology, the field that studies cryptosystems generally (Figure 1). The art and science of cryptography come together to build cryptosystems, which provide strong protection for sensitive data (M. N. Reza, and M. Islam, 2021). This field revolves around the practical aspect of safeguarding digital data, involving the design and implementation of mechanisms based on mathematical algorithms. These mechanisms serve as the foundation for essential information security services, effectively forming a versatile toolkit for security applications. In parallel, Cryptanalysis serves as the complementary counterpart to Cryptography within the realm of cryptology. While cryptography generates ciphertext for secure transmission or storage, cryptanalysis is concerned with the analysis and potential decryption of these cryptographic systems. Cryptanalysts study cryptographic mechanisms with the aim of breaking them, revealing vulnerabilities, and identifying weaknesses (Kumar, Pullela SVVSR, & Chaturvedi, Abhay, 2023). Additionally, cryptanalysis plays a crucial role in the development of new cryptographic techniques by rigorously testing their security strengths and assessing their resilience against potential attacks. These two branches, cryptography and cryptanalysis, coexist in the ongoing quest for information security and encryption advancements.

Figure 1. Context of cryptology

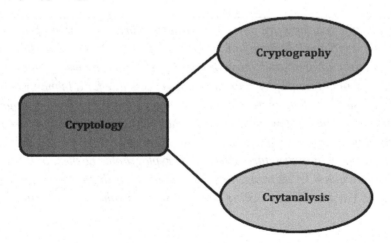

Cryptography: Safeguarding Secrets Through the Ages

The ancient practice of cryptography, dating back millennia, has been a silent sentinel guarding secrets and sensitive information from prying eyes. From the rudimentary ciphers of ancient civilizations to the complex algorithms of today, cryptography has evolved in response to the ceaseless quest for secure communication- (Kumar, R and B. Ashreetha, 2023). We traverse the annals of history, tracing the evolution of cryptographic methods and their pivotal role in wars, diplomacy, and espionage. Yet, it is in the contemporary digital age that cryptography finds its most significant challenges and opportunities. With the advent of symmetric and asymmetric encryption, the establishment of Public-Key Infrastructure (PKI), and the ubiquity of cryptographic hashing, we are compelled to explore the intricate mechanisms that safeguard our digital world. The inception of cryptography coincided with the development of written language. As human societies progressed, forming tribes, groups, and kingdoms, concepts such as power, warfare, dominance, and politics emerged. These ideas fueled the ever-changing landscape of encryption, which in turn fueled people's natural inclination to communicate discreetly with chosen receivers (S. Tan, B. Knott and D. J. Wu, 2021). The ancient Egyptians used hieroglyphs for encrypted communication some 4000 years ago, which is the first known application of cryptography. This code remained the exclusive knowledge of scribes entrusted with transmitting messages on behalf of kings. The use of basic mono-alphabetic substitution ciphers was subsequently adopted by intellectuals between 500 and 600 BC. The secret rule that allowed one to decode the original message was used as a replacement for letters inside the message using this approach (P. H. Kumar and T. Samanta, 2022). One well-known early Roman cryptography system was the Caesars Shift Cipher, which included moving a message's characters around by a certain number, usually three. To get the original message back, the receiver would have to move the characters backwards by the same amount (Figure 2).

Figure 2. Oldest cryptographic technique

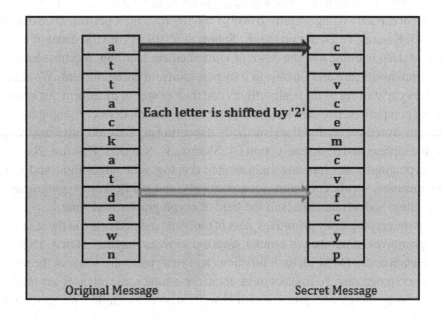

While both encryption and steganography aim to hide information, steganography adds an extra degree of complexity. With this method, we want to make sure that no one outside of the intended recipients knows that sensitive information is hidden away(A.Singla, N. Sharma, 2022). Invisible watermarking is a prime example. By design, steganography ensures that the observer of the data is utterly oblivious to the fact that it contains secret information. Cryptography, on the other hand, usually allows an attacker to deduce that data is being communicated, albeit in a coded or jumbled form, since they may see the message in some form that is encrypted (Figure 3).

Figure 3. Steganography (invisible watermarking)

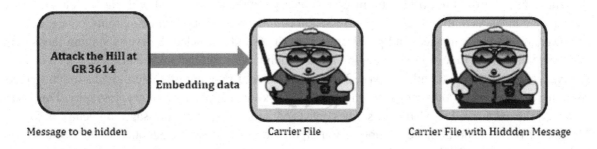

Machine Learning: The Quest for Intelligence in Data

In parallel, machine learning stands as a testament to the potential of artificial intelligence. It bestows upon computers the remarkable ability to learn, adapt, and make informed decisions by discerning patterns in data. Our journey through machine learning begins with an exploration of its core principles, revealing the inherent capacity of algorithms to evolve and improve their performance through exposure to empirical data(G. Karatas, O. Demir and O. K. Sahingoz, 2019). From the dawn of neural networks to the resurgence of deep learning and the dawn of reinforcement learning, machine learning has redefined industries, from healthcare and finance to transportation and entertainment. We shine a spotlight on the extraordinary capabilities of these algorithms and their power to transform our world. The figure 4 provides a visual comparison between classic cryptography and modern cryptography.

Classic cryptography represents traditional methods of securing information, often involving techniques such as substitution ciphers and basic encryption (A. Sharma, K. S and M. R. Arun, 2022). Conversely, state-of-the-art cryptography incorporates sophisticated cryptographic algorithms and methodologies, such as digital signatures, secure communication protocols, and public-key cryptography. This figure illustrates the evolution and advancements in the field of cryptography over time.

Figure 5 depicts the cryptography primitives, a set of tools and methods used in the area. By selectively exploiting these primitives, a number of crucial security services may be offered. Digital signatures, message authentication codes (MACs), hash functions and encryption are some of the most significant building blocks for cryptography. To find out more about these topics, as well as many others in modern-day information security theory and practice visit H million at www.etoilegenieecom G. Govardhana

Figure 4. Traditional cryptography vs. contemporary cryptography

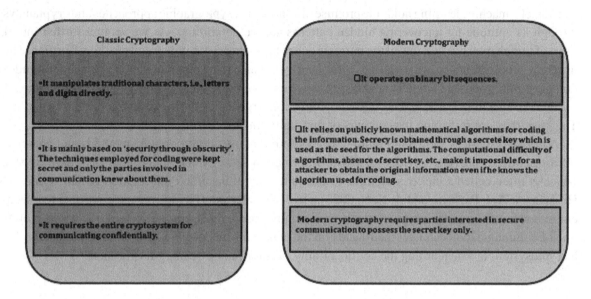

Figure 5. Cryptography primitives

Primitive Sevice	Encrption	Hash Function	MAC	Digital Signature
Confidentiality	Yes	No	No	No
Integrity	No	Sometimes	Yes	Yes
Authentication	No	No	Yes	Yes
Non Reputation	No	No	Sometimes	Yes

Reddy & K. Raghavendra (2022), In most security environments, these components are a very important part of premises for data and sys-tem protection against jamming, tampering or removal.

The Confluence of Cryptography and Machine Learning

Where everything thickens, however is where the nexus of cryptography and machine learning lies. This cross-fertilization has created thrilling prospects in recent years, while at the same time raising tremendous obstacles. But because they are inevitably sources of sensitive data, learning machines require the use of encryption to shield such information from peeping eyes and hackers (A. Musa & A Mahmood, 2021). Conversely, machine learning holds the promise of enhancing cryptographic approaches and cryptanalysis through its aptitude for uncovering hidden patterns and vulnerabilities. As we venture further into the heart of this chapter, we will unveil the intricate dance between cryptography and machine learning. Their interplay promises not only to redefine cybersecurity but also to inspire innovation across a multitude of domains. Join us on this intellectual odyssey as we explore the intricacies of modern cryptography, the wonders of machine learning, and the captivating convergence of these two extraordinary disciplines. Together, they are reshaping the contours of our digital future.

A cryptosystem, as shown in Figure 6, is a system that uses cryptographic methods and associated infrastructure to provide services related to information security. The main goal of a cryptosystem, which is often called a cipher system, is to guarantee that transmitted information remains secret (N. Hussain, A. A. J. Pazhani, and A. K. N, 2023). Here, a sender wants to deliver sensitive data to a recipient in a safe way, and the cryptosystem's architecture ensures that anyone trying to eavesdrop on the line of communication can't get their hands on the data. This model showcases the fundamental role of a cryptosystem in safeguarding the confidentiality of information during transmission.

Figure 6. Model of a cryptosystem

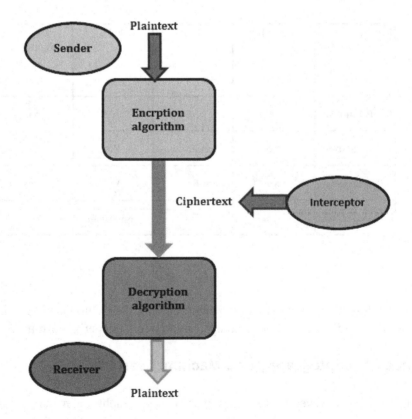

1.1 Understanding Cryptography

In the digital age, the importance of cryptography in safeguarding sensitive information cannot be overstated. This section offers an in-depth exploration of cryptography, its historical evolution, and the pivotal role it plays in modern-day cybersecurity. We also delve into the various types of cryptographic algorithms and elucidate how they function to ensure secure communication.

In this figure 7, the essential elements that constitute a basic cryptosystem are illustrated. These components work in tandem to enable the secure transmission and protection of sensitive information.

Figure 7. Components of a basic cryptosystem

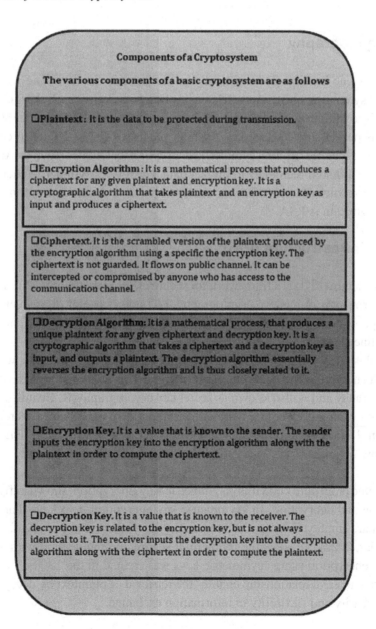

1.2 A Journey Through History

Cryptography is a practice with an ancient lineage, and as the needs of human societies change it has changed its face many times. We start our story at the earliest days, when civilizations such as those of Egypt and Greece used simple encryption methods to discourage people from meddling with confidential messages. Cryptography has always been used covertly in war, diplomacy and espionage (Shivashankar & S. Mehta 2016). Julius Caesar, for example, used the famous Caesar cipher to encrypt his private correspondence. In fact, the real breakthrough in terms of cryptography occurred during World War II when mechanical and electromechanical ciphering machines like the Enigma machine appeared. These devices posed unprecedented difficulties for Allied codebreakers to overcome.

1.3 Modern Cryptography

The cryptographic scene has changed drastically in the last few decades. The world of cryptography now includes both symmetric and asymmetric encryption techniques, each designed to suit a different environment. With asymmetric encryption, one key is private and the other public; with symmetric encryption there is only a single secret key for both processes (L. R. Knudsen och J. E. Mathiassen 2000). We go into the specifics of how symmetric encryption techniques, such as Advanced Encryption Standard (AES), use a shared secret key to protect data. However, asymmetric encryption schemes use the mathematical properties of large prime numbers to permit safe communication free from a common secret. One such algorithm is RSA.

1.4 Public-Key Infrastructure (PKI)

Public-Key Infrastructure (PKI) is a framework for secure electronic communication and digital identity verification that forms part of modern cryptography. PKI makes use of digital certificates, which pair public keys with people or institutions. We examine the inner workings of PKI, and how it serves as a foundation for online commerce.

This figure 8 illustrates Symmetric Key Encryption, a cryptographic process where the same key is employed for both encrypting and decrypting information. This area of study falls under the domain of symmetric cryptography and is also known as secret key cryptography(R. Beaulieu, D. Shors, J. Smith, 2018) . The transmitter and receiver in a symmetric cryptosystem must share a secret key in order for the system to function. Digital Decryption Standard (DES), Triple-DES (3DES), IDEA, and BLOWFISH are a few well-known symmetric key encryption algorithms that effectively secure data using symmetric key cryptography.

The cryptographic procedure known as Asymmetric Key Encryption, shown in figure 9, uses separate keys for encrypting and decryption. In asymmetric key encryption, two keys that are mathematically linked but distinct are employed, as opposed to one key in symmetric key encryption (P. Gope, O. Millwood and B. Sikdar, 2022). To solve the problem of secure communication without pre-shared secret keys, a method of encryption using asymmetric keys was created in the 1900s. Despite the keys being different, their mathematical relationship enables the retrieval of plaintext by decrypting ciphertext, offering enhanced security and flexibility in information exchange.

Figure 8. Symmetric key encryption

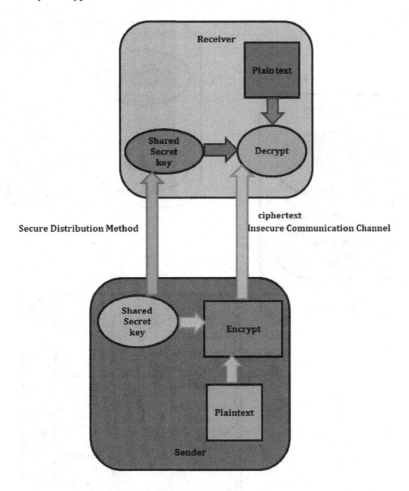

1.5 Cryptographic Hash Functions

Cryptographic hashing is another integral aspect of modern cryptography. We elucidate the role of cryptographic hash functions, which transform variable-length input data into fixed-length strings of characters. These functions are used for data integrity check, password storage and digital signatures. This section presents a detailed review of cryptographic algorithms. It outlines the principles and existing applications in real life (Kumaraswamy & Gupta, Anand Kumar 2023). Readers will become familiar with how cryptography has developed from ancient practices to sophisticated mathematical algorithms, an essential pillar of modern cybersecurity.

2. THE NEED FOR MODERN CRYPTOGRAPHY

Internet use is proliferating, complexity abounds-in an age where information flows ceaselessly across the digital highways of the world, it's never been more important to ensure secure communications.

Figure 9. Asymmetric key encryption

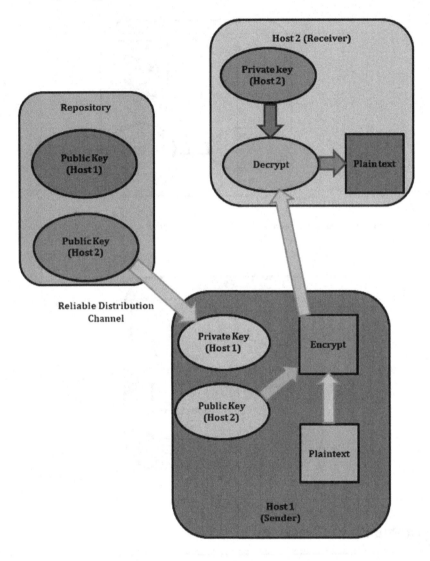

This part explores how the need to protect our data and channels for communication is increasingly greater, pointing out that traditional cryptography doesn't have a solution. Beginning now with modern cryptography we can solve today's problems in security issues.

2.1 The Era of Digital Ubiquity

The digital age has brought about an unparalleled era of interdependence. Through online banking, e-commerce and telemedicine; to social networking--the internet has become part of our everyday life. But the digital ubiquity has also seen a breed of new threats emerge. Cyberattacks, data breaches and identity theft are now commonplace incidents backed by powerful forces that remind us how essential effective security systems have become.

2.2 The Limits of Traditional Cryptography

Traditional cryptographic methods, while still a solution to the intricacies of contemporary digital communication when they were first designed for use in this medium may indeed not remain so. Symmetric encryption makes use of shared secret keys (K.D.V., Gite, Pratik, Sivakumar 2023). Such a method requires the secure exchange of keys between communicating parties, which is another weak link exploited by perpetrators who constantly check for weaknesses.

The transmission and storage of large amounts of data are two obstacles that traditional cryptography has difficulty dealing with. The massive growth of data and the coming quantum threat mean a crisis for classical encryption. Our trusted time-hallowed cryptographic algorithms, which have served us well for decades will eventually be brought to their knees by the arrival of quantum computing.

2.3 Modern Cryptography: A Necessity

Modern cryptography has emerged as the necessary technology to burnish our digital ramparts. Its innovative technology and powerful encryption algorithms overcome the functional shortcomings of traditional methods.

A principal advantage of modern cryptography is the use of asymmetric encryption, which requires two different keys for encryption and decryption. This eliminates the need for safe key exchange, and solves a problem with symmetric encryption. ECC and RSA, prime examples of asymmetrical encryption in practice. Moreover, with the application of cryptographic hashing and digital signatures modernized crypto can enhance data integrity and authentication (S. Zhu & Y. Han 2021). These methods are important in proving the authenticity of digital documents, and to keep data intact during transmission.

2.4 Quantum-Resistant Cryptography

Not only that, modern cryptography takes this one step further by including such quantum-resistant algorithms. In the post-quantum world our data will be safe because these encryption methods are immune to quantum computers 'calculating power. This is particularly important, since quantum computers (once they are realized in full) will have the power to break conventional cryptographic systems within seconds. This is a weakness in modern cryptography. It prepares us for the quantum age.

In summary, the digital age requires a change in paradigm with regard to security and communications. While they have a long and honored history, traditional cryptographic methods are inadequate for protecting our digital lives. The next generation of cryptography, featuring new attacks and tailored algorithms that can withstand the onslaught of quantum computers, becomes a must-have defense against rapidly changing dangers. In the course of this chapter, we will dive into these state-of-the art cryptographic techniques in detail and reveal their central place at regents junction between cryptography and machine learning.

3. COURSES IN MACHINE LEARNING

Let us now enter the world of machine learning, where ways to teach computers how to learn and make judgments have dramatically changed. Many universities offer courses in machine learning these days, and anyone can emerge to wield data like a sword or shield. As a result, we will examine the essentials of supervised learning, unsupervised learning and reinforcement. Second, consider that machine data blood.

3.1 The Unveiling of Machine Learning

Artificial intelligence is concerned with thinking in new ways about problems and decision-making; one of its offshoots is machine learning. In other words, through a process of digging out patterns from the data--using what is found or changing to adapt as needed--and then based on precedent (a similar experience), making predictions and judgements, machine learning allows a computer to learn things all by itself. It converts data into actionable information and opens up an infinite new world to many fields.

3.2 The Trio of Learning Paradigms

Machine learning encompasses three primary learning paradigms, each with its own unique applications and characteristics:

Supervised Learning: Supervised learn ing is one of the methods in which labeled data (data that already has ($ continue) The principle behind this algorithm is to map the input into an output. It is useful in image category classification, spam detection and translation.

Unsupervised Learning: The study of patterns and structures within unlabeled data is called unsupervised learning. For example, clustering similar data points and dimensionality reduction in large datasets are examples of applications that fit this paradigm.

Reinforcement Learning: Reinforcement learning takes inspiration from behavioral psychology, where agents learn to interact with an environment to maximize a reward signal. It finds applications in fields like robotics, gaming, and autonomous systems, enabling machines to learn and adapt through trial and error.

3.3 The Data Fueling Machine Learning

At the heart of every machine learning endeavor lies a fundamental truth: data is the lifeblood of the process. The quality, quantity, and relevance of data directly impact the performance and accuracy of machine learning models. Machine learning algorithms rely on vast datasets to uncover patterns, make predictions, and optimize decision-making(P. Pavankumar, N. K. Darwante, 2022). The importance of data cannot be overstated. It serves as the raw material from which machine learning models extract knowledge. Through the careful collection, cleaning, and preprocessing of data, we empower these algorithms to distill insights, identify trends, and ultimately drive informed decision-making. In the absence of sufficient and high-quality data, machine learning models falter. Erroneous predictions, biased outcomes, and suboptimal performance become the norm. Therefore, data engineering and data governance are essential components of any machine learning initiative, ensuring that the data used for training and testing is representative, unbiased, and reliable.

3.4 Unlocking the Potential of Machine Learning Courses

As machine learning continues to proliferate across industries, the demand for skilled practitioners grows in tandem. Machine learning courses, offered by academic institutions and online platforms, provide individuals with the knowledge and tools to harness the potential of this transformative technology. These courses offer a structured curriculum covering the theoretical foundations of machine learning, hands-on experience with popular machine learning libraries and frameworks, and real-world projects to apply newfound knowledge. Whether you are a data scientist seeking to sharpen your skills or a newcomer eager to explore the world of machine learning, these courses provide a pathway to expertise(Suryawanshi and Abhay Chaturvedi, 2022). In a nutshell, machine learning is an evolving discipline that can deliver what the data has to say. Robust, well-curated data undergirds the triad of supervised learning paradigms; unsupervised and reinforcement. This is machine learning's power to revolutionize. During this chapter, we will take a closer look at the applications and breakthroughs emerging between machine intelligence and cryptography.

4. CONVERGENCE OF CRYPTOGRAPHY AND MACHINE LEARNING

Cryptography and machine learning share an intriguing point of intersection where data-driven brain power collides with the needs for security and privacy. So let's take a closer look at how machine learning can be used with cryptography. Its complexities and pros we weigh alike. Even better, real life examples show that there is great practical value to this convergence.

4.1 Challenges and Benefits of Integration

Cryptography using machine learning has many advantages and disadvantages that must be shouldered. However, machine learning can also lead to a cracking of the cryptographic code. Murder solving Even send key control; cryptanalysis which decrypts the cipher texts. But this assimilation is not without its problems. But the safety of machine learning models is especially relevant to cryptographic applications. Because inside hidden in machine-learning algorithms are vulnerabilities which the malicious actor can take advantage of once it pleases.

In addition, balancing the computational needs of machine learning against those of cryptography is no easy matter. Nonetheless, the hope of this convergence could bring with it better security protocols and more effective cryptographic algorithms.

4.2 Real-World Examples

In practice, examples of the cryptography-machine learning nexus provide real food for thought about the potency of such linkages. For instance, in cryptographic systems one uses machine learning for intrusion detection. These machine learning models analyze patterns of network traffic to detect abnormal behavior, safeguarding cryptographic protocols from attacks. Another interesting application is the use of machine learning in computer passwords. Using the power of machine learning algorithms, organizations can enhance their policies for passwords and strengthen authentication methods. They will also be able to detect cases where a thief has already hatched into an egg (indicating that your company is in serious trouble), or they can figure out whether you just had three eggs at breakfast this morning through analysis of what kind of dishes its brethren around it have.

Today, information is the energy that powers just about everything companies do and nearly all aspects of human life. Therefore, keeping vital data safe from criminals 'actions and attacks is becoming an absolute necessity. The various information-related threats should be looked into. There are two primary ways to classify these assaults, depending on the activities taken by the attacker: include passive assaults (Figure 10) and active assaults (Figure 11).

Figure 10. Passive attacks

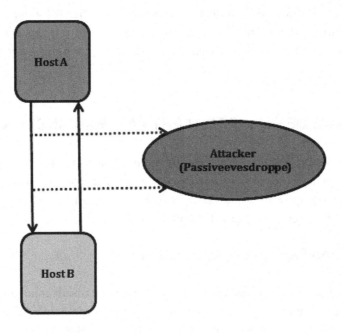

Figure 11. Active attacks

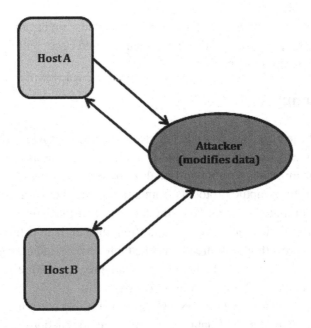

Making changes to data directly represents the characteristic of active attacks. Passive assaults, on the other hand, entail gaining unauthorized access to information without changing it in any way. Passive attacks, for instance, include bugging and monitoring communications lines. These are examples of passive behaviors. They don't change the data and they don't interfere with transmission. But a passive attack is really more like data theft. Perhaps the most significant difference between data theft and ordinary stealing of tangible items lies in that when some one's personal information has been stolen, although it may have become crippled due to forgery or other means, its owner still remains its legitimate rightful holder. It means that information attacks pass unnoticed for a long time, becoming more insidious than theft. In contrast, active attacks involve changing the information in some way by running it through various processes. In contrast to passive attacks, actively modifying or destroying information is the object of these attacks. Passive and active attacks are both a threat to information. While the former can often show up as more immediate, visible consequences; it is essential that strong security measures prevent either from hurting data integrity.

4.3 Opportunities for Innovation and Advancement

This union of cryptography and machine learning paves many paths towards innovation. A means of integrating cryptography and machine learning Leaving the old behind, many times over. Combining cryptography with machine learning yields all manner of prospects for KKLs to develop and build further. The development of post-quantum cryptographic algorithms is one area offering hope. An increasingly pressing question is whether machine learning can help devise encryption methods resistant to attack by quantum computers, as the technology for such machines develops.

Two privacy-preserving methods, secure multi-party computing and homomorphic encryption offer great potentials for machine learning. Through extending these kinds of techniques in machine learning, the ability to do calculations on encrypted data without compromising indeed sensitive information is possible. In addition, the applicability of machine learning to cryptographic key management can give rise to stronger and economical approaches for secure generation, distribution and retention of keys. In summary, the combination of cryptography and machine learning certainly has great potential to remodel our digital security and privacy. Despite these challenges, the benefits and opportunities for innovation are considerable. As we move through this chapter, we will examine particular applications as well as how machine learning is helping to improve the discipline of cryptography. This contributes in turn toward a safer and data-driven future.

5. MACHINE LEARNING-BASED CRYPTANALYSIS

The combination of cryptography and machine learning has enormous potential. Great potential exists for research into post-quantum cryptographic algorithms. However, given the rapid development of quantum computer technology machine learning can be used to design encryption algorithms not vulnerable to a future quantum computer.

From such a perspective, the field of machine learning-supported cryptoanalysis is one frontline in the battle between artificial intelligence and encryption. But what are the benefits and drawbacks of using machine learning in cryptanalysis? In order to give you some idea of precisely how much computerized algorithms have affected the relationship between a man and his work, we provide several case examples.

5.1 The Machine Learning and Cryptanalysis

Cryptanalysis, the art of cracking cryptographic codes and deciphering encrypted messages, is a cat-and-mouse game between code makers and code breakers that dates back more than 40 centuries. Machine learning is a new power player in this arena. Cryptanalysis is all about pattern recognition and inference, skills which are core to machine learning algorithms.

5.2 Advantages of Machine Learning in Cryptanalysis

Efficiency: Machine learning algorithms can greatly speed up the process of cryptanalysis. Unlike conventional procedures that are forced to laboriously pore over the whole solution area, a computer operated by industrial machine learning can easily discover potential solutions.

Pattern Recognition: A particular strength of machine learning is drawing fine distinctions from within larger sets. This ability exists in cryptanalysis and can be used to discover chinks in the encryption armour, reconstruct clues from vulnerabilities or even predict key combinations.

Adaptability: But adversaries adapt their encryption techniques and tactics, so that machine learning models must follow suit. This adaptability is essential in the ever-changing field of cryptography.

5.3 Disadvantages and Challenges

Data Dependency: Thus in cryptanalysis, whether or not machine learning techniques work depends more on the state of training data. If data is insufficient, machine learning models can underperform.

Computational Resources: Deep learning is one of the most processing intensive types of machine-learning. This could be a stumbling block for cryptanalysts working in environments with few resources or no access to HPC.

Ethical Considerations: The use of machine learning in cryptanalysis also creates ethical questions about privacy and security.Techniques that might affect the security of encrypted information must be treated with extreme care.

5.4 Real-World Breakthroughs

Already machine learning-based cryptanalysis is making remarkable progress in the field of encryption. Here are some notable examples:

5.4.1 AES Key Recovery

A machine learning-based attack on the Advanced Encryption Standard (AES) was demonstrated by researchers in 2017. They could then train a neural network to search for similar patterns in ciphertext and the corresponding plain text; using this, they were able to recover AES encryption keys with speed and accuracy unprecedented there before. This breakthrough exposed AES's weakness vis-a-vis machine learning attack methods, and spurred the development of stronger security models. Shift Cipher The described cryptosystem is one of the simplest kinds of substitution cipher schemes. How it works The Caesar Cipher, frequently employed with a shift of three to create cipher text, simply substitutes each letter in the plain by another possible one. This encryption key is a "secret shift number" from 0 to 25 which the sender and recipient decide on between themselves.

Figure 12 shows the Shift Cipher method broken down: A first step in encryption is that the sender uses a sliding ruler placed under an original set of plaintext characters, moving it left by the secret shift-specified number of positions. Next, use the sliding ruler beneath to find the ciphertext letter that matches to the plaintext letter. The word "tutorial" would become "WXWRULDO" with a three-position shift, for instance. The following graphic depicts the cipher text alphabet for a 3-shift Shift Cipher. Cryptographic systems of today differ from its alphabetic predecessors in that they express digital data as sequences of binary digits (bits). To encrypt and process these binary strings, symmetric encryption

Figure 12. Process of shift cipher

Plaintext Alphabet	Ciphertext Alphabet	Ciphertext Alphabet	Plaintext Alphabet	Plaintext Alphabet	Ciphertext Alphabet
a	D	A	x	a	K
b	E	B	y	b	D
c	F	C	z	c	G
d	G	D	a	d	F
e	H	E	b	e	N
f	I	F	c	f	S
g	J	G	d	g	L
h	K	H	e	h	V
i	L	I	f	i	B
j	M	J	g	j	W
k	N	K	h	k	A
l	O	L	i	l	H
m	P	M	j	m	E
n	Q	N	k	n	X
o	R	O	l	o	J
p	S	P	m	p	M
q	T	Q	n	q	Q
r	U	R	o	r	C
s	V	S	p	s	P
t	W	T	q	t	Z
u	X	U	r	u	R
v	Y	V	s	v	T
w	Z	W	t	w	Y
x	A	X	u	x	I
y	B	Y	v	y	U
z	C	Z	w	z	O

schemes are employed. These schemes can be classified into two main categories based on how they handle binary strings:

Block Ciphers: Bits or blocks of a certain size are used to encrypt and decrypt plaintext binary data in the Block Cipher algorithm. By applying a sequence of cryptographic operations on a chosen block of plaintext bits, we may convert it into a matching block of ciphertext bits. The fixed and fixed-in-prediction block size does not change. Data Encryption Standard (DES) and Advanced Encryption Standard (AES) are two popular encryption algorithms with 64-bit and 128-bit block sizes, respectively.

Stream Ciphers: Stream Cipher is a method that processes the plaintext bit by bit. This method requires bit-by-bit execution of cryptographic operations on the plaintext in order to generate a single bit of ciphertext. Stream ciphers are ideal for encryption data streams in immediate communication since, technically speaking, they are merely a kind of block cipher with a block size of one bit.

Figure 13 provides an overview of these two main categories of modern symmetric key encryption, highlighting the essential differences in their data processing approaches.

The Feistel Cipher, a fundamental cryptographic design model, serves as the blueprint for numerous block ciphers, with DES (Data Encryption Standard) being a notable example. The encryption and decryption processes of a cryptographic system that relies on Feistel Ciphers are executed by the same

Figure 13. Modern symmetric key encryption

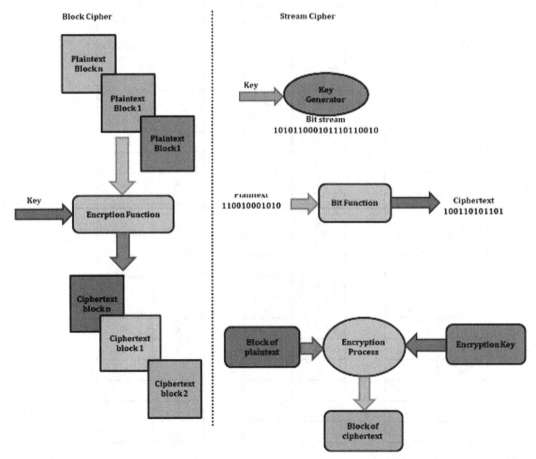

algorithm. As shown in Figure 14, the method of encryption within this framework is composed of numerous rounds, with each round including a "substitution" phase and a permutation step. The input block is split in half, L for left half and R for right half, at the beginning of each round. The right half (R) stays the same from round to round, whereas the left half (L) changes depending on R and the key used for encryption. In order to accomplish this change, we use an encrypting function 'f,' which accepts two arguments, R and the key (K), and returns f(R, K). Then, L is XORed with this output. The next step is a permutation that finishes a "round" by exchanging the changed L for the original R. The exact design of the cipher dictates the number of rounds. The last step in creating the ciphertext block is to join the R and L subblocks together once all rounds have finished. In DES and other realistic implementations, round-dependent subkeys are created from the original key instead of employing the complete decryption key in each round. While all of the subkeys are tied to the original encryption key, this guarantees that a new key is used in each cycle. Designing a Feistel Cipher poses the challenge of selecting a suitable round function 'f.' This function must possess specific properties to ensure the cipher's security, a topic that extends beyond the scope of this discussion.

Figure 14. Feistel block cipher

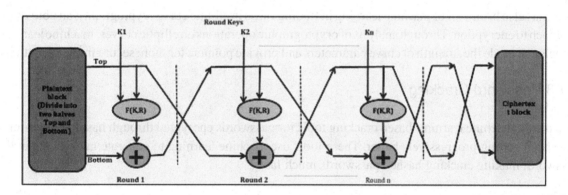

Decryption in the Feistel Cipher follows a process quite similar to encryption, with a few key distinctions. The Feistel structure starts with the ciphertext block rather than the plaintext block. Moving further, the procedure is identical to encryption, as mentioned before. Importantly, decryption and encryption are quite similar; however, there is a major difference in the use of subkeys, which are used in the opposite sequence during decryption. Last but not least, the Feistel Cipher's last swap of 'L' and 'R' is a crucial phase that is the same in encryption and decryption. Without this critical step, the decryption of the generated ciphertext using the original method would fail. How many rounds a Feistel Cipher uses is dependent on how secure the system has to be. Encryption and decryption get slower as the number of rounds increases, but security is improved. Therefore, a compromise between speed and safety dictates the total number of rounds. One prominent use of the Feistel Cipher is the Data Encryption Standard (DES), a block cipher with a symmetric key developed by the National Institute of Technology and Standards (NIST). The block size of DES is 64 bits, and it uses a 16-round Feistel structure. Even though there are 64 bits in the key, DES only uses 56 bits since 8 of those bits are check bits and aren't used by the encryption process. Figure 15 provides a general overview of the structure of DES.

Figure 15. Data encryption standard

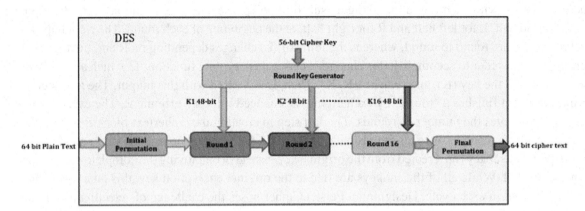

5.4.2 Elliptic Curve Cryptography (ECC) Vulnerability

There has also been uses of machine learning in finding flaws in elliptic curve cryptography, an ubiquitous approach to encryption. Through analysis of cryptographic operations on elliptic curves, machine learning models can grade the strength of curve parameters and provide pointers for more secure implementations.

5.4.3 Password Cracking

As a result, machine learning-based cracking tools for passwords encrypted through hashing algorithms have been getting progressively better. These tools use machine learning to generate guesses about the password, making cracking hashed passwords much faster.

5.5 The Transformative Impact

The application of machine learning to cryptanalysis isn't just an evolutionary shift, it is a revolutionary one. It calls into question traditional concepts of cryptographic security and forces the design of more robust encryption methods. In this chapter we will proceed to dig deeper, and consider the changing relationship between cryptography and machine learning. Two warring sides are playing an intense chess- like struggle for advantage in a high stakes game of wits which determines digital security on one hand; while another highlights how they complement each other's strengths, fortifying defense lines on the other?

6. MACHINE LEARNING FOR CRYPTOGRAPHIC SECURITY

In this section, we explore how machine learning can transform cryptographic security. We are focusing on its key role in attack detection and prevention, thereby strengthening the security of cryptographic protocols. We cite a number of illustrative examples to show how machine learning can enhance cryptographic security. With the increasingly global and data-based nature of our world, machine learning means that sensitive information should be in safer hands than ever before.

6.1 The Synergy of Machine Learning and Cryptographic Security

Cryptographic security is the wall that keeps sensitive data free from prying eyes and malevolent hands. Yet, as the digital world develops so do cyber criminals 'methods. Machine learning complements traditional cryptographic techniques with a dynamic, agile defensive shield.

6.2 Attack Detection and Prevention

6.2.1 Anomaly Detection

Machine learning algorithms can spot anomalous data patterns. Such a capability is particularly valuable in the field of cryptographic security. For instance, through the use of machine learning algorithms, aberrant access patterns or unsuccessful attempts to decrypt without authorization could be flagged for further examination.

6.2.2 Intrusion Detection

Network monitoring and system logs are used by machine learning intrusion detection systems to look for suspicious activity. Systems that operate by the book based on previous data can also effectively identify intruders and contain breaches.

6.2.3 Zero-Day Vulnerability Detection

This is because the more serious security risks are those that arise from zero-day vulnerabilities, which software developers don't know about. Through monitoring the system's behavior, machine learning can anticipate zero days that are about to occur. This gives organizations enough time to fix vulnerabilities before they are exploited.

6.3 Strengthening Cryptographic Security: Examples

6.3.1 Advanced Malware Detection

Machine learning has completely changed the landscape of malware detection. By examining file attributes, behavior patterns and network communications we can accurately identify malicious software using machine learning models. It not only resists compromise but also can strengthen the security of cryptographic keys and data.

6.3.2 Anomaly-Based Cryptographic Key Management

And keys used by machine-learning based cryptographic key management systems are always tracked for use. The moment any deviation from the norm is detected, an alert goes up. By this means organizations can early on detect such threats to their encryption keys. This provides the security of cryptographic operations in complicated, changing ones.

6.3.3 Secure Multi-Party Computation (SMPC)

One application of multi-party trusted techniques is for parties to jointly calculating a function on their own input without interfering with the privacy of that input. The security and cost efficiency of SMPC protocols can be improved using machine learning techniques. This is a powerful weapon at their disposal for applications where collaborativeuse of data is required but not sharing.

Artistic process The combination of machine learning and cryptographic security is an evolutionary journey. Now that adversarial tactics have developed, defensive mechanisms also must change. Data-driven wisdom and flexibility make machine learning an important weapon in the fight against new threats. Therefore machine learning is a force for change, helping to enhance cryptographic security. It detects abnormalities, keeps out attacks and strengthens cryptographic protocol. active defense against constantly changing threats With Combat Cloud, a new cloud service. This is machine learning and cryptographic security 'interdependent relationship, which we'll play around with this chapter. Today, in our networked society how can we maintain secrets? Let's look.

7. ETHICAL AND PRIVACY ISSUES

Furthermore, as for researching a combined approach to machine learning and cryptography indeed creates all kinds of basic ethical dilemmas along with privacy concerns. This coming together of these two fields is the place with great promise to advance security. This should be done, however, in the most responsible and ethical manner. In this section, the problems involving ethics and confidentiality created by such a connection are examined. Though it is reasonable that we maintain security in order to live peacefully every day of our private life there must be constraints on making personal information public or getting rid of these restrictions will threaten people's sensitive feelings as well as their human dignity.

Invasion of Privacy: The big data-handling power of machine learning undermines personal privacy-- and the public's. Guarding personal and sensitive information Advanced encryption techniques are used, combined with anonymization to the fullest extent possible.

Surveillance and Monitoring: Media Reports on Monitoring Systems Humanize for Subtitle Although machine learning-based surveillance and intrusion. detection systems effectively reduce risk, they can also potentially lead to mass"surveillance. There is a strict necessity to walk the line walking between defense against threats and respect for basic civil liberties.

Responsible Data Use: Using training data (sensitive, private) for machine learning models. But whatever measures are taken to guard against misuse or invasion of privacy become absolutely critical in how ethical data treatment methods such as anonymization and collection by consent must be applied.

7.1 Privacy Challenges

Privacy challenges loom large in the ethical discourse surrounding machine learning in cryptography:

Data Collection: The fact is that one side effect of training a machine learning model, most companies amass huge data bases in which are stored rich troves of private or sensitive personal information. Yet, of course, preventing break-ins and unsanctioned access is super important.

Data Retention: Old training and testing data is a privacy risk. The balance between system needs and privacy of individual's data Organisations should develop a policy for retaining information.

Algorithmic Bias: Machine learning algorithms are prone to bias, which can filter into cryptographic applications. Fairness and impartiality in decision-making is a basic ethical obligation.

Addressing these ethical and privacy issues necessitates the responsible and ethical use of machine learning in cryptography:

Transparent Algorithms: Fairness, privacy and security. Research on transparent algorithms suitable for auditing is important work to be done. As for transparency, open-source development and peer review are key.

Data Minimization: Data collection should follow the principle of data minimization. Minimal essential data should be collected, and wherever possible anonymized or pseudanymized.

Security by Design: In its design, machine learning model and cryptographic systems should implicitly consider security and privacy. The system design should integrate privacy-preserving techniques like federated learning and differential privacy starting on day one.

Multidisciplinary Collaboration: Cryptographers, ethicists, policymakers and technologists have to cooperate. They can also see the ethical issues surrounding machine learning in cryptography, and plot out together a set of guidelines for appropriate use.

In general, the application of machine learning to cryptography demonstrates that security and secrecy need proper balancing. Maintaining security remains a top priority. However, this cannot come at the expense of individual rights and basic ethics.

8. FUTURE DIRECTIONS AND CHALLENGES

An outlook In this last part we look into the future of notable developments in modern cryptography and machine learning before ending this essay. But today's digital environment is changing more than ever. So we're left with sore feet and the need to change as rapidly as the ever-changing world outside us. In speaking, moreover about possible obstacles to us and Utopian horizons still being dreamt of by mankind we deepest hope that our readers are encouraged on the way toward a lifelong study in these fields.

8.1 Anticipated Challenges

Quantum Computing Threats: This type of system is facing the arrival of an extremely serious threat in powerful quantum computers. And transitioning to quantum-proof encryption will become an urgent issue.

Privacy Preservation: In the era of data-driven technology, this conflict between utility and privacy will be a recurring theme. The right mix It takes a fine balance to achieve this blend, but new cryptographic techniques will need crafting that allow information analysis without sacrificing personal privacy.

Ethical and Regulatory Frameworks: In terms of the ethical and administrative realm of machine learning, cryptography will continue to be examined further. For a comprehensive framework, that is still beyond us.

Scalability and Performance: This presents a technical challenge, and especially in terms of blockchain-defined decentralized ledger technology.

8.2 Promising Horizons

Homomorphic Encryption: Having your computations do not require decryption and having it done on the actual, encrypted data set is a very exciting idea. There are also prospects for further development and application.

Post-Quantum Cryptography: The digital battlement No more gem hong radios Knowing how important this is, we will keep data safe in the post-quantum era.

Explainable AI for Security: In terms of security, future explainable AI will help us better understand a variety of machine learning models 'decisions.

Privacy-Preserving Machine Learning: The development of new privacy-preserving machine learning techniques such as federated learning and differential privacy will ensure that organizations can still glean intelligence from sensitive data while respecting the limits on personal information. endless possibilities and ominous challenges The weapons of modern cryptography are inseparable from machine learning. If we want to live in this changing world, then all must study their whole lives and keep on researching and developing. Let us continue to stay informed, organize cross-disciplinary teams and participate in discussions on ethical problems and data privacy--we can influence the future of such vital fields as big data. With this chapter in the books, readers are encouraged to look into these fields of modern cryptography and machine learning for themselves. High barriers but huge potential rewards--technological innovation and progress toward a safe and secure digital environment constructed on solid ethics.

9. CONCLUSION

More specifically, this chapter provides a detailed introduction to modern cryptography and machine learning. These technologies have emerged from the front line in our rapidly changing information age. They started out with a reminder of this urgent need to secure communications in the age of interconnection and data exchange. In this chapter we have looked both at the fundamental principles and applications of these two big domains, a truly remarkable overlap. The historical development of modern cryptography begins with an examination of ancient means up to today's encryptions and ciphers. This chapter explained the subtleties of secure communications. It covered symmetric and asymmetric encryption, public-key infrastructure and cryptographic hashing. At the same time, research into machine learning brought out some basic concepts-supervised and unsupervised learning as well as reinforcement; all depends upon data. Indeed, the core of exploration was at the intersection between modern cryptography and machine learning. Only in this way can one try to discover how new input from tools such as neural networks will cause old exploitation techniques to disappear completely. Real-world examples. Examples ranged from passphrase recovery to vulnerability detection and password cracking, revealing the interesting connections between these transformative domains. Ample evidence that it had much to offer for strengthening cryptographic security was seen in applications of machine learning such as those involving attack detection and intrusion prevention, and protocol enhancement. The chapter emphasized the ethical and privacy problems arising from this, warning of responsible use while at the same time pointing out that there is a need for compromise between securtiy and personal liberty. The chapter also looked ahead, looking at problems and hope. From threats in the fields of quantum computing, privacy preservation and ethical frameworks to scaling needs. Yet the potentials for homomorphic encryption, post-quantum cryptography, explainable AI and privacy preserving machine learning justify this quest. At the end, readers are encouraged to participate actively in this ongoing study of modern cryptography and machine learning. The obstacles are huge, but the room for invention is endless. Similarly, to the protectors of our global village itself that are today well known-cryptography and machine learning -- have indispensable roles in how our digital society is evolving.

REFERENCES

Gope, P., Millwood, O., & Sikdar, B. (2022). A Scalable Protocol Level Approach to Prevent Machine Learning Attacks on Physically Unclonable Function Based Authentication Mechanisms for Internet of Medical Things. *IEEE Transactions on Industrial Informatics*, *18*(3), 1971–1980. doi:10.1109/TII.2021.3096048

Govardhana Reddy, H. G., & Raghavendra, K. (2022). Vector space modelling-based intelligent binary image encryption for secure communication. *Journal of Discrete Mathematical Sciences and Cryptography*, *25*(4), 1157–1171. doi:10.1080/09720529.2022.2075090

Gowda, V. D., Prasad, K. D. V., Gite, P., Premkumar, S., Hussain, N., & Chinamuttevi, V. S.K.D.V. (2023). A novel RF-SMOTE model to enhance the definite apprehensions for IoT security attacks. *Journal of Discrete Mathematical Sciences and Cryptography*, *26*(3), 861–873. doi:10.47974/JDMSC-1766

Hussain, A. A. J., Pazhani, & A. K., N. (2023). A Novel Method of Enhancing Security Solutions and Energy Efficiency of IoT Protocols. *IJRITCC, 11*(4), 325–335.

Karatas, G., Demir, O., & Sahingoz, O. K. (2019). A Deep Learning Based Intrusion Detection System on GPUs. *2019 11th International Conference on Electronics, Computers and Artificial Intelligence (ECAI)*, 1-6. 10.1109/ECAI46879.2019.9042132

Knudsen, L. R., & Mathiassen, J. E. (2000). A chosen-plaintext linear attack on DES. *Proceedings of the International Workshop on Fast Software Encryption (FSE)*, 262–272.

Kumar, P. H., & Samanta, T. (2022). Deep Learning Based Optimal Traffic Classification Model for Modern Wireless Networks. *2022 IEEE 19th India Council International Conference (INDICON)*, 1-6. 10.1109/INDICON56171.2022.10039822

Kumar, R., & Ashreetha, B. (2023). Performance Analysis of Energy Efficiency and Security Solutions of Internet of Things Protocols. *IJEER, 11*(2), 442–450. doi:10.37391/ijeer.110226

Kumar & Chaturvedi. (2023). Securing networked image transmission using public-key cryptography and identity authentication. *Journal of Discrete Mathematical Sciences and Cryptography, 26*(3), 779-791. doi:10.47974/JDMSC-1754

Musa, A., & Mahmood, A. (2021). Client-side Cryptography Based Security for Cloud Computing System. *2021 International Conference on Artificial Intelligence and Smart Systems (ICAIS)*, 594-600. 10.1109/ICAIS50930.2021.9395890

Pavankumar, P., & Darwante, N. K. (2022). Performance Monitoring and Dynamic Scaling Algorithm for Queue Based Internet of Things. *2022 International Conference on Innovative Computing, Intelligent Communication and Smart Electrical Systems (ICSES)*, 1-7. 10.1109/ICSES55317.2022.9914108

Reza, M. N., & Islam, M. (2021). Evaluation of Machine Learning Algorithms using Feature Selection Methods for Network Intrusion Detection Systems. *2021 5th International Conference on Electrical Information and Communication Technology (EICT)*, 1-6. 10.1109/EICT54103.2021.9733679

Sharma & Arun. (2022). Priority Queueing Model-Based IoT Middleware for Load Balancing. *2022 6th International Conference on Intelligent Computing and Control Systems (ICICCS)*, 425-430. 10.1109/ICICCS53718.2022.9788218

Sharma, A. (2023). A novel approach of unsupervised feature selection using iterative shrinking and expansion algorithm. *Journal of Interdisciplinary Mathematics*, *26*(3), 519–530. doi:10.47974/JIM-1678

Shivashankar & Mehta. (2016). MANET topology for disaster management using wireless sensor network. *International Conference on Communication and Signal Processing, ICCSP 2016*, 736–740. . doi:10.1109/ICCSP.2016.7754242

Singla, A., & Sharma, N. (2022). IoT Group Key Management using Incremental Gaussian Mixture Model. *2022 3rd International Conference on Electronics and Sustainable Communication Systems (ICESC)*, 469-474. 10.1109/ICESC54411.2022.9885644

Suryawanshi, V. A., & Chaturvedi, A. (2022). Novel Predictive Control and Monitoring System based on IoT for Evaluating Industrial Safety Measures. *IJEER*, *10*(4), 1050–1057. doi:10.37391/ijeer.100448

Tan, S., Knott, B., & Wu, D. J. (2021). CryptGPU: Fast Privacy-Preserving Machine Learning on the GPU. *2021 IEEE Symposium on Security and Privacy (SP)*, 1021-1038. 10.1109/SP40001.2021.00098

Zhu, S., & Han, Y. (2021, August). Generative trapdoors for public key cryptography based on automatic entropy optimization. *China Communications*, *18*(8), 35–46. doi:10.23919/JCC.2021.08.003

Chapter 2
Future Outlook:
Synergies Between Advanced AI and Cryptographic Research

Dankan Gowda V.

https://orcid.org/0000-0003-0724-0333

BMS Institute of Technology and Management, India

Joohi Garg

https://orcid.org/0000-0003-1008-0350

Mody University of Science and Technology, India

Shaifali Garg

https://orcid.org/0000-0002-5647-3347

Amity Business School, Amity University, Gwalior, India

K. D. V. Prasad

https://orcid.org/0000-0001-9921-476X

Symbiosis Institute of Business Management, Symbiosis International University, India

Sampathirao Suneetha

Andhra University College of Engineering, Andhra University, India

ABSTRACT

Artificial intelligence (AI) and cryptography have recently made rapid progress respectively, forming a surprising mutual relationship. With the development of AI, it is now evolving to a point where an AI can study and even design cryptography systems. Cryptographic researchers are continually bringing out new ways to protect AI infrastructures from the ever-changing nature of attack, however. So, in this area, the authors examine the future topography and consider various possible ways these two breaking fields of study could meet up. Meanwhile, quantum computing and neuromorphic technology could push advanced AI further than any computer has been able to go before. On the one hand, cryptographic methods also help keep AI models open, safe, and within legal privacy regulations even facing attack. In a nutshell, cutting-edge AI and cryptography research are together reinventing the frontier of internet security within artificial intelligence. What lies ahead? This chapter lays out the problems and prospects of this exciting intersection.

DOI: 10.4018/979-8-3693-1642-9.ch002

1. INTRODUCTION

In the rapidly evolving field of technology, AI and cryptography are a good case for such interdisciplinary cooperation. The impact of AI and cryptography combined As well as being fascinating reading in their own right, the developments described here will have many interesting outcomes.

The twenty-first century has witnessed unprecedented progress in AI and cryptography, and their convergence represents a pivotal moment in technological history. Cryptography is a perfect fit for artificial intelligence because to AI's pattern recognition, intelligent decision-making, and capacity to analyze massive volumes of data. Cryptography, on the other hand, has long been the guardian of data privacy and security, ensuring that sensitive information remains shielded from prying eyes. Artificial Intelligence (AI) is a specialized field within computer science focused on creating rational agents. These agents are designed to perceive their environment, process this information internally, and then select the most suitable action from various possibilities. Improving the agent's function of objective is the goal of this decision-making procedure (N. Hussain, A. A. J. . Pazhani, and A. K. . N, 2023). Once the agent decides what to do, it modifies its internal model of the environment and goes to work. Some of the many kinds of agents that fall under the umbrella of artificial intelligence are learning agents, logical agents, planning agents, antagonistic search agents, and search agents. Learning agents stand out because of their data-driven decision-making capabilities and use of machine learning methods. A set of data pairs is used to infer these activities.

At the heart of artificial intelligence (AI) lie Artificial Neural Networks (ANNs). ANNs are defined by their structure, which includes the amount of cells or perceptual neurons in each layer, the specific activation processes used by the neurons, the cost function for training, and the number and setup of densely interrelated hidden layers (Figure 1). The weights of the interconnections are adjusted during ANN training using gradient descent and backpropagation, which are based on the slope of the cost function within the weight space (as shown in Figure 2). The three most important areas of interest for artificial neural networks (ANNs) are input categorization, sequence learning, and function approximation. An important AI tool, ANNs can easily represent complex nonlinear functions thanks to their use of the nonlinear activation functions such as Sigmoid, Tanh and RELU.

1.1 The Convergence of AI and Cryptography

The role of AI in cryptography is broad and profound. The most notable aspect of this convergence is the advent of AI-driven encryption. Traditional encryption is based on algorithms and mathematical structures, effective but by no means adapted to today's computer environment. This aspect is handled by AI, as it can learn to adjust encryption techniques to the very purpose of protecting data (Shivashankar, and S. Mehta, 2016). But the convergence between AI and cryptography is truly a fascinating phenomenon. The two are becoming ever more intertwined, with each promoting the other in turn. The application of AI in cryptography has completely transformed how we think about data security and information protection. In fact, AI is the motor that drives cryptographic innovation to its limits.

For instance, AI sifts through data-traffic patterns to increase encryption on the fly. In this way, important information is well protected even when in transit. It can also improve key generation procedures, lowering the workload and time spent on encrypting. These AI-based encryption algorithms are constantly learning and evolving, staying one step ahead of potential attackers. Another major area where AI and cryptography overlap is that of the targeted use known as cryptanalysis. Breaking codes is secret

Figure 1. Fundamental building block of an artificial neural network is the perceptron

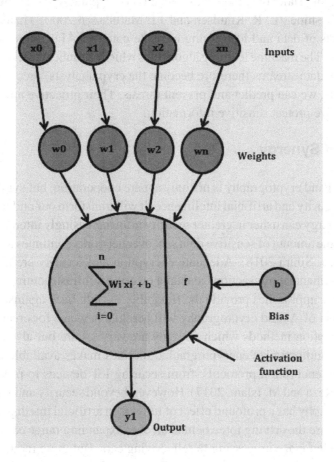

Figure 2. Multi-layer perceptron

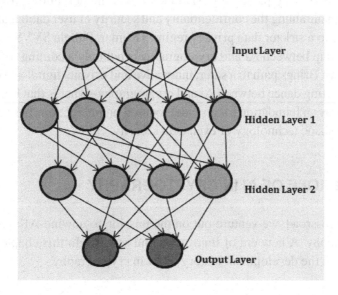

decoding, while discovering flaws in an encryption method is cryptanalysis. It is here in fact, where AI's analytical abilities really shine. (L. R. Knudsen and J E Mathiassen 2000) Thanks to its capability for processing huge amounts of data and identifying intricate patterns, AI can uncover shortcomings that human analysts overlook. The machine learning algorithms which are unbeatable in identifying anomalies and irregularities within data streams therefore become the cryptanalysts 'precious weapons. By using AI to drive cryptanalysis, we can predict and prevent threats. Their proactive approach to security may change forever the way we protect sensitive information.

1.2. Significance of Synergy

The synergy between AI and cryptography is not only a mere cooperation, but symbolizes the difference in thinking about data security and artificial intelligence. It will transform our understanding of the digital landscape. First, this synergy can usher in greater security in an increasingly interdependent world. While technology progresses, the amount of sensitive data sent over networks continues to expand exponentially (R. Beaulieu, D. Shors, J. Smith 2018). Adequate encryption and security are also now critical, from personal information to financial transactions and data on critical infrastructure. These solution-driven, AI-infused cryptographic approaches provide the flexibility to fight back against new threats.

Also, the combination of AI and cryptography will herald a new age for creativity. We thereby can imagine advanced encryption methods which not only are very secure but also efficient and flexible. AI's capability to learn and optimize encryptographic routines makes available an expanded range of solutions for developing encryption protocols, from securing IoT devices to protecting the privacy of healthcare data. (M. N. Reza and M. Islam, 2017). However, beyond security and innovation, the synergy between AI and cryptography has a profound effect of its own on artificial intelligence itself. Deep learning and neural networks are the driving force behind an ever-expanding range of applications, including everything from natural language processing to self-driving cars. But these models work with sensitive user data, raising privacy and data protection issues. Cryptography offers a solution to this problem with its experience in data encryption and privacy-protecting techniques. The partnership between AI and cryptography gives rise to privacy-preserving AI models. These models allow AI systems to make intelligent decisions, while maintaining the confidentiality and security of user data. It also makes users more confident and conforms to a stricter data privacy regime (Kumar, Pullela SVVSR & Chaturvedi Abhay 2023). In short, the overlap between AI and cryptography is not only a coming together of methods but also comeback of visions. Brings path to a safer, innovative and private digital world. In this section, we look at the highly fascinating dance between Ai and cryptography--what is that bread made with banana in? At the same time it lays a foundation for a sequel focused on interactions between these two worlds, and their potential to reshape technology or even data security.

2. THE EVOLVING ROLE OF AI IN CRYPTOGRAPHY

On this technological crossroad, we venture out on the mission to unwind AI's rapidly evolving capabilities-within cryptography. A new era of innovation and security In this chapter, we take you on an interesting trip to explore the development history of AI in cryptography.

2.1 AI-Powered Encryption

A marriage made in heaven The combination of AI and cryptography is a new frontier for information protection. This convergence centers on AI-driven encryption, a breakthrough development that may well change the paradigm of data security.

While effective, traditional encryption methods generally follow relatively fixed protocols and algorithms, making them easy targets for evolving threats. Encryption with artificial intelligence introduces a new dynamic and unfixed method to protect data. Here's how it works: AI algorithms have the capacity to learn from data patterns. Analyzing large sets of data to detect trends, and anomalies which they adapt encryption techniques in turn (Kumar R & B Ashreetha 2023). In today's quickly changing digital environment, in which new cyber threats emerge on an almost daily basis, this adaptability is especially significant.

Take for example the case of a company that has data traffic which fluctuates from day to night. Real-time adjustment of the encryption level with AI encryption. In high traffic times, stronger encryption is used; in light load periods a lighter scheme is selected. Not only does it enhance security; it also optimizes computational resources, raising overall efficiency.

Another area where AI has an impact is key generation. Cryptographic key generation is an important facet of encryption, and the complexity of this process generally reflects the strength of the encryption. By analyzing historical data and user behavior, AI can help key generation become more secure and friendly. This lessens the risk of weak keys and makes encrypted data more secure generally. In addition, AI can recognize potential holes in encryption algorithms. AI constantly watches data traffic and system haviation, looking for unusual patterns or signs of intrusion. If anomalies are detected, the encryption system can automatically change its parameters or send alarms to reduce potential risks (S. Tan et al., 2021). AI-driven encryption isn't just about stronger encryption, it's also about smarter and more efficient. It allows organizations to change with the threat landscape. And in an ever more interwoven world, sensitive data will be protected.

created in 1999 by Daemen and Rijmen, the Rijndael algorithm or Advanced Encryption Standard (AES) is a symmetric block cipher. Built on this kind of encryption technology, it superseded the Data Encryption Standard (DES) in 2001 when the United States National Institute of Standards and Technology, or NIST, officially accepted it. AES has a constant 128-bit block size and supports key sizes of 128, 192 or 256 bits. Its flexibility is another major strength (P. H. Kumar and T. Samanta, 2022). The number of rounds used in AES encryption depends on key sizes; a 128-bit key uses 10, a 192-bit key uses 12 and a 256-bit key usese s. AES begins the decryption and encryption phases, as detailed in Figure 3. The two main factors here are a key K and a 128-bit block B (a so-called state). The key may be of length 128, 192 or even 256 bits. A special feature of AES is the use of state arrays during encryption and decryption. In these procedures, the blocks B (with components $B0$ to $B15$) are arranged into matrices of four rows and four columns. Bytes correspond with squares, or if you will terms like square by square.. These are called state arrays, and are important to the operation of the AES algorithm.

2.2. Cryptanalysis and AI

Cryptanalysis, today's name for the art of breaking encryption codes, has long been a game of cat and mouse between attackers and defenders. But with the incorporation of artificial intelligence (AI), this game is evolving into a whole new ball-game. In essence, cryptanalysis is the analysis of encrypted data

Figure 3. Illustration of the block and the subkey, both represented in bytes

B0	B1	B2	B3
B4	B5	B6	B7
B8	B9	B10	B11
B12	B13	B14	B15

K0	K1	K2	K3
K4	K5	K6	K7
K8	K9	K10	K11
K12	K13	K14	K15

to determine the hidden message or key (P. Gope, O. Millwood and B. Sikdar, 2022). It takes a detailed knowledge of encryption algorithms and keen perception of weaknesses. In terms of history, cryptanalysts have used the human brain and calculating machines to crack codes. Now AI is changing the game.

One reason for the potential revolution in cryptanalysis is AI's exceptional ability to analyze, speed and adaptability. Here's how AI is reshaping the landscape of cryptanalysis:

Rapid Analysis: This enormous amount of data can be processed by these AI algorithms in a flash. They are particularly good at detecting patterns and oddities within encrypted messages or data streams. With this ability, AI can rapidly find any weak points or gaps in encryption systems. Pattern Recognition: Traditionally, cryptanalysts use human intuition and experience to detect patterns in encrypted data. However, AI can automate this process (A.Singla, N. Sharma 2022). With machine learning algorithms, one can find the subtlest patterns often overlooked by human analysts. This affords a more complete picture of encrypted data.

Attack Automation: Cryptographic attacks can be launched automatically by AI. It can, for instance, perform brute-force attacks by trying all possible keys systematically; or it could use more refined techniques such as differential cryptanalysis. These processes are automated with the use of AI, which greatly speeds up the cryptanalysis.

Adaptation to New Algorithms: However, as encryption algorithms are developed to be more secure, cryptanalysts must break ever more complex codes. But human limitations are not a problem for AI. It can quickly adapt to new encryption techniques and devise novel ways of attacking.

Proactive Threat Detection: AI's ability to monitor in real time makes it possible for threats to be detected preemptively. It can analyse network traffic and encrypted communications in a continuous manner to detect suspicious activities or possible intrusions. This early warning system improves cybersecurity and enables organizations to respond quickly to threats.

A more modern method of artificial intelligence is based on a concept called Deep Learning. Artificial Neural Networks (ANNs) with a high data throughput are used to handle raw, original data in Deep

Learning, essentially replacing conventional signal processing approaches(G. Karatas, O. Demir and O. K. Sahingoz, 2019). The contrast between a traditional ANN with a single hidden layer, sometimes known as a "shallow" ANN, and a deep network with three hidden layers is seen in Figure 4. The dramatic rise in processing power and efficiency is the primary motivator for the widespread use of deep learning. An example of such a network is the one used by Google's Inception-V3 model; it has 49 levels and more than 20 million connections. But, in order to calculate the numerous weights needed by these deep networks, a large quantity of training data is essential for deep learning to be successful. Luckily, the required training data is now more easily accessible online because to the combination of rising processing power and the exponential expansion of the World Wide Web of Things (IoT). Now that we live in the Age of Big Data Society, when both large datasets and the computing power to process them are readily available, deep ANNs are a reality(A. Sharma, K. S and M. R. Arun, 2022). Industry behemoths like Google and Facebook, together with national security agencies, are the primary drivers of the increase in computer power that has allowed deep learning to evolve. The recent trend of supercomputers being consolidated into single graphic processing unit (GPUs) has enabled deep learning and high-resolution gaming possible in a much smaller form factor, and applications such as facial recognition and tracing and tracking have emerged as key issues.

Figure 4. Simple neural network and deep neural network

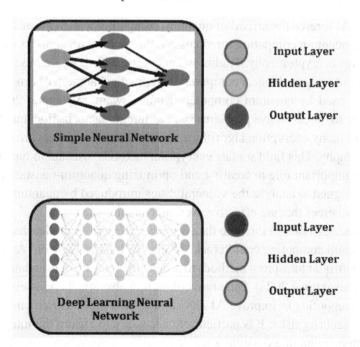

Additional examples of such ciphers can be found in the functions or maps provided in Figure 5. These functions define the structure of the function $x_{k+1} = f\left(x_k\right), x_o \epsilon \left(0,1\right)$. In order to build stream ciphers, these particular functions take a starting key x0 from the interval (0, 1) and optimize their output by changing the value of r to produce a chaotic number-stream. Next the output is processed to produce a stream with uniform distribution quality (H G Damodara Reddy & K Raghavendra, 2022).

These stream ciphers are intended to raise the security and randomness of generated encryption keys and data streams.

To sum up, the pairing of AI and cryptanalysis is changing the face of data security. AI-aided cryptanalysis is not only more effective and easier it operating, but also preemptive in countering threats (A. Musa and A. Mahmood, 2021). At the same time, it makes attackers' skills even more potent, but also means that defenders can stay one step in front in this continuing fight over data security. The development of this function stresses the ongoing need for innovation and vigilance in an ever-changing world of cryptography.

3. STRENGTHENING AI AGAINST EMERGING THREATS

In today's rapidly changing world of technology, artificial intelligence (AI) is a game-changer. But with this rapid progress also come several kinds of emerging threats. To address such challenges, it's important to fortify AI against possible weaknesses. This chapter delves into two key aspects of this process: quantum computing and the interplay between neuromorphic technology and AI security.

3.1 Quantum Computing Challenges

New developments in AI foresee the arrival of quantum computing, which promises both opportunities and threats. The more quantum computing threatens AI, the more it threatens its own security. Among the most basic problems is cryptography. Traditional encryption methods that use complex mathematical problems which would take a classical computer an impractical amount of time to solve, suffer from the brute force attack used by quantum computers(Kumaraswamy & Gupta, 2023). Also, quantum computers may be able to quickly solve problems such as integer factorization and discrete logarithms, which lie at the root of many encryption algorithms. In response, researchers are currently working on post-quantum cryptography. This field studies encryption methods resistant to quantum attacks. In this endeavor, AI plays an important role in creating and optimizing quantum-resistant cryptographic techniques. Algorithms designed to analyze the vulnerabilities introduced by quantum computing can help formulate encryption schemes that are effective even in a quantum age.

And quantum computing is also a threat to data privacy. Because AI models handle masses of sensitive information, quantum computing could crack the encryption they rely on. As a result, AI systems should be developed with quantum-proof methods to protect the security of user data in a Quantum World (K.D.V., Gite, Pratik, Sivakumar 2023). Quantum computing also affects AI itself. QML is a new field which uses quantum computing to improve AI algorithms. This presents tremendous potential for AI, but it also brings new security risks. It is particularly necessary to ensure the integrity and security of AI models in a quantum computing environment.

3.2. Neuromorphic Technology and AI Security

Based on the architecture of the human brain, neuromorphic technology is remodeling the area of AI. It holds the prospect of more agile, versatile, and capable AI systems. On the other hand, as AI becomes increasingly intertwined with neuromorphic technology, it introduces new security challenges. The way in which neuromorphic systems process information is one of the biggest problems. (S. Zhu and Y. Han,

2021) In contrast with traditional AI models, which require explicit instructions, neuromorphic systems learn and adjust themselves through synaptic connections in the same way as human brains. This offers advantages in terms of cognitive capacities, but is also a source of potential weakness. For example, adversarial attacks on neuromorphic AI systems can twist the subtleties of synaptic learning to change the behavior of artificial intelligence models. Such attacks can have severe repercussions, from incorrectly classifying data to a serious compromise of decision-making processes. Thus securing neuromorphic AI against adversarial attacks is an urgent priority. Improving AI's perceptual capabilities is another aspect of neuromorphic technology. In terms of low power consumption and high-speed processing, sensors based on biological vision systems are decidedly advantageous. Yet now that such sensors have been manufactured, they become vulnerable to new channels of attack. In particular, sensor-level attacks threaten the integrity of sensory data. To address these security challenges, research is going on toward developing solid defense systems for neuromorphic AI systems (P. Pavankumar, N. K. Darwante 2022). AI is necessary in this process. It also tries to locate the weaknesses and design strong learning algorithms capable of fighting existing weakness, as well designing security protocols particularly for neuromorphic technology. Finally, to strengthen AI against such emerged threats is a complex process. Rise of the quantum computer and interactions between artificial intelligence and neuromorphic technology both demand active defenses in order to protect the stability, security (safety) if AI systems- Suryawanshi& Abhay Chaturvedi2021. In this chapter, we have considered the difficulties associated with overcoming these challenges and explained why AI can be an important way to do so. An age of AI capable of taking up the challenges that lie ahead on the horizon is now ready to begin.

4. COLLABORATIVE INNOVATIONS IN CRYPTOGRAPHIC PROTOCOLS

In addition, the combination of artificial intelligence (AI) and cryptography will make systems more secure not only about stealing information but also integration inventions in crypto-cryptographic protocols. In this chapter we examine how the development of AI-based protocols and new encryption techniques are redrawing the data protection map.

4.1 AI-Driven Protocol Development

Data security includes cryptographic protocols. Traditional protocols use mathematical principles and fixed algorithms to protect sensitive information. However, with the advent of AI. Protocol development has entered a new era of mobility and elasticity. Designing, designing cryptographic schemes-AI develops protocols driven by machine learning algorithms. In these rapidly changing digital surroundings, more resilient protocols can adapt in real time to threats and the methods of attack. In particular, the core advantage of intelligent AI-driven protocol development is that it allows you to analyze and respond to new threats as they occur. Due to artificial intelligence systems, all transfers of data across networks can be overseen and analyzed. Anomalies or flaws in security will thereby come clearly into view. If the threat is detected, the protocol can adjust dynamically its parameters or encryption methods in an attempt to lower risks. Further, AI can help design encryption protocols suitable for particular applications. For example, when dealing with Internet of Things (IoT) devices that have limited computational resources available to them, suitable lightweight cryptographic protocols need to be developed. AI can optimize encryption schemes to strike a balance between security and efficiency, ensuring that IoT devices remain secure without compromising performance.

The fundamental motivation for using EC and ANNs to produce stream encryption algorithms is the need to design or modify example maps, as shown in Figure 5, to suit the unique demands of cryptographic applications. EC offers the advantage of automatically initiating the evolutionary process using real-world noise, allowing for the creation of customized stream ciphers that are compatible with cryptographic applications. Contrarily, ANNs have their uses, but when it comes to building PRNGs based on iterated nonlinear functions, they aren't as versatile as they may be. The use of evolutionary algorithms, which use a stochastic search process based on populations and designed to simulate natural selection, is essential for this goal. Due to their capacity to discover optimum solutions for complicated and dynamic problems within tolerable processing timescales, evolutionary algorithms have attracted attention from different sectors. In 2013, the use of Eureqa and other evolutionary computation algorithms was first investigated for potential cryptographic applications. Using this method, nonlinear functions may be repeatedly developed to characterize complicated input signals, which are often seen in chaotic system experimental data. No nonlinear function can, in theory, provide an evolutionary model that accurately captures really random (delta uncorrelated) noise. Natural noise, on the other hand, has the ability to "trick" a system into repeatedly trying to mimic the noise, which might make it work as a PRNG. To determine its appropriateness, it is subjected to a battery of tests, as shown in Figure 6 (where ticks show successful test results), which include checking if the cipher stream is uniformly distributed, calculating

Figure 5. Illustrations of chaotic maps used for stream cipher generation

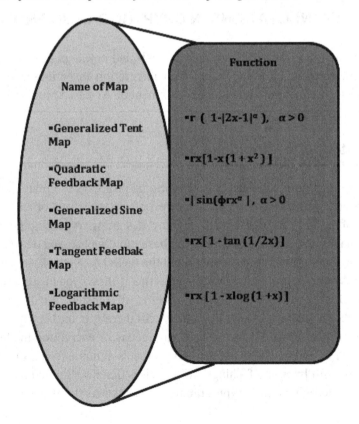

Figure 6. Schematic diagram illustrating the process of stream cipher generation with an elliptic curve as the basis

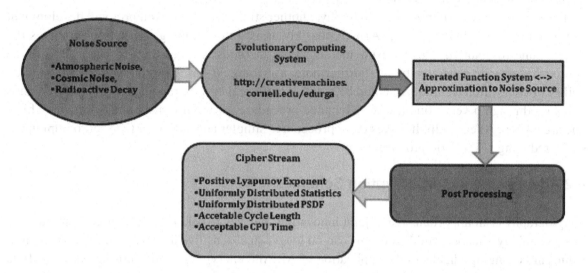

the Power Spectral Distribution Function (PSDF), and more. On the other hand, a design for creating a stream cipher using an ANN is shown in Figure 7. It is clear from comparing the two methods that the ANN architecture and weights are similar to an evolving function generated by EC. Both scenarios include testing against Figure 6 and 7, as well as the updated PRNG evaluations provided by the Cryptographic Algorithm Validation Program (CAVP) by the National Institute of Standardization (NIST) the

Figure 7. Overview of the methods employed in generating a stream cipher with an artificial neural network (ANN), presented schematically

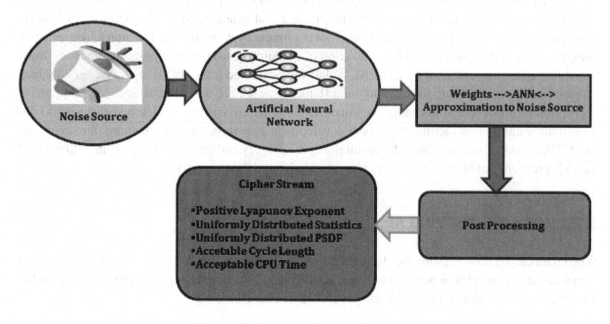

Computer Security Resource Center. Any cryptographic algorithm must pass these NIST tests, which are the gold standard for evaluating a cypher's cryptographic strength.

In the field of post-quantum cryptography, another strength is AI-driven protocol development. In the era of quantum computing, AI will possibly assist in developing encryption protocols that are immune to quantum attacks. New mathematical methods and quantum-resistant algorithmic approaches may be generated by AI. Furthermore, ascribing AI-based protocol development to usability of encryption techniques should be noted. Traditional cryptographic protocols must in most cases go through a very complex key exchange procedure, or require manual adjustment. This is one area where AI can help. It makes these procedures simpler and easier for the user to implement, while reducing risk of compromise.

4.2 Advancements in Encryption Schemes

Cryptography is an important area of joint innovation. The key to data protection is encryption. With this technology, the most ruthless enemy can no longer steal sensitive information. Encryption algorithms are changing, thanks to the application of AI. And encryption algorithms based on artificial intelligence not only keep up with changes in data security requirements, but also switch the level of encrypted to a certain extent according to even real-time traffic. This flexibility not only strengthens security, it weakens computational efficiency. Progress with artificial intelligence contributes to key generation, a significant element of encryption. AI will study past data and user behavioral trends, then can produce encryption keys that are both secure but also easy to use. Thus it adds a degree of protection against poor keys, and improves overall data security. AI also plays an important role in the security of encryption keys. Potential Threats or Unauthorized AccessMonitoring and protecting encryption keys are important aspects of data protection. An intelligent system can help here as well. Development has also extended into areas including safe multi-party computing and homomorphic encryption. Critical in many applications, including safe data sharing and cloud computing, these methods allow calculations on encrypted information without a need to first decrypt. Private quantum-resistant encryption is another frontier of development. For fear that quantum computing will eat away at the underpinnings of encryption, researchers are looking for encryptions resistant to attack by a quantum computer. Faster development and optimization of quantum-resistant encryption methods are made possible by the computational speed of AI. At last the combined forces of AI and cryptography have given us an exponential rate like leaping on a flame. Now we are watching as new combinations of encryption protocols begin to change our concepts about data security completely. Advanced AI and evolutionary encryption facilitates protocol development in response to the changing threat environment. These innovations are routes for maintaining the privacy and security of data in an online world. This chapter looks at how AI is changing cryptography and data security.

5. PRIVACY-PRESERVING AI

When data can be both treasure and damaging, even to the private life of individuals--just at this time comes about such an idea as personal artificial intelligence. This chapter explores two key facets of this paradigm: zero-knowledge proof systems and locked machine learning.

5.1 Zero-Knowledge Proof Systems

The key to balancing privacy and AI-enabling data information is finding just that point of balance. This is a major breakthrough in zero-knowledge proof systems. The method of zero-knowledge proofs is a cryptological technique that allows the prover to tell if the verifier knows anything without ever getting it out. This idea has a profound influence on privacy-preserving AI. So let's say someone wants to use an AI-generated service without giving away any privacy. It is accomplished through zero knowledge proof systems. So a user can show he meets certain criteria without having to reveal underlying figures. For example, if a user needs to prove that they are over 18 for age verification reasons without revealing their full date of birth (DOB). Besides the obvious example of authentication and identity verification, zero-knowledge proof systems have found application in numerous other fields. Users can log in with no personal information disclosed. As a result, both online security and privacy are improved. Most importantly, zero-knowledge proofs are used to protect privacy in AI calculations. In addition, security sensitive data transmission can be proven correct without disclosing any private information through use of zero-knowledge proofs. This can be particularly true in an environment of collaborative AI, where there are many parties providing data and don't show their cards to let others see what they have received. Another application of DeFi and blockchain is also important. In addition, the use of proof-of-knowledge systems provides greater privacy for transactions and smart contracts. Financial transactions are private but they're precise and believable. With the spread of AI into diverse industrial domains, and as technologies connected with privacy-preserving artificial intelligence are becoming more and more mature, this zero knowledge proof system provides a firm foundation for such systems. In the digital age of information exchange, they offer a means for users to transparently and fairly share data--and protect their dignity.

5.2. Encrypted Machine Learning

Encrypted machine learning, which allows organizations to safely enjoy all the benefits offered by a powerful new and rapidly developing technology while keeping secure boundaries around sensitive data, forms one of the cutting edges on privacy-preserving AI. Stealing information Put simply, most machine learning models have to run using an open door- all raw crackable and unprotected data must be fed into the model for training or prediction. Nevertheless, this method is not without privacy risks. For example, in the case of bank records or medical records. Cloud-based encrypted machine learning thus offers a way for companies to avoid these dangers by performing calculations on the raw materials. One of the main encryption methods in machine learning is homomorphic cryptography; another is secure multi-party computing. Therefore, homomorphic encryption means that the AI models can process encrypted data without first decrypting it. Thus, from the start of machine learning to its completion private data is secure. Take the case of a healthcare provider. They could use encrypted machine learning to train a predictive model on patient data, without ever seeing the patients 'actual raw medical records. SMPC ensures that privacy protection moves onto the shared platforms of machine learning. SMPC allows many parties to jointly train a machine learning model with different data sources, while keeping each party 'data private from the others. This is particularly crucial in sensitive areas like finance, where many different institutions depend on each other to set up prediction models while protecting their own proprietary data. This ensures data security in machine learning, and AI can also learn with decentralized sources of training data on users 'devices. This is a method often used in programs such as personalized recommendations and mobile keyboards. By insisting that sensitive data remain encrypted throughout the life cycle of an AI model, organizations can use encryption-based machine learning to satisfy stringent laws such as GDPR and HIPAA governing what may be done with patient health information. Service users can have access to the AI-driven services and insights, but still retain control over their own personal information. In the end, privacy-preserving AI is not an empty dream but a reality ushered in by zero-knowledge proof systems and encrypted machine learning. These new innovations give organizations and users the power to utilize AI without having to divulge their most prized data. However, as the digital universe evolves, these technologies will still stay at the cutting edge of artificial intelligence and data security. We introduce their importance and novelty in helping it build trusting, innovative privacy-preserving AI.

AUTONOMOUS CRYPTOGRAPHIC SYSTEMS

That is why the future lies in autonomous cryptographic systems. Systems designed to drive back the frontiers of data protection are experiments that marry artificial intelligence (AI) with breakthroughs in cryptography. AI Hunts Down Cryptographic Flaws This chapter discusses how artificial intelligence can be used to find cryptographic weakness.

6.1 AI's Role in Detecting Flaws

A fundamental aspect of data security is the strength of cryptographic systems. As cryptographic technology has become more and more complex and powerful, so too have the tools that malicious actors use to seek out flaws in existing encryption systems. With such a changeable scene, there is no choice but to be more active in identifying and solving these problems-AI has been the pioneer. The ability of AI to handle big data and analyze complex patterns has made it a formidable weapon in the cryptanalyst's arsenal. Its ability to analyze is naturally of great value in identifying flaws in cryptographic systems.

The biggest strength of AI is its ability to spot flaws, through security audits. Cryptographic protocols and encryption algorithms are constantly probed for weaknesses by AI systems both on-line as well. The method narrows the time window for attackers to find flaws. AI can design various attack scenarios and search for vulnerable points. For example, it can use brute force or frequency analysis to attack cryptographic systems. Or else it may resort to the more sophisticated differential cryptanalysis. If AI observes an anomaly or a weakness, it can sound the alarm to alert the security people and allow them action immediately. The use of AI in flaw detection is based on machine learning models identifying fine distinctions and variations in the cryptographic data. These patterns may indicate an impending threat or a weakness in the cryptography that should be patched up. With AI-assisted flaw detection, an organization is able to counter potential attackers and protect data.

Further, AI's role in fault detection reaches to post-quantum crypto. With the development of quantum computing, cryptographic systems must change to stay safe. AI can help find the weak links introduced by quantum computing and devise encryption schemes resistant to quantum computers. The issue at hand is to find out whether a finite-length binary string includes understandable information (perhaps owing to determinism) or if it only contains true noise. Here, determinism encompasses the idea that the digital string might represent naturally occurring language that has developed from repetition and use, even if the process of encoding is intentional and premeditated, as in ASCII encoding. A technique for comparing the corresponding order and chaos of the individual bits in two byte strings of any length has to be defined. For this reason, a simple binary entropy test won't cut it. This restriction is a result of its inability to differentiate between really random binary sequences and those that display regularity. When p=0 or p=1, the binary string entropy H(p) is 0, which occurs for fully ordered binary strings when every one of the elements are equal (e.g., all 0s or all 1s). On the other hand, a maximum of 1 for H(p) indicates complete randomness or irregularity when p=0.5. But think of a string like "01010101," which has the number "01." repeated many times. Here, with p=0.5 and H(p)=1, we get the false impression that the string is random while, in fact, it is periodic. Accordingly, the work required is to design a

binary information entropy metric more sharply differentiating than what Equation $H = -\sum_{n=1}^{2} P_n log_2{}^{p_n}$

alone offers. This problem is presented in quantitative terms in Figure 8, which shows examples of order and disorder characteristics for some 8-bit binary strings. The purpose of this metric is to show more clearly the underlying structure and determinism in binary strings, beyond what conventional entropy calculations can indicate. We conclude that AI has an important role to play in the detection of cryptographic flaws, thereby maintaining the security of data and communications. Its ability to analyze complex cryptographic systems, identify weaknesses, and immediately respond to new threats means that AI can be a trusted guardian of data security in the age of digital.

Figure 8. Samples showcasing both ordered and disordered characteristics in connection with compact binary sequences

Example Binary String	Description	Reason
11111111	Perfectly ordered	All 1's
00000000	Perfectly ordered	All 0's
10101101	Mostly Ordered	Mostly01's
101010101	Regular ,not disordered	Repeating 01's
11001100	Regular ,not disordered	Repeating 1100's
10100101	Mostly Ordered	1010 then 0101
1101011	Somewhat disordered	No apparent pattren
10110101	Somewhat disordered	No apparent pattren

6.2. Self-Healing Cryptographic Systems

Self-healing cryptographic systems are nothing less than a new paradigm for data security. The systems don't just passively react to cryptographic mistakes, they go out scuffling for weaknesses. Cryptographic systems incorporating artificial intelligence constantly monitor the evolution—and adaptation and development in real time-of cryptographic protocols everywhere, aiming to detect signs of compromise or degradation. Protecting against the threat A knowledgeable system can act rapidly and directly. These actions may include:

Dynamic Reconfiguration: Vulnerability discovered? The self-healing systems change encryption algorithms or whatever to tighten security.

Isolation of Threats: For example, a cryptographic failure. Self-healing systems can remove infected components or links, so that the problem does not then spread to other members.

Adaptive Updates: The system provides automatic updating or patching of vulnerable cryptographic components.

Anomaly Mitigation: Anomaly detection in self-healing systems can detect abnormal behavior or threats within cryptographic procedures.

Additionally, decentralized ledger technologies such as blockchain can also be used by self-healing cryptographic systems to improve security and transparency. These systems create an immutable audit trail by recording cryptographic events and actions on a blockchain. This does have value for use in forensic analysis or compliance.

In critical infrastructure, secure communications and financial transactions the most significant benefits of self-healing cryptography. Protecting information that must remain effective Such systems also work to shield against unexpected dangers from novel, undetected risks and flaws. Ultimately, AI and self-healing cryptographic systems will be the future of data security. These systems find and fix cryptographic bugs autonomously. But they make themselves the enemy of all threats--even those that aren't conceived yet. As our future belongs to digital information, protection of data and communication security through self-healing cryptographic systems will be all the more important.

7. POST-QUANTUM SECURITY

Data security may bring new opportunities or perils with quantum computing. The Butradent combination of artificial intelligence (AI) and the most advanced cryptography has been an integral part of what we call in the Quantum Future "guarding data". This section looks at the role played by AI in allowing quantum-resistant cryptography and long term solutions to be deployed.

7.1 AI-Enabled Quantum-Resistant Cryptography

Data security is threatened by the possibility that quantum computing will crack conventional encryption methods. A potential answer, nevertheless, has emerged from the merging of AI and encryption: quantum-resistant cryptography. The goal of quantum-resistant cryptography is to create encryption techniques that are immune from attacks using a quantum computer. Inside is a role for AI in the design and development of quantum-resistant cryptographic techniques.

One of the biggest problems for post-quantum cryptography is designing secure algorithms. So quantum mechanics has to have secure encryption to protect the cryptographic methods and mathematical structures that we use from being cracked by quantum computers' processing power. These constructs are precisely what AI algorithms specialize at discovering and probing. Because AI-driven optimization can make such cryptographic protocols both safe and speedy, quantum-resistant encryption is possible.

For example, AI changes encryption parameters such as key length and types of arithmetic operations to strike a balance between speed and security. As a result, quantum-resistant encryption does indeed have practical applications. Moreover, AI can mimic quantum attacks and determine how resistant cryptographic systems are. Because of threats recognized by quantum computing, artificial intelligence has an advantage in designing unbreakable encryption methods. Simulated quantum attacks can even teach machine learning models to build more secure algorithms themselves. One other advantage of AI-aided quantum cryptography is its flexibility. The development of quantum computing technology leads to new attack surfaces. Relying on quantum computing, AI can comb through the threat landscape as things change day by day and alter or upgrade existing cryptographic protocols whenever necessary to protect data.

7.2 Long-Term Security Solutions

In the era of quantum computing, long-term security is an essential. Additionally, the formulae of today's cryptographic systems and encryption methods must stand up to time. They are being required downing entire generations-to keep secrets safe for several decades or more years at a stretch. AI shapes these long-term security plans. And essential to long-term security is the development of so called post quantum safe standards. These standards set out the conditions any cryptographic algorithm needs to satisfy in order for it be immune from quantum computer attacks. AI helps pick those standards, and confirms that they are healthy ones for the future. Second, AI research into other encrypted methods also is better than tradition encryption. Lattice-based cryptography is one possible route to quantumresistant security. This increases the speed of creation and optimization for lattice-based cryptographic protocols, opening up possibilities to long term secure solutions. The concept of QKD is included in long-term security as well. At the level of key distribution, QKD protects communications by exploiting quantum physics. AI can help put applications of the QKD system one step closer to being practical and mass-produced. In this way, it proclaims itself as long-term stable pillar in the market for security products. Blockchain also offers long-term security. Distributed ledger technologies electronically encode cryptographic events and transactions in such a way that it is impossible to change what was done; the effect this has throughout time forms an electronic historical archive which can always be examined as part of auditing cryptography systems, so long as they are constructed on distributed-ledger technology. So, with quantum computing threatening data security, post-quantum security is essential. The coming of the age of quantum means that there must be AI-enabled, quantum resistant cryptography and long-term security to protect important information. This chapter stresses that the role of AI is especially significant for data security and resisting quantum threats.

8. FUTURE HORIZONS

But now that a new age of technology is coming, the marriage between artificial intelligence (AI) and cryptography will completely change this online security game. In that brave new world, we only have a taste of the boundless value there is to be gained by working with AI and crypto.

8.1 Realizing the Potential of AI-Crypto Synergy

The future of AI and crypto is limitless, transforming the way we nab digital information. This section covers all the possible ways this synergy can be accomplished and applied to ensuring online safety. One of the big ways to do that is democratizing security. Security enabled by AI? AI-driven cryptographic implementations could allow strong security to be widely available to users and organizations. It's a decentralization; people and small units can protect their digital assets better. But the AI-cryptography synergy also initiates prospects for customized security schemes. According to user behavior analysis and according to users 'specific security needs, algorithms can determine the cryptographic protocols that best meet their special requirements. Not only does this give the users a better experience, it also strengthens security by reducing excessive friction. And integrating AI into cryptographic systems means threats can be detected and addressed in real time. AI algorithms constantly watch over network traffic and data flow to look for abnormalities or security threats. Either way, it's early intervention of external threats to diminish the damage from breaches and flaws. In terms of privacy, this overlap between AI and cryptos results in better techniques. methods, such as differential privacy securities for users 'data and zero knowledge proof that information always remains in the hands of consumers when it comes into practical application AI to assist them. A second frontier is the weaving of an AI-crypto ecology. For one thing, threads are being spun from a string of potential applications for AI models and cryptographic protocols; furthermore warps come with blockchain technology itself. So these ecosystems are constantly improving, and data exchange is transparent. It's not an exaggeration to say that they will completely transform industries such as healthcare, finance and supply chain management.

8.2. Challenges and Promises

This marks the future AI-crypto synergy, which is at once attractive and problematic. This chapter explores the obstacles and opportunities on this transformative process. One of the biggest problems is lack of training in strong AI and cryptography. When people and organizations get a handle on the subtleties of both fields, this synergy is at its fastest. This is the chasm in knowledge which progress will have to bridge, cultivating interdisciplinary expertise. Furthermore, as AI-crypto synergy develops, ethical considerations are increasingly important. Examples of the problems that need to be resolved in a responsible manner for cryptographic systems include those related to privacy, bias and social responsibility. Interoperability is another challenge. A smooth linking of different components and platforms (i.e., between emerging AI-crypto ecosystems) is an important prerequisite for the success or failure of these systems. As for assurances, online safety and data protection will reach unprecedented levels in the future. A combined AI-crypto could means a world where data cracks are the exception, privacy is king and digital trusts spread like dust. When it comes to the promise of AI in developing post-quantum cryptography, making sure data remains secure as a new generation of quantum computing technology emerges--they mean even more. But AI-based cryptographic innovation will keep advancing to anticipate new dangers, ensuring long term data security. In a nutshell, the concurrence of AI and cryptography is redefining online security. You can have democratized security, personalized solutions, and above all real-time threat detection--as well as privacy-preserving techniques. They are all accessible to you now. To take full advantage of this synergetic power, we must overcome obstacles such as education, morality and interoperability. Forward we march, and the online safety/data protection frontier has never looked so auspicious.

9. CONCLUSION

In the concluding chapter, "Future Outlook: The Synergies Between Advanced AI and Cryptographic Research, in which we've taken you on a truly interesting journey to the cutting edge of artificial intelligence (AI) and cryptography is one such synthesis. That symbiosis embodies a modern reconception of information security and privacy in the digital age. In the course of this chapter, we've seen that these two have had a great impact on one another. The meeting of AI and cryptography is not just overlap; it has washed away the boundaries that online safety had long relied upon. This chapter describes in concrete terms how this synergy is unfolding. From AI-assisted encryption and cryptanalysis, raising both the security and efficiency of a cryptographic system to new levels; through combined breakthroughs in co-orbiting influenza vaccines. This wave of artificial intelligence is further reinforced by privacy-preserving AI which uses systems like zero-knowledge proof and encrypted machine learning. Such technology is helping such companies and people to strike the right balance between data insights and user privacy. What's more, self-healing cryptographic systems which are based on AI greatly hasten the prediction and proactive avoidance of possible flaws in data protection. A world of democratized security, and personalize remedies to problems On the horizon. A trusted online world The future is digital. On the other hand, one should be aware of these difficulties in front. And we have to make sure our education is there, and people are aware that this relationship is symbiotic. Ethical aspects also come into play; as does the importance of interoperability. This convergence takes readers past a single technology, creating limitless chances to strengthen data security and the safety of the Web. It is a new era. A time when AI plus cryptography will transform the way we protect our digital lives.

REFERENCES

Gope, P., Millwood, O., & Sikdar, B. (2022). A Scalable Protocol Level Approach to Prevent Machine Learning Attacks on Physically Unclonable Function Based Authentication Mechanisms for Internet of Medical Things. *IEEE Transactions on Industrial Informatics*, 18(3), 1971–1980. doi:10.1109/TII.2021.3096048

Govardhana Reddy, H. G., & Raghavendra, K. (2022). Vector space modelling-based intelligent binary image encryption for secure communication. *Journal of Discrete Mathematical Sciences and Cryptography*, 25(4), 1157–1171. doi:10.1080/09720529.2022.2075090

Gowda, V. D., Prasad, K. D. V., Gite, P., Premkumar, S., Hussain, N., & Chinamuttevi, V. S.K.D.V. (2023). A novel RF-SMOTE model to enhance the definite apprehensions for IoT security attacks. *Journal of Discrete Mathematical Sciences and Cryptography*, 26(3), 861–873. doi:10.47974/JDMSC-1766

Hussain, Pazhani, & A. K. (2023). A Novel Method of Enhancing Security Solutions and Energy Efficiency of IoT Protocols. *IJRITCC, 11*(4), 325–335.

Karatas, G., Demir, O., & Sahingoz, O. K. (2019). A Deep Learning Based Intrusion Detection System on GPUs. *2019 11th International Conference on Electronics, Computers and Artificial Intelligence (ECAI),* 1-6. 10.1109/ECAI46879.2019.9042132

Knudsen, L. R., & Mathiassen, J. E. (2000). A chosen-plaintext linear attack on DES. *Proceedings of the International Workshop on Fast Software Encryption (FSE)*, 262–272.

Kumar, P. H., & Samanta, T. (2022). Deep Learning Based Optimal Traffic Classification Model for Modern Wireless Networks. *2022 IEEE 19th India Council International Conference (INDICON)*, 1-6. 10.1109/INDICON56171.2022.10039822

Kumar, R., & Ashreetha, B. (2023). Performance Analysis of Energy Efficiency and Security Solutions of Internet of Things Protocols. *IJEER*, *11*(2), 442–450. doi:10.37391/ijeer.110226

Kumar & Chaturvedi. (2023). Securing networked image transmission using public-key cryptography and identity authentication. *Journal of Discrete Mathematical Sciences and Cryptography, 26*(3), 779-791. doi:10.47974/JDMSC-1754

Musa, A., & Mahmood, A. (2021). Client-side Cryptography Based Security for Cloud Computing System. *2021 International Conference on Artificial Intelligence and Smart Systems (ICAIS)*, 594-600. 10.1109/ICAIS50930.2021.9395890

Pavankumar, P., & Darwante, N. K. (2022). Performance Monitoring and Dynamic Scaling Algorithm for Queue Based Internet of Things. *2022 International Conference on Innovative Computing, Intelligent Communication and Smart Electrical Systems (ICSES)*, 1-7. 10.1109/ICSES55317.2022.9914108

Reza, M. N., & Islam, M. (2021). Evaluation of Machine Learning Algorithms using Feature Selection Methods for Network Intrusion Detection Systems. *2021 5th International Conference on Electrical Information and Communication Technology (EICT)*, 1-6. 10.1109/EICT54103.2021.9733679

Sharma & Arun. (2022). Priority Queueing Model-Based IoT Middleware for Load Balancing. *2022 6th International Conference on Intelligent Computing and Control Systems (ICICCS)*, 425-430. 10.1109/ICICCS53718.2022.9788218

Sharma, A. (2023). A novel approach of unsupervised feature selection using iterative shrinking and expansion algorithm. *Journal of Interdisciplinary Mathematics*, *26*(3), 519–530. doi:10.47974/JIM-1678

Shivashankar & Mehta. (2016). MANET topology for disaster management using wireless sensor network. *International Conference on Communication and Signal Processing, ICCSP 2016*, 736–740. . doi:10.1109/ICCSP.2016.7754242

Singla, A., & Sharma, N. (2022). IoT Group Key Management using Incremental Gaussian Mixture Model. *2022 3rd International Conference on Electronics and Sustainable Communication Systems (ICESC)*, 469-474. 10.1109/ICESC54411.2022.9885644

Suryawanshi, V. A., & Chaturvedi, A. (2022). Novel Predictive Control and Monitoring System based on IoT for Evaluating Industrial Safety Measures. *IJEER*, *10*(4), 1050–1057. doi:10.37391/ijeer.100448

Tan, S., Knott, B., & Wu, D. J. (2021). CryptGPU: Fast Privacy-Preserving Machine Learning on the GPU. *2021 IEEE Symposium on Security and Privacy (SP)*, 1021-1038. 10.1109/SP40001.2021.00098

Zhu, S., & Han, Y. (2021, August). Generative trapdoors for public key cryptography based on automatic entropy optimization. *China Communications*, *18*(8), 35–46. doi:10.23919/JCC.2021.08.003

Chapter 3
Artificial Intelligence–Supported Bio–Cryptography Protection

K. Sriprasadh
https://orcid.org/0000-0003-2494-6151
SRM Institute of Technology, India

ABSTRACT

Cryptography is a technological term to protect a secret message or information. The practices of converting the normal text into unreadable form are called encryption. It is possible through key management. Artificial intelligence is a technology that supports all domain in decision making. Bio-inspired cryptography is bio-cryptography that can identify the human unique features and covert as a key and incorporate in the encryption process through artificial intelligence multiple bio-cryptographic keys that can be linked into a single key module with artificial intelligence decision-making support in the decryption part. Through decision-making support, exact and accurate authentication can be made possible.

1. INTRODUCTION

Cryptography is normally is done as a practice in the form of converting normal text into encrypted text the through key. Key may be symmetric and asymmetric, In the process of cryptography key is involved in converting the data into inaccessible format with the support of key. In the bio cryptography similar process can be considered .Initially bio cryptography should be analysed to know the knowledge about the bio cryptography. Cryptographic ideology which involves the human unique features in identifying and authenticating a user for provisioning the service is can be coined as bio cryptography (Alroobaea et al., 2022).

Organizations needs of security in a better manner the multiple types of authentication can be provided based on the various aspects of credentials, those data can be duplicated in one or in another form, so that such data for security should be replaced with the data or credentials that are not matched or duplicated for authentication trials. As the cyber criminals act in precise manner to match the security data with the fake data to satisfy the authentication, bio inspired cryptographic system is recommended for data

DOI: 10.4018/979-8-3693-1642-9.ch003

protection. The told authenticating system works with unique features of human. It can be considered for authentication purpose for providing ultimate security for human data.

Authentication in many ways can be considered for security of data or for accessing a device. Authentication is based on the users the authentication can be varied for the company staff and authentication can be different for the end users. Different level of authentication can be considered for people to people based on the knowledge level. Those security should be in a standardize manner assuring total security for the device or a service.

To understand in the better manner end users cannot use multiple or two level authentication as technical or educated person does. But similar level security should be provided to their earning and belongings. For this reason Bio cryptography can provide a multi or similar protection. In this book chapter multiple unique human features are matched and mapped in a single verification term. That will provide them an authentication proven system.

Authentication model can considered in two ways they are

1. Based on the security model
2. Based on the User level of usage

Let's take a closer look at the many sorts of authentication techniques available:

Figure 1. Different types of authentication

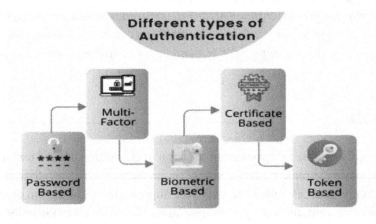

2. LITERATURE REVIEW

A literature review has been done on various biometrics factor for authenticating a user, based on users' own identical property that the user possesses to provide the security to the user and user data.

Through table 1, the following error correction ideology are studied, and show cased for the user as for the understanding from the table 1, keystroke-based bio-metric security and voice recognition, error correction is made through discretization it was referred from Monrose et al. (1999). Signature identification ideology is understood from Hao and Chan (2002). In this ideology, signature velocity forward features and backward features are understood in the form of graphical representation here error

Table 1. Biometric features for authentication

Biometrics	Identifying Features	Error Correction	Ref.
Keystroke	Duration, latency: a computer user's typing patterns consist of durations for each letter typed and latencies between keystrokes	Discretization	Monrose et al., 1999
Voice	Text-dependent or text-independent speaker utterance units	Discretization	Monrose et al., 2001
Signature	Dynamic signature features, such as pen-down time, max forward Vx (Velocity in x direction), max backward Vy (velocity in y direction), time when the last peak of Vx or Vy occurs, pressure, height-to-width ratio, and so on.	Averaging	Hao et al., 2002
Face	Facial features: positions, sizes, Angles, etc	RS code	Chen & Chandran, 2007
Iris	Digital representation of iris image processed with Gabor wavelet	RS code Hadamard	Hao et al., 2006
Fingerprint	Minutiae points: ridge ending and ridge bifurcation	Quantization	Uludag et al., 2005
Palmprint	Unique and stable features such as principal lines, wrinkles, minutiae, delta points, area/size of palm	RS code	Kumar & Kumar, 2008
Head	Acoustic signals modulated by physiological structures of human head	Neural-network	Rodwell et al., 2007
Mouse	Types of mouse actions, such as mouse-move, drag-and-drop, point-and-click, and silence; traveled distance (in pixels); elapsed time (in seconds); and movement direction	Neural-network	Nazar et al., 2008

correction is made averaged. Facial movement and face recognition error are identified by RS code it was referred from Chen and Chandran (2007). Iris identification and authentication as refereed from Hao et al. (2006) here the learned element is iris image being processed gabot wavelet. Fingerprint identification or detection user authentication is refereed through Uludag et al. (2005) here error correction is being identified as quantization. Considering the palm print biometrics, it was referred through Kumar and Kumar (2008) here the error correction through RS code and it has unique and stable feature such as principal lines. Head is considered for the authenticating a person neural network-based error correction has been considered it was referred through O'Connell-Rodwell (2007).

3. SECURITY MODELS IN PRACTICES

3.1 Based on the Security Model

Model based security is based on the level of the security the user prefers the user can single level of security, two level security or multi-level security. The complexity of the security based on the value of the data or the application that to be used. For better understanding if the security of the mere data single or two levels security authentication is preferred. If the securing credentials like property documents or any investing banking bonds or while transferring money a multi-level security can be considered (miniOrange, n.d.).

3.2. Based on the User Level Usage

This way of security authentication is based on the user level of security. Users very much aware of the technology and other authentication complexities they prefer the multi-level of authentication for their applications. Coming to the layman normal person, who doesn't have much knowledge about the authentication procedures and complexities mostly prefer for the single level security authentication and two-level authentication.

Before discussing about combination of the authentication aspects different types of authentication methodologies are elaborated for the better understanding.

3.2.1. Protection Through Passwords

Most prominent method of protection is provided through password protection, The most commonly used login authentication system is through password protection, on the regular daily based login system is password authentication system. To utilize the online services to enter the using system all required to passwords, while using password-based authentication system the user is providing his username and password as self-authenticating him. Mostly password will be informed of remembered by the user. The password types will be numeric, alphabetical, or alpha numeric symbolic. Mostly the password will be the combination of all the these. Password length will be varied product to product the password length will be minimum four character for the mobile phones length will be eight characters for mail or other services protection. The password is matched with the previous stored set of integers in the data base, if it matches the service access is enabled or otherwise it is disabled.

Figure 2. Password protection process

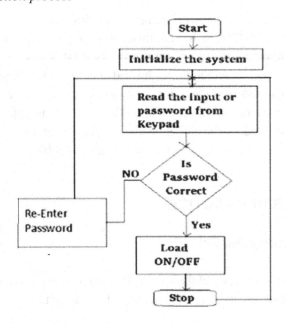

The password protection can be easy challenged and able to break by the cyber criminals. For the best password protection, password should often change at regular intervals, If the use of same password prolongs there is chances of attack of cybercriminals by that operation similar to phishing and data breeches is possible. Due to the foretold drawback's user requires furthermore protection over the password protection for their working applications. Organizations using the password protection in their systems, looking for better protection now for their systems for protecting their data credentials.

3.2.2. Authentication With Multiple Parameters

Authentication with multiple parameters is a verification method in which a user should pass multiple parameters conditions. To gain the access of the services multiple parameter kind of factors must be proven by the user. With the support of password protection and other multi-level of other security aspect also considered here. User should prove his authentication. It may be answering his personal questions, which he only may know. A single time password will be generated and provided to the user through his mail or mobile number, based on the above said parameters the user will try to gain the service with their Username and Password.

Figure 3. Multi parameter authentication control flow

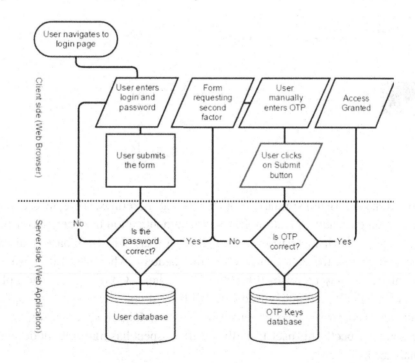

The user may choose any of the methodology to prove his authentication on any of muti-factor methodologies, it may be single time password or with replying to the personal questions or through clicking the time stamp link that has been sent to your mail as a part of authentication. This security aspect can be considered as most trusted as multiple parameters are involved in the authentication procedures.

Comparing to the password protection system is somewhat it is secured. Most organisation follows multi parameter authentication system. In day-to-day examples we can look after this systems in bank transaction application.

3.2.3. Authentication Through Biometric

Every user has unique features that others don't possess. The users possess unique features in the following aspects in human body, thumb, retinas, palms, voice, facial reorganisation, finger impression. These features collectively grouped under a attribute aspect and a security model is developed biometric oriented authentication. These physicals can be verified individually or collectively matched with the previous data and authentication provided. These aspects are already in the usage in market for attendance marking and device accessing and in biometric money transaction cards.

Figure 4. Biometric authentication methodology

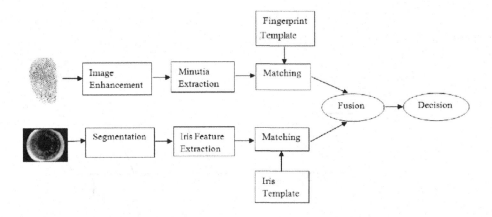

Entity corporeal characteristics similarly fingerprints, palms, retinas, voice, face, and voice identification being used in biometric authentication. Biometric authentication has been performed by upcoming steps: formerly, the physical characteristics of individuals are saved in a database. Individuals' corporeal features are checked against the data contained in the database whenever a user wants to access any device or physically enter any premises (Organization, School, Colleges, and Workplace). Biometric user verification ideological technique is used worldwide by almost everywhere its applications are from providing attendance to confirming the citizenship of a nation. It has been employed in all sectors where security is an essential aspect. This user-friendly security aspect has multiple modesamong them some methods are analyzed as follows.

3.2.1 Fingerprint Impression

To work with fingerprint security access over the security enables access. The fingerprint impression initially taken and stored in the database, while proving the authentication it is been checked with the previously stored record if the fingerprint matches with the previous record the service is provided or otherwise the service is denied. Fingerprint is a unique feature in all humans which will differ from person to person; even twins differ with their finger impression. Even in some advanced authentication system even a minute finer impression lines called as papillary ridges, furrows, loops, whorls, and arches., are recorded in some advanced Fingerprint authentication systems, As the biometric is useful to the user and it has high accuracy comparable to other authentication devices. This Biometric system considering it a real time example, it is common to see nowadays the system is utilized in user mobiles where any of the finger impression is stored as a key and it is matched with the Biometric' similarly user is identifies and security is provided In self-proving applications like, attendance to citizenship of the users.

3.2.2 Securing Through Retina and Iris

In this mode of biometric system, scanners scan the retina and the iris through a strong light. This light impinged into the human eyes and the retina and iris get scanned and the pattern of retina and iris is get stored in the database. This pattern is compared when the user attempts to access the product or the service.

3.2.3 Biometric Security Through Facial

Human face is used as the security aspect for locking the device in facial authentication, multiple angles and multiple aspects of the face is captured and stored in database.

Figure 5. Biometric authentication methodology through facial recognize

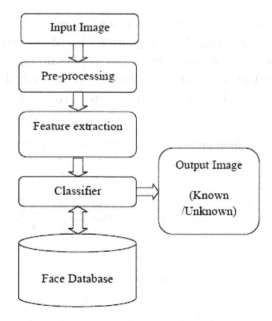

User attempts to use the device or application. The face features are compared with previous stored data and the access or denial is provided to the user.

3.2.4 Biometric Voice Recognition

Humans voice tone will differ person to person. Initially the voice tone is stored in a data base with various angles with a various modulations. A secret code is trained and stored in the database with the modulations.

Figure 6. Biometric authentication methodology through voice

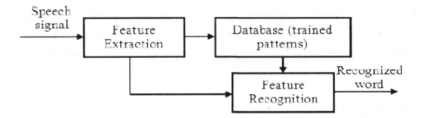

recognised. So, while the users access the device with the code with his or voice it accepts and allows user to access. So, if the code or voice is not acceptable form the access id denied.

3.2.5 Certificate-Based Authentication

This authentication involves only software not on other human features it is different compared to bio metric based. In this authentication certificate is generated based on the request of the user users should prove their identity, It may be by their username or password or through the challenging questions. The user should answer the secret question and sign with public key and private key. Based on this a one-time accessible certificate is provided. The certificate will be provided based on valid username and password.

Figure 7. Certificate-based authentication

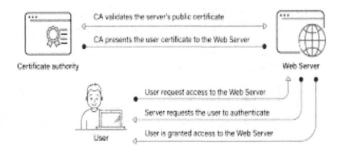

This certificate is valid for a single session and with the particular time interval. These modes of authenticating provide better security without any external hardware tool. The digital signature is linked with the certificate to strengthen the security. In this authentication method the Certificate-based authentication identifies people, servers, workstations, and devices by using an electronic digital identity. In our daily lives, a digital certificate functions similarly to a driver's licence or a passport. A certificate is made up of a user's digital identity, which contains a public key and a certification authority's digital signature. This certificate verifies that the public key and the person who issued the certificate are both the same person. When a user attempts to log in to a server, they must first present their digital certificate. The server checks the digital certificate's identity and credibility by confirming that the user has a correctly associated private key with the certificate using cryptography.

3.2.6 Token-Based Authentication

In this system of Token-Based Authentication the users are allowed to enter their identifications once at a time and to receive a link to encrypted string in return of exchange. You will be allowed to access the service. There will no requirements re input your credentials latter. This digital link token will ensure the gained access of the service. This authentication system are mostly use use-cases, similar to Restful APIs that are accessed by many frameworks and clients.

Figure 8. Token-based authentication

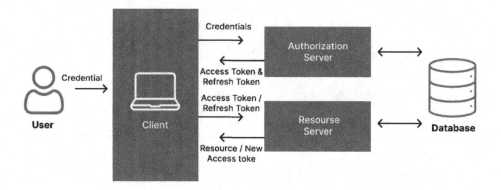

Authentication through token based consists of authentication tokens that will be provided through server, Token based authentication performs in the following manner, and authentication is performed in four stages as initially as Demand, Confirmation, Tokens and Determination.

In Demand, the user client demands for acceptance to protection to asset interestingly. With the support of username and user credentials the demand for the link is generated. In the verification process after proving the client's certificates the user confirms his presence in using the service, and then the tokens are exchanged between clients and server. After exchanging of authentication tokens, the access is granted to the user to access the service.

Considering the pros and cons of the method of token-based authentication it is having good effectiveness, adaptability and security. In the cons part secret key can be compromised and the authenticate period of access has been comparatively will provide the chance attackers to access over it.

3.2.7 One-Time Sign-On Authentication (SSO)

In the method of One Time –sign on it is similar to username and password system. In this initially created when the user the creates the account to get any of the service, he /she provided with secret single sign on key through that entire service are provided, for example a Gmail account is created through that username password entire Google service can be obtained. As the Google is providing multiple service mail services to money transaction, here they can make a single sign on to access entire services. This sign on can considered double sided sword at one end you can experience a smooth access of services through a single sign on, on another end your username and password exposed multiple times and chances to pave way for the security breach.

Figure 9. One-time sign on

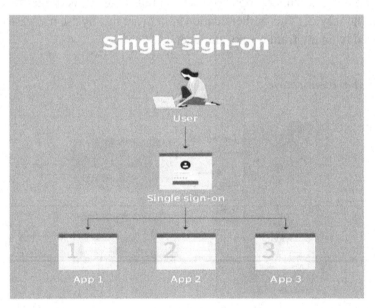

The user should remember his username and password only. The user has to create the username and password, if they forget their username and password, they can contact the admin and proving the identity and authentication they can re-sign in their account and start access their services.

3.2.8 Dual Factor Authentication

In the dual factor authentication user is to pass to two different authentication sign in procedures to prove their identity as the proper user, there is chances of attack if the eaves dropper attempt to access the account when it comes to dual authentication mode there is s chances, the attempter will be locked any one of the point.

Figure 10. Dual factor authentication

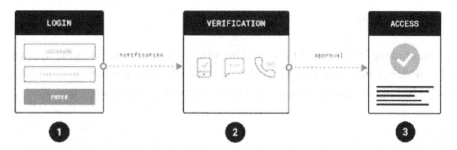

In this method even though user login with his username and his password an OTP is generated and it is forwarded to his mobile or to his email the user should type the message to prove that he is the right person accessing his own account or a challenge for proving his identity is triggered to the user while the time of login Most of the multiple service providers like money apps banking apps utilize dual factor authentication system for protecting their device and their account

3.2.9 Adaptive Authentication

In this authentication methodology multiple factors like users device IP, Location data, device data and access time of the device are considered while authentication approval it is apart from two factor authentication it can be considered as multi factor authentication .In this authentication methodology the user are enabled enter the username and password, while entering the information his device ip address, device address and time of device access in taken into consideration matching all the factors verifying the user is accessing from prominent area or device the approval is provided based on the request.

Figure 11. Adaptive authentication

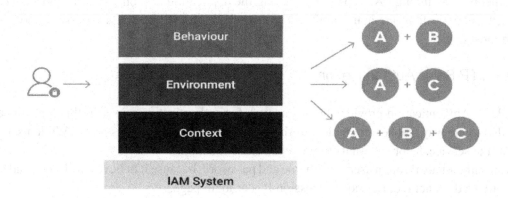

You could have experienced this authentication, while using Gmail services, when you use the Google in different or new device initially apart from your old device it provides a approval call or message to the old device you mostly use, After getting authenticated from the user only it allows to access the service. Through this security authentication methodology user genuineness is proved.

3.2.10 API Authentication

Application programming Interfaces (API's)are a important links which allows the applications to communicate and provide services and to exchange required authentication before imitating the access of any applications, the targeted application really requires the authentication of the client .

Figure 12. API authentication

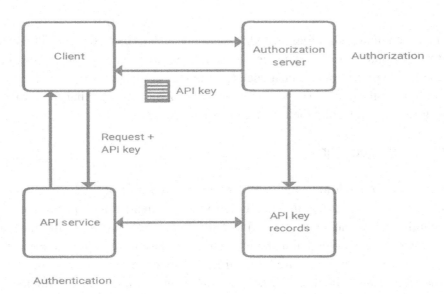

Individual applications have their application security gate ways in that each end user will be proving their authentication through APIs before accessing the application it is one security aspect. There are many API authentications are in use in that HTTP Basic, Auth, API keys and OAuth are most popular one and most in use.

3.2.11 HTTP Basic Authentication

HTTP Basic Authentication provides the framework for authenticating a user in this form of security it provided in the way that server challenges the user with username and password. While user tries to access of the service, he or she wants to prove his authentication.

It is an authenticity through user's username and password, because it believes in HTTP header itself. This approach does not require cookies, session IDs or login page.

Figure 13. HTTP authentication

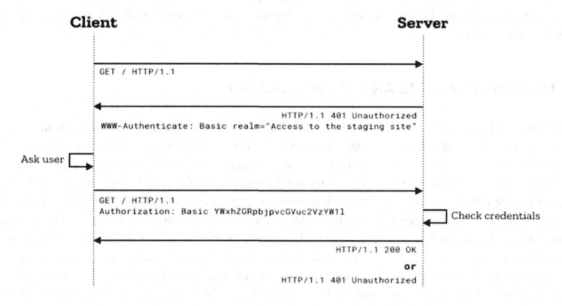

3.2.12 API Passwords

API key is an unique solution for the web service queries it identifies the user request based on the source, when the request arises from the user a secret key is generated a key token is enabled and provided to the user. The user should use this key while using it first time through registration. This key token is made pair with the API. If the user attempts user the service subsequent times, previously generated token similar link will be activated, and verification is made, and service is provided.

Figure 14. API password transaction

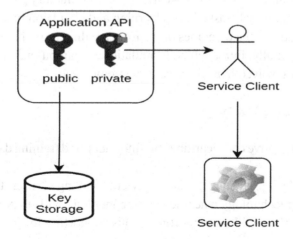

Simply saying an ID is created based on the user credentials; this id is used entry all service access to better understanding UPI money transactions works under this concept of API password security (Anees et al., 2022).

4. MACHINE LEARNING AND CRYPTOGRAPHY

Still, they will have a series of input/ affair dyads for the unknown function f, if the cryptanalyst possesses a set of matching plaintext/ cipher text bits. Exercising a learning algorithm that can conclude f from this data collection can serve as a precious cryptanalytic tool. Also, a chosen- cipher text attack subventions the cryptanalyst the capability to query the unknown function f at any given point. Thus, a learning algorithm that can infer f through queries can prove to be an effective cryptanalytic tool. It's worth noting that a description of learn ability that allows for" approximate" learning is well- suited for this problem. However, they will be suitable to decipher 99 of the plaintext, if the cryptanalyst can learn an approximation of f that aligns with f 99 of the time. Let us first consider a known plaintext attack. Sound cryptographic design principles mandate that f should have an equal liability of outputting 0 or 1. This generally implies that the contents of the shift register can be viewed as a aimlessly named illustration from {0, 1} n, drawn according to the invariant distribution. (We emphasize that this supposition is what makes our statements academic; thorough analysis or trial is necessary to validate the reasonableness of this supposition in each proposed direction.) There live colourful learning- proposition results that assume exemplifications are drawn from {0, 1}" grounded on the invariant distribution. While this supposition may feel unrealistic and restrictive in utmost learning operations, it aligns impeccably with a cryptographic script. What assignments can be deduced from cryptography?

A deep learning model cannot be trained with only one source of training data in some applications. As a result, many data owners want the set up to study both their data from all the form. In order to attain the target, they can use one cloud and let the model in the cloud learn from their data. The cloud largest data storage possesses a huge amount of different data sources. To protect the data of the users cloud storage security should be ensured for that a homomorphic form of encryption is recommended.

Participating translated training data aimed two tricks (i.e. introductory gambit and improved gambit) to save sequestration for druggies who asked deep learning and cloud combine each other to ensure the data security. It is understood that the outcomes of the form are direct to achieve to be obliged, but there have chances to disclose. Initially, introductory formulation of gambit and the cloud are grounded to community-key completely involved in encryption of homomorphic.

4.1 The Multi-Level Complexity

There are two types of collaborative deep learning: sharing encrypted training data and sharing encrypted gradients.

Even though cryptography is protecting the data transaction among the users the security aspect should be upgraded with upcoming technology machine learning ideology will support in this aspect. Some of the machine learning algorithms will be supporting in this supporting for providing better security. In this section machine learning algorithms is discussed.

Encryption programs are not necessarily used on machines model learning, and this decade, machine learning must be in the field of encryption Here Machine learning recognition can be divided into two types(1) non-adversarial adaptive machine learning and (2)Resistance to adversarial machine learning. A non-adversarial machine learning scripting used neural network models Create an encryption scheme and it improves on the previous ones by using a hybrid approach and establishing nonlinear properties of neural network models Encryption and decryption scheme.

4.2 Non-Adversarial Adaptive Machine Learning

The secret key for this program is network parameters (weights and biases) or mixed with some random numbers. The situation is like, if the network is exposed, the solution is not secure. Building a scheme based on symmetric encryption and decryption based on genetic algorithms and DNA software. It consists based on `the key output section and an encryption and decryption section part. First, use the general algorithm for doing the lock Generation, the process of mutation and transmission and choice. The main candidate for the double string is to initialize, then change to delay Get the number of candidates by randomly changing some bits of each candidate the forum. After that, there is a transition to increase Get as many candidates as possible by simply changing a section a couple of major candidates. And the most important candidate obtained from this result is best fitness functionality is maintained. This process continues this continues until the random value reaches the threshold. Then the encryption scheme can be achieved by: DNA computing. Convert a plaintext bit string Create a DNA series by assigning 00 to A (adenine) and 01 to A (adenine). C (cytosine), 10 to G (guanine), 11 to T (thymine). This DNA strand is processed by transcription and translation. Processed and converted to a binary string. This string is performed using an exclusive OR (XOR). An operator using generated keys. Decryption this process is the reverse of the encryption process.

4.3 Resistance to Adversarial Machine Learning

Currently, researchers are focusing on neural cryptography, an encryption and decryption algorithm. You can learn to increase privacy there are enemies in this program. and proposed methods based on deep learning Provides privacy for communications with adversarial neural networks Cryptography. A simple example is Alice, Bob and Eve. Alice and Bob use asymmetric encryption to communicate. They want privacy. Eve refused Communicate with the desire to get a clear text from the communication Encrypted message. For example, it can be seen in the picture. 3. Alice asymmetric constructs the cipher text C from the plaintext P Lock K and send it to Bob. At the same time, Eve also agreed Text C. Bob receives the cipher text C, and tests it Use the K key to decode the C text to save the P text and Print the returned ten text P Bob. Even so, Eve tried Returns the text P and produces the plain text P Eve. Note that Bob has an advantage over Eve because he has the K key, But Eve did not do that (Basu et al., 2019).

5. BIOMETRICS AUTHENTICATION AND MACHINE LEARNING

In terms of safety, enhancing accuracy and performance of biometric authentication structures can't usually be completed with human programming. Artificial intelligence and device getting to know can assist us make our structures greater cosy as well as resourceful. This technique can be understood into two aspects for consideration into domains, Corporal as well as manners.

5.1 Corporal Bio-Metric Technique

Corporal bio-metrics comprises of the whole thing so as to be got previously talked about in proposed research outcome. Those are idea from a individual features similarly unique i.e. (face or fingerprints, DNA, and iris). These features ought to transform as facts, these facts data are taken as input for the analysing grouping the features and decision making through AI gadget that can be analyzed by technology. In a comparison the opposition to a record for substantiation functions.

At one instance in which Artificial Intelligence and Machine Learning proves to be handy is with recognising the human face. Worked significantly to amplify fact elucidation, Artificial Intelligence be capable of assist craft human face recognition with the support of computer systems multiple feature of single face based image are compared and the actual face is indentified to provide authentication.

5.2 Behavioural Bio-Metric Practice

The maximum appealing developments with the intention of AI create feasible is actions bio-metric generation. It makes use of specific actions traits of ways they interact with the arena, matters that the consumer won't even recognise approximately themselves. The defending factor against the cavernous faux swindle tries. A number of famous human feature authentication techniques are analyzed in this section:

- Mousy interests
- Key-stroke activity
- Touch-screen pushes length, region, and force
- Cell tool activity

Through lab research outcome Bio-metrics and information sample are self reliant. The University of Madrid advanced invented *BeCAPTCHA*, an anomaly revealing technique which makes use of human activity based bio-metrics. The technique is achievable that human activity based bio-metrics may be used without any technical support, getting rid of the want for stressful check of person's human act based CAPTCHA demanding situations made to perform. In this technology the users are challenged by clicking a set of pictures of similar images for proving users are not robots .User must prove him that he or she is not robot.

Importantly, behavioural biometrics can help in ensuring safety in the course of a whole consultation. For instance, the person validates himself as well as following it he goes away from system for a instance, if someone takes the control over the system. The user uses the same system, based on the activity the unauthorised access can be detected based on behaviour. For stopping the access systems restricts them by providing self proving questions. By this security in ensured to the users system.

Working Procedure of Multi-Model Bio-Metric Authentication

Bio-metric has its own advantages and disadvantages. The layer based security as well as multi –model verification is recommended to improve accuracy and effectiveness of bio-metric verification, it's essential to layer security with multimodal biometric recognition answers.

Figure 15. Working of biometric authentication multi model

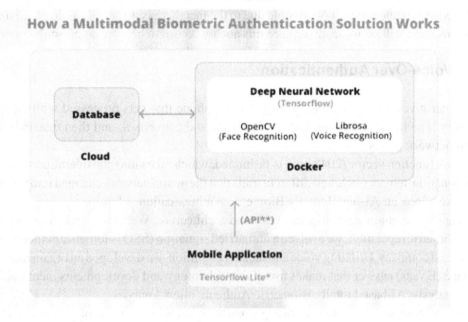

Mobile networks possessed neural networks are tough increase and implement. Neural networks can be integrated into applications the usage of Tensor Flow Lite, but there are various boundaries. Training your neural network models with the Tensor Flow library can help. You may need to thoughtfully layout the structure of the software in advance and placed those necessities into attention.

If a local application isn't viable, this technique may be offloaded to the cloud to procedure the statistics like relaxation API. However, this will incur extra networking sources and require an internet connection.

There is an Nvidia Docker which could simplify the deployment of the device, whilst a carrier company (such as AWS) can provide an uninterrupted communication channel, computing electricity for neural networks, and a convenient interface for scaling your gadget.

Case 1: Facial Identification

The user creates a photograph-imprint that's stored at the tool the use of a digicam. This biometric imprint is transformed and normalized the usage of the OpenCV library.

The face is diagnosed the use of a photograph, and every of the sixty four landmarks detected by way of OpenCV are highlighted. A biometric verification landmark consists of such things as a distance from the bridge of the nose to the attention and other facial features.

Those landmarks and a cutout image of the face are transferred to a deep neural community, that's trained using the TensorFlow library.

An eDNA characteristic vector is formed after neural network processing is finished. The function vector collects the biometric traits of a selected man or woman. The duration of the vector is typically 2048 bits. The lengths depend upon the DNN architecture.

In the course of verification, eDNA is issued and in comparison with the anchor file that become formed earlier. Opposite engineering is not possible due to the fact there is no get admission to to the vector. The biometric machine will periodically replace this anchor record to healthy an person's converting seems.

Case 2: Voice-Over Authentication

The consumer gives a voice sample through a microphone that gets processed with the aid of the Librosa library. The library reads the audio, transforms and converts it, and then transmits biometrics to the neural network (DNN).

An eDNA function vector (2048 bits) is fashioned, which takes into consideration such biometrics as timbre, intonation, tempo, pitch, and different traits that the neural network changed into trained to reply to.

Case take a look at: AI-based totally Biometric Authentication solution

By means of combining a microservice-based architecture, WebRTC, and gadget getting to know powered biometric reputation, we evolved a unmarried signal-on (SSO) biometric authentication solution for a US-based company. Utilizing voice and facial recognition, we developed an organization verification as-a-service (EVaas) answer that makes use of the technology and developments mentioned in advance.

Case Analysis: AI-based totally Biometric Authentication Analysis

By way of combining a microservice-primarily based structure, WebRTC, and gadget studying powered biometric recognition, we developed a single signal-on (SSO) biometric authentication solution for a US-based totally company. Using voice and facial recognition, we developed an organisation verification as-a-carrier (EVaas) solution that uses the technologies and trends mentioned in advance.

This product proved that biometric authentication structures may be tremendously customizable and clean to apply, powering a completely simple consumer interface from behind the scenes. In addition, this case was able to combine with existing systems through API.

Figure 16. Working of biometric authentication multi model

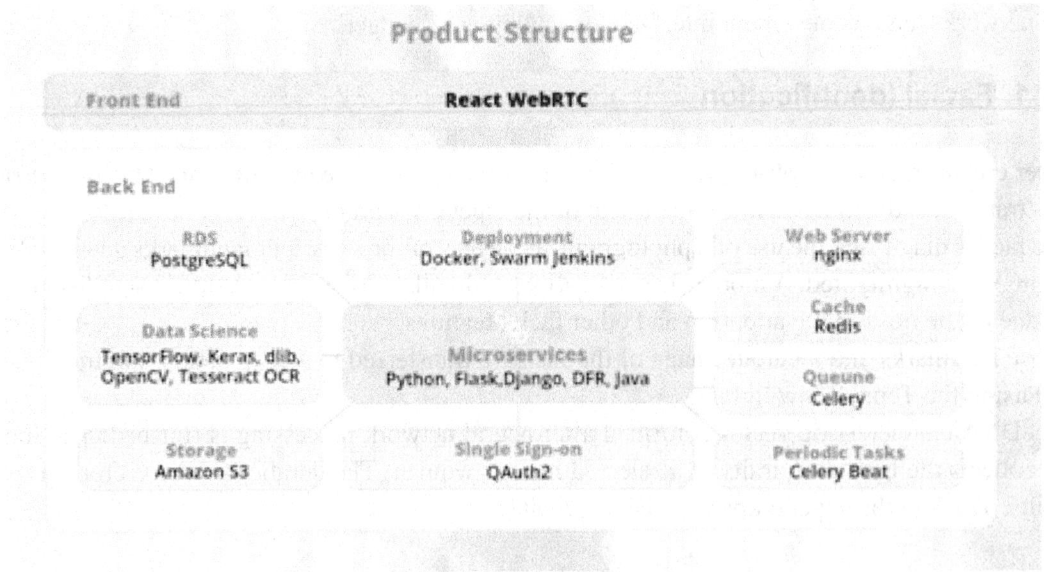

Securing systems isn't a count number to take lightly. While touchy statistics is on the road like covered health records or institutional facts is on the line, it's miles extremely vital to take the measures important to save you statistics breaches. Failure to maintain an excessive level of security surrounding this information can bring about fraud which could value groups tens or even hundreds of tens of millions.

Biometric authentication and verification technology, in particular the ones powered by using synthetic intelligence aren't smooth and frequently require specialists inside the discipline to correctly combine them with present systems. If you are thinking about your alternatives for enforcing new safety features into your device to your business or on your customers, we encourage you to attain out to our ML team to have a communiqué about your need.

Workspace security may be a fiddly money drain, specially for corporations that cope with touchy information, or run multiple offices with heaps of employees. Digital keys are one in every of the standard options for the way safety structures may be automated, but in truth there are lots of downsides like misplaced, forgotten, or faked keys (Rivest, 1991).

Biometrics has proven strong options to the traditional safety features, considering the fact that they represent a concept of "what-you-are" authentication. This indicates, someone can use their unique characteristics like fingerprint, iris, voice, or face to show they have got get right of entry to a positive area. The use of biometrics as a way to authenticate ensures the important thing can't be lost, forgotten, or fabricated. So these days we'll talk about our enjoy with aspect biometrics, that is the combination of area gadgets, AI, and biometrics to put in force AI protection tracking structures for places of work.

5.3 Edging Biometrics

First matters first, what is edging AI? In a traditional architecture of artificial intelligence, a not unusual exercise is to install models and statistics in the cloud, cut loose the working tool or hardware sensor. These forces us to maintain the cloud server in a proper nation, hold a strong internet connection, and pay for the cloud carrier. If the garage seems inaccessible in case a web connection is misplaced, the complete AI utility will become useless. The best brilliant pitfall is that as all of the processing needs to be accomplished on the tool in a short amount of time, and the hardware components need to be effective sufficient and up to date for this function.

For obligations like biometric authentication with face or voice recognition, rapid response and reliability of the security machine are vital. On account that we need to make certain seamless person enjoy in addition to proper safety, counting on edge devices gives those advantages.

Biometric records like worker faces and voices appears to be cozy sufficient, due to the fact they constitute particular styles that may be diagnosed by neural networks. Additionally, this type of information is easier to acquire, as maximum corporations have already got pix of their personnel in their CRM or ERP. This way you can additionally avoid any privacy worries through accumulating, say, fingerprint samples of your people.

Combined with area, we can create a flexible AI safety dig cam device for workspace front. So allows discuss the implementation of this sort of system primarily based on our very own experience of automating workplace entrance tactics with the assist of part biometrics.

A comparative analysis is been processed between various bio-metric ideology those ideas are shared in the table, here characteristic features of each bio metric devices are analyzed with multiple factors and best of the biometric approach is identified.

Table 2. Characteristics features of biometric technologies

Characteristics	Fingerprints	Hand Geometry	Retina	Iris	Face	Signature	Voice
Easy of Use	high	high	Low	Medium	Medium	High	High
Error Incidence	Dryness, dirt, age	Hand injury, age	Glasses	Lighting	Lighting, age, glasses, hair	Changing signature	Noise, colds
Accuracy	High	High	Very high	Very high	High	High	High
User Acceptance	Medium	Medium	Medium	Medium	Medium	High	high
Long Term Stability	High	Medium	high	high	Medium	Medium	Medium

In this table comparison is made between the various characters of bio metric technology and bio metric factors each ideology its own advantages and disadvantages. So the combination of multiple biometric techniques will make security system strong for the usage.

5.4 AI-Based Place of Business Surveillance Machine Design

The main concept in the back of the challenge becomes to authenticate personnel on the workplace entrance with only a look inside the camera. The laptop vision model is capable of discover a person's face, compare it with the formerly obtained picture and release the door. Voice verification turned into brought as an extra step to avoid tricking the system in any manner. The complete pipeline includes 4 models that bring distinct obligations from face detection to speech recognition.

Figure 17. Work flow diagram of multi model of biometric authentication system

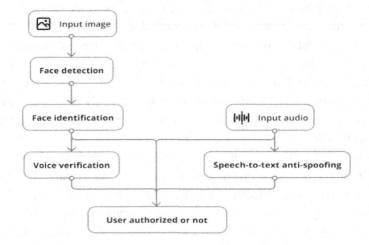

All of those steps are carried out thru a lone facet device that serves as a video/audio enter sensor, in addition to a controller for sending instructions to fasten/release doors. As an part device, NVIDIA Jetson Xavier has been selected. The primary reasons in the back of this choice were the presence of GPU reminiscence (that's important for accelerating inference for deep learning initiatives) and the supply of Jetpack – SDK from NVIDIA, which permits coding on devices in Python3. Therefore, there is no strict need to convert the DS version to another layout and almost all the codebase may be tailored to the device with the aid of DS engineers, so no rewriting from one programming language to some other is required (Vasilchenko, 2024).

5.5 Challenges of Bio Cryptography

As AI supported bio cryptographic has many positive parts there are some challenges to still to meet out also to be discussed in three aspects there is threat to authentication of Bio cryptography.

Identity Spoofing: With the support of same AI technology a Spoof of personality can created with many AI tools .This spoof can take place in image based bio metrics, With support of AI techniques mitigated identity of finger print, iris, face, voice and palm can be created in fake. Fake photos can be replaced to fake photo to prove the authentication. This spoof mirage blinds the human, by that they can't able to differentiate between real and replica. Solution for this challenge should sort in near future.

Deep fakes: Deep fakes is the new threat was reported currently that is artificially created personalities are created as moving images that is videos .This fake videos make false proof and damages their personal image. Deep fakes combines morphed image and voice of the person and created as a moving image .That is portrayed as a real image, Human eye cant able differentiate between real and fake . This is really big challenges to be provided solution.

Legal and Civil challenges: There is huge need of rules and regulation for protecting the identity of human credentials. The personal details can be revealed with some compromises in the real world today. To protect the details proper laws should be framed accordingly and punishment also should be strong for the defaulters .This also can be considered as a challenges to be sorted out (Incode, 2022).

6. CONCLUSION AND FUTURE STUDY

Bio cryptography and authentication based on the bio cryptography is future of protecting humans credentials, as there is no replacement for the human individuality this mode of protection may provide better security. With support of Artificial intelligence supported algorithms will map the multiple human aspect make a relative cryptographic cipher lock of encryption which will be stronger, and the decryption key would be the personal identity will make the better bound of security to the data.

This may happen in near future within a half a decade the biometric based authentication can be act as a key for all kind of banking transactions. For all kind of locking aspects and can used for security locking, medical record locking, for travelling and can make your data safe by using biometric keys. In future for all kind of daily activities will be act as an essential feature (Mthunzi et al., 2019).

REFERENCES

Alroobaea, R., Arul, R., Rubaiee, S., Alharithi, F. S., Tariq, U., & Fan, X. (2022). AI-assisted bio-inspired algorithm for secure IoT communication networks. *Cluster Computing*, *25*(3), 1805–1816. doi:10.1007/s10586-021-03520-z

Anees, A., Hussain, I., Khokhar, U. M., Ahmed, F., & Shaukat, S. (2022). Machine learning and applied cryptography. *Security and Communication Networks*, *2022*, 1–3. doi:10.1155/2022/9797604

Basu, S., Karuppiah, M., Nasipuri, M., Halder, A. K., & Radhakrishnan, N. (2019). Bio-inspired cryptosystem with DNA cryptography and neural networks. *Journal of Systems Architecture*, *94*, 24–31. doi:10.1016/j.sysarc.2019.02.005

Chen, B., & Chandran, V. (2007, December). Biometric based cryptographic key generation from faces. In *9th Biennial Conference of the Australian Pattern Recognition Society on Digital Image Computing Techniques and Applications (DICTA 2007)* (pp. 394-401). IEEE. 10.1109/DICTA.2007.4426824

Hao, F., Anderson, R., & Daugman, J. (2006). Combining crypto with biometrics effectively. *IEEE Transactions on Computers*, *55*(9), 1081–1088. doi:10.1109/TC.2006.138

Hao, F., & Chan, C. W. (2002). Private key generation from on-line handwritten signatures. *Information Management & Computer Security*, *10*(4), 159–164. doi:10.1108/09685220210436949

Incode. (2022, December 12). *The Future of Biometrics Technology: An Overview by Industry*. Retrieved from https://incode.com/blog/future-of-biometrics/

Kumar, A., & Kumar, A. (2008, March). A palmprint-based cryptosystem using double encryption. In *Biometric technology for human identification V* (Vol. 6944, pp. 115–123). SPIE. doi:10.1117/12.778833

miniOrange. (n.d.). *What is Authentication? Different Types of Authentication*. Retrieved from https://blog.miniorange.com/different-types-of-authentication-methods-for-security/

Monrose, F., Reiter, M. K., & Wetzel, S. (1999, November). Password hardening based on keystroke dynamics. In *Proceedings of the 6th ACM Conference on Computer and Communications Security* (pp. 73-82). ACM.

Mthunzi, S. N., Benkhelifa, E., Bosakowski, T., & Hariri, S. (2019). A bio-inspired approach to cyber security. *Machine Learning for Computer and Cyber Security: Principle, Algorithms, and Practices*, 75.

O'Connell-Rodwell, C. E. (2007). Keeping an "ear" to the ground: Seismic communication in elephants. *Physiology (Bethesda, MD)*, *22*(4), 287–294. doi:10.1152/physiol.00008.2007 PMID:17699882

Rivest, R. L. (1991, November). Cryptography and machine learning. In *International Conference on the Theory and Application of Cryptology* (pp. 427-439). Springer Berlin Heidelberg.

Uludag, U., Pankanti, S., & Jain, A. K. (2005, July). Fuzzy vault for fingerprints. In *International Conference on Audio-and Video-Based Biometric Person Authentication* (pp. 310-319). Springer Berlin Heidelberg. 10.1007/11527923_32

Vasilchenko, A. (2024, January 23). *AI Biometric Authentication for Enterprise Security*. Retrieved from https://mobidev.biz/blog/ai-biometrics-technology-authentication-verification-security

ADDITIONAL READING

Ahamed, F., Farid, F., Suleiman, B., Jan, Z., Wahsheh, L. A., & Shahrestani, S. (2022). An Intelligent Multimodal Biometric Authentication Model for Personalised Healthcare Services. *Future Internet*, *14*(8), 222. doi:10.3390/fi14080222

Ahmed, K. I., Tahir, M., Habaebi, M. H., Lau, S. L., & Ahad, A. (2021). Machine Learning for Authentication and Authorization in IoT: Taxonomy, Challenges and Future Research Direction. *Sensors (Basel)*, *21*(15), 5122. doi:10.3390/s21155122 PMID:34372360

Alkadi, R., Al-Ameri, S., Shoufan, A., & Damiani, E. (2021). Identifying drone operator by deep learning and ensemble learning of imu and control data. *IEEE Transactions on Human-Machine Systems*, *51*(5), 451–462. doi:10.1109/THMS.2021.3102508

Alsarhan, A., Al-Ghuwairi, A.-R., Almalkawi, I. T., Alauthman, M., & Al-Dubai, A. (2020). Machine Learning-Driven Optimization for Intrusion Detection in Smart Vehicular Networks. *Wireless Personal Communications*, *117*(4), 3129–3152. doi:10.1007/s11277-020-07797-y

Ananthi, J. V., & Jose, P. S. H. (2021). A Perspective Review of Security Challenges in Body Area Networks for Healthcare Applications. *International Journal of Wireless Information Networks*, *28*(4), 451–466. doi:10.1007/s10776-021-00538-3 PMID:34690480

Arora, P., Kaur, B., & Teixeira, M. A. (2022). Security in Industrial Control Systems Using Machine Learning Algorithms: An Overview. In *ICT Analysis and Applications* (pp. 359–368). Springer. doi:10.1007/978-981-16-5655-2_34

(2018, December). Ashraf Darwish Bio-inspired computing: Algorithms review, deep analysis, and the scope of applications Faculty of Science. *Helwan University, Cairo, Egypt Future Computing and Informatics JournalVolume*, *3*(2), 231–246.

Balamurugan, E., Mehbodniya, A., Kariri, E., Yadav, K., Kumar, A., & Haq, M. A. (2022). Network optimization using defender system in cloud computing security based intrusion detection system withgame theory deep neural network (IDSGT-DNN). *Pattern Recognition Letters*, *156*, 142–151. doi:10.1016/j.patrec.2022.02.013

Bhattacharya, M., Pujari, S., Anand, A., Kumar, N., Jha, S. K., Raj, A., & Hossain, S. M. (2021). Intruder Detection System using Posture Recognition and Machine Learning. *International Journal of Computer Applications*, *183*(19), 17–23. doi:10.5120/ijca2021921533

Brindha, N. V., & Meenakshi, V. S. (2022). A secured optimised AOMDV routing protocol in MANET using lightweight continuous multimodal biometric authentication. *Journal of Ambient Intelligence and Humanized Computing*, *40*, 1–17.

Chiroma, H. (2021). Deep Learning Algorithms based Fingerprint Authentication: Systematic Literature Review. *J. Artif. Intell. Syst.*, *3*(1), 157–197. doi:10.33969/AIS.2021.31010

Gayathri, M., & Malathy, C. (2021). A Deep Learning Framework for Intrusion Detection and Multimodal Biometric Image Authentication. *J. Mob. Multimed.*, *1*, 393–420. doi:10.13052/jmm1550-4646.18212

Gupta, R., Tanwar, S., Tyagi, S., & Kumar, N. (2020). Machine Learning Models for Secure Data Analytics: A taxonomy and threat model. *Computer Communications, 153*, 406–440. doi:10.1016/j.comcom.2020.02.008

Iwendi, C., Anajemba, J. H., Biamba, C., & Ngabo, D. (2021). Security of things intrusion detection system for smart healthcare. *Electronics (Basel), 10*(12), 1375. doi:10.3390/electronics10121375

Kumar, K. S., Nair, S. A. H., Roy, D. G., Rajalingam, B., & Kumar, R. S. (2021). Security and privacy-aware Artificial Intrusion Detection System using Federated Machine Learning. *Computers & Electrical Engineering, 96*, 107440. doi:10.1016/j.compeleceng.2021.107440

Latif, S. A., Wen, F. B. X., Iwendi, C., Wang, L.-L. F., Mohsin, S. M., Han, Z., & Band, S. S. (2022). AI-empowered, blockchain and SDN integrated security architecture for IoT network of cyber physical systems. *Computer Communications, 181*, 274–283. doi:10.1016/j.comcom.2021.09.029

Mittal, M., Iwendi, C., Khan, S., & Javed, A. R. (2020). Analysis of security and energy efficiency for shortest route discovery in low-energy adaptive clustering hierarchy protocol using Levenberg-Marquardt neural network and gated recurrent unit for intrusion detection system. *Transactions on Emerging Telecommunications Technologies, 32*(6), e3997. doi:10.1002/ett.3997

Sedik, A., Faragallah, O. S., El-Sayed, H. S., El-Banby, G. M., El-Samie, F. E. A., Khalaf, A. A. M., & El-Shafai, W. (2021). An efficient cybersecurity framework for facial video forensics detection based on multimodal deep learning. *Neural Computing & Applications, 34*(2), 1251–1268. doi:10.1007/s00521-021-06416-6

Shafiq, M., Tian, Z., Bashir, A. K., Du, X., & Guizani, M. (2020). CorrAUC: A malicious bot-IoT traffic detection method in IoT network using machine-learning techniques. *IEEE Internet of Things Journal, 8*(5), 3242–3254. doi:10.1109/JIOT.2020.3002255

Shafiq, M., Tian, Z., Bashir, A. K., Du, X., & Guizani, M. (2020). IoT malicious traffic identification using wrapper-based feature selection mechanisms. *Computers & Security, 94*, 101863. doi:10.1016/j.cose.2020.101863

Shafiq, M., Tian, Z., Bashir, A. K., Jolfaei, A., & Yu, X. (2020). Data mining and machine learning methods for sustainable smart cities traffic classification: A survey. *Sustainable Cities and Society, 60*, 102177. doi:10.1016/j.scs.2020.102177

Shafiq, M., Tian, Z., Sun, Y., Du, X., & Guizani, M. (2020). Selection of effective machine learning algorithm and Bot-IoT attacks traffic identification for internet of things in smart city. *Future Generation Computer Systems, 107*, 433–442. doi:10.1016/j.future.2020.02.017

Suresh, P., Logeswaran, K., Keerthika, P., Devi, R. M., Sentamilselvan, K., Kamalam, G. K., & Muthukrishnan, H. (2022). Contemporary survey on effectiveness of machine and deep learning techniques for cyber security. In *Machine Learning for Biometrics* (pp. 177–200). Academic Press. doi:10.1016/B978-0-323-85209-8.00007-9

Chapter 4
An Adaptive Cryptography Using OpenAI API:
Dynamic Key Management Using Self Learning AI

R. Valarmathi
https://orcid.org/0000-0002-1535-4552
Sri Sairam Engineering College, India

R. Uma
https://orcid.org/0000-0002-0053-0162
Sri Sairam Engineering College, India

P. Ramkumar
Sri Sairam College of Engineering, India

Srivatsan Venkatesh
Sri Sairam Engineering College, India

ABSTRACT

Security functions which are present now, such as the SHA series of hash functions, other brute force prevention protocols, and much more, are keeping our cyber fields safe from any script-kiddies and professional hackers. But the recent study shows that penetration tools are optimised in numerous ways, enabling the hackers to take in a big advantage over our key logging and brute forcing prevention tactics, allowing them to make a clean hit over the fragile databases. Many of the existing domains now are optimised with the added benefit of artificial intelligence support. Specifically, the OpenAI API market has grown plentiful of their uses, and the password hash automation now has a time to get upgraded.

DOI: 10.4018/979-8-3693-1642-9.ch004

1. INTRODUCTION

The Idea is to create a self-learning and bug withstanding AI. A tremendous data is fed and worst case history of bugs and hackers are collected, using the trustworthy OpenAI's API. Their algorithm is used to train and get the response of a threat immediately instead of a 24hr monitoring of status of the medium. The AI will replace few tedious tasks, making sure to give a complete log of an error or a breach. It locks the important databases and other codes from getting spread, into completely removing any bugs if the bugs which are in active attacking module that has previously encountered by some other instance of this same AI. Moreover, this AI can also be used to shift few keys in the current encryption status, creating new keys over the user location, as well as the domain location systems. This is the future of the great vault of security and privacy.

OpenAI Models are easier to retrieve and train, due to its increasing popularity and their dataset training methods. The dynamic key encryption requires predictive hash generation as well as key storage by AI. The AI model that we are about to train and analyse is the slight variation of OpenAI's API, specifically GPT-3 language model for NLP. First is the analysis phase, in which the data is collected from previously faulty dataset of cryptographic environments, security incidents and its respective cyber protection, the ways of bypassing the history of cyber malfunctions and data breaches, anomalies in existing system, and all the other defects within a system, and finds preventive measures. This form of data collection is especially useful when providing and feeding it to an OpenAI API connected Cryptography machine. It finds the error, if the symptoms of the attack are related to any previous known attack strategy, or if it encounters a new kind of attack, it must store the attack pattern in its database, and must adapt to the upcoming attack by another form of defence, dynamic key management.

Dynamic key Management ensures that the key of certain hash or information gets randomised multiple times in our systems, servers as well as host systems. Dynamic key Management AI also must be responsible for storage, delivery and generating new forms of key hash, either by random generation, or by seeded noise generation. When using a seeded noise generated key, it is a good practice to choose the seed of randomised noise with another randomizer with a unique seed, which ensures that even the seed of the current key gets blown; the decisive algorithm changes the seed of the randomizer responsible for changing seeds of key randomizer. And thus, a triple layer key protection as well as Dynamic key handling is done by OpenAI tool. This Layered Security in any form of media is fool proof and easily operable to an admin as well. Thus the next security encryption comes in the format of protection of this AI from a hack-insider or key logger for API of AI.

Together with all these qualities, we are going to create an AI capable of detection of all forms of intrusion

2. BACKGROUND

Cybersecurity is the most required field of division in this modern era, which solely runs on the digital media for data transfer and usage. In this day and age, thieves may not require your wallet to get your identification, but may readily steal it from the systems you are trusting. This unfolds the term "cybercrime". Traditional security measures face challenges due to evolving hacking techniques, including the use of script bots and AIs (Pearce et al., 2023), rendering manual penetration avoidance and security measures less effective.

Notably, the advent of AI has introduced new complexities, such as spear-phishing using GPT (Khan et al., 2021), overpowering some network-based intrusion detection systems (Gala et al., 2023). Researchers like Joshi et al. (2022), explored automatic penetration methods like SQL Injections, influencing our project's scope. Gallus et al. (2023) investigated how Generative Neural Networks, akin to DALL-E and ChatGPT, can serve as web application penetration testing tools, leveraging Large Language Models (LLM) and Generative Neural Networks.

Research by Li and Oprea (2016), on breach detection using security logs in an enterprise, inspired our AI-IDS to detect breaches through security logs. Memos and Psannis (2020) highlighted the use of AI in honeypots for botnet detection, a crucial component in countering Distributed Denial of Service (DDoS) attacks. Prasad et al. (2023), emphasized the role of GPT models in the cybersecurity domain, guiding our project's direction.

Srinivasan and Deepalakshmi (2021) contributed insights into AI-driven malware detection, González, et al. (2023), explored anomaly detection using Generative AI, influencing our use of AI for detecting anomalies. Kandhro, et al. (2023), delved into real-time detection of malicious intrusions and attacks, guiding our understanding of attacker identification.

Cova et al. (2010), identified the anomalies and analysed the JavaScript code. Bailey et al. (2007), proposed a classification technique and analysed the behaviour of malware.

Song et al. (2008) provided a binary analysis on BitBlaze project. Kruegel et al. (2005) demonstrates to detect the cyber stealth attacks. Zhang et al. (2010) discussed about the challenging threats in Web applications.

Bilge et al, (2011), analyses the DNS queries to detect the domains that involves in malicious activities. Grier et al. (2012) investigated the exploit as a service model by analysing the malicious URLs. Canali et al. (2011), explored the vulnerabilities in the firmware images.

These resources and researchers lay the foundation for the Antibody AI project, reflecting the collective wisdom and advancements in the field of cybersecurity. Their work informs our efforts to develop a robust defense mechanism against emerging cyber threats.

3. PROCESSING WAYS

The Creation of this revolutionary AI comes with a 4-part training and programming method, each of the processes used for some component of the bigger AI, The Antibody so we speak. The process of creation of this AI is dependent on following factors such as,

- Breach Detection using SUND factors
- Historical breach data Detection and Comparison of current breach with previous attempts.
- Security Protocols and Attack Alerting Systems
- Lockdown Protocols and Aftermath Response Mechanisms

3.1 Breach Detection Using "SUND" Factors

"SUND" stands for the four main components as the raw inputs for this protection system, (i.e.) Software Logs, User-Entry Logs, Network Logs, and Database Logs. The Breach Detection system embedded within this AI serves as the primary line of defence, playing a vital role in protecting systems against potential threats posed by key loggers and other malicious entities attempting a brute force attack. The Antibody AI is equipped with a vast array of inputs strategically designed to monitor and ensure the security of systems. These inputs are easily configured to track various parameters, both internal and external to the organization, thereby providing a secure surveillance approach. The primary objective of the Antibody AI is to swiftly identify any irregularities or signs of a breach within the system from the usage of given inputs, enabling proactive measures to be taken promptly. By constantly monitoring the safety of the systems and employing a sophisticated set of inputs, the Antibody AI enhances the overall resilience of the cybersecurity framework, ensuring a robust defence against emerging threats.

The Inputs required by the AI for Breach Monitoring are,

- Software Logs
- User Entry Logs
- Network Traffic Logs
- Database Logs

Additionally, the Antibody AI needs another Parameter to use, which is the IRS access (Intrusion Response System Access).

Each of those inputs is used separately in accordance with the AI's own dataset of "History of Breaches" set. The AI is trained with the History of Breaches Dataset, and when the AI detects a Breach environment using the above given inputs and proceeds to further steps. Input Samples acquired from the logs shown in Table 1.1

Table 1. Input samples acquired from the Logs

Data No.	IP Address	Network Ping of the IP	Software Code Usage of the IP	Sql Injection Detection
1	192.168.0.71	345ms	72% memory	False
2	192.168.0.72	228ms	68% memory	True
3	192.168.0.73	315ms	45% memory	False
4	192.168.0.74	12ms	30% memory	False

3.1.1 Software Log Usage

The AI here uses software logs as a part of any in-app code maliciously runs any key logging or if an outsider/hacker tries Reverse-Brute forcing through some employee's old password. Such cases are still prevailing as a go-to means of penetrating through the security of the company. The AI supposedly detects any form of malicious activity present within an application

- if any Brute forcing is occurring from within the application
- if the application uses any malware code to steal user data
- if the application has any unnecessary backdoors

Whenever there is a malicious code using an innocent part of any software as a host, it is bound to leave its traces within the software, and those traces will definitely be collected via the log. Some of the software code usage is cleared as it may be of over-usage of a singular function, ranging from small memory and ram usages to collectively using a large part of the software. Sometimes, the malicious code doesn't keep track of how much ram it has consumed, while the AI scours through the software checking for valid signatures for the software and the software's memory usage validity. The first defence is to note the usage down and report it to authorities whilst writing the ip of the memory usage. When specific threshold is reached and once the AI detects it, it causes its protocols to activate, decreases secure points and detects the malware to be sent to IRS (Intrusion Response System). Sample Software code log shown in Figure 1.

3.1.2 User Entry Log Usage

User Entry and Exit logs are stored as a part of code in the biometrics attendance section. The AI checks for stray IPs and checkout times to detect any strange activity of any of the IP Addresses within the network, proceeding to alert the Division responsible to handle, also triggering the lockdown protocol series-1 (refer lockdown protocols section) with the instance of the suspicious IP, thus protecting others from the network. If an Optimised Brute Force Algorithm user uses botnets or zombies to enter, a number of trials and entries can be detected and the lockdown protocol series-2(refer lockdown protocols section) is triggered to protect the users. Other users are safe to work since their work is forcefully and temporarily moved to a virtual working environment until the attacker is contained or the botnets are removed by safety measures. User Sign in log shown in Figure 2.

Figure 1. Software code log

Name	Description	Status
Microsoft Exchange Active Directory Topology	Provides AD topology information to Exchange services. If this service is stopped, most Exchange services ar...	Started
Microsoft Exchange EdgeSync	The Exchange EdgeSync Service.	Started
Microsoft Exchange File Distribution	Microsoft Exchange File Distribution Service.	Started
Microsoft Exchange Hygiene Update	The Exchange Hygiene Update Service.	Started
Microsoft Exchange IMAP4	Provides Internet Message Access Protocol (IMAP4) Services to clients. If this service is stopped, clients are u...	
Microsoft Exchange Information Store	Manages the Microsoft Exchange Information Store. This includes mailbox stores and public folder stores. If t...	Started
Microsoft Exchange Mail Submission Service	Submits messages from the Mailbox server to the Hub Transport servers.	Started
Microsoft Exchange Mailbox Assistants	Performs background processing of mailboxes in the Exchange store.	Started
Microsoft Exchange Monitoring	Allows applications to call the Exchange diagnostic cmdlets.	
Microsoft Exchange POP3	Provides Post Office Protocol version 3 (POP3) Services to clients. If this service is stopped, clients are unable...	
Microsoft Exchange Replication Service	The Exchange Replication Service provides replication functionality used by Local Continuous Replication and ...	Started
Microsoft Exchange Search Indexer	Drives indexing of mailbox content, which improves the performance of content search.	Started
Microsoft Exchange Service Host	Provides a host for several Microsoft Exchange services	Started
Microsoft Exchange System Attendant	Provides monitoring, maintenance, and Active Directory lookup services, for example, monitoring of services ...	Started
Microsoft Exchange Transport	The Microsoft Exchange Transport Edge Service.	Started
Microsoft Exchange Transport Log Search	Provides remote search capability for Microsoft Exchange Transport log files.	Started

NOTE: *Antibody AI here is not the entire IDPS and IRS package, it is just the cryptography securer and breach detector IDS, so depending on the IRS in the systems and the cyber division of respective company uses, the time of stay in virtual work environment for other users is depended.*

Figure 2. User sign-in log

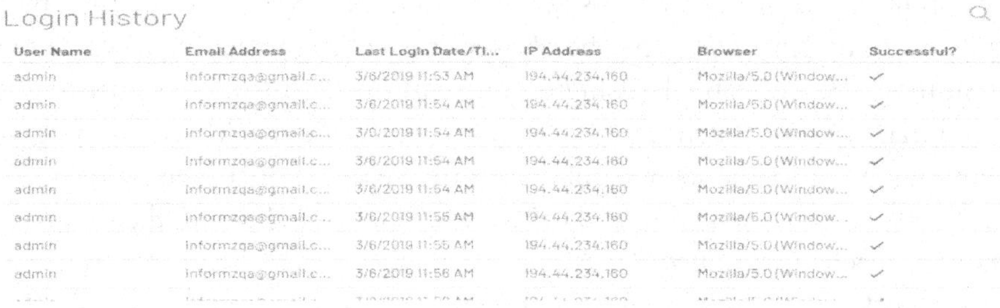

Login History

User Name	Email Address	Last Login Date/Ti...	IP Address	Browser	Successful?
admin	informzqa@gmail.c...	3/6/2019 11:53 AM	194.44.234.160	Mozilla/5.0 (Window...	✓
admin	informzqa@gmail.c...	3/6/2019 11:54 AM	194.44.234.160	Mozilla/5.0 (Window...	✓
admin	informzqa@gmail.c...	3/6/2019 11:54 AM	194.44.234.160	Mozilla/5.0 (Window...	✓
admin	informzqa@gmail.c...	3/6/2019 11:54 AM	194.44.234.160	Mozilla/5.0 (Window...	✓
admin	informzqa@gmail.c...	3/6/2019 11:54 AM	194.44.234.160	Mozilla/5.0 (Window...	✓
admin	informzqa@gmail.c...	3/6/2019 11:55 AM	194.44.234.160	Mozilla/5.0 (Window...	✓
admin	informzqa@gmail.c...	3/6/2019 11:55 AM	194.44.234.160	Mozilla/5.0 (Window...	✓
admin	informzqa@gmail.c...	3/6/2019 11:56 AM	194.44.234.160	Mozilla/5.0 (Window...	✓

3.1.3 Network Traffic Log Usage

Network Traffic Logs are monitored along with other inputs in any case there is a halt in any of the systems within the network. The halt in the network may denote an additional traffic that may be caused due to brute forcing algorithms using botnets or zombie PCs to enter the mainframe. If that is a halt due to any other hindrances, the reason is noted and sent to the Response mechanism as well as the network admin, cyber security admin present within the campus to alert them of any malicious activities. If the network's jam is nothing but a ping resends, or a slow network, the AI's precision detects those and reports to corresponding staff members and measures are taken to prevent slow network traffic by any other means.

This Network log usage is directly translated into the base value of the "Secure points", allowing the AI to detect breaches shown in Figure 3.

Figure 3. Network traffic log

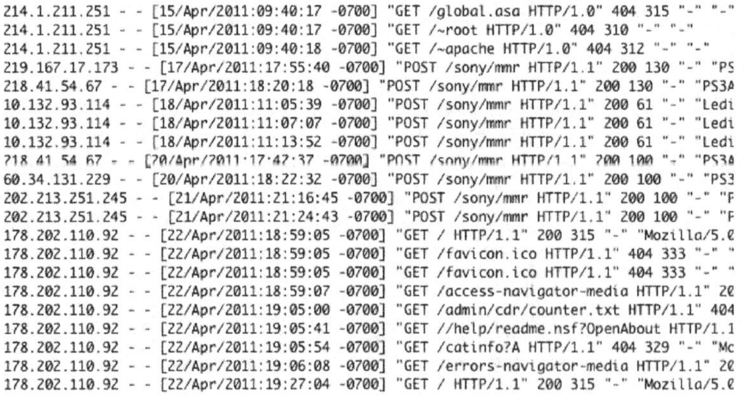

```
214.1.211.251 - - [15/Apr/2011:09:40:17 -0700] "GET /global.asa HTTP/1.0" 404 315 "-" "-"
214.1.211.251 - - [15/Apr/2011:09:40:17 -0700] "GET /~root HTTP/1.0" 404 310 "-" "-"
214.1.211.251 - - [15/Apr/2011:09:40:18 -0700] "GET /~apache HTTP/1.0" 404 312 "-" "-"
219.167.17.173 - - [17/Apr/2011:17:55:40 -0700] "POST /sony/mmr HTTP/1.1" 200 130 "-" "PS
218.41.54.67 - - [17/Apr/2011:18:20:18 -0700] "POST /sony/mmr HTTP/1.1" 200 130 "-" "PS3A
10.132.93.114 - - [18/Apr/2011:11:05:39 -0700] "POST /sony/mmr HTTP/1.1" 200 61 "-" "Ledi
10.132.93.114 - - [18/Apr/2011:11:07:07 -0700] "POST /sony/mmr HTTP/1.1" 200 61 "-" "Ledi
10.132.93.114 - - [18/Apr/2011:11:13:52 -0700] "POST /sony/mmr HTTP/1.1" 200 61 "-" "Ledi
218.41.54.67 - - [20/Apr/2011:17:42:37 -0700] "POST /sony/mmr HTTP/1.1" 200 100 "-" "PS3A
60.34.131.229 - - [20/Apr/2011:18:22:32 -0700] "POST /sony/mmr HTTP/1.1" 200 100 "-" "PS3
202.213.251.245 - - [21/Apr/2011:21:16:45 -0700] "POST /sony/mmr HTTP/1.1" 200 100 "-" "F
202.213.251.245 - - [21/Apr/2011:21:24:43 -0700] "POST /sony/mmr HTTP/1.1" 200 100 "-" "F
178.202.110.92 - - [22/Apr/2011:18:59:05 -0700] "GET / HTTP/1.1" 200 315 "-" "Mozilla/5.0
178.202.110.92 - - [22/Apr/2011:18:59:05 -0700] "GET /favicon.ico HTTP/1.1" 404 333 "-" "
178.202.110.92 - - [22/Apr/2011:18:59:05 -0700] "GET /favicon.ico HTTP/1.1" 404 333 "-" "
178.202.110.92 - - [22/Apr/2011:18:59:07 -0700] "GET /access-navigator-media HTTP/1.1" 20
178.202.110.92 - - [22/Apr/2011:19:05:00 -0700] "GET /admin/cdr/counter.txt HTTP/1.1" 404
178.202.110.92 - - [22/Apr/2011:19:05:41 -0700] "GET //help/readme.nsf?OpenAbout HTTP/1.1
178.202.110.92 - - [22/Apr/2011:19:05:54 -0700] "GET /catinfo?A HTTP/1.1" 404 329 "-" "Mc
178.202.110.92 - - [22/Apr/2011:19:06:08 -0700] "GET /errors-navigator-media HTTP/1.1" 20
178.202.110.92 - - [22/Apr/2011:19:27:04 -0700] "GET / HTTP/1.1" 200 315 "-" "Mozilla/5.0
```

3.1.4 Database Log Usage

The AI uses the Logs and Errors from Database in any of the client computers to check if any botnet is trying to enter into the system using the SQL injection method, it checks for error logs occurred at a specific time to check if any zombies are trying to penetrate into the Database. To make the prevention easy and the zombies unharmed, the AI detects this as an "anomaly" tag, and returns to the Cyber Security division in the company and leaves the zombies trouble alone. The Database is also vulnerable to some script-kiddies using SQL Injection tags within the Text Fields, so the AI monitors the inputs from the Text Fields to checks for these vulnerable Tags, and if it is detected, it is forwarded to Cyber Division of the company; also the Security protocol for this specific problem is triggered. The Database logs are shown in Figure 4.

Figure 4. Database log (SQL)

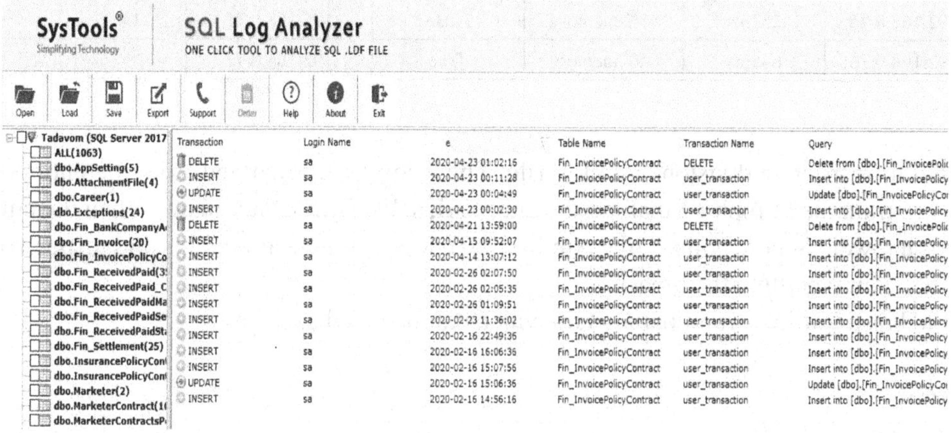

3.1.5 IRS Access

Like the previous note explains, This AI is not the Response System, but merely a detection and protection system. It needs access to the IRS system each network uses, in order to alert the systems as well as to Respond or counter-attack any threat which the systems withstand. In any case if there is a detection of intrusion, either by brute force, SQL injection, botnets or zombies, then the AI must activate the IRS situated within the company systems and alerts the other users that a situation is going on. The Final input that is required for this detection AI and key-changing AI is the access to the response system that can be used for the correct response to the intrusion.

3.2 Historical Breach Data Detection and Comparison of Current Breach With Previous Attempts

The Antibody AI uses the inputs given here not as separated as the raw numbers provided, but as a part of bigger inputs to detect what we call now as the "secure points" for a system at that specific time. The AI is fed these secure points through another AI we create called the "Lymph AI". This Lymph AI is just a simple CNN based AI which collects the logs and its respective factors to create the "secure points" that we spoke of. The Lymph AI is trained with a dataset of Breaches which occurred in the past and their respective logs in the specific formula given in the table 1.2.

This Historical data can be used to train the Lymph AI, and to collect the Data from Antibody AI and check for breaches. These occur in the intervals of 30 seconds for each system, and reports of this

Table 2. Example dataset of previous breaches and output of lymph AI producing the secure points for the data received and calculating the breach percentage of the data

Data No.	IP Address	Network Ping of the IP	Software Code Usage of the IP	Sql Injection Detection	Similar Tries of Other Users	Secure Points	Potential Breach Percentage
1	192.168.0.71	345ms	72% memory	False	192.168.0.75	20	89%
2	192.168.0.72	228ms	68% memory	True	192.168.0.76	10	92%
3	192.168.0.73	315ms	45% memory	False	NIL	64	25%
4	192.168.0.74	12ms	30% memory	False	NIL	85	8%
5	192.168.0.75	562ms	81% memory	False	192.168.0.71	14	90%
6	192.168.0.76	645ms	84% memory	True	192.168.0.72	8	96%

are submitted to respective divisions as a log file. These log files generated from the antibody AI can also be used to train the Lymph AI making the entire AI, self-learning automata. When the current data collected has a lower "Secure points", the Antibody AI detects the Secure points and respective counter measures are taken regarding the breach.

The Table has a few important parameters which can be listed as follows:

- IP address
- Network ping of the IP
- Software code usage of the IP
- SQL injection detection
- Similar tries of other users
- Secure points
- Potential breach percentage

First the IP address is received to detect and pinpoint the malicious PC which has been affected/which is behind the breach. If the IP is detected, after the countermeasures, the IP and its respective machine are cleared throughout the process.

Network Ping of the IP is used to detect any High traffic in the system, and that specific system has a higher rate of doing a Brute force process, or has malware which affected the IP. The Protocol which gets triggered after detecting this is the Lockdown Protocol series-1. Other IPs within the network are secured using this. Wireshark is used to detect network traffic within an IP, by ping round-trip shown in Figure 5.

Code Usage of that specific IP is used to detect if any Virus or Trojan are active within that specific system. Even the keylogging can be detected once the data is sent. The aftermath of the IRS triggers the Antibody AI to Reinstall the Software in that specific IP. This protection is not specifically useful for the "secure points" but in the off-chance of this monitoring another stray IP leads to Prevention of a bigger threat, rather than to keep this useless. :HTOP used to detect Memory usage within an IP, by remote access from admin is shown in Figure 6.

SQL Injection detection is the easy and crucial part of this intrusion detection. It checks for a few keywords which are often used in SQL Injection by the user, or the temporary PCs by tools such as

Figure 5. Wireshark is used here to detect network traffic within an IP, by ping round-trip from its usage

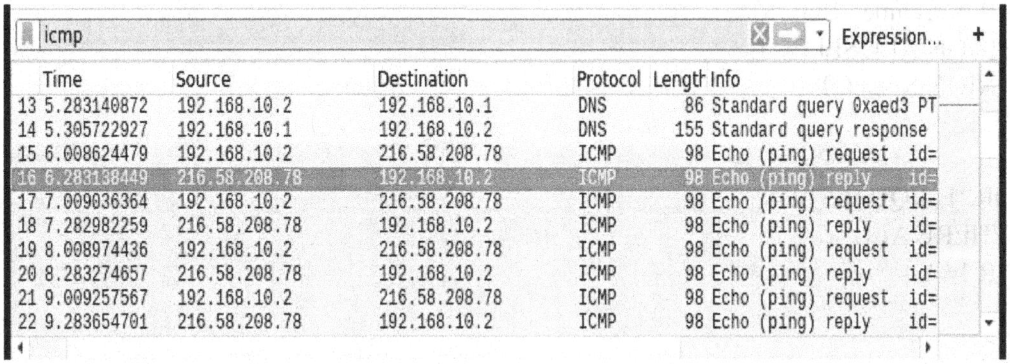

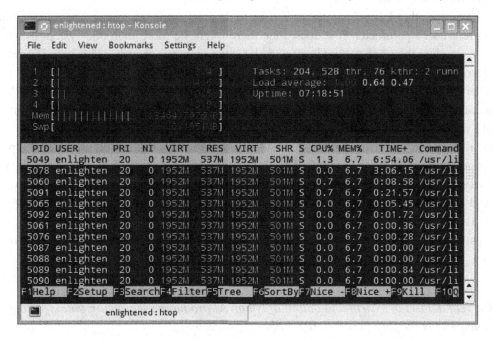

Figure 6. HTOP is used here to detect Memory usage within an IP, by remote access from admin

SQLMap, etc. If there is an input from some IP which looks like an SQL Injection, it switches the SQL Injection Flag to True, instantly decreasing the Secure points. This is by far the easiest but essential parameter for the AI, allowing easier breach detection as well as to locate the individual responsible easily.

Some of the Parameter for detection are as follows:

- " OR 1=0 –
- " OR 1=1 –
- " OR 1=1 OR ""="
- ' OR (EXISTS)
- ' OR uname LIKE '%

- ' OR userid LIKE '%
- ' OR username LIKE '%
- ' UNION ALL SELECT
- ' UNION SELECT
- '
- "
- " OR '1' EQUALS '1'
- ' WHERE ALL
- ' OR 1=1 –
- ' --

These are few tags that are used for SQL injections. Usually people trying SQL injections use a script or a bot to continuously try out all these parameters just so that one of them could crack the text box and penetrate the system.

"Similar Tries of other Users" parameter is used to detect if some other users' parameters match up with the current user's parameter. If it does, then there might be more than one system overruling all the protocols, or more than one system is affected by same malware or virus. This case is prominent in many huge companies' breaches, so it is better to be safe than sorry.

Secure points are points which are given after the analyzation of lymph AI. It is the result of evaluation of all the data obtained by Lymph AI as the dataset. This Secure point is used to evaluate if the system is safe or if it is prone to be infiltrated in the real-time. To make an added evaluation, the "secure points" are also accompanied by the added parameter, "potential breach percentage" and "trigger flag". The potential breach percentage detects the amount of vulnerability or the possibility of the IP or system being breached currently, and the trigger flag is used to switch on the IRS and safety measures included with the Antibody AI. Table 1.3 shows the data received at that moment's notice, and detecting the breach. As you can see, the systems which are responsible for the breach along with the status which triggered the flag are stored.

Table 3. Current dataset of system and output of lymph AI producing the secure points for the data received and triggering the flag to call in IRS within the division

Data No.	IP Address	Network Ping of the IP	Software Code Usage of the IP	SQL Injection Detection	Secure Points	Potential Breach Percentage	Trigger Flag
1	192.168.0.71	345ms	72% memory	False	20	89%	True
2	192.168.0.72	228ms	68% memory	True	10	92%	True

3.3 Security Protocols and Attack Alerting Systems

Once the Antibody AI has initiated the trigger, the Security protocols are activated and the alert systems are notified. The Security protocols have a specific set of ordered workflow, each of it are as:

- **Security Protocol SP (1) - Backup of log and initiation of alert** – the current logs responsible for the trigger is backed up into a folder named "black box", in case if any event causes the entire system to crash, this black box is stored in an external cloud device and can be taken after the problem is solved, to find the cause of the problem.
- **Security Protocol SP (2) – Triggering the IRS and Lockdown protocols** – Using the IRS present in the systems, the AI starts the response operations while simultaneously shifting the non-infected users to the virtual work environment as a safety procedure, whilst showing the following error in the screen of the non-infected users.

"ATTENTION: Antibody AI has detected a potential Breach level: ____. To proceed safely, we have moved your files to a remote Virtual Work Environment. Apologies for the inconvenience." Alert message shown in Figure 7.

Figure 7. Alert message of the AI when there is a "GAMMA" level of intrusion threat happening

With the rising levels of potential breach each varying over the results of secure points as follows,

- **Delta Level:**
  The breach is not severe, but just annoying. Maybe the result of,
  - Minor SQL Injection trials
  - Password logins using any scripts or bots.
  - Continuous failed attempts in a lower time-frame

And the preventive measures include, calling Lockdown Protocol Series – 1 with the malicious IP as its parameter.

- **Gamma Level:**
  Breach conditions are satisfied for more than one machine, but threat level is minimal. Possible results include,
  - Weak botnets or zombies trying SQL Injection.
  - Same Malicious code running in multiple devices.
  - Rogue employee remote accessing and using some form of hacking technique.

And the preventive measures include, calling Lockdown Protocol Series – 1 with the malicious IP(s) as its parameter.

- **Beta Level:**
  Threat level is high and many Systems are affected. Possibly,
    - Near-Successful breach attempts in any of the systems.
    - Network Lags and spikes.
    - Severe amount of attempts from many IPs

  And the preventive measures include, calling Lockdown Protocol Series – 2 with the malicious IP(s) as its parameters.
- **Alpha Level:**
  Severe Breaching indicated. Some Scenarios include,
    - File Damages.
    - IP Hoarding.
    - Illegal Access already entering.
    - Successful Breach Attempts.

  And the preventive measures include, calling Lockdown Protocol Series – 2 with the malicious IP(s) as its parameters.

Phase 2 of this security system relies on the IRS present in the System, or the Network. After the SPs (Security Protocols) are initiated, The Attack Alerting Systems call out for the IRS present in the Systems. These IRS proceed to respond to the imminent attack, whilst the Antibody AI goes to its main duties it has been designed to perform, Cryptography.

3.4 Lockdown Protocols and Aftermath Response Mechanisms

3.4.1 Lockdown Protocols

Lockdown protocols present in this AI are used to safely eliminate the other unaffected IPs or Systems within the network. These protocols are triggered by the security protocol 2 (SP2). Lockdown protocols take IP addresses as parameters, to safely lockdown and quarantine the unaffected from the affected. Antibody AI Has 2 Lockdown Protocols (LPs for Short),

- **Lockdown Protocol Series 1 (LPS-1) –** This protocol is used whenever One or Two specific systems within a given network is affected/malicious. This lockdown protocol gets called with the affected IP Addresses as its parameters and it locks down the affected IPs to protect the unaffected or safe systems.
- **Lockdown Protocol Series 2 (LPS-2) –** This protocol is used whenever there is more than one system in the network is malicious or tagged. In this case, the protocol LPS 2 is called with the malicious/affected systems' IP Addresses, but it locks down other innocent systems away from these Tagged and affected systems to ensure a spread or clearance from the affected to unaffected systems is not possible, thus protecting the other systems in the network.

When the Lockdown procedures are engaged, the Systems will automatically shift to its respective Virtual Work Environment. Then it proceeds to aftermath of the Breach.

3.4.2 Aftermath Response Mechanisms

After the intrusion is over and the IRS has done its job, Aftermath Response Mechanism is activated. This is the Cryptography part of the AI and the main motive of this project. Several layered steps are present in this ARM (Aftermath Response Mechanism) such as,

- **Aftermath Response Mechanism – Sector 1**

  ○ **Layer 1** – The Antibody AI searches for any malicious code within the systems after the IRS has responded.
  ○ **Layer 2** – The Antibody AI restores all the files which are evacuated to the Virtual Working Environment.
  ○ **Layer 3** – The AI Again Searches for any malicious code or any Breach signs after restoring the Files to their respective systems
  ○ **Layer 4** – The Antibody AI uses Lymph AI and the Black Box backup of the last breach, and trains the Lymph AI of another Threat to watch out, thereby Self-learning.
  ○ **Layer 5** – The AI Proceeds to provide the IRS log and Lymph AI log to the Cyber Division of its respective workplace.
  ○ **Layer 6** – The Users are removed from their lockdown status and are back to work.
  ○ **Layer 7** – The AI performs one last search throughout the systems as the user works to check if the piece of code is present or not.

After Sector 1 has been successfully executed without any mishap, the whole network goes to maintenance for a fixed time period and the Response Mechanism moves to the most crucial step, Sector 2.

- **Aftermath Response Mechanism – Sector 2**
  ○ **Layer 1** – The Antibody AI proceeds to backup all of the passwords and collective information of the Database to a random location within the database, to ensure that nobody can find out its location, not even the admins.
  ○ **Layer 2** – The AI strips the old Encryption function key and proceeds to generate a new, Random key.
  ○ **Layer 3** – This new key will now be used to encrypt all the passwords stored within the random location, and stored to respective users' password field.
  ○ **Layer 4** – Final step is to make the users login again to check for any encryption errors, and if there are errors, the backup passwords within the random folder specified can be used to enter and change.

After the Sector 2 of this Aftermath Response Mechanism is loaded, then the whole network returns back to normal with a new encryption, changed from breach to breach and undetectable, even by the admins. Then the maintenance period ends with an information alert, **"THANK YOU FOR WAITING: Antibody AI has now changed the encryption of the password. To check if your password is encrypted correctly, please try to login to your software. If you encounter any error, contact your administrator,"** shown in Figure 8, and the Antibody AI completes its work. And thus is the workflow of this Antibody AI along with its other parts such as the Lymph AI and protocols in action.

Figure 8. Info message of the AI when the ARM Sector 2 is completed

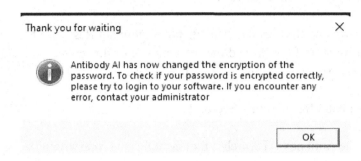

4. SYSTEM ARCHITECTURE

Figure 9 shows the architecture of the Antibody AI. The users section is of the users who use the software or the network, and it consists of few legit users and a few hacker's/key loggers. The network section depicts the network in which the users' systems are used and the Database denotes the storage location of all the crucial data. The Antibody AI consists of

- **Lymph AI**
- **Protocols**

Figure 9. System architecture of antibody AI and all the components present within it

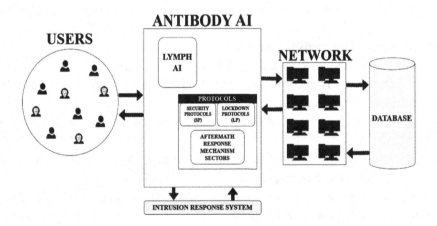

4.1. Lymph AI

This part of the Antibody AI is responsible for collective training with the datasets and generation of "secure points" which are used by Antibody AI and its protocols. Since the Antibody AI is an LLM based/ Generative AI based Neural Network, it must take few easy inputs in order to act accurately. For the sole reason, the Antibody AI comes with an embedded smaller AI model specifically used for converting the raw data (i.e.) the Logs and other inputs from the user, directly to processed output points. These points determine if the system is safe or there is a breach on-going. These outputs from the lymph AI is then sent to the main AI, the Antibody AI, which uses these points in accordance with its own processing methods to convert the points into a usable format to detect if the System is breached. Figure 10 shows the Working of Lymph AI and returning the output

Figure 10. Working of lymph AI and returning the output

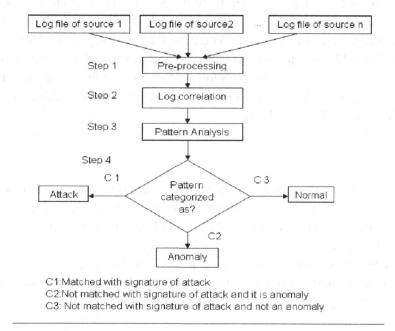

4.2. Protocols

Protocols play a major part of this Antibody AI. To do a process this huge, the AI cam sometimes get randomized and gets mixed up while trying to protect or contain a breach. To avoid it as well as to label the processes for the users, this AI has few protocols to secure and protect the network as well as itself.

Some of the Protocols that are previously explained are as follows:

- **Security Protocol (SP)** - These protocols are triggered once the AI identifies breach possibility
- **Lockdown Protocol (LP)** - These protocols are triggered once the IRS has received its trigger message and used to protect other users within the same network.
- **Aftermath Response Mechanism Sector (ARMS)** - These protocols are triggered once the IRS has completed its work on the intruders or the hackers. This is the Main algorithm which is responsible for Dynamic key change of the Antibody AI.

5. PARAMETERS INFLUENCING ACCURACY

This project consists of Two AIs with different parameters and different workflows, so each of the AI has a few notable parameter precedence and influence over their accuracy. These are categorized as follows,

5.1. Parameters Influencing Lymph AI

Lymph AI is the first layer of this total Antibody AI. Every Input we directly give to the Antibody AI, (i.e.) the SUND inputs that we give to the Antibody AI, gets into the Lymph AI first. The Lymph AI accepts these inputs in order to create an output through selective formula method and dataset training method. The output that is given by the Lymph AI is called the "secure points". These secure points are given out to the Antibody AI. The Antibody AI only accepts the inputs which are from Lymph AI. These secure points are in turn converted into different forms of parameters that are used by the Antibody AI for different purposes. Those parameters are PBP or potential breach percentage and Trigger flag. The input parameters influencing Lymph AI are,

5.1.1. IP Address

IP Address of the computer scanned determines the System we are trying to access. It is like the Id of the computer and we are using it to denote which computer we are deriving the data of. This is the Primary key of the Lymph AI and is not used in the formula for calculation of "Secure points", yet still important for the AI to detect any intrusions.

If by any chance there is a detection of any kind of intrusion, the lymph AI sends the Secure points along with the IP of the affected PCs or the IP which is the reason. These IPs are used as parameters for Lockdown protocols, thereby providing the case of use for the protocols.

5.1.2. Network Ping of the IP

Network ping of the IP or Network ping of the System is used to find the Network traffic, a crucial data to analyse about brute force attempts or botnet attempts. This important part of the parameter is set to the unit millisecond. This parameter is used prominently within the Lymph AI as the base detection detects this parameter first.

This is the base value parameter for the Secure points of the Lymph AI. This when set to high (i.e.) Network ping becoming high, decreases the Secure points vastly, but it doesn't decrease the value higher than 20 points.

5.1.3. Software Code Usage of the IP

The Software code usage of the system can detect if any malicious code runs within the software. The main way to detect that is by using the memory consumption of the selected application or the OS. By remote logging into the OS, we can detect the memory and RAM usage of the selected IP. If it crosses a certain threshold, then we come to a conclusion that the software is either running malicious code (i.e. automated keygen or bruteforce codes) or the software is hanged. This parameter has the least priority within the Lymph AI.

5.1.4. SQL Injection Detection

The Detection of SQL injection is the simplest, and the most important parameter that we require for the Lymph AI. It detects if any SQL Injection based tags are put within any text fields, and it immediately switches from its default value (False) to True, and drastically lowering "Secure points", since we know that it is a possible intrusion once any tag is detected from the user. But when the SQL injection is detected via a simple textbox input searching or a simple validation script flag, then we will know that a system is trying to penetrate and is trying to get to the database of the System.

This SQL Injection detection has a massive Secure Point Drop value (i.e.) when the Lymph AI gets the input of SQL Injection as true, then the Secure points which are outputted from the Lymph AI is Dropped in value heavily, but the Alert level for this is systemically low.

5.2. Parameters Influencing Antibody AI

Antibody AI has a few parameters, but not its own. specifically, these parameters are the parameters which are outputs of Lymph AI. These parameters are generally what are used to trigger a few protocols and IRS. These Parameters are therefore as follows:

5.2.1. Secure Points

The main output of Lymph AI is the generation of secure points, which subsequently serve as the foundation for deriving two additional parameters. These parameters play an important role whenever a breach occurs or an attempt is made within the networked systems. The secure points, crucial in creation of another layer of security infrastructure, are carefully composed into defined limits. These limits, in turn, give rise to two new parameters that are used in the functionality of Antibody AI. By establishing a systematic relationship between the secure points and these derived parameters, the overall security architecture is reinforced, providing a robust defence mechanism against breaches and unauthorized attempts within the network. The Secure points are also used in simplification of AI inputs for the GPT AI (i.e.) the Antibody AI, allowing the Antibody AI to just detect the upcoming inputs we are about to describe, scanning them and then decide if the system is in a breach condition, instead of feeding all the raw parameters to the Antibody AI.

5.2.2. Potential Breaching Percentage

Since the breach detection is still not adapted to plain numeric points for Detecting if the breach is occurred, the secure points are processed into a percentage type variable, specifically the "Potential Breaching Percentage". This parameter can be used by the admins and users to verify the possibility of an intrusion occurring in real-time. Potential Breach Percentage is just a semi-raw parameter which is optimized then, but mainly is used to show the users and Cyber intellects about the crucial breach they have observed.

This Percentage value is used to determine the level of Threat the breach is and is used to determine the Security protocols and Lockdown Protocol Series are to be used. But since the percentage also is not an optimal way to be used for this AI to detect breach effectively, it is still processed into last form of parameter, the Trigger flag.

5.2.3. Trigger Flag

Trigger flag is a Boolean based parameter processed from "potential Breaching Percentage" parameter. If the Breaching percentage is below 50%, trigger flag is false. If the Breaching Percentage is above 50%, Trigger flag is true. This way, it is easy for the OpenAI API inputs to detect and do something about the intrusion easily, rather to check for intrusion using some function and to detect intrusion.

And these parameters are used to detect breaches and trigger the protocols of the Antibody AI. Figure 11 shows the UML diagram of Antibody AI and all the Components present within it

Figure 11. UML diagram of antibody AI and all the components present within it

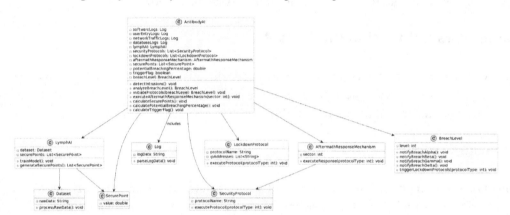

6. FUTURE RESEARCH DIRECTIONS

The Antibody AI along with the Lymph AI is the first instalment to a wide array of other plans our team has planned, and while the detection is the crucial part of security, it is just a showcase, not but a mere pointing to the problem.

Our future plans include that of an Ultimate collection of AI or a Single AI controlling a vast collection of tools and everything consisting upon all the problems of Cyber mass media. The Future of the Computer Era is the birth of Artificial Intelligence. Our Master AI plans are of high value, using AI to reconnaissance, Troubleshoot, Detection, Prevention, respond to Attack, Categorize the Attack, Perform Attack on the Attacker, perform healing measures within the System, Collectively Restoring and protecting some important files, And much more, through this Larger Language Models.

Simple yet subtle motives are often faster and easier to execute. The plan revolves around a Master AI or the Brain AI, controlling all parts of other AIs or other tools such as our Antibody AI, to detect and as an added benefit, the Master AI trains the other AI through raw input factors with increased possibility like finding a virus code within a software immediately, creating a new firewall, detecting remote access through shell or batch executables and much more, thus making our work environment and the systems safe from all possible malware breaches and Hackers.

If the AI field of the domain gets even more plentiful upgrades, we shall use this AI and collection of other AIs in creation of a bigger part of the project, AGI models and AGI simulation models for this specific crypto graphical purpose, and use it across all the infrastructures and business systems to increase the Safety effectively.

7. CONCLUSION

This chapter explains the use of AI for dynamic cryptographic key exchanges and breach detection through the integration of OpenAI's API and other algorithms. This chapter uses the OpenAI API and other machine learning algorithms to create an ultimate IDS based AI which takes as input, four different logs, processed through another AI that gives as output few parameters such as "secure points". Such flags, tries to check for any intrusion or breach in any of the system in surveillance of the AI, and when the breach is detected, it uses its security protocols to call for action, lockdown protocol to isolate and protect the unaffected systems. Finally, the aftermath response mechanism sectors clean up the damage and randomly changes the encryption dynamically. We hope this information serves as a key for further research, encouraging individuals to explore and develop this concept within this endless realm of knowledge. The collaborative nature of scientific exploration thrives on the collective efforts of researchers, and we aspire for this paper to contribute to the ongoing hive mind of knowledge in this field.

REFERENCES

Bailey, M., Oberheide, J., Andersen, J., Mao, Z. M., Jahanian, F., & Nazario, J. (2007). Automated classification and analysis of internet malware. In *International Workshop on Recent Advances in Intrusion Detection*. Springer. 10.1007/978-3-540-74320-0_10

Bilge, L., Kirda, E., Krügel, C., & Balduzzi, M. (2011). EXPOSURE: Finding Malicious Domains Using Passive DNS Analysis. *Network and Distributed System Security Symposium.*

Canali, D., Robertson, W., Kirda, E., Kruegel, C., & Vigna, G. (2011). A Large-Scale Analysis of the Security of Embedded Firmwares. *Proceedings of the 18th Annual Network and Distributed System Security Symposium.*

Cova, M., Kruegel, C., & Vigna, G. (2010, April). Detection and analysis of drive-by-download attacks and malicious JavaScript code. In *Proceedings of the 19th international conference on World wide web* (pp. 281-290). ACM. 10.1145/1772690.1772720

Gala, Y., Vanjari, N., Doshi, D., & Radhanpurwala, I. (2023). AI based Techniques for Network-based Intrusion Detection System: A Review. *2023 10th International Conference on Computing for Sustainable Global Development (INDIACom),* 1544-1551.

González, G. G., Casas, P., & Fernández, A. (2023, July). Fake it till you Detect it: Continual Anomaly Detection in Multivariate Time-Series using Generative AI. In *2023 IEEE European Symposium on Security and Privacy Workshops (EuroS&PW)* (pp. 558-566). IEEE. 10.1109/EuroSPW59978.2023.00068

Grier, C., Ballard, L., Caballero, J., Chachra, N., Dietrich, C. J., Levchenko, K., Mavrommatis, P., McCoy, D., Nappa, A., Pitsillidis, A., Provos, N., Rafique, M. Z., Rajab, M. A., Rossow, C., Thomas, K., Paxson, V., Savage, S., & Voelker, G. M. (2012). Manufacturing compromise: the emergence of exploit-as-a-service. *Proceedings of the 2012 ACM conference on Computer and communications security*. 10.1145/2382196.2382283

Holz, T., Gorecki, C., Rieck, K., & Freiling, F. C. (2009). Measuring and Detecting Fast-Flux Service Networks. *Proceedings of the 14th European Conference on Research in Computer Security*.

Joshi, N., Sheth, T., Shah, V., Gupta, J., & Mujawar, S. (2022). A Detailed Evaluation of SQL Injection Attacks, Detection and Prevention Techniques. *2022 5th International Conference on Advances in Science and Technology (ICAST)*, 352-357. 10.1109/ICAST55766.2022.10039662

Kandhro, I. A., Alanazi, S. M., Ali, F., Kehar, A., Fatima, K., Uddin, M., & Karuppayah, S. (2023). Detection of Real-Time Malicious Intrusions and Attacks in IoT Empowered Cybersecurity Infrastructures. *IEEE Access: Practical Innovations, Open Solutions, 11*, 9136–9148. doi:10.1109/ACCESS.2023.3238664

Khan, H., Alam, M., Al-Kuwari, S., & Faheem, Y. (2021). Offensive AI: Unification of Email Generation Through GPT-2 Model With A Game-Theoretic Approach For Spear-Phishing Attacks. Competitive Advantage in the Digital Economy (CADE 2021), 178 – 184. doi:10.1049/icp.2021.2422

Kruegel, C., Vigna, G., & Robertson, W. (2005, August). A multi-model approach to the detection of web-based attacks. *Computer Networks, 48*(5), 717–738. doi:10.1016/j.comnet.2005.01.009

Memos, V. A., & Psannis, K. E. (2020). AI-Powered Honeypots for Enhanced IoT Botnet Detection. *2020 3rd World Symposium on Communication Engineering (WSCE), Thessaloniki, Greece*, 64-68. 10.1109/WSCE51339.2020.9275581

Pearce, H., Tan, B., Ahmad, B., Karri, R., & Dolan-Gavitt, B. (2023). Examining Zero-Shot Vulnerability Repair with Large Language Models. In *Proceedings - 44th IEEE Symposium on Security and Privacy, SP 2023* (pp. 2339-2356). Institute of Electrical and Electronics Engineers Inc. 10.1109/SP46215.2023.10179324

Petr Gallus. (2023). *Generative Neural Networks as a Tool for Web Applications Penetration Testing*. Institute of Electrical and Electronic Engineers.

Prasad, S. G., Sharmila, V. C., & Badrinarayanan, M. K. (2023). Role of Artificial Intelligence based Chat Generative Pre-trained Transformer (ChatGPT) in Cyber Security. *2023 2nd International Conference on Applied Artificial Intelligence and Computing (ICAAIC)*, 107-114. 10.1109/ICAAIC56838.2023.10141395

Song, D., Brumley, D., Yin, H., Caballero, J., Jager, I., & Kang, M. G. (2008). BitBlaze: A New Approach to Computer Security via Binary Analysis. *Proceedings of the 4th International Conference on Information Systems Security*. 10.1007/978-3-540-89862-7_1

Srinivasan, S., & Deepalakshmi, P. (2021). Malware Multi Perspective Analytics with Auto Deduction in Cybersecurity. *2021 Fifth International Conference on I-SMAC (IoT in Social, Mobile, Analytics and Cloud) (I-SMAC)*, 1627-1630. 10.1109/I-SMAC52330.2021.9640803

Zhang, Y., Sharif, M., Chen, H., & Lee, W. (2010). Side-Channel Leaks in Web Applications: a Reality Today, a Challenge Tomorrow. *Proceedings of the 17th ACM Conference on Computer and Communications Security*.

Chapter 5
Optimized Deep Learning–Based Intrusion Detection Using WOA With LightGBM

R. Jayashree
SRM Institute of Science and Technology, India

J. Venkata Subramanian
(iD) https://orcid.org/0000-0003-2343-6790
SRM Institute of Science and Technology, India

ABSTRACT

Machine learning is a powerful tool in both cryptosystem and cryptanalysis. Intrusion detection is a significant part of cyber defence plans where improvements are needed to deal with the challenges such as detection of false alarms, everyday new threats, and enhancing performance and accuracy. In this chapter, an optimized deep learning model is proposed to detect intrusion using whale optimization algorithm (WOA) with light gradient boosting machine (LightGBM) algorithm. To increase the performance of the model, the collected network data from the KDD dataset are pre-processed with feature selection and dimensionality reduction methods. The WOA-LightGBM algorithm processes the pre-processed data for training. The outcomes of these experiments are compared with the performance of benchmarking algorithms to prove that this intrusion detection model provides better performance and accuracy. The proposed model detects the intrusion with high accuracy in short period of time.

1. INTRODUCTION

Cryptography is the art of generating secure systems for secret data through encryption and decryption techniques (Yan et al., 2022). Machine learning (ML) Techniques are used to automates the analytical model facilitating continuous learning even for big data inputs. This is the major reason for the application of ML in cryptosystems (CS). Moreover, ML and CS both process a huge amount of data with large search spaces. Private Key generation in cryptography is supported through reinforcement learning ML techniques (Yan et al., 2022). From the steganography perspective, ML classification methods, Bayesian

DOI: 10.4018/979-8-3693-1642-9.ch005

classification, AdaBoost and Support Vector Machine (SVM) are popularly used to perform classification of encrypted traffic and conversion of objects to steganography (Yan et al., 2022). The intrusion is an effort for influence upon the security mechanism and its regulations. This intrusion detection structure is in the direction to watch the network traffic and discover unfamiliar behaviour that may causes a harm (Ahmad and Mirvaziri, 2019). The techniques of detection are used to spot the attributes of data sets that they appear to be homogeneous and typical but these are rare (Sahil et al., 2020). These unusual cases are also referred as outliers, variations, exceptions, divergences, peculiarities, etc. (Sahil et al., 2020).

A Swarm Intelligence based approach detects the intrusion effectively for dynamic system (Hanieh et al., 2019). Here, a cryptosystem is viewed as a communication network in which individual node's dynamic behaviour is fully or partially observed by another node. Changes in system behaviour might be directly change the system's domestic communication structure by including or removing or altering i.e., strengthening or weakening of existing communication channels. Thus, the changes in the communication structure may replicate changes in the operating conditions of the system, and the detection of these modifications is a key component for intrusion detection (Hanieh et al., 2019). The familiar Whale Optimization Algorithm (WOA) is a novel meta-heuristic population-based optimization algorithms used for clustering which cohorts the hunting behaviour of humpback whales. In WOA, each whale represents a potential solution to the optimization problem, and the whales move through the search space to find the optimal solution.

The ML model such as XGBoost has been utilized in the networks or IoT (Internet of Things) intrusion detection. Zhang and Hamori (Zhang and Hamori, 2020) and Deng et al. (Deng et al., 2021) utilized intense gradient boosting (XGBoost) as an investigational model for prediction, and the outputs shown that the XGBoost model was capable to attain the exactness value of 86%. In (Cheng and Shi, 2021) Yan Song et al. proposed an intrusion detection model that is mostly based on the XGBoost, and uses the WOA to discover the suitable constraints for this. Though if accuracy rate is not bad, the drawback of the XGBoost model is found to traverse the dataset even during the node dividing process which tremendously increases the computational load (Xiang et al., 2022) and has particular boundaries in selecting or optimizing model parameters (Huang et al., 2021 and Chaofei et al., 2020). Light Gradient Boosting Machine (LightGBM) is an enhanced version of the gradient boosting decision tree model using an exclusive leaf-wise developing idea based on the huge depth limit, which may decrease many issues and obtain the improved accuracy while using the equivalent amount of splits (Xiang et al., 2022). Therefore, the detection methods become more efficient and more precise when WOA optimized parameters are combined with LightGBM model, which is planned in this article to enhance the correctness of intrusion detection. The architectural diagram of the proposed model is shown in the Figure 1.

2. LITERATURE REVIEW

In (Yan et al., 2022), Amir Anees et al. made a review on a number of latest works on proceed in various features of ML applications in cryptosystems and cryptanalysis. Developing anomaly detection models directly on data has a huge fault rate with respect to exactness and detection (Sahil et al., 2020). The dimensionality of datasets can be considerably condensed using feature selection methods. Deep learning approach, Restricted Boltzmann Machine is highly effective in extracting high-level features and creating clusters at various scale levels (Sahil et al., 2020).

Figure 1. WOA with LightGBM intrusion detection model

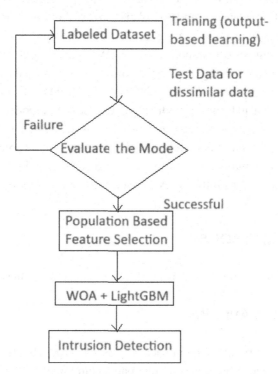

Hongjiao Wu et. al. in (2024) presented an improvised network attack detection method using Naïve Bayes with feature weight value based on the context. Zhao et al. (Zhao et al., 2021) described ID archetypal using deep ANN (Artificial Nural Network) for larger dataset. In (Maheswari and Arunesh 2020), authors provided a model with fusion of KNN (K-nearest neighbor) and network traffic. Privacy preserving model maintain security of the data and effectively predicts intrusion even in limited resources (Mourad et al., 2020 and Rahman et al., 2020). Deep learning with LSTM (long short-term memory) and GRU (gated recurrent unit) contexts is more effective in model classification of some attacks (Gautam et al., 2022 and Esmaeili et al., 2022).

Unbalanced training data distribution is one of the challenges which is tackled by the author using one-sided gradient oversampling with binded mutually exclusive features (Cong et al., 2022). Tu et al. (Chung-Jui et al., 2007) proposed a model to extract features with crossbreeding of PSO and SVM where classification is carried out using PSO fitness function.

Kamel et al. (Rongfeng et al., 2020) introduced in the article about, machine learning systems and honeypots, and based on these skills, prepared a smart agent for the avoidance and forecast of cyber attacks. Zheng et al. (Muhammed et al., 2011) studied pioneer statistical features for differentiating benign and malicious traffic for training the clustering model. In (Chen et al., 2021), the authors demonstrated the feasibility of deep learning-based cryptanalysis by attacking lightweight block ciphers such as basic Data Encryption Standard, Simon, and Speck. The outputs proven, that deep learning-based cryptanalysis can effectively recover key bits when the key space is limited to 64 ASCII characters.

The swarm intelligence is utilized for mining the internal communication topology of dynamic systems (Chen et al., 2016). The authors of (Ahmad and Mirvaziri, 2019) applied a swarm intelligence-based algorithm with finding data extracted from Gaussian and non-Gaussian distributions. The WOA is a new meta-heuristic optimization algorithm that replicates the hunting mechanism of humpback whales by simulating the bubble net feeding and attack mechanisms of humpback whales (Wang and Wang, 2021, Sharma and Singh, 2020, Alsabti et al., 1998). In the article (Xiang et al., 2022), the authors proposed a collective predicting model of hog futures prices is developed by using WOA-LightGBM and CEEMDAN that represents, the weakness of single machine learning models in terms of predicting correctness and model stability.

In (Cheng and Shi, 2021), XGBoost is an excellent machine learning algorithm with notable execution speediness along with exactness and is widely used in classification problems. In the article (Nadiya et al., 2020), the authors were explained the shortfalls of currently available intrusion detection systems and evaluate the functionality of LightGBM-AE-based intrusion detection categorization types.

3. MATERIALS AND METHODS

In this section various methods and materials used in the proposed archetypal is discussed in detail.

3.1 Whale Optimization Algorithm

This algorithm is a replicated form of the humpback whales' cleverness hunting behaviour which is called as "bubble-net". The whales create bubbles in a circular path encircling their feed and then make a spiral shape like '9' around the prey (Mohamed et al., 2022). In similar pattern, a force system is necessary to identify intruders and to create a seamless security system for the protection of network. The WOA-based system efficiently detects and protects the network. However, WOA simply lead to local optimization, therefore this paper combines LightGBM with WOA to improve the success rate of Intrusion detecting (Mohamed et al., 2022).

The WOA algorithm is a population based meta-heuristic optimization algorithm that resembles the hunt behaviour of humpback whales by producing bubble net like a circle or number '9' (Xiang et al., 2022). There main components of WOA are,

- Prey search – encircling
- Roundup – spiral search and random search
- Net bubble attack

In this approach, the whale (candidate solution) hunts by changing its moving direction, vector, in a single/multidimensional space which balance the exploration phases effectively.

In WOA, the whales one by one begins from an accidental spot, and then, each entity whale enhances its place according to the appropriate individual whale spot found following every iteration or arbitrarily found individual whale (Xiang et al., 2022). Table 1 consist of terminologies used in this paper.

3.2 Prey Search

Each and every whale shares the knowledge regarding the location and prey group quantity with other whales or closest whale x to that prey to obtain optimal solution.

Table 1. Terminology

Notation	Description
K	closest whale to the prey
$x^{\wedge}(\tau)$	Optimal position of the whale at current time τ
$x_{rand}(\tau)$	Random position of the whale at iteration number τ
R_1 and R_2	Random numbers where $0<R1, R2<1$
A'	Convergence factor (linearly decrease from 2 to 0)
τ_{max}	Global maximum number of iterations
α and β	Coefficient matrices
q	Constant parameter (determine the spiral shape)
Z	Homogeneously distributed random number, where $-1<Z<1$

All whales move closer to the whale, which is presently near to the prey's position, $x^{\wedge}(\tau)$. This contracts the circumference of the encirclement. This concept can be mathematically represented as below,

$$x(\tau+1) = x^{\wedge}(\tau) - [\alpha \cdot (|\beta \cdot x^{\wedge}(\tau) - x(\tau)|)] \tag{1}$$

where,

$$\alpha = (2A' \cdot R_1) - A'$$

$$e = 2R_2$$

$$A' = 2 - (2\tau/\tau_{max})$$

3.3 Spiral Search

In this searching, the whale targets prey in spiral ascending format which can be represented as follows,

$$x(\tau+1) = x^{\wedge}(\tau) - [|\beta \cdot x^{\wedge}(\tau) - x(\tau)| \cdot e^{qZ}\cos(2\Pi Z] \tag{2}$$

Whale decreases the search space as it approaches its prey in a rotational search. Assuming the probability of rotational search as 0.5, we get from (1) and (2),

$$x(\tau+1) = \begin{cases} x^{\wedge}(\tau) - \left[\alpha \cdot \left(\left|\beta \cdot x^{\wedge}(\tau) - x(\tau)\right|\right)\right], & when\ p < 0.5 \\ x^{\wedge}(\tau) - \left[\left|\beta \cdot x^{\tau} - x(\tau)\right| \cdot eqZ\cos(2\Pi Z)\right], & when\ p \geq 0.5 \end{cases} \tag{3}$$

3.4 Random Search

This search algorithm enhances the global search ability of the whale by increasing the search range. Therefore,

If $|\alpha| \geq 1$, then Random Search and

If $|\alpha| < 1$, then Spiral Search.

This expression is represented as,

$$x(\tau+1) = x_{rand}(\tau) - [\alpha \cdot (|e \cdot x_{rand}(\tau) - x(\tau)|)] \tag{4}$$

3.5 LightGBM

LightGBM is a machine learning algorithm that can be used for intrusion detection, which is the task of identifying malicious or unauthorized activities on a network. LightGBM is a fast and efficient enactment of gradient boosting, which is a technique that combines numerous feeble learners (such as decision trees) into a sturdy learner that can make precise predictions (Tian 2022)

Some of the advantages of using LightGBM for intrusion detection are:

- It can handle large-scale and high-dimensional data efficiently, as it uses a histogram-based algorithm that reduces the number of split points and memory usage.
- It can deal with imbalanced data, which is common in intrusion detection, as it uses a sampling technique called Gradient-based One Side Sampling that retains the most informative instances and discards the less informative ones.
- It can automatically handle missing values and categorical features, which can reduce the need for data preprocessing and feature engineering.
- It can perform feature selection, which can improve the model performance and interpretability, as it uses a regularization technique called Exclusive Feature Bundling that groups together mutually exclusive features and reduces the number of features.

The LightGBM is a decision based gradient boosting model which enables parallel learning (Xiang et al., 2022). Fast training rate and minimum memory usage are the advantages of LightGBM compared to XGBoost model (Machado 2003). Let M represent a set of data with input values x = {x1,..,xn} and prediction label y={y1,..yn}. Let f(x) represent model function and L(y, f(x)) is the losing function. Then, according to gradient boost approach, gij, where j is the iteration number, we get

$$g_{ij} = -\left[\frac{\partial L(y_i, F(x_i))}{\partial F(x_i)}\right]_{F(x)=F_{1-i}(x)} \tag{5}$$

The LightGBM tears the tree leaf-wise as contrasting to other boosting algorithms that develop tree level-wise as shown in Figure 2. Since the leaf is predetermined, the leaf-wise algorithm has a minimal loss compared to the level-wise algorithm. Furthermore, histogram-based procedures in LightGBM enables transferring continuous attribute values from bucket to discrete bins (Ping et al., 2007, Liang et al., 2019, Devan and Khare 2020). This increased speedup training and decrease memory usage. LightGBM uses graph deduction to speed up training. Based upon this, we may converse histograms only for one leaf, and get its neighbor's histograms by deduction as fine. Thus, in LightGBM depth limit is exploited to obtain highest prediction accuracy without overfitting problem.

Figure 2. LightGBM leaf-wise tree growth

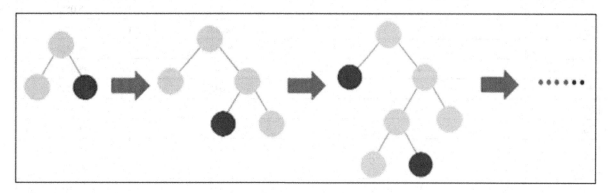

4. DATASET AND METHODOLOGY

Narrow search is the limitations of popular grid search method and also difficult in finding optimal parameters (Cheng and Shi, 2021). Python provides toolkits to optimize parameters using WOA, learning rate, sampling rate and identifying depth of a tree (Zhou et al., 2018, Wu 2024). The dataset, NSL-KDD, is the benchmark dataset of the proposed model. The KDD dataset is utilized for experiments and this model reduces the frequency of false detection. This dataset is a boosted modification of the 'KDDCup99' dataset with a larger set of features that afford the basis for the accuracy of archetypal in sensing and prevention intrusions (Theepa 2023). The dataset is free off redundant and repeated data which enables instant use of dataset in the training and testing stages (Nadiya et al., 2020). Training data includes around 126,000 data and 4 types of threats classes such as

- Gathering information regarding networks and identifying security control system avoidance techniques.
- Causing the machine network to slow down or stop service access.
- Illegal system accessing through remote packets spoofing.
- Finding system vulnerability and using it as a normal handler.

Initially preprocess the dataset and then normalize dataset by applying MIN-MAX normalization technique. One-hot-encoding method converts symbolic features into numerical values which can be further processed for feature selection from 41 existing features. The highest accuracy of 99.2% is obtained when number of features is reduced to 21 using LightGBM algorithm (Nadiya et al., 2020). Several features along with threshold values for feature selection and their respective accuracy percentages are shown in Table 2.

Table 2. Features with threshold and accuracy values (Nadiya et al., 2020)

S. No	Number of Features	Threshold Value	Accuracy
1	1	0.154	88.55%
2	2	0.087	92.88%
3	3	0.061	94.17%
4	4	0.049	95.05%
5	6	0.048	98.40%
6	7	0.047	98.34%
7	9	0.044	98.37%
8	10	0.037	98.55%
9	11	0.036	98.67%
10	13	0.031	98.72%
11	14	0.029	98.69%
12	17	0.019	99.06%
13	20	0.013	99.07%
14	21	0.009	99.20%
15	23	0.007	99.18%
16	25	0.006	99.13%
17	28	0.005	99.10%
18	29	0.004	99.07%
19	30	0.003	99.07%
20	31	0.002	99.10%
21	33	0.001	99.10%
22	41	0	99.12%

4.1 Whale Optimization Algorithm With LightGBM Methodology

Assign the LightGBM parameters such as learning rate, number of boosted trees to fit, Maximum number of tree depth and tree leaves. These parameters define the position vector for every whale. The WOA finds the global optimal point through iterative search which is the ending parameter of the LightGBM model (Cheng and Shi, 2021 and Xiang et al., 2022).

This paper proposes WOA optimization parameters with LightGBM algorithm. Python toolkit LightGBM optimizes the parameters with fast learning rate and maximum depth limit of the decision tree without overfitting (Xiang et al., 2022).

The following steps involved in the proposed method are as follows:

Step 1: Preprocess the data set with normalization and perform the dimensionality reduction.

Step 2: Initialize the WOA and set whales in a 3-D space with population density, number of iterations

Step 3: Set Upper and lower limits of LightGBM and generate initial whale population within the search space boundary.

Step 4: Calculate fitness of each whale location based on LightGBM model where the strength task is opted as the Mean Square Error (MSE) task.

Step 5: Identify the location of whale according to the following three components prey search, spiral and random search within predetermined boundary.

Step 6: Find the best whale location of the current whale by sorting all extracted fitness values. This best location is considered as the current global optimal location.

Step 7: Using equations (1) to (5) update the whale position.

Step 8: Repeat steps 2 to 4 to produce iterative optimization until the maximum number of iterations is reached. Thus, the best parameter and absolute whale position is obtained.

Step 9: The finest parameters and WOA search results are integrated with the LightGBM model to find the best intrusion detection model once trained.

5. EXPERIMENTS AND RESULTS

The experimental environment consists of a windows 10 operating system, Python 3.6, PyTorch 1.3 and system with 64 GB of memory. For the given dataset, the experiment result of 10-fold CV is concise as shown in Table 3. The WOA with LightGBM model detects intrusion effectively compare to all other models, WOA with SVM, WOA with XGBoost and GirdSearch with XGBoost. The proposed model WOA with LightGBM algorithm results in high accuracy which is depicted in the Table 3.

Table 3. Model with specificity, sensitivity, and accuracy

Model	Specificity	Sensitivity	Accuracy
GridSearch with XGBoost	0.981	0.907	0.981
WOA with SVM	0.998	0.906	0.980
WOA with XGBoost	0.996	0.955	0.991
WOA with LightGBM	0.999	0.976	0.998

While comparing the accurateness of our projected type and general machine learning algorithms XGBoost -78.61 LightGBM – 89.82 as shown in Table 3.

On average WOA- LightGBM model is more than 10 times faster than WOA-XGBoost as shown in Figure 3.

4.2 Performance Evaluation for Intrusion Detection

The system of measurement used to evaluate the performance of a binary classification model are Precision, Recall, and F1-score. These systems of measurement are valuable in gauging the performance of

Figure 3. Comparison chart for WOA-XGBoost and WOA-LightGBM

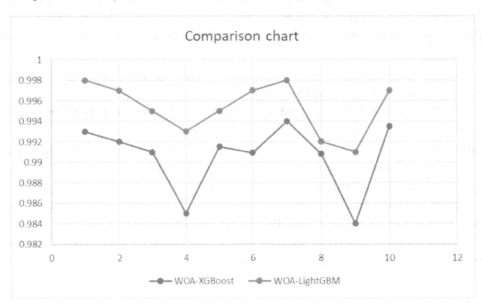

an archetypal when the classes are imbalanced. Measure the effectiveness of intrusion detection using a confusion matrix (see below) (Zhao et al., 2021) to deduct normal or abnormal (intrusion) with the subsequent notations,

TP - true positive
FP - false positive
TN - true negative, and
FN - false negative

Actual \ Predict	*Norm*	*Abnorm*
Norm	*TP*	*FN*
Abnorm	*FP*	*TN*

Figure 4. depicts how system of measurements are related to the notations TP, FP, FN and TN diagrammatically. The most intuitive classification metric is accuracy percentage which measures correctly predicated attack to the total number of attacks in the network.

$$\text{Accuracy} = \frac{\left(\text{TP} + \text{TN}\right)}{\left(\text{TP} + \text{TN} + \text{FN} + \text{FP}\right)} \qquad (6)$$

When the dataset is imbalanced Precision and recall measures performance better than accuracy. Precision measures the accuracy of true positives to the total number of positive predictions.

Figure 4. Relationship of precision, recall, and specificity with TP, FP, FN, and TN

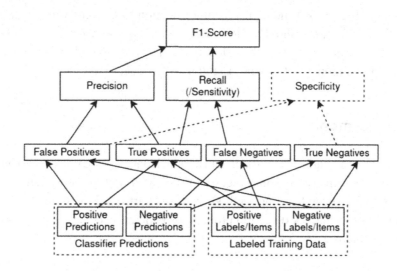

$$Precision = \frac{TP}{\left(TP + FP\right)} \tag{7}$$

The ability of the model in identifythe ratio of true positives to the total number of actual positive occurences.

$$Recall = \frac{TP}{\left(TP + FN\right)} \tag{8}$$

The F1-score harmonic mean of precision and recall. Thus, from eq. (6), (7) and (8), we get,

$$F1\text{-score} = 2 \times \frac{\left(precision \times recall\right)}{\left(precision + recall\right)} \tag{9}$$

The proposed model results in high accuracy of 90.96%, high precision of 92.87% that indicates our proposed model predicts a positive class correctly. Recall percentage of our proposed model is 95.11% which indicates that the model identifies most of the positive instances successfully. The F1-score is 93.98%, to find a balance between FP and FN.

6. CONCLUSION

Though XGBoost classification is popularly used in ML algorithm, the adjustment of trainer parameters is required to improve the performance and obtaining optimal parameters is a challenging task (Cheng and Shi, 2021). To overcome these problems, we use LightGBM method for intrusion detection instead of XGBoost. We apply LightGBM model for feature selection based on the importance of the feature score (Nadiya et al., 2020). A threshold value is set to identify whether a data is normal or attacked. From the experimental result we get 91% classification accuracy compared to the benchmark, XGBoost, model. Thus, the proposed model, WOA with, LightGBM, produces better accuracy and faster intrusion detection models.

6.1 Future Enhancement

Cybersecurity deals with the high-dimensional data as attack datasets are too large to handle. Hence, the advanced technique of learning comes into picture to deal with high-dimensional data. The advanced learning techniques such as deep learning methods and latest artificial intelligence techniques can provide better solutions for cyberattack detection problem by efficiently covering the classification as well as feature selection problems.

ABBREVIATIONS

ML: Machine learning
CS: Cryptosystems
SVM: Support Vector Machine
WOA: Whale Optimization Algorithm
LightGBM: Light Gradient Boosting Machine
IoT: Internet of Things
MSE: Mean Square Error

REFERENCES

Ahmad, S., & Mirvaziri, H. (2019). Performance improvement of intrusion detection system using neural networks and particle swarm optimization algorithms. *International Journal of Information Technology : an Official Journal of Bharati Vidyapeeth's Institute of Computer Applications and Management, 12,* 849–860.

Chaofei, T. (2020). An Efficient Intrusion Detection Method Based on LightGBM and Autoencoder. *Semantic Scholar, Symmetry, 12*(1458), 1-16.

Chen, J. H., Ma, S. F., & Wu, Y. (2021). International carbon financial market prediction using particle swarm optimization and support vector machine. *Journal of Ambient Intelligence and Humanized Computing, 2021,* 1–15.

Chen, R. Y., Pan, B., & Lin, X. D. (2016). Chinese stock index futures price fluctuation analysis and prediction based on complementary ensemble empirical mode decomposition. *Mathematical Problems in Engineering, 2016,* 1–13. doi:10.1155/2016/3791504

Chung-Jui, T., Chuang, L.-Y., Jun-Yang, C., & Yang, C.-H. (2007). Feature selection using PSO-SVM. *IAENG International Journal of Computer Science*, 33.

Cong, Y.-Q., Guan, T., Cui, J., & Cheng, X. (2022). LGBM: An Intrusion Detection Scheme for Resource-Constrained End Devices in Internet of Things. *Security and Communication Networks*, 2022, 1–12. doi:10.1155/2022/1761655

Devan, P., & Khare, N. (2020). An efficient XGBoost-DNN-based classification model for network intrusion detection system. *Neural Computing & Applications*, 32(16), 16. doi:10.1007/s00521-020-04708-x

Esmaeili, M., Goki, S. H., Masjidi, B. H. K., Sameh, M., Gharagozlou, H., & Mohammed, A. S. (2022). ML-DDoSnet: IoT Intrusion Detection Based on Denial-of-Service Attacks Using Machine Learning Methods and NSL-KDD. *Wireless Communications and Mobile Computing*, 2022, 1–16. doi:10.1155/2022/8481452

Gautam, S., Henry, A., Zuhair, M., Rashid, M., Javed, A. R., & Maddikunta, P. K. R. (2022). A Composite Approach of Intrusion Detection Systems: Hybrid RNN and Correlation-Based Feature Optimization. *Electronics (Basel)*, 11(21), 3529. doi:10.3390/electronics11213529

Hanieh, A., Richard, M. K., Wanchat, T., & Kenneth, A. L. (2019). A swarm intelligence-based approach to anomaly detection of dynamic systems. *Swarm and Evolutionary Computation*, 44, 806–827. doi:10.1016/j.swevo.2018.09.003

Li, P., Qiang, W. & Christopher, J. B. (2007). McRank: Learning to rank using multiple classification and gradient boosting. Advances in Neural Information Processing Systems, 20.

Liang, Y., Wu, J., & Wang, W. (2019). ACM Product Marketing Prediction Based on XGboost and LightGBM Algorithm. Association for Computing Machinery.

Ma, L., Cheng, S., & Shi, Y. (2021). Enhancing learning efficiency of brain storm optimization via orthogonal learning design. *IEEE Transactions on Systems, Man, and Cybernetics. Systems*, 51(11), 6723–6742. doi:10.1109/TSMC.2020.2963943

Ma, L., Huang, M., Yang, S., Wang, R., & Wang, X. (2021). An adaptive localized decision variable analysis approach to large-scale multi-objective and many-objective optimization. *IEEE Transactions on Cybernetics*, 52(7), 6684–6696. doi:10.1109/TCYB.2020.3041212 PMID:33476273

Machado, F. P. (2003). *Communication and memory efficient parallel decision tree construction*. Academic Press.

Mohamed, S. A., Alsaif, O. I., & Saleh, I. A. (2022). Intrusion Detection Network Attacks Based on Whale Optimization Algorithm. *Ingénierie Des Systèmes D Information*, 27(3), 441–446. doi:10.18280/isi.270310

Mourad, A., Tout, H., Wahab, O. A., Otrok, H., & Dbouk, T. (2020). Ad-hoc Vehicular Fog Enabling Cooperative Low-Latency Intrusion Detection. *IEEE Internet of Things Journal*, 1–1. doi:10.1109/JIOT.2020.3008488

Muhammed, S., Gianni, A. D. C., & Muddassar, F. (2011). Swarm intelligence based routing protocol for wireless sensor networks: Survey and future directions'. *Information Sciences, 181*(20), 4597–4624. doi:10.1016/j.ins.2010.07.005

Nadiya El, K., Mohamed, E., Youssef, L., & Raja, T. (2020). A Smart Agent Design for Cyber Security Based on Honeypot and Machine Learning. *Security and Communication Networks, 2020*, 1–9.

Rahman, S. A., Tout, H., Talhi, C., & Mourad, A. (2020). Internet of Things intrusion Detection: Centralized, On-Device, or Federated Learning? *IEEE Network, 34*(6), 310–317. doi:10.1109/MNET.011.2000286

Rongfeng, Z., Jiayong, L., Weina, N., Liang, L., Kai, L., & Shan, L. (2020). Preprocessing Method for Encrypted Traffic Based on Semisupervised Clustering. *Security and Communication Networks, 2020*, 1–13.

Sahil, G., Kuljeet, K., Shalini, B., Gagangeet, S. A., Graham, M., Neeraj, K., Albert, Y. Z., & Rajiv, R. (2020). En-ABC: An ensemble artificial bee colony based anomaly detection scheme for cloud environment. *Journal of Parallel and Distributed Computing, 135*, 219–233. doi:10.1016/j.jpdc.2019.09.013

Sharma, A., & Singh, B. (2020). AE-LGBM: Sequence-based novel approach to detect interacting protein pairs via ensemble of autoencoder and LightGBM. *Computers in Biology and Medicine, 103964*, 103964. Advance online publication. doi:10.1016/j.compbiomed.2020.103964 PMID:32911276

Theepa Sri, S., & Rama, A. (2023). Efficient Intrusion Detection System Using Convolutional Long Short Term Memory Network. doi:10.1109/CSITSS60515.2023.10334106

Uma Maheswari, S., & Arunesh, K. (2020). Unsupervised Binary BAT algorithm based Network Intrusion Detection System using enhanced multiple classifiers. *2020 International Conference on Smart Electronics and Communication (ICOSEC)*. 10.1109/ICOSEC49089.2020.9215453

Wang. (2021). A new hybrid forecasting model based on SW-LSTM and wavelet packet decomposition: A case study of oil futures prices. *Computational Intelligence and Neuroscience, 2021*, 1–22. PMID:34335724

Wu, H. (2024). Feature-Weighted Naive Bayesian Classifier for Wireless Network Intrusion Detection. *Security and Communication Networks, 2024*, 1–13. doi:10.1155/2024/7065482

Xiang, W., Shen, G., Yibin, G., Shiyu, Z., Yonghui, D., & Daqing, W. (2022). A Combined Prediction Model for Hog Futures Prices Based on WOA-LightGBM-CEEMDAN. *Complexity, 22*, 1–15.

Yan, S., Haowei, L., Xu, P., & Dan, L. (2022). A Method of Intrusion Detection Based on WOA-XGBoost Algorithm. *Discrete Dynamics in Nature and Society, 22*, 1–9. doi:10.1155/2022/7771216

Zhang, Y. L., & Hamori, S. (2020). Forecasting crude oil market crashes using machine learning technologies. *Energies, 13*, 10.

Zhao, R., Yin, J., Zhi, X., & Gui, G. (2021). An Efficient Intrusion Detection Method Based on Dynamic Autoencoder. *IEEE Wireless Communications Letters, 10*(8), 1707–1711. doi:10.1109/LWC.2021.3077946

Zhou, Y., Qin, R., Xu, H., Sadiq, S., & Yu, Y. (2018). A Data Quality Control Method for Seafloor Observatories: The Application of Observed Time Series Data in the East China Sea. *Sensors (Basel), 18*(8), 2628. doi:10.3390/s18082628 PMID:30103440

Chapter 6
A Survey of Machine Learning and Cryptography Algorithms

M. Indira

P.K.R. Arts College for Women (Autonomous), Gobichettipalayam, India

K. S. Mohanasundaram

P.K.R. Arts College for Women (Autonomous), Gobichettipalayam, India

M. Saranya

P.K.R. Arts College for Women (Autonomous), Gobichettipalayam, India

ABSTRACT

The intersection of machine learning and encryption has emerged as a key area in technology. A model shift in technology and data security has brought the combination of machine learning and encryption. In order to provide insight on the underlying algorithms and techniques, this survey was taken between the domains. It presents an overview of machine learning and cryptography algorithms. A wide variety of algorithms are examined in the field of machine learning. This survey also clarifies the interaction between machine learning and cryptography, demonstrating how these two fields work together to produce privacy-preserving ML, secure authentication, anomaly detection, and other benefits. A new era of data privacy and security has methods like secure multi-party computation (SMPC) and homomorphic encryption, which allow calculations on encrypted data. An updated overview of machine learning techniques used in cryptography is presented in this survey. The report offers recommendations for future study initiatives and summarizes the work.

INTRODUCTION

The integration of machine learning (ML) with encryption has caused an unprecedented shift in the field of modern technology, opening up previously unheard-of opportunities in the areas of security, privacy, and data-driven insights. Combining the strong principles of cryptography with machine learning's capacity to identify patterns and extract useful information from large datasets creates a potent coalition

DOI: 10.4018/979-8-3693-1642-9.ch006

against new threats and difficulties. The domains of privacy preservation, secure model training, and better adversarial resilience are undergoing significant changes due to this mutually beneficial interaction (Biggio et al., 2023).

In almost every industry conceivable, the modern community has incredible access to cutting-edge hardware and software at a pace that is unparalleled. On the other hand, this has given rise to an entirely new set of security and privacy risks. As a result, it is imperative to address the security and privacy aspects of various cyberthreats, which are growing dramatically faster than before due to undiscovered malware. More than 10 billion of the world's people, according to a special report, depend upon mobile phones or other smart devices for banking, shopping, financing, healthcare, blockchain applications, social media posts, and professional information and updates.

Therefore, there is a good probability that data will be hacked or disclosed when downloading apps on smart devices. In addition, malicious software can be activated via faulty system processes, unapproved network entry, and the collection of private data. Numerous anti-virus programmes, intrusion detection systems, defenders, and the most recent firewalls with security updates are available to address these problems.

Enormous search areas and handling enormous amounts of data are two commonalities between encryption and machine learning (ML). While machine learning (ML) has long been used in cryptography, given the daily cohort of over 5 quintillion bytes of data, ML approaches are now more pertinent than ever. In order to continuously learn from and adapt to the massive quantity of data being provided as input, machine learning (ML) typically automates the creation of analytical models. The relationship between the input and output data produced by cryptosystems can be shown using machine learning techniques.

To generate the private cryptographic key, machine learning techniques like boosting and mutual learning can be applied. Classification techniques like naive Bayesian, Artificial Neural Networks, support vector machine, and AdaBoost can be applied to categorise objects and encrypted traffic into steganograms that are utilised in steganography. In addition to being used in cryptography, the art of building safe systems for encrypting and decrypting private information, machine learning techniques can also be used in cryptanalysis, the art of cracking cryptosystems to carry out specific side-channel attacks.

The ways in which cryptography and machine learning differ and are similar show how one discipline can affect another. Cryptography and machine learning have attracted a lot of interest. Generally speaking, cryptanalysis and machine learning share more similarities than does machine learning and cryptography. This is because their shared goal searching across expansive search spaces is the reason for this. The goal of a cryptanalyst is to decipher the correct key, but the goal of machine learning is to select an appropriate answer from a wide range of potential answers. Over the past few years, applications of various machine learning approaches have drawn increasing attention.

There are other study fields as well, such as machine learning modification to mislead its application to incorrect classification, quantum machine learning, and privacy preservation. The fields of machine learning and cryptography mutual research are not new. The computational complexity of machine learning and its computational components were covered by Kearns in his dissertation. This research cleared the path for further machine learning and cryptography research. Machine learning has several uses in the field of information and network security, in addition to cryptography and cryptanalysis.

LITERATURE SURVEY

In the paper entitled "Distributed Outsourced Privacy-Preserving Gradient Descent Methods among Multiple Parties," Z. Tan et al. (2021) provided two novel techniques for the outsourced privacy-preserving gradient descent method over data that is divided vertically or horizontally across several parties

In the paper entitled "Fusion of Machine Learning and Privacy Preserving for Secure Facial Expression Recognition," A. Ullah et al. (2021) offered a unique framework and a reliable, efficient method for recognising facial expressions in an unrestricted setting; it also assisted in the classification of facial photos in the client/server model while maintaining anonymity.

Sayed Ali et al. (2021), in "Machine Learning Technologies for Secure Vehicular Communication in Internet of Vehicles: Recent Advances and Applications," facilitated the Internet of Vehicles, has carried out a thorough review using analytical modelling for offloading mobile edge-computing decisions based on deep reinforcement learning and machine learning techniques.

"Multicriteria Decision and Machine Learning Algorithms for Component Security Evaluation: Library-Based Overview" (J. Zhang et al., 2020) presented reusing components is advised to save time, effort, and resources because they are already built; hence, a new system was developed using these reusable components.

In the paper titled "Android Malware Detection Based on a Hybrid Deep Learning Model," T. Lu et al. (2020) suggested a hybrid deep learning model that combines a gate recurrent unit and a deep belief network as the basis for an algorithm for detecting Android viruses.

"A Smart Agent Design for Cyber Security Based on Honeypot and Machine Learning" (N. E. Kamel et al., 2020) introduced honeypot systems and machine learning, using these technologies, created a smart agent for predicting and preventing cyberattacks.

"Spam Detection Approach for Secure Mobile Message Communication Using Machine Learning Algorithms" (L. G. Jun et al., 2020) suggested using machine learning to detect spam in order to get precise detection. This method classified spam and ham messages from mobile device communications using machine learning classifiers like logistic regression, K-nearest neighbour, and decision trees.

Vyas et al. (2015) provide an overview of supervised machine learning techniques for email spam filtering. The Naïve Bayes method outperforms all other techniques examined in terms of speed and reasonable precision.

RESEARCH GAP

- Improvements in these cryptographic algorithms' capacity and effectiveness can be the main focus of research for machine learning that protects privacy (Chen et al., 2018). It is very important to develop multi-key homomorphic encryption systems that are both practical and efficient. To investigate the novel methods for incorporating differential privacy into machine learning models without losing their usefulness is challenging one.
- In order to make multi-key homomorphic encryption more feasible for contexts with limited resources, research might concentrate on creating more effective schemes, refining already-existing schemes, and investigating hardware-accelerated alternatives.

- The majority of applications allow the encoding strategy for a considerable amount of time, which aids the analyst in concentrating on this approach till acknowledging the key or creating a method for knowing the key each time it is modified.

PROPOSED METHOD

Detecting anomalies in data involves finding unusual or unexpected behaviour. By examining network data and spotting trends that point to a possible attack, machine learning algorithms can be used to spot possible security lapses or assaults. This may lessen the possibility of illegal access to encrypted data. In collaborative data analysis, several parties work together on sensitive data to analyse and draw conclusions without sharing any of their personal information.

The suggested proposed method uses secure multi-party compute approaches to overcome privacy issues (Chen et al., 2022) related to collaborative data analysis. The significance of privacy-preserving data analysis and the requirement for safe collaboration frameworks are discussed. With the ability to manipulate encrypted data directly and the property that altering the ciphertext directly yields the same outcome as altering the plaintext first and then encrypting it, Multi-key homomorphic encryption is used for encryption, in scenarios involving outsourced computing. When using Multi-key homomorphic encryption, each side encrypts its personal information. A third party performs the computations directly on the encrypted data, and the resultant output is also encrypted. The third party, who carries out the computation without decrypting the secret data, receives the encrypted data from each party.

CONTRIBUTION TO THE RESEARCH

- By utilising a multi-key homomorphic encryption proxy to re-encrypt the provided data, a safe multi-party computing system based on encrypted data is implemented. Proxy re-encryption allows the data owner to go offline after encrypting the uploaded data and eliminates the need for them to remain online during safe multi-party computing. This solves the issue where the multi-key homomorphic encryption technique cannot be decrypted individually when the result is acquired.
- A neural network-based secure multi-party computing strategy is suggested, which combines multi-key fully homomorphic encryption agents with re-encryption.
- This secure multi-party computing solution satisfies all requirements (Hunag et al., 2021).

MACHINE LEARNING AND ITS APPLICATIONS

Algorithms are used in machine learning classification approaches to group data into preset classes or labels. These methods can be used in a variety of cryptography applications to address privacy and security issues. The following are a few machine learning classification methods with applications in cryptography:

Algorithms for Supervised Learning

In the domain of cybersecurity, supervised learning algorithms are employed for tasks like spam filtering, virus detection, and intrusion detection. For example, by learning patterns of typical network behaviour and recognising abnormalities, Support Vector Machines (SVMs) can be utilised for intrusion detection. Random Forest algorithms work well for categorising malware according to characteristics taken from its behaviour or code.

Neural Networks

Neural networks are used for cryptography tasks such as cryptographic key generation, intrusion detection, and encrypted data analysis. For example, deep learning for anomaly detection uses a neural network to learn typical network traffic patterns and spot anomalies that might be signs of security risks. Secure cryptographic key generation is one cryptographic procedure that neural cryptography can improve.

Decision Trees

In cybersecurity, decision trees are used to categorise network traffic and differentiate between benign and malevolent activity. For example, network packets can be classified as benign or malicious using Decision Trees for Intrusion Detection, which can be trained to identify information such as port numbers, source and destination IP addresses, etc.

Ensemble Learning

The general accuracy and resilience of classification models used in cryptography can be increased by employing ensemble learning techniques like bagging and boosting. AdaBoost, for instance, can be used to enhance the efficacy of weak classifiers in tasks such as malware detection.

Naive Bayes

In cryptography, Naive Bayes classifiers are used for spam detection and email filtering. For example, spam detection: Naive Bayes algorithms are capable of analysing email content and characteristics to ascertain whether or not an email is likely to be spam.

K-Nearest Neighbours (KNN)

In network traffic analysis, KNN algorithms can be utilised for anomaly detection and categorization. As an illustration: Network Anomaly Detection: KNN can spot odd network traffic patterns that could point to an intrusion or security risk.

Regression Techniques in Cryptography Applications

In machine learning, regression techniques are primarily applied to forecast continuous or numerical outcomes based on feature-based inputs. Regression techniques are used when the goal variable is a continuous value, whereas classification approaches concentrate on allocating data points to preset groupings or categories. Regression techniques are useful in the field of cryptography for a number of tasks that entail making numerical predictions or determining correlations between variables.

- Using models, one can determine the ideal key length for cryptographic algorithms by taking into account variables like processing power, security needs, and possible threats.
- Analysis can be used to simulate the link between different input parameters or configurations and the performance of a cryptographic algorithm (e.g., encryption/decryption speed).
- It can help to fine-tune cryptographic protocol security parameters, such choosing the right values for things like a block cipher's number of rounds.
- By simulating the effects of different parameters on the performance or vulnerability of cryptographic protocols, techniques can be used to analyse their security or efficiency.
- It can be applied to the estimation of entropy levels in cryptographic key creation procedures or random number generators.
- Analysis models the link between important factors and attack resistance, which aids in assessing the cryptographic strength of algorithms.

When an algorithm is given unlabeled data and entrusted with identifying patterns, relationships, or structures within the data without explicit instruction in the form of labelled outputs, this sort of machine learning is known as unsupervised learning. Unsupervised learning aims to find hidden patterns or explore the data's innate structure without explicit guidance on what to look for. In unsupervised learning, dimensionality reduction and grouping are frequent problems.

Two types of unsupervised learning techniques:

- Clustering is the process of assembling comparable data points according to a similarity metric. Natural groupings or clusters within the data are found by the algorithm.
- The goal of dimension reduction approaches is to decrease a dataset's feature count while maintaining its key attributes.

In machine learning, unsupervised learning is also applicable. In situations where reference output is unavailable for comparison, learning is accomplished only through input data. Unsupervised learning or training is what it is known as. Clustering is a prevalent unsupervised learning technique. Finding structures or clusters in input data is done by clustering.

Reinforcement Learning

- The processes of key creation, distribution, and management can be optimised with the use of RL. As usage patterns and the security environment change, the agent can be trained to dynamically modify important parameters.
- Adaptive cryptography algorithms that can modify their parameters in response to a changing threat landscape can be created using reinforcement learning. This can entail adapting key lengths or dynamically altering encryption techniques in response to shifting security requirements.

- RL can improve cryptographic network intrusion detection systems (Borges et al., 2017). The agent can be trained to identify unusual patterns of behaviour, react to security events, and modify its tactics over time to increase the system's overall resilience.

APPLICATIONS IN CRYPTOGRAPHY

Al-Rawe and Naimi (2023) discussed the primary focus of this study is secure MPC techniques for co-operative recommender networks. It looks at recent developments and tactics designed to preserve user privacy while enabling accurate and useful cooperative recommendations.

Lee and Wang (2021) explained An extensive analysis of secure MPC techniques used in coopera-tive machine learning settings is provided by this paper. It looks at the issues with collaborative ML that protects privacy and provides an overview of the solutions that have been proposed in the literature.

Al-Shammari and Zincir-Heywood (2009) presented a classification technique, to categorise encrypted traffic using machine learning. The task was completed in order to evaluate the machine learning cat-egorization of encrypted traffic's robustness.

Blum (2007) discussed the possibilities of connecting machine learning and cryptography. The study claims that there are substantial technological overlaps between machine learning and cryptography systems. This is related to techniques for enlarging cryptosystems.

Klien et al. (2005) presented mutual learning as a novel phenomenon. In cryptography, this mutual learning effect can be useful. Mutual learning can facilitate the creation of a shared secret key between the two communication parties over a public channel.

Rosen-Zvi et al. (2002) proposed that a public-key cryptosystem can be implemented via mutual learning in a tree parity machine. The synchronisation state of the tree parity machine is utilised as the key in a specific encryption and decryption rule, which explains how the machine can be used as a public-key cryptosystem.

Secure Multi-Party Computation (SMPC) and Multi-Key Homomorphic Encryption

Innovative methods for data privacy and security include Secure Multi-Party Computation (SMPC) and Homomorphic Encryption, which enable calculations on encrypted data without disclosing the underly-ing information (Brown & Davis, 2020).

Multi-Key Homomorphic Encryption

A cryptographic method called Multi-key homomorphic encryption makes it possible to compute on encrypted material without having to decrypt it. When the computation is decrypted, the result matches the result that would have been obtained if the operations were conducted on the plaintext.

- Users can store encrypted data on a cloud server and use it for computations without having to first decode it, which improves privacy.

- During training and inference, Multi-key homomorphic encryption can be utilised to safeguard private information that is used in machine learning models.
- Companies can contract with outside organisations to do data processing functions without disclosing the real data.

Figure 1. Multi-key homomorphic algorithm

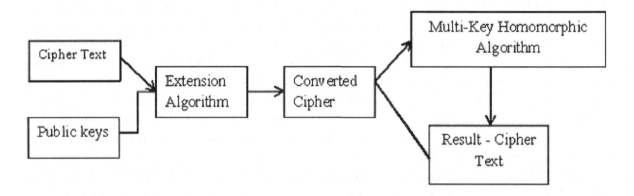

Secure Multi-Party Computation (SMPC)

SMPC protects the privacy of the inputs by enabling multiple parties to concurrently compute a function over them (Zhang & Zhang, 2020). Without disclosing specific inputs to one another, each party computes the required function collectively while maintaining the privacy of its own private input through cryptographic methods.

- In domains where data sharing is restricted, such as healthcare, finance, or research, many parties can work together to analyse datasets without disclosing the raw data (Liu et al., 2022).
- SMPC can be used to create private, secure electronic voting systems that protect each voter's vote.
- SMPC can be used when several entities need to decide based on their separate inputs without sharing those inputs (Smith & Johnson, 2019).

ATTACKS ON MACHINE LEARNING IN CRYPTOGRAPHY

A study with incorrect predictions made by a classifier was suggested by Dalvi et al. (2005). The adversarial classification problem is the name given to this issue. An adversarial learning problem, first identified by Lowd and Meek (2005), allows attackers to send queries to a classifier in order to reverse engineer it and locate harmful instances that the classifier is unable to identify.

Olakunle Ibitoye et al. (2019) state that machine learning in network security is also susceptible to different adversarial assaults, which may result in inaccurate predictions. In order to better understand how adversarial assaults affect machine learning and network security, they carried out an extensive

Figure 2. Secure multi-party computation (SMPC)

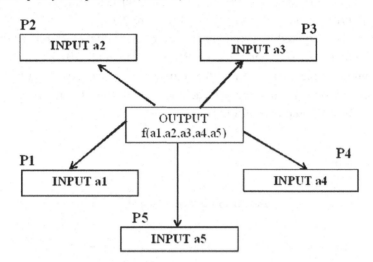

investigation. They came to a risk grid map that shows which adversarial attacks (Athalye et al., 2018) ML systems in network security are susceptible to. Many learning methods are available online these days and can be used from a distance. According to accountability, a summary of machine learning assaults was provided by K. Auernhammer et al. (2019). An adversarial attack that targets and compromises the security of connected and autonomous automobiles is proposed by Prinkle Sharma et al. (2019).

A comprehensive analysis of security and privacy in machine learning was presented by Peprnot et al. (2016). The paper presents an adversarial framework with an extensive threat model for machine learning and an appropriate classification scheme for assaults and defences. An effective adversarial black-box approach that allows the attacker to take control of a remotely hosted DNN without needing to know the model or training data

The backdoor study in machine learning systems is provided by Yujie Ji et al. (2020). Backdoors are introduced by third-party primitive learning modules (PLMs). Under specific circumstances, malicious PLMs have the ability to create system malfunctions. Using this technique, model parameters can be changed to introduce backdoors. A strategy for adding a backdoor to deep learning models using data poisoning is proposed by Chen et al. (2017). Even without any prior understanding of the model or input data, this model functions well.

Backdoor attacks, as demonstrated by Liao et al. (2018), can be introduced into convolution neural network models by the use of covert perturbations. The target label is recognised as the attacker's label. Bagdasaryan et al. (2018) discussed backdoor attacks on federated learning and suggested a secure privacy protecting learning system.

RESULTS

To ensure that data integrity is maintained, the proposed approach also challenges the problem of un-trusted third parties executing homomorphic operations on encrypted data. This is crucial because it guards against threats like data change and tampering. Data alternation attacks cause inaccurate decryption outcomes by modifying encrypted data without the secret key.

When the ciphertext is decrypted, the attacker can alter it to create a different plaintext, which could result in data loss, illegal access, or other negative effects (Yang et al., 2020). The suggested work provides a multi-key homomorphic encryption with Security multi-party computation (SMPC) technique that uses a unique key to independently encrypt each decimal digit of the input integer number. Where individual data cannot be activated by multi parties.

Figure 3. Encryption of text

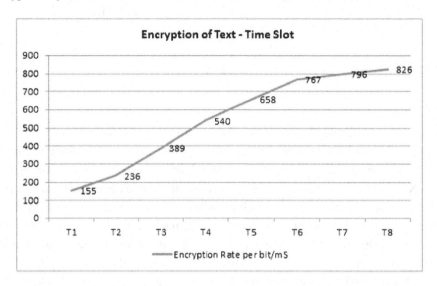

Figure 4. Decryption of text

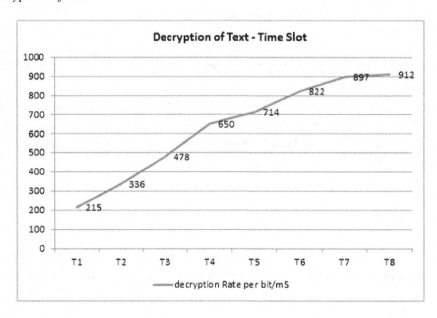

CONCLUSION AND FUTURE WORKS

Our presentation provided an overview of the use of machine learning in the fields of multi-key homomorphic encryption, secure multi-party computation, and cryptography. The literature review revealed that these study topics have a great deal of untapped potential. Additionally, the report covered security flaws in machine learning methodologies and machine learning-based systems.

Due to the fact that machine learning is heavily reliant on data quality in security applications, new dangers resulting from cyber-attacks have the potential to destroy vital data infrastructure. It is difficult to identify protected data using machine learning-based techniques in security applications because they gather and predict many samples. A new field of study is made possible by the sharp rise in security events and the security of machine learning-based decision systems in security settings. Malicious users may occasionally be able to minimise false-positive rates and raise false-negative rates proportionately. This allows them to maintain an overall error rate while deceiving the system and giving attackers a tactical advantage in more complex attacks. Investigating this kind of problem is necessary to effectively identify assaults on ML-based systems. All data privacy fields have made enormous strides, but their effectiveness is still limited by the intricate workings of machine learning algorithms that depend on a vast number of parameters. Thus, it is necessary to research very effective privacy-preserving techniques in cryptographic data. A performance trade-off between scalability and accuracy for machine learning classifiers was identified.

FUTURE WORKS

There are many interesting possibilities for tackling issues related to data security, privacy, and cryptographic protocols at the intersection of machine learning and cryptography.

- Providing sophisticated ways for training machine learning models on encrypted data by utilising privacy-preserving approaches such as homomorphic encryption. When open data sharing is not possible, this can improve privacy.
- Using machine learning to create dynamic, adaptable key management systems that can react to changing security risks. This can guarantee ongoing security and increase the resistance of cryptographic systems to attackers.
- Finding abnormalities and possible security lapses in cryptographic systems, apply machine learning methods. This can help detect unusual activity or efforts to undermine the security of cryptographic systems early on.
- Examining how blockchain systems' privacy and security can be improved by machine learning approaches. This covers transactions in blockchain networks that protect privacy, safe consensus techniques, and anomaly detection.

REFERENCES

Al-Rawe, Y. H. A., & Naimi, S. (2023). Project construction risk estimation in iraq based on delphi, RII, spearman's rank correlation coefficient (DRS) using machine learning. *International Journal of Intelligent Systems and Applications in Engineering, 11*(5s), 335–342. www.scopus.com

Ali, E. S., Hasan, M. K., Hassan, R., Saeed, R. A., Hassan, M. B., Islam, S., Nafi, N. S., & Bevinakoppa, S. (2021). Machine Learning Technologies for Secure Vehicular Communication in Internet of Vehicles: Recent Advances and Applications. Security and Communication Networks, (1), 1-23.

Alsadhan, A. A., & Alani, M. M. A. (2018). Detecting ndp distributed denial of service attacks using machine learning algorithm based on flow-based representation. *Developments in eSystems Engineering (DeSE), 2018 Eleventh International Conference on.* 10.1109/DeSE.2018.00028

Alshammari, R., & Zincir-Heywood, A. N. (2009). Machine learning based encrypted traffic classification: Identifying ssh and skype. *Computational Intelligence for Security and Defense Applications, 2009. IEEE Symposium on CISDA 2009,* 1–8.

AthalyeA.EngstromL.IlyasA.KwokK. (2018). *Synthesizing robust adversarial examples.* arXiv:1707.07397v3

Auernhammer, K., Kolagari, R. T., & Zoppelt, M. (2019). Attacks on Machine Learning: Lurking Danger for Accountability. *Conf. of AAAI Workshop on Artificial Intelligence Safety.*

Bagdasaryan, E., Veit, A., Hua, Y., Estrin, D., & Shmatikov, V. (2018). *How to backdoor federated learning.* arXiv preprint arXiv:1807.00459.

Banerjee, S., & Mondal, A. C. (2023). An intelligent approach to reducing plant disease and enhancing productivity using machine learning. *International Journal on Recent and Innovation Trends in Computing and Communication, 11*(3), 250–262. doi:10.17762/ijritcc.v11i3.6344

Bhattacharyya, D. K., & Kalita, J. K. (2013). *Network anomaly detection: A machine learning perspective.* Chapman and Hall/CRC. doi:10.1201/b15088

Biggio, B., Corona, I., Maiorca, D., Nelson, B., Šrndić, N., Laskov, P., Giacinto, G., & Roli, F. (2023). Evasion attacks against machine learning at test time. *ECMLPKDD'13: Proceedings of the 2013th European Conference on Machine Learning and A Survey on Security Threats to Machine Learning Systems at Different Stages of its Pipeline,* 15, 387–402.

Blum, A. (2007). Machine learning theory. Carnegie Melon University, School of Computer Science.

Bonawitz, K., Ivanov, V., Kreuter, B., Marcedone, A., McMahan, H. B., Patel, S., Ramage, D., Segal, A., & Seth, K. (2017). Practical secure aggregation for privacy-preserving machine learning. *Proceedings of the 2017 ACM SIGSAC Conference on Computer and Communications Security,* 1175–1191. 10.1145/3133956.3133982

Borges, P., Sousa, B., Ferreira, L., Saghezchi, F. B., Mantas, G., Ribeiro, J., & Simoes, P. (2017). Towards a Hybrid Intrusion Detection System for Android-based PPDR terminals. In *Proceedings of the 2017 IFIP/IEEE Symposium on Integrated Network and Service Management (IM).* IEEE. 10.23919/INM.2017.7987434

Brown, M., & Davis, R. (2020). Efficient Secure Multi-Party Computation for Collaborative Genomic Analysis. *Journal of Bioinformatics and Computational Biology*, *18*(3), 235–257.

Chen, Liu, Li, & Lu. (2017). *Targeted Backdoor Attacks on Deep Learning Systems Using Data Poisoning*. arXiv:1712.05526 v1 [cs.CR]

Chen, L. (2018). Privacy-Preserving Data Analytics using Secure Multi-Party Computation: A Survey. *ACM Computing Surveys*, *51*(3), 1–35. doi:10.1145/3190507

Chen, Z. (2022). Secure Multi-Party Computation for Collaborative Fraud Detection: A Systematic Review. *Journal of Financial Crime*, *29*(2), 345–367.

Dalvi, Domingos, Mausam, & Sanghai. (2004). Adversarial Classification. *Proceedings Of The Tenth ACM SIGKDD International Conference On Knowledge Discovery And Data Mining*, 99–108.

Dang, H., Huang, Y., & Chang, E. C. (2017). Evading classifiers by morphing in the dark. *CCS '17: Proceedings of the 2017 ACM SIGSAC Conference on Computer and Communications Security*, 119–133. 10.1145/3133956.3133978

Dwork, C., & Roth, A. (2014). The algorithmic foundations of differential privacy. Foundations and Trends® in Theoretical Computer Science, 9(3-4), 211–407.

El Kamel, Eddabbah, Lmoumen, & Touahni. (2020). A Smart Agent Design for Cyber Security Based on Honeypot and Machine Learning. *Hindawi Security and Communication Networks*, 1-9.

Grosse, K., Papernot, N., Manoharan, P., Backes, M., & McDaniel, P. (2017). Adversarial examples for malware detection. In *ESORICS* (pp. 62–67). Computer Security – ESORICS.

Huang, Y. (2021). Privacy-Preserving Collaborative Natural Language Processing using Secure Multi-Party Computation. *Journal of Artificial Intelligence Research*, *70*, 965–988.

Klein, E., Mislovaty, R., Kanter, I., Ruttor, A., & Kinzel, W. (2005). Synchronization of neural networks by mutual learning and its application to cryptography. *Advances in Neural Information Processing Systems*, 689–696.

Lee, H., & Wang, S. (2021). Secure Multi-Party Computation for Collaborative Machine Learning: Challenges and Solutions. *IEEE Transactions on Knowledge and Data Engineering*, *33*(8), 1234–1256.

Li, H., Wang, Y., Xie, X., Yang, L., Wang, S., & Wan, R. (2020). Light can hack your face! Black-box backdoor attack on face recognition systems. *arXiv preprint arXiv:2009.06996*.

Liu, X. (2022). Secure Multi-Party Computation for Collaborative Financial Analysis: A Systematic Review. *Journal of Financial Data Science*, *2*(1), 45–68.

Lowd & Meek. (2005). Good word attacks on statistical spam filters. In CEAS-2005, Palo Alto, CA.

Lu, Du, Li, Chen, & Wang. (2020). Android Malware Detection Based on a Hybrid Deep Learning Model. *Security and Communication Networks*, 1–11.

Luo, Nazir, Khan, & Ul Haq. (2020). Spam Detection Approach for Secure Mobile Message Communication Using Machine Learning Algorithms. *Security and Communication Networks*, 1–11.

Mohassel, P., & Zhang, Y. (2017). Secureml: A system for scalable privacy-preserving machine learning. *2017 38th IEEE Symposium on Security and Privacy (SP),* 19–38. 10.1109/SP.2017.12

Ohrimenko, O., Schuster, F., Fournet, C., Mehta, A., Nowozin, S., Vaswani, K., & Costa, M. (2016). Oblivious multi-party machine learning on trusted processors. *USENIX Security Symposium,* 619–636.

Papernot, N., McDaniel, P., Sinha, A., & Wellman, M. (2016). *Towards the science of security and privacy in machine learning.* arXiv preprint arXiv:1611.03814.

Ristè, da Silva, Ryan, Cross, Córcoles, Smolin, Gambetta, Chow, & Johnson. (2017). Demonstration of quantum advantage in machine learning. *NPJ Quantum Information, 3*(1), 16.

Rosen-Zvi, M., Klein, E., Kanter, I., & Kinzel, W. (2002). Mutual learning in a tree parity machine and its application to cryptography. *Physical Review. E, 66*(6), 066135.

Sharma, P., Austin, D., & Liu, H. (2019). Attacks on Machine Learning: Adversarial Examples in Connected and Autonomous Vehicles. *IEEE International Symposium on Technologies for Homeland Security (HST).*

Sheng, Y.-B., & Zhou, L. (2017). Distributed secure quantum machine learning. *Science Bulletin, 62*(14), 1025–1029. doi:10.1016/j.scib.2017.06.007 PMID:36659494

Smith, J., & Johnson, A. (2019). Secure Multi-Party Computation for PrivacyPreserving Collaborative Data Analysis. *Journal of Privacy and Security, 15*(2), 123–145.

Tan, Z., Zhang, H., Hu, P., & Gao, R. (2021). Distributed Outsourced Privacy-Preserving Gradient Descent Methods among Multiple Parties. *Hindawi Security and Communication Networks,* 1–16.

Ullah, A., Wang, J., Anwar, M. S., Ahmad, U., Saeed, U., & Fei, Z. (2019). Facial expression recognition of nonlinear facial variations using deep locality de-expression residue learning in the wild. *Electronics (Basel), 8*(12), 1487.

Vyas, T., Prajapati, P., & Gadhwal, S. (2015). A survey and evaluation of supervised machine learning techniques for spam e-mail filtering. In *Proceedings of the 2015 IEEE international conference on electrical, computer and communication technologies (ICECCT).* IEEE.

Xu, W., Qi, Y., & Evans, D. (2016). Automatically Evading Classifiers: A Case Study on PDF Malware Classifiers. *Conference of Network and Distributed System Security Symposium,* 1–15. 10.14722/ndss.2016.23115

Yang, C. (2020). Privacy-Preserving Collaborative Social Network Analysis using Secure Multi-Party Computation. *Social Network Analysis and Mining, 10*(1), 1–22.

Zhang, J., Nazir, S., Huang, A., & Alharbi, A. (2020). Multicriteria Decision and Machine Learning Algorithms for Component Security Evaluation: Library-Based Overview. *Hindawi Security and Communication Networks,* (September), 1–14.

Zhang, W., & Zhang, L. (2020). Secure Multi-Party Computation for Collaborative Internet of Things Data Analysis. *IEEE Internet of Things Journal, 7*(5), 3789–3807.

Chapter 7
Quantum Cryptography:
Algorithms and Applications

R. Thenmozhi
SRM Institute of Science and Technology, India

D. Vetriselvi
 https://orcid.org/0009-0001-3870-9061
SRM Institute of Science and Technology, India

A. Arokiaraj Jovith
SRM Institute of Science and Technology, India

ABSTRACT

Cryptography is the process of encrypting data or transforming plain text to ciphertext so that it can be deciphered only by appropriate key. Quantum cryptography employs quantum physics principles to encrypt and transport data in an unpackable manner. Quantum key distribution (QKD) is a technique for creating and exchanging private keys over quantum channels between two parties. Then, using standard cryptography, the keys can be used to encrypt and decrypt messages. Unbreakable encryption is something we really must have. The integrity of encrypted data is now in danger due to the impending development of quantum computers. Fortunately, quantum cryptography, via QKD, provides the answer we require to protect our information for a very long time to come. This is all based on the intricate principles of quantum mechanics. This chapter is discussing the various algorithms used and the applications of quantum cryptography.

INTRODUCTION

Quantum Computing

Quantum computing is a multidisciplinary field that integrates computer science, mathematics, and physics. We can solve complex problems far faster with quantum physics than we can with conventional

DOI: 10.4018/979-8-3693-1642-9.ch007

computers. Quantum computing includes both hardware and software development and research. Two examples of quantum mechanical characteristics that quantum computers employ to surpass classical computers in particular problem types are superposition and quantum interference. This is so that quantum computers may make use of these phenomena. Machine learning (ML), optimisation, and simulation of physical systems could all profit from the faster processing rates provided by quantum computers. Potential applications in the future include enhancing financial portfolios and modelling chemical reactions, two tasks that require resolving issues that are beyond the capabilities of even the most potent supercomputers available today.

Quantum bits, or qubits, are represented by symbols called quantum particles. The control devices play a major role in the success of the attempt to maximise the processing capabilities of a quantum computer by manipulating qubits. The bits found in traditional computer types are comparable to the qubits seen in quantum computers. A traditional machine's CPU is primarily in charge of manipulating bits to accomplish its tasks. Parallel to this, the manipulation of qubits is the only way the quantum processor can perform its duties (Raymer, 2017).

An electronic signal that can exist in one of two states—on or off—is referred to as a "bit" in the context of classical computing. Depending on the circumstance, the classical bit's value can be either one (on) or zero (off). Owing to its foundation in the concepts of quantum physics, the qubit can exist in a superposition of states.

BACKGROUND

Quantum Mechanics

In the study of very small-scale particle behaviour, physics offers a field known as quantum mechanics. The equations governing particle behaviour at the subatomic scale are not the same as those describing the macroscopic environment. The utilisation of these phenomena by quantum computers results in computational processes that are radically novel (Sasaki, 2012).

Basic Concepts Behind Quantum Computing

The application of quantum ideas forms the foundation of quantum computing. A new lexicon of terms is required to fully comprehend quantum principles. These include concepts like decoherence, entanglement, and superposition. Let us get a deeper comprehension of these principles (Banafa, 2023).

- **Superposition**
  Superposition is the idea that two or more quantum states can be combined in a way that is like how waves are combined in conventional physics, and the outcome will be another valid quantum state. Conversely, any given quantum state can also be defined as the sum of two or more other unique states. The inherent parallelism of quantum computers, which allows them to perform millions of tasks simultaneously, comes from this superposition of qubits.

- **Entanglement**

    When two systems are connected in such a way that knowledge about one system instantly provides knowledge about the other, regardless of the distance between the two systems, this phenomenon is called quantum entanglement. Quantum computers can infer information about the initial particle by measuring another particle. They can determine, for example, that when one qubit spins upward, the other will necessarily spin downward, and vice versa. By utilising quantum entanglement, quantum computers can solve complex issues faster. When a quantum state is measured, the wavefunction collapses, and the state is measured as either a zero or a one depending on the measurement outcome. When in this known or predictable state, the qubit behaves similarly to a conventional bit. Entanglement occurs when qubits can correlate their states with those of other qubits.

- **Decoherence**

    Decoherence is the process by which a qubit loses its quantum state. The collapse of the qubits' quantum state can occur under a variety of environmental circumstances, including radiation. The design of the many features that try to postpone the state's decoherence is one of the biggest engineering hurdles in the process of creating a quantum computer. As an illustration, the creation of specific structures that protect the qubits from outside fields.

Components of Quantum Computer

In the same way that classical computers have hardware and software, quantum computers also operate in this manner.

Figure 1. Components of Quantum Computing

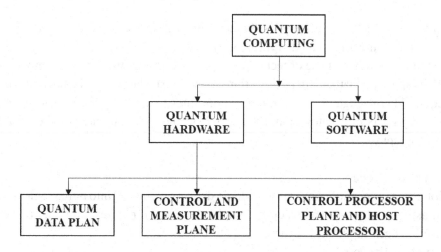

Quantum Hardware

Hardware for quantum computing consists of three primary components.

- **Quantum Data Plane**
  - The core of the quantum computer is the quantum data plane, which contains all the physical qubits and the structures required to hold them in place.
- **Control And Measurement Plane**
  - The control and measurement plane converts digitalized signals into either wave control signals or analogue signals.
  - The analogue signals in the quantum data plane are responsible for executing the qubit operations.
- **Control processor plane and host processor**
  - The control processor plane implements both the sequence of operations and the quantum algorithm.
  - The host processor communicates with the quantum software and sends a digital signal or a set of classical bits to the control and measurement plane.

Quantum Software

Using quantum circuits to implement unique quantum algorithms is known as quantum software. A kind of computing process known as a quantum circuit describes a series of logical quantum operations that are carried out on the qubits that make up the circuit. To write quantum algorithms, programmers can make use of a broad range of software development tools and libraries.

Cryptography

The translation of the word "cryptography" is "hidden," and the suffix "-graph" denotes writing. Hence, writing that is secure or hidden is called cryptography.

Cryptography is the study and use of techniques to shield information and communication from attackers. It involves applying mathematical algorithms to transform data into a format that is unintelligible without the required knowledge or key. Authentication, integrity, confidentiality, and non-repudiation are the four primary goals of cryptography (Nitaj, 2023). The following are some essential ideas and elements of cryptography:

- **The Encryption Process**
  Encryption is the process of converting readable data, or plaintext, into unreadable data, or ciphertext, using an algorithm and a cryptographic key. The ciphertext can only be decrypted and converted back to plaintext by the owner of the correct key.
- **The Decryption Process**
  Decryption is the opposite of encryption. To convert ciphertext back into plaintext, the decryption algorithm and the appropriate key must be used.

- **Symmetric Cryptography**

  In symmetric cryptography, the same key is used for both encryption and decryption. The sender and the recipient need to exchange the secret key.

- **Asymmetric Cryptography**

  Asymmetric cryptography uses two sets of keys: public and private. The public key is used for encryption, but the private key is required for decryption. Only the recipient should be in possession of the private key.

- **Infrastructure for Public Keys (PKI)**

  PKI is a set of roles, policies, and procedures that are used to create, manage, distribute, use, store, and revoke digital certificates as well as supervise public-key encryption.

Cryptography is a fundamental component of information security and is used in a wide range of applications, including secure communication, digital signatures, access control, and data protection. The field of cryptography is always evolving, with new challenges arising due to changes in technology and threat landscape.

Quantum Cryptography

The term "quantum cryptography" describes an encryption method that uses the properties of quantum physics to protect and transfer data in a way that prevents unauthorized access.

The methodical process of encoding and protecting data so that only those with the right secret key can decrypt it is referred to as cryptography. Unlike traditional cryptography, quantum cryptography bases its security framework primarily on physics rather than mathematics. This sets it apart from other cryptographic systems. The technique of quantum cryptography is intrinsically secure, as it effectively blocks unauthorised access without requiring the sender and recipient of the encrypted message to be aware of it (Bhushan, 2022).

When it comes to quantum communication, information that is encoded within a quantum state cannot be replicated or accessed without resulting in detection by the sender or the recipient. Maintaining the security of quantum cryptography against adversaries using quantum computing capabilities is essential. Photons, which are discrete light particles, are used in quantum cryptography to transfer data over fibre optic cables. Binary information is based on photons as its fundamental unit. Quantum mechanics and its applications are necessary for the system to function properly. These are the properties that are considered secure:

- Particles can exist in several places or states at once.
- Any quantum characteristic that is observed must be changed or disrupted.
- Moreover, complete particles cannot be replicated.

These properties make it impossible to measure the quantum state of any given system without causing some kind of disturbance. Since photons have the necessary property, they are used in quantum cryptography. As information carriers, the behaviour of optical fibre cables is well understood. Known as one of the most notable examples of quantum cryptography, quantum key distribution (QKD) provides a strong mechanism for exchanging cryptographic keys.

A field of study called quantum cryptography uses the ideas of quantum mechanics to create secure communication channels. In contrast to classical cryptography, which depends on mathematical formulas and specific difficulties (like factoring big numbers), quantum cryptography leverages the essential characteristics of quantum mechanics to provide security (Barnett, 2009).

Here are some key concepts and principles of quantum cryptography:

- Quantum Key Distribution (QKD): This is one of the main uses of quantum cryptography in practice. By using QKD, two parties can create a shared secret key over a communication channel that may not be secure. The laws of quantum mechanics ensure the security of this key distribution.

- Superposition: A concept from quantum mechanics, superposition refers to the simultaneous existence of multiple states in particles like photons. Information is encoded using this property in quantum key distribution protocols.

- Entanglement: Regardless of the distance between two or more particles, quantum entanglement is a phenomenon in which the states of those particles are directly related to one another. Establishing secure quantum communication channels involves the use of entanglement.

- Uncertainty Principle: According to the Heisenberg Uncertainty Principle, it is impossible to know two properties of a particle exactly at the same time, such as momentum and position. Quantum cryptography protocols use this intrinsic uncertainty to identify eavesdropping attempts.

- Quantum Measurement: A quantum system is disturbed when it is measured. This disturbance has applications in quantum cryptography to identify potential eavesdroppers. The quantum states will unavoidably be disrupted if a third party attempts to measure them, and this disruption can be identified.

- BBM92 Protocol (BB84 Protocol): One of the first and most well-known quantum key distribution protocols was put forth by Charles Bennett and Gilles Brassard in 1984 (thus the name BB84). It involves the transfer of photons with various polarizations, and quantum mechanical principles ensure its security (Brassard, 2005).

Figure 2. Key Concepts in Quantum Cryptography

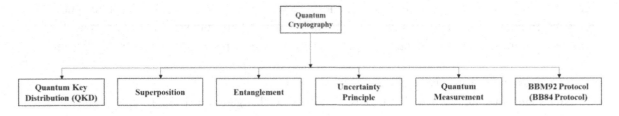

Communication that is truly secure could be possible thanks to quantum cryptography, since any attempt to decipher messages encrypted with this technique would upset the fragile quantum states that are being sent. It is crucial to remember that there is still much to learn about quantum cryptography, and that developing trustworthy quantum communication hardware and dealing with the fragility of quantum states will present difficulties for any real-world applications. However, it has the potential to offer never-before-seen levels of communication security

RELATED WORKS

The utilisation of a distinctive quantum key distribution (BB84 protocol) and its integration with traditional encryption techniques to enhance the security of data transmission. Furthermore, it evaluates the encryption, decryption, avalanche effect, and performance of both QKD free versions, as well as QKD for these operations, to analyse the efficiency of different cryptographic methods across different file sizes. The study investigates the potential applications of quantum cryptography in secure communication systems, building upon previous research on the topic (Khodakhast Bibak and Robert Ritchie, 2021) (Chankyun Lee, Ilkwon Sohn, and Wonhyuk Lee, 2022), (J Zhou, L Lu, Y Lei, and X Chen, 2014).

Concrete evidence employing a communicative architectural model and implementation to replicate the principles of quantum physics. The quantum key distribution (QKD) implemented using the BB84 protocol utilises both the presence and absence of an eavesdropper. Simulation data suggest that the utilisation of Heisenberg's uncertainty principle and the no-cloning principle can help in detecting an eavesdropper. Based on simulation data, the probability of precisely anticipating the polarisation state to eavesdrop on is extremely low (Dariush Abbasinezhad-Mood and Morteza Nikooghadam, 2018), (Amritha Puliadi Premnath, Ju-Yeon Jo, and Yoohwan Kim, 2014).

The present state of quantum computing and its applications in cryptography. This study examines the resilience of current encryption methods against quantum computing and explores the potential of quantum computers in predicting secret keys for decrypting communication. The paper also discusses the creation of an application that allows users to employ this method for deciphering encrypted messages (Jia-Lun Tsai and Nai-Wei Lo., 2015), (Vanga Odelu, Ashok Kumar Das, Mohammad Wazid, and Mauro Conti, 2016).

This article will analyse quantum computing algorithms, namely Shor's algorithm, to explore its potential in replacing traditional methods for decrypting encryption systems. The evaluation of several quantum computing techniques will encompass an analysis of their storage capacity, computational time precision, correctness, integrity, availability, and efficiency (Neetesh Saxena and Santiago Grijalva, 2016).

This study presents a factorial quantum technique for cracking RSA without explicitly determining the modulus of n. The basis of this is the utilisation of phase estimation and the quantum inverse Fourier transform. The Shanks' SQUARE Form Factorization method, the Lehman methodology, and the RSA Quantum Polynomial-Time Fixed-Point Attack have all been studied as potential methods to the Integer Factorization Problem (IFP) (Baokang Zhao, Bo Liu, Chunqing Wu, Wanrong Yu, Jinshu Su, Ilsun You, and Francesco Palmieri, 2016).

Detailed analyses of state-of-the-art quantum key distribution (QKD) secured optical networks that will significantly influence communication networks in the upcoming decades. This text provides a comprehensive description of the fundamental setup approach, as well as the procedures and methods employed in optical networks protected by Quantum Key Distribution (QKD). The text provides a comprehensive discussion and comparison of several approaches suggested in the literature for addressing networking-related challenges (J Zhou, L Lu, Y Lei, and X Chen, 2014).

The utilisation of wireless body sensor networks (WBSN) for distant medical monitoring during the COVID-19 epidemic. After analysing the latest security weaknesses in WBSN data, a novel enhanced BB84 Quantum Cryptography Protocol (EBB84QCP) is suggested as a reliable method for secure key distribution without the need for directly exchanging secret keys (Yonghong Ma, Xiuyu Wang, and Dandan Cui, 2013).

METHODOLOGY

Quantum Key Distribution (QKD)

Within the field of information security, quantum key distribution (QKD) and machine learning are two separate but related fields. A variety of cybersecurity scenarios, such as intrusion detection, anomaly detection, and threat intelligence, can benefit from the application of machine learning. On the other hand, QKD is a cryptographic technique that secures communication channels by utilizing the concepts of quantum mechanics. Although they are not usually used together directly, there are some circumstances in which they might be (Chindiyababy, 2022).

This is a conceptual overview of possible joint research projects between machine learning and quantum key distribution:

Figure 3. Steps to Integrate Quantum Key Distribution and Machine Learning

Enhancing Quantum Key Distribution Security

Based on the ideas of quantum mechanics, QKD offers a secure key exchange mechanism. It is intended to provide information-theoretic security, which means that rather than being ensured by computational complexity, the security is based on the rules of physics. The application of machine learning can help detect and reduce possible security holes or assaults on QKD systems. Machine learning algorithms, for instance, could be used to identify patterns or unusual behaviours in a quantum communication channel that might point to a security risk.

Key Management and Authentication

Key QKD management tasks can be aided by machine learning. This covers user or device authentication for the purpose of quantum communication. Machine learning algorithms can analyse key usage patterns and generate alerts if anomalous patterns are found, which may point to a security breach.

Network Security and Anomaly Detection

For tasks like key distribution, classical data transmission, and network management, classical communication infrastructure is still required, even though QKD secures the quantum communication channel. These traditional communication channels can be monitored and secured with the use of machine learning techniques. For instance, in traditional network infrastructure, machine learning algorithms can assist in identifying unusual activity or possible cyberthreats.

Quantum Random Number Generation

The generation of random numbers, which is necessary for cryptographic applications, can be done with quantum computers. Quantum-generated random numbers can be evaluated and verified using machine learning techniques to make sure they adhere to the necessary cryptographic standards.

Post-Processing of Quantum Key Material

Post-processing tasks pertaining to the generated quantum key material may be investigated using machine learning techniques. This could entail improving the key material's efficacy or resistance to specific kinds of attacks by refining or optimizing it.

It is crucial to remember that the field of study integrating QKD and machine learning is still developing, and that practical applications may be constrained by the state of quantum technologies now and the needs of the involved cryptographic systems. Depending on the particular use case and developments in machine learning and quantum computing, these technologies may be combined. Cybersecurity and quantum information science experts are always looking for new approaches to improve communication system security using these technologies.

Optimising Quantum Key Distribution (QKD)

Investigating machine learning techniques can help QKD systems operate more efficiently. Using machine learning algorithms to dynamically adjust system parameters in response to environmental conditions and real-time measurements could be one way to achieve this (V. Srividya,2021).

- **Quantum Error Correction:**
  Quantum error correction, which is essential for maintaining the accuracy of quantum information in the face of errors and noise, may be improved by machine learning.
- **Quantum Random Number Generation:**
  A key element of quantum cryptography is the production of random numbers by quantum processes, which can be assessed and validated using machine learning techniques.
- **Post-Processing and Key Distillation:**
  Machine learning has the potential to improve the efficiency of critical distillation processes by optimizing post-processing operations associated with quantum crucial material.

Enhancing Quantum Key Distribution (QKD) Protocols

Techniques for quantum key distribution (QKD) that rely on entangled particles can benefit from the application of machine learning. This entails real-time parameter adjustments based on experimental results to enhance the security and efficiency of the key distribution process.

- **Correction of Errors in Entangled States:**
  Maintaining the accuracy of quantum information, including entangled states, requires quantum error correction. The development of error correction codes or procedures that are more ef-

fective at fixing mistakes and especially made for complex scenarios may be facilitated by machine learning techniques.

- **Analysis of Entanglement:**
  The analysis and description of entanglement properties can be done with machine learning techniques. This involves determining relevant characteristics from the experimental data to assess the degree of entanglement and other relevant parameters.

Uncertainty Principle

The Uncertainty Principle, as proposed by Werner Heisenberg, states that the accuracy with which some pairs of properties (like momentum and position) of a particle can be simultaneously determined is intrinsically limited in quantum physics. The Uncertainty Principle plays a central role in the field of quantum cryptography, and machine learning can be used to address various aspects related to quantum uncertainty (Faulkner, 2021). The following lists suggested connections between machine learning, quantum cryptography, and the Uncertainty Principle:

- **Quantum Key Distribution (QKD) and Uncertainty:**
  Quantum Key Distribution (QKD) protocols, like the well-known BBM92 (Bennett-Brassard 1992) protocol, employ the Uncertainty Principle and other concepts from quantum mechanics to facilitate secure key exchange. Measurement of the quantum state by nature breaks the corresponding conjugate property, making it possible to identify eavesdropping attempts.
- **Quantum State Characterization Using Machine Learning:**
  Quantum states, particularly those affected by the Uncertainty Principle, can be characterized through the application of machine learning techniques. For example, this might involve using machine learning techniques to extract relevant properties from quantum states or improve the measurement process.
- **Quantum Sensing and Parameter Estimation:**
  The intrinsic uncertainty of quantum mechanics is harnessed by quantum sensors to achieve remarkable precision in parameter estimation. Algorithms for machine learning can analyse data from quantum sensors and enhancing parameter estimation accuracy.
- **Quantum Random Number Generation (QRNG):**
  By taking advantage of the unpredictable nature of quantum states, QRNG uses quantum uncertainty to produce genuinely random numbers. The quality of randomness generated by QRNG devices can be examined and confirmed through the application of machine learning techniques.
- **Quantum Error Correction and Uncertainty:**
  Errors arising from uncertainty and associated measurement disruption are common in quantum systems. Using machine learning algorithms, quantum error correction processes can be improved, lowering uncertainties that may arise during quantum operations.
- **Enhancing Quantum Measurement Strategies:**
  Making measurements on quantum states is a common task in quantum cryptography, and choosing a measurement strategy is crucial. By considering the conditions and uncertainties of the experiment, machine learning algorithms can optimize measurement procedures.

- **Quantum Tomography and Uncertainty-Aware Reconstruction:**
  The method of determining a new quantum state from measurements is known as quantum state tomography. Rebuilding quantum states while accurately and efficiently accounting for uncertainty is possible with machine learning techniques.

It is necessary to acknowledge the dynamic field of study that is the application of machine learning to quantum cryptography. Researchers are currently looking into how machine learning could enhance the capabilities of quantum technologies, particularly in addressing measurement disturbance and uncertainty-related problems. The applications and approaches used can vary based on the goals and circumstances of the current quantum cryptography project. It is essential to stay up to date with the latest research and literature in quantum information science and machine learning to fully understand the ongoing developments in this multidisciplinary field.

Quantum Measurement

Quantum measurement plays a crucial role in quantum cryptography, especially in quantum key distribution (QKD) protocols. The security of quantum communication hinges heavily on the identification of these perturbations, which can occur during the measurement of a quantum state (Ekert, 2005). Machine learning finds applications in the field of quantum measurement in a wide range of situations. The following are some applications for machine learning:

- **Improving the Bases of Measurement:**
  A common step in quantum key distribution is choosing measurement bases, and the optimal choice depends on the properties of the quantum states being used. Machine learning algorithms can be used to optimize the selection of measurement bases by taking performance evaluation and real-time feedback into account.
- **Adjustable Metrics:**
  Machine learning techniques can be utilized to create procedures for adaptive measurement. Because the system can learn from previous measurement results, it can dynamically modify measurement parameters to maximize information gain while reducing disturbance.
- **Adjusting Errors in Measurement Disturbances:**
  Quantum measurements are inherently unstable, so errors may occur during the taking process. Machine learning techniques can be used to develop efficient error correction methods that reduce the impact of disruptions and increase the accuracy of the key generation process.
- **States Rebuilt and Quantum Tomography:**
  Quantum state tomography aims to reconstruct an unknown quantum state from measurement data. Reconstructing quantum states could be improved and expedited with the use of machine learning techniques, especially when measurement uncertainties are present.
- **Adversarial Attack Detection:**
  Machine learning can be used to detect adversarial attacks or eavesdropping attempts during the quantum measurement process. In order to alert the parties involved in the communication, abnormal patterns in measurement outcomes can be detected by machine learning algorithms.

- **Quick and Easy Post-Processing**

  Post-processing steps that can be optimized with machine learning come after quantum measurements. This includes privacy amplification and distillation, two tasks where machine learning algorithms can help increase the efficiency of the classical processing of quantum measurement outputs.

- **Online Monitoring and Calibration:**

  Quantum measuring apparatus needs to be continuously observed and calibrated to preserve the reliability of quantum cryptography systems. Machine learning algorithms can be used to detect and correct drifts or discrepancies in measurement equipment, enabling online calibration.

- **Characterizing Quantum Channels:**

  Machine learning techniques support the characterization of the quantum channel, including its noise and characteristics. Using this information to adjust measurement procedures can optimize the performance of quantum communication protocols.

Machine learning within the quantum measurement framework allows for intelligent and adaptive approaches to quantum key distribution. It provides a means of fortifying quantum cryptography systems against measurement errors and other disturbances, optimizing protocols, and strengthening security. The development of this multidisciplinary field of study may lead to the emergence of new methods and uses for the combination of machine learning and quantum cryptography.

QUANTUM KEY DISTRIBUTION (QKD) ALGORITHMS

1. BBM92 Protocol (BB84)

Objective:
- ◦ Advised for quantum key distribution (QKD)-based secure communication.
- ◦ Seek to make it possible for two people to exchange a private key for safe traditional communication.

Key Features:
- ◦ Makes use of quantum mechanical properties, in particular the no-cloning theorem and quantum superposition concepts.
- ◦ The protocol entails the transmission of qubits (quantum bits) using two non-orthogonal states in a different basis (usually represented as "+" and "×") and two additional non-orthogonal states in the standard basis (typically represented as "0" and "1").
- ◦ Alice, the sender, encrypts each bit using a random combination of the two bases.
- ◦ Additionally, Bob, the receiver, selects a basis for measurement at random.
- ◦ An eavesdropper's attempt to intercept the qubits introduces errors that the legitimate parties can detect because of the non-orthogonality of the states.

Security Basis:
- ◦ The fundamental ideas of quantum mechanics, such as the impossibility of cloning an unknown quantum state and the disturbance brought on by measurements, are what underpin the security of BB84.

Figure 4. BBM92 Protocol

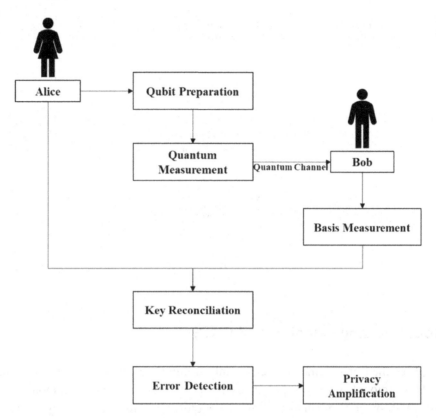

Key Exchange Process:

i.   **Qubit Preparation**: Alice gets a series of qubits ready in two of the four possible states—the standard basis and the Hadamard basis.
ii. **Quantum Transmission**: Bob receives Alice's qubits via a quantum channel.
iii. **Basis Measurement**: Bob selects a basis at random for each qubit that is received.
iv. **Key Reconciliation**: Alice and Bob interact freely to contrast their measurement bases and eliminate data that was measured using a different basis.
v.   **Error Detection**: Alice and Bob look for mistakes in their critical information that might point to the existence of an illegal listener.
vi. **Privacy Amplification**: By processing the final shared key, privacy amplification techniques are applied to improve its security.

The BB84 protocol proved that secure key exchange utilizing quantum principles was feasible and established the groundwork for quantum key distribution. In the realm of quantum cryptography, it continues to be an essential protocol (Ciesla, 2020).

Figure 5. E91 Protocol (Entanglement-based QKD)

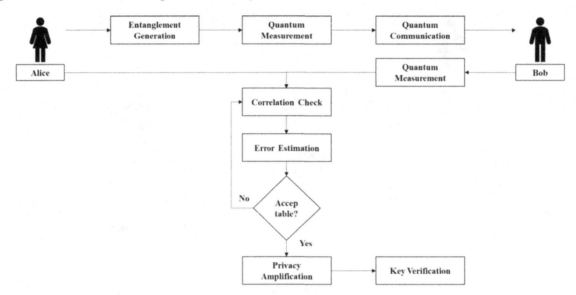

2. E91 Protocol (Entanglement-Based QKD)

Artur Ekert proposed the Entanglement-based Quantum Key Distribution (QKD) protocol, or E91 protocol, in 1991. This protocol allows for the safe exchange of keys between two remote parties by taking advantage of the phenomenon known as quantum entanglement. This is a summary of the E91 protocol:

E91 Protocol Overview:

Entanglement Generation:
- In an entangled state, Alice produces pairs of entangled particles, usually photons. Regardless of their distance from one another, entanglement indicates that the states of the two particles are directly correlated.

Quantum Measurement:
- Alice measures her particles in a variety of bases, selecting the basis at random for each measurement. Selecting a basis is essential for security.

Quantum Communication:
- Alice sends one particle to Bob, who is located far away, from each entangled pair. The usual medium for this communication is a quantum channel.

Quantum Measurement at Bob's End:
- For every particle received, Bob selects at random a measurement basis and conducts measurements in accordance with that basis.

Correlation Check:
- Alice and Bob exchange information regarding the bases they used for their measurements following the quantum communication phase. They keep only the measurements made with the same foundation.

Error Estimation:
- ◦ Bob and Alice calculate the measurement error rate. Elevated mistake rates could suggest the existence of a listener.

Privacy Amplification:
- ◦ Alice and Bob use privacy amplification techniques to distil a shorter, but more secure, final shared key if the error rate is judged acceptable.

Key Verification:
- ◦ Alice and Bob take extra precautions to make sure their key is secure against possible eavesdropping and to confirm that it is correct.

Security Basis:
- ◦ Entanglement provides non-local correlations that are essential to the security of the E91 protocol.
- ◦ Any attempt to eavesdrop would cause the entangled particles to become disoriented, which would result in observable mistakes in the key generation process.

Significance:
- ◦ The E91 protocol highlighted the non-local and quantum nature of the security features by demonstrating the potential to use entanglement for secure key distribution.
- ◦ Even though the E91 protocol may not be as useful in practice, it has sparked additional study and the creation of more sophisticated entanglement-based QKD protocols.

In the search for workable quantum communication systems, several entanglement-based protocols have been put forth and investigated. Quantum entanglement offers a special resource for secure key distribution.

Figure 6. SARG04 Protocol (Six-state QKD)

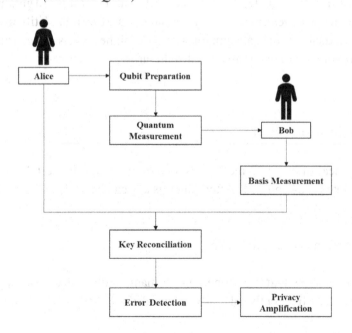

3. SARG04 Protocol (Six-state QKD): Six-State Quantum Key Distribution

- Qubit Preparation:
  Like BB84, Alice prepares qubits in one of six non-orthogonal states. These states are often represented as $|0\rangle$, $|1\rangle$, $|+\rangle$, $|-\rangle$, $|i\rangle$, and $|-i\rangle$, where $|+\rangle$ and $|-\rangle$ are superpositions of $|0\rangle$ and $|1\rangle$, and $|i\rangle$ and $|-i\rangle$ are superpositions of $|0\rangle$ and $|1\rangle$ with a phase factor.
- Quantum Transmission:
  Alice sends the qubits to Bob over a quantum channel.
- Basis Measurement:
  Bob randomly chooses a basis for measuring each received qubit.
- Key Reconciliation:
  Alice and Bob communicate openly to compare their measurement bases and discard bits measured in different bases.
- Error Detection:
  Alice and Bob check for errors in their key bits, which would indicate the presence of an eavesdropper.
- Privacy Amplification:
  The final shared key is processed to enhance its security through privacy amplification techniques.

The Six-State Protocol provides an improvement over the BB84 protocol by using additional non-orthogonal states, which can increase the efficiency of quantum key distribution in certain scenarios.

QDS (QUANTUM DIGITAL SIGNATURES)

A subfield of quantum cryptography known as "quantum digital signatures" (QDS) uses quantum computing and quantum key distribution (QKD) to create secure digital signatures. To guarantee the integrity and authenticity of electronic messages or data, digital signatures are essential. Utilizing the special qualities of quantum mechanics, quantum digital signatures provide higher levels of security (Bykovsky, 2018).

This is a basic introduction to quantum digital signatures:

Key Concepts

Quantum Key Distribution (QKD)

- By utilizing the ideas of quantum mechanics, two parties can safely establish a secret key through QKD protocols like BB84 and E91. After that, this key can be utilized for traditional cryptography operations.

Quantum Superposition and Entanglement

- To create quantum states that are vulnerable to manipulation or eavesdropping attempts, quantum digital signatures frequently take advantage of the concepts of quantum superposition and entanglement.

Figure 7. Quantum Digital Signature Process

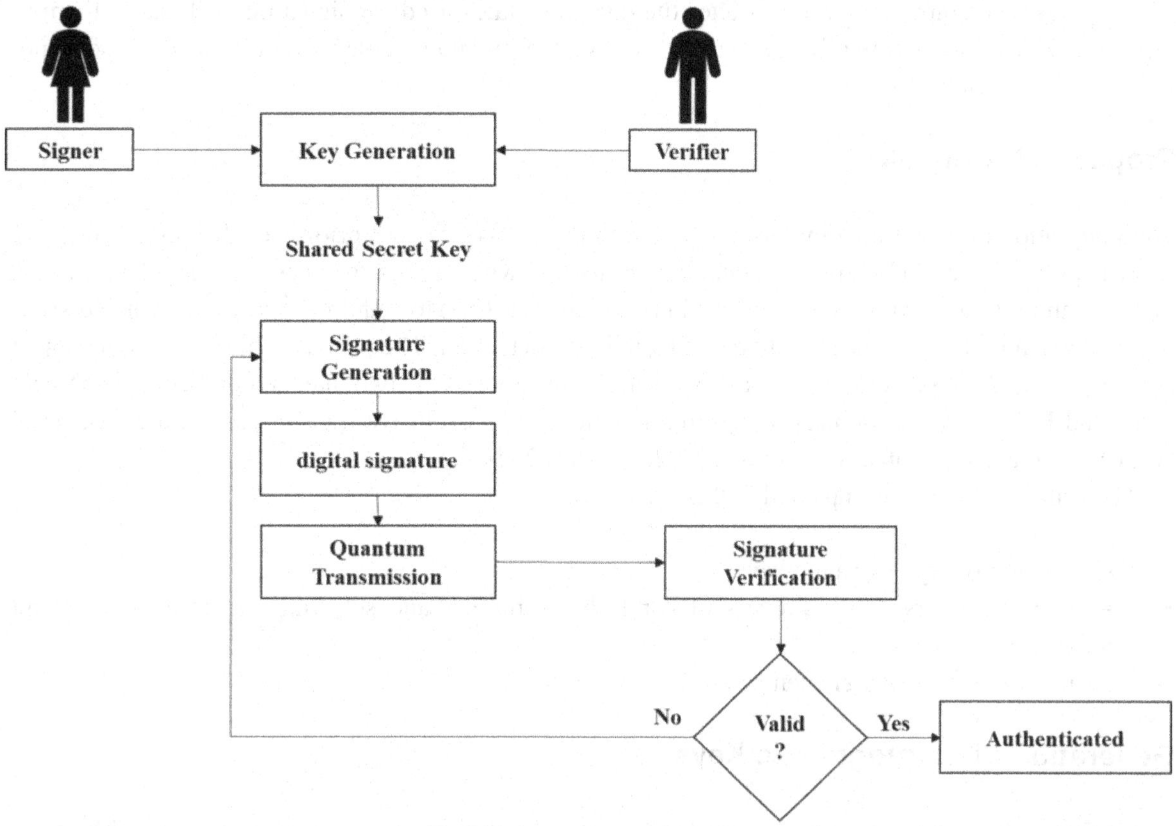

Quantum Digital Signature Process

- Key Generation: Using a QKD protocol, two parties—referred to as the signer and the verifier—establish a shared secret key.
- Signature Generation: The digital signature is generated by the signer using the secret key to create a quantum state. The message to be signed determines the creation of this quantum state.
- Quantum Transmission: A quantum communication channel is used to send the verifier the quantum signature.
- Signature Verification: Using the shared secret key, the verifier measures the received quantum state. The verifier acknowledges the signature as authentic if it is valid.

Security Aspects

Quantum Resistance:

○   The purpose of quantum digital signatures is to withstand attacks from quantum computers, which can defeat classical digital signature algorithms (like RSA and ECC) by using Shor's algorithm.

Tamper Detection:

    ◦   Any attempt to measure or alter the quantum states used for signatures will cause them to change. Consequently, the signer or the verifier would be able to identify any eavesdropper tampering.

Proposed Methodology

The integration of Quantum Key Distribution with the BB84 protocol prioritises the enhancement of security proof. Alice and Bob utilise quantum bits, also known as qubits, to generate the key. Every effort made by an individual who secretly listens in (referred to as Eve) to acquire the key results in a disruption in the quantum signal, ultimately resulting in Eve's detection. The primary objective of our project is to provide a safe mode of communication exclusively between the two intended participants, namely Alice and Bob. This communication ensures security by the exclusive transmission of a confidential key. (Anilkumar, C., Lenka, S., Neelima, N., & V E, S., 2024)

The primary stages encompassed in this system are:

- Generation of cryptographic keys
- Key Sifting refers to the process of carefully examining and selecting important or relevant information.
- Extraction of essential elements

Generation of Cryptographic Keys

The emitter sends out a photon with a randomly selected polarisation from a set of four possible states for each bit. He maintains a record of the orientation in a list.

- The photon is transmitted across the quantum channel.
- The recipient selects either a horizontal or diagonal direction for a filter, which enables them to distinguish between two randomly occurring polarisation states for each photon received. He meticulously records both the orientations and the outcomes of the detections, specifically noting whether the photons were deflected to the right or left.

Key Sifting

Key sifting refers to the process of carefully examining and sorting through a set of keys to identify and select the most relevant or important ones. The emitter utilises this information to compare the orientation of the photons he has transmitted with the corresponding filter orientation. He provides the recipient with information regarding the specific instances in which the orientations are compatible and those in which they are not. In the BB84 protocol diagram, it is observed that after sifting, the two parties possess a sequence of bits called the sifted key, which is identical if there is no eavesdropper present. Additionally, it has the capability to serve as a covert cryptographic key.

Key Distillation

Process of extracting essential information or distilling the most important elements. If there was no unauthorised listener during the broadcast and the equipment used was perfect, the key should be completely free of errors after Key Sifting. All these inaccuracies are attributed to the eavesdropper to prevent compromising the security of the key. Subsequently, a post-processing technique known as Key Distillation is performed.

Figure 8. Proposed Methodology

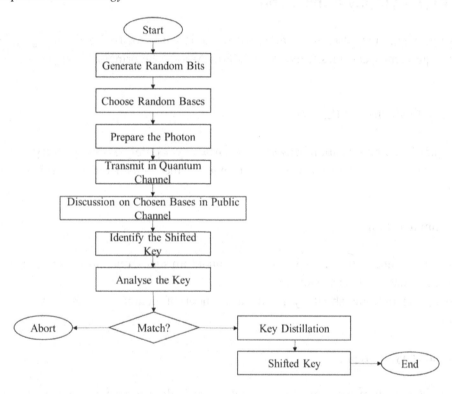

Challenges and Future Developments

Implementation Challenges

- One of the biggest challenges is creating useful quantum communication networks and devices that can carry out QDS. The state of quantum technologies today is still experimental.

Combining With Conventional Systems

- It is a difficult task to integrate quantum digital signatures seamlessly with current classical cryptography systems.

Quantum-Safe Cryptography

- Long-term security requires quantum-resistant (post-quantum) cryptographic algorithms as quantum computers develop.
- In quantum cryptography, quantum digital signatures are a promising field of study that tackles the threats that quantum computers might pose to traditional cryptographic systems. Current research endeavours to devise pragmatic applications and surmount the obstacles linked to quantum communication technologies.

Quantum Cryptography Applications

Applications for quantum cryptography are numerous and mainly focused on securing communication channels using quantum mechanics (Mohamed, 2020). Among the principal uses of quantum cryptography are:

Quantum Key Distribution (QKD)

- Enables private communication between two parties by securely exchanging cryptographic keys;
- Uses the ideas of quantum mechanics to provide a mechanism for identifying eavesdropping attempts.

Secure Communication

- By taking advantage of the intrinsic security of quantum states, quantum cryptography guarantees the privacy of data that is transmitted.
- The disruption brought about by the measurement of quantum states makes eavesdropping detectable.

Quantum-Safe Cryptography

- Creating post-quantum cryptography, or cryptographic algorithms resistant to quantum attacks, to get ready for the era of quantum computers.
- Preserving information from quantum computers' potential to decrypt it.

Quantum Digital Signatures

- Ensures the integrity and authenticity of electronic messages in a quantum-safe way;
- Generates digital signatures that are safe from quantum attacks using quantum states.

Quantum Secure Direct Communication (QSDC)

- Making secure communication possible between two parties without requiring the distribution of keys beforehand;
- Directly utilizing quantum entanglement to achieve secure communication.

Quantum Key Exchange (QKE)

- Enabling safe communication even when a possible quantum adversary is present.
- Safely exchanging cryptographic keys via quantum protocols.

Quantum Networks

- Developing quantum communication networks to enable safe multiparty communication.
- Putting quantum cryptography into more extensive and useful applications.

Quantum Token Passing

- securing token transfers via quantum communication to make sure that only authorized parties have access to resources or systems

Quantum-Secured Cloud Computing

- Improving cloud computing security through the application of quantum-resistant cryptography.
- Keeping private information safe from potential quantum computer decryption

Satellite-Based Quantum Communication

- Using satellites to deploy quantum communication systems to create secure connections between far-off places.
- Overcoming obstacles in the way of long-distance quantum communication on Earth

Quantum Internet

- Creating a global quantum internet that will enable users to communicate securely and instantly with each other anywhere in the world.
- Combining different quantum communication protocols and technologies into a unified network.

Financial Transactions

- Utilizing cryptographic algorithms that are resistant to quantum fluctuations to safeguard financial transactions;
- safeguarding digital signatures; and guaranteeing the accuracy of financial information.

By offering answers to problems with traditional cryptographic techniques and potential dangers from quantum computing in the future, quantum cryptography has the potential to completely transform the field of secure communication. The goal of ongoing research and development is to increase the practicality and accessibility of quantum cryptography technologies for use in everyday situations.

Applications of Quantum Computing

• Artificial Intelligence (AI) and Machine Learning (ML)

The capacity to process solutions to problems in parallel, as opposed to sequentially, holds great promise for machine learning (ML) and artificial intelligence (AI). Artificial intelligence (AI) and machine learning (ML) are tools used by modern organizations to find ways to automate and improve task performance. Optimisation can happen more quickly and broadly when quantum computing is used in conjunction with optimisation techniques, especially when dealing with complex or disorganised large data sets.

- **Financial modelling:**
  The large-scale modelling capabilities of quantum computing can help financial organizations better understand the behaviour of securities and assets. This could help with risk mitigation, portfolio optimization on a large scale, and improving financial organizations' understanding of global financial economic trends and oscillations.
- **Cybersecurity:**
  Encryption and privacy may be directly impacted by quantum computing. Quantum computers have the potential to improve data encryption by guaranteeing its security during both transmission and storage, providing protection in transit and at rest, because of the dynamic and quickly changing nature of the cybersecurity environment.
- **Optimisation of routes and traffic:**
  For smooth transportation and supply chain operations, route design is essential. The main challenge is how to use the abundance of real-time data—which includes dynamic traffic and weather patterns—to effectively inform this planning process. This is the field in which quantum computers can operate very well. They could adjust routes for an entire fleet of vehicles at once, making sure that every vehicle took the most efficient route, because they could analyse and manage all the data in real time.
- **Production:**
  Higher precision and realism in prototyping and testing can be achieved with quantum computers. In terms of manufacturing, this could produce more refined designs that require less extensive testing and result in lower prototype costs.
- **Pharmaceutical and chemical investigation:**
  More precise models of atomic interactions can be produced by quantum computers, leading to a more precise and advanced understanding of molecular structure. This might directly impact chemical and medical research and change how new products and drugs are developed. Quantum computers can predict how chemicals and drugs will behave in the future and how they will interact with other elements as well as how they will evolve.
- **Energy storage devices:**
  The understanding of manufacturers regarding the incorporation of new materials into products, like semiconductors and batteries, could be improved by quantum computing. This may provide more insight into improving the longevity and efficiency of batteries. Manufacturers' understanding of lithium compounds and battery chemistry can be improved by quantum computing. Protein docking energy may be analysed and understood by quantum computing, which could improve the performance of electric car batteries.

RESULTS AND DISCUSSION

The topic of discussion is Shor's Algorithm. Decrypting the RSA Encryption. Shor's algorithm has effectively decrypted the RSA algorithm by determining the factors of the supplied N number and discovering the secret key. The figure labelled as Fig.9 displays the outcomes obtained from the execution of Shor's algorithm. Here, the time required to decipher the elements of the N value is directly proportional to the value of N.

Figure 9. Time Required for Shor's Algorithm to Defeat the RSA Scheme

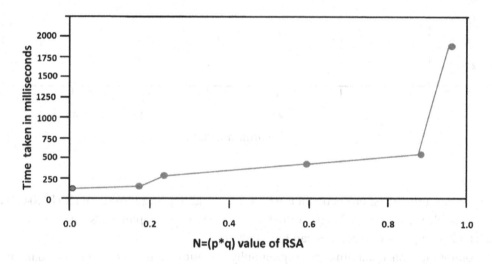

Fig.10 Evaluation of the time complexity involved in generating Quantum keys. Quantum Key Distribution involves three distinct stages: key generation, key filtering, and key distillation. The figure labelled 10 illustrates the duration required for generating cryptographic keys using Quantum Key Distribution. The following data indicate that the duration of quantum key generation is significantly shorter in relation to the number of bits, and even shorter when compared to other traditional key generation techniques like RSA.

CONCLUSION

Utilizing the ideas of quantum mechanics, quantum cryptography is a novel and exciting field that aims to solve the problems with classical cryptographic systems. Particularly considering developing quantum technologies, the development of quantum cryptographic algorithms and their applications has the potential to completely transform how we secure communication.

Based on the fundamental ideas of quantum mechanics, quantum cryptography makes use of the no-cloning theorem, superposition, and entanglement. The intrinsic sensitivity of quantum states to any attempt at measurement or eavesdropping is the foundation for the security of quantum cryptography systems.

Figure 10. Analysis of the Time Complexity of Quantum Key Generation

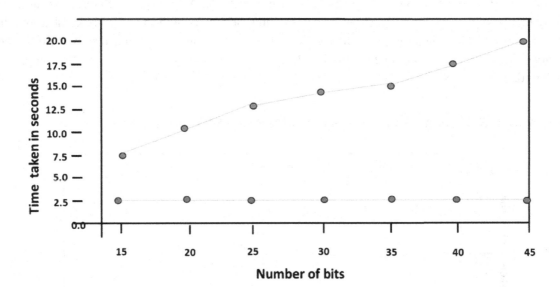

Using quantum principles, protocols like BB84, E91, and Six-State Protocol (SARG04) have been developed to enable secure key exchange. With QKD, secret cryptographic keys can be created between two parties and attempts at interception can be detected.

Secure communication, quantum-safe cryptography, quantum digital signatures, and quantum secure direct communication are just a few of the many uses for quantum cryptography. Financial transactions, cloud computing, satellite-based communication, and the creation of quantum internet infrastructure are among the applications of this technology that are being investigated.

The development of quantum-resistant cryptographic algorithms, integration with classical systems, and the practical deployment of quantum communication networks are some of the obstacles facing quantum cryptography. Research is still being done to try to solve these issues and get quantum cryptography closer to useful, real-world applications.

Quantum-resistant cryptographic algorithms are becoming more and more necessary to guarantee the long-term security of data and communication as quantum computers develop. Global effects could result from the development of quantum cryptography technologies, which could significantly improve communication security and privacy beyond what can be achieved with traditional cryptography systems.

In the quickly developing field of quantum cryptography, physicists, mathematicians, computer scientists, and engineers must work together across disciplinary boundaries. To overcome present obstacles and realize the full potential of quantum cryptography applications, innovation and collaboration must continue.

In conclusion, quantum cryptography is leading the way in secure communication technologies and has the potential to offer never-before-seen levels of protection against constantly changing threats. The future of secure communication is anticipated to be significantly impacted by the incorporation of quantum cryptographic solutions into real-world applications as research and development in quantum technologies advances.

REFERENCES

Abbasinezhad-Mood, D., & Nikooghadam, M. (2018). An anonymous ecc-based self-certified key distribution scheme for the smart grid. *IEEE Transactions on Industrial Electronics, 65*(10), 7996–8004. doi:10.1109/TIE.2018.2807383

Amritha, Jo, & Kim. (2014). Application of ntru cryptographic algorithm for scada security. In *2014 11th international conference on information technology: new generations* (pp. 341–346). IEEE.

Anilkumar, C., Lenka, S., Neelima, N., & v e, S. (2024). A secure method of communication through BB84 protocol in Quantum Key Distribution. *Scalable Computing: Practice and Experience, 25*(1), 21–33. doi:10.12694/scpe.v25i1.2152

Banafa, A. (2023). Quantum Computing trends. *Introduction to Quantum Computing, 31–35*, 31–35. Advance online publication. doi:10.1201/9781003440239-8

Barnett, S. (2009). *Quantum cryptography*. Quantum Information. doi:10.1093/oso/9780198527626.003.0006

Bhushan, S. (2022). Quantum cryptography. *Holistic Approach to Quantum Cryptography in Cyber Security*, 193–206. doi:10.1201/9781003296034-11

Bibak, K., & Ritchie, R. (2021). Quantum key distribution with prf (hash, nonce) achieves everlasting security. *Quantum Information Processing, 20*(7), 228. doi:10.1007/s11128-021-03164-3

Brassard, G., & Crépeau, C. (n.d.). Quantum cryptography. Encyclopedia of Cryptography and Security, 495–500. doi:10.1007/0-387-23483-7_338

Bykovsky, A. Y., & Kompanets, I. N. (2018). Quantum cryptography and combined schemes of Quantum Cryptography Communication Networks. *Quantum Electronics, 48*(9), 777–801. doi:10.1070/QEL16732

Chindiyababy, Jayaraman, R., & Kumar, M. (2022). Quantum cryptography and Quantum Key Distribution. *Holistic Approach to Quantum Cryptography in Cyber Security*, 179–192. doi:10.1201/9781003296034-10

Ciesla, R. (2020). Quantum cryptography. *Encryption for Organizations and Individuals*, 227–234. doi:10.1007/978-1-4842-6056-2_11

Ekert, A. (2005). Quantum cryptography. *Optical Science and Engineering*, 1–15. doi:10.1201/9781420026603.ch1

Faulkner, J. S. (2021). *Quantum cryptography*. Modern Quantum Mechanics and Quantum Information., doi:10.1088/978-0-7503-2167-9ch11

Jia-Lun & Lo. (2015). Secure anonymous key distribution scheme for smart grid. *IEEE Transactions on Smart Grid, 7*(2), 906–914.

Lee, C., Sohn, I., & Lee, W. (2022). Eavesdropping detection in bb84 quantum key distribution protocols. *IEEE Transactions on Network and Service Management, 19*(3), 2689–2701. doi:10.1109/TNSM.2022.3165202

Mohamed, K. S. (2020). New trends in cryptography: Quantum, blockchain, lightweight, chaotic, and DNA cryptography. *New Frontiers in Cryptography*, 65–87. doi:10.1007/978-3-030-58996-7_4

Neetesh & Grijalva. (2016). Dynamic secrets and secret keys based scheme for securing last mile smart grid wireless communication. *IEEE Transactions on Industrial Informatics*, *13*(3), 1482–1491.

Nitaj, A., & Rachidi, T. (2023). Applications of neural network-based AI in cryptography. *Cryptography*, *7*(3), 39. doi:10.3390/cryptography7030039

Odelu, V., Das, A. K., Wazid, M., & Conti, M. (2016). Provably secure authenticated key agreement scheme for smart grid. *IEEE Transactions on Smart Grid*, *9*(3), 1900–1910. doi:10.1109/TSG.2016.2602282

Raymer, M. G. (2017). *Application: Quantum computing*. Quantum Physics. doi:10.1093/wentk/9780190250720.003.0010

Sasaki, Y. (2012). Quantum computing and number theory. *Quantum Information and Quantum Computing*. doi:10.1142/9789814425223_0005

V. Srividya, B., & Sasi, S. (2021). An emphasis on quantum cryptography and quantum key distribution. *Cryptography - Recent Advances and Future Developments*. doi:10.5772/intechopen.95383

Yonghong, Wang, & Cui. (2013). Secure communication mechanism for smart distribution network integrated with subcarrier multiplexed quantum key distribution. *Power Syst. Technol., 11*, 36.

Zhao, B., Liu, B., Wu, C., Yu, W., & Su, J. (2016). A novel ntt-based authentication scheme for 10-ghz quantum key distribution systems. *IEEE Transactions on Industrial Electronics*, *63*(8), 5101–5108.

Zhou, J., Lu, L., Lei, Y., & Chen, X. (2014). Research on improving security of protection for power system secondary system by quantum key technology. *Power Syst. Technol*, *38*(6), 1518–1522.

Chapter 8
Minimizing Data Loss by Encrypting Brake–Light Images and Avoiding Rear–End Collisions Using Artificial Neural Network

Abirami M. S.

https://orcid.org/0000-0002-7401-454X

SRM Institute of Science and Technology, India

Manoj Kushwaha

SRM Institute of Science and Technology, India

ABSTRACT

Rear-end collisions are a threat to road safety, so reliable collision avoidance technologies are essential. Traditional systems present several issues due to data loss and privacy concerns. The authors introduce an encrypted artificial neural network (ANN) method to prevent front-vehicle rear-end collisions. This system uses encryption techniques and ANN algorithm to recognize the front vehicle brake light in real time. Information can't be deciphered without the appropriate key using encryption. Intercepting data during transmission prevents reading. The system works day and night. ANN outperforms LR, SVM, DT, RF, and KNN in accuracy. An encrypted ANN-based ML model distinguishes between brake and normal signals. ANN accuracy was 93.7%. Driver receives further alerts to avoid rear-end collisions. This work proposes a lightweight, secure ANN-based brake light picture encryption method. The proposed approach may be applied to other collision circumstances, including side and frontal strikes. The technique would be more adaptable and applicable to many road safety circumstances.

DOI: 10.4018/979-8-3693-1642-9.ch008

1. INTRODUCTION

Rear-end collisions are common and often fatal in third-world nations. In complex surroundings with many unknowns, it might be challenging for conventional systems to reliably identify and predict the likelihood of a rear-end collision. Accidents come from drivers who do not respond quickly enough to potential threats (Feng et al., 2020). Sixty percent of crashes can be avoided with a half-second notice, and an astounding ninety percent can be avoided with a 1.5-second warning (Karungaru et al., 2021). Existing methods for collision detection tend to depend largely on a single intelligence algorithm, despite the advantages that may be gained from using a hybrid approach. Furthermore, they frequently fail to account for adverse weather that might reduce vision, rendering their detection systems useless.

Our encrypted images analysis with Artificial Neural Network (ANN) is capable of doing in-depth analyses, identifying patterns, and making very accurate predictions (Guo et al., 2022). It's like having a very intelligent passenger who can foresee potential accidents. One of the most common causes of accidents on the road is rear-end collisions. Distracted driving, driver weariness, and following too closely are just a few of the causes of these (Shang et al., 2021). To prevent front-vehicle rear-end crashes, we present an encrypted technique with ANN in this research.

If the ANN determines that the driver will not be able to respond quickly enough to avoid a collision, an alarm will be triggered. The findings demonstrated that the proposed method might minimize rear-end accidents by as much as 50%. Rear-end collisions are a major cause of traffic accidents (Shen et al., 2023). They account for about 25% of all traffic fatalities in the United States (Zhang et al., 2022). There are many different things that can lead to rear-end collisions, including distracted driving, exhaustion, and following too closely (Kushwaha, 2023).

There are a number of techniques that can be used to avoid rear-end collisions. These include: The driver should always maintain a safe following distance from the vehicle in front of them. This will give them enough time to react if the vehicle in front of them stops suddenly. The driver should avoid distractions while driving, such as talking on the phone or texting. These distractions can prevent the driver from paying attention to the road and can lead to a rear-end collision. The driver should be aware of their surroundings and be prepared to stop if necessary. This includes being aware of the speed and distance of the vehicles around them.

The use of Artificial Intelligence (AI) to prevent rear-end crashes has gained popularity in current years (Fu et al., 2021; Pu et al., 2021). With the help of AI, we can create systems that study the driving habits of individual motorists and foresee when they will cause an accident (Kushwaha & Abirami, 2023). The data collected by these systems can then be utilized to issue warnings or conduct other preventative measures.

This system makes an effort to detect the brake light coming from the forward vehicle by making use of an ANN Machine Learning (ML) algorithm in real-time (Hadjidimitriou et al., 2020; Yang et al., 2020). The accuracy of the ANN method is superior to that of other ML classifiers, including Logistic Regression (LR), Support Vector Machine (SVM), Decision Tree (DT), Random Forest (RF), and K-Nearest Neighbor (KNN), Naïve Bayes (NB), Decision Tree (DT), Stochastic gradient Descent (SGD), Gradient Boosting (GB), AdaBoost. In order to distinguish between normal and brake signals, ML model based on ANN is utilized.

Researchers and policymakers in government will find this information valuable in their efforts to reduce the number of traffic fatalities (Abirami et al., 2021). ANN is used in the suggested method to prevent rear-end collisions and detect brake light from front vehicle. The vehicle speed, distance from the front vehicle, and the driver's reaction time are only some of the sensory inputs used to train the ANN. If the ANN determines that the driver will not be able to respond quickly enough to avoid a collision, an alarm will be triggered. The ANN, which is a type of ML method. A value is produced by each neuron in the ANN after it gets input from the layer above it. To forecast the driver's response time, we use the data returned by the neurons in the output layer. Encryption is the process of encoding information such that it can't be deciphered without the right key (Alsafyani et al., 2023). If the data is intercepted while being sent, this can prevent anybody from reading it. Mobile alert message data can be protected using encryption methods, which transform the information into a code that can't be deciphered without the right key (Silva et al., 2023). In this way, the information is extremely secure, even if it is intercepted in transit.

Although various methods exist for encrypting data, the most prevalent ones are: For symmetric encryption, the same key is used for both the encryption and the decryption of the data. This facilitates its implementation, but necessitates secrecy surrounding the key. Since the private key is never divulged, this method is more secure than symmetric encryption. Protected information may include the name of the driver, the location of the incident, and the severity of the collision when delivering alert messages to drivers following rear-end crashes. Access to sensitive information can be restricted via authentication and permission procedures. All data access can be logged to assist in revealing any efforts at unauthorized entry. Data can also be shielded from prying eyes with the use of physical security measures.

The proposed solution offers a novel way to prevent front-vehicle rear-end incidents. This paper has proposed a secure, lightweight encryption technology with ANN to protect the information in the vehicles brake light images. The method relies on an ANN that has been developed and trained using a vehicle brake light image dataset. If the ANN determines that the driver will not be able to respond quickly enough to avoid a collision, an alarm will be triggered. The research found that the proposed method might cut the frequency of rear-end crashes by as much as half (Wang et al., 2020). These results imply that the proposed method may be able to dramatically enhance road safety. There are several ways in which the proposed method might be enhanced. The ANN, for instance, may be taught using a more extensive collection of brake light information. As a result, the ANN would be better able to understand the driver's behavior and make reliable predictions. The suggested method may be generalized to encompass a broader range of collision scenarios, including but not limited to side impacts and frontal collisions. This would make the method more flexible, allowing it to be used in a broader range of scenarios in which road safety is being addressed. This method has several benefits. Protecting critical brake-light data from unwanted access and harmful assaults with ANN-based encryption. Optimization for real-time processing allows ANNs to identify and respond to collisions quickly. Training ANNs on large data sets ensures precise brake-light identification and accident risk assessment. By integrating secure encryption with real-time collision avoidance techniques, this approach minimizes data loss while maximizing safety on the roads (Li et al., 2021).

The following are some of the contributions that this research has made:

(i) We presented a new method that uses ANN and other ML models to encrypt brake light frames. A novel encryption algorithm is developed to secure brake-light images during transmission and storage. This ensures privacy compliance while maintaining the integrity of the dataset.

(ii) Encrypted brake-light images are used to train the ANN. The model is optimized using backpropagation and fine-tuning techniques to achieve high accuracy.

(iii) During real-time operation, the encrypted brake-light images are decrypted for analysis. The ANN's output triggers collision avoidance mechanisms, contributing to enhanced road safety.

(iv) LR, KNN, SVM, NB, DT, RF, SGD, ANN, GB, and AdaBoost are some of the ML algorithms that will be compared.

Rest of this paper is arranged as follows. Section 2 of this publication covers similar work. Section 3 discusses unique brake light images encryption using ML models. Result analysis and discussion are in Section 4. This paper's conclusion is in Section 5.

2. RELATED WORK

This area comprises typical research that are exclusively focused on encryption of brake light image safety. Additionally, the literature employs image encryption utilizing ML algorithms with different methods and databases, as shown in Table I.

Majed Alsafyani et al. (2023) proposed a fresh approach to image encryption using an innovative method for picture encryption that makes use of adaptive control parameters and a generalized symmetric map in a multi-coupled map lattice system. For DL to work at its best, a big training dataset is necessary.

Syed Muhammad Unsub Zia et al. (2022) presented a new picture cryptosystem based on linked map lattice systems that generates pseudo-random sequences using generalized symmetric maps. By adjusting a single control parameter, the user may select the source of pseudo-random sequence creation using the generalization of symmetric maps. Three separate pseudo-random sequence generators are used by the proposed encryption method; they are re-randomized prior to the final encryption procedure.

Xiuhui Chen et al. (2022) lifted scheme and cross-component permutation to create a unique color image encryption method. CIE-LSCP is a new color image encryption method based on lifting and cross-component permutation. The Loren-z-Haken laser chaotic system's initial parameters are constructed from plaintext picture and external key SHA256 hash values. The chaotic system creates encryption sequences. PSLS is proposed for plaintext images.

Liang Liu et al. (2022) created AlexNet, an upgraded convolutional neural network that uses a pre-processing module to encrypt the data. Additionally, the visual text is encrypted by means of a chaotic sequence that is created by a one-dimensional chaotic system known as Logistic-Sine and a multi-dimensional chaotic system known as Lorenz. This guarantees the system's real-time performance as well as its security effect. Here, the chaotic function and AlexNet are utilized to develop a model for real-time image text encryption.

Yang Gao (2022) executed data, physical, and digital security all encompass a wide range of uses for image processing. Steganography and watermark conceal information by imperceptibility, whereas encryption aims to challenge hackers and the secret technique that is revealed in advance.

Zhongyun Hua et al. (2019) developed an image encryption method called IES-JPFD that takes into account both the Josephus scrambling, which is derived from the Josephus issue, and the filtering technology. The encryption algorithm follows the classical diffusion and confusion framework. The Josephus scrambling generates random sequences to quickly separate the picture pixels, and image filtering is commonly used for image smoothing.

Shima Ramesh Maniyath (2020) related about data security arise whenever data is sent for processing, storage, or transmission across any kind of network system. There are many different kinds of data security algorithms out there today, each with its own set of pros and cons. Implementation of data security measures over a centralized or distributed system, as well as the specific data types and structures, determine their utilization. The primary concern with many hosted business apps has always been security.

Kartik Sharma et al. (2019) proposed A new, significantly more secure method for image steganography. While it does make use of some standard steganography methods, the combination of these with cryptography and neural networks makes it very difficult to decipher.

Zhenzhou Wang et al. (2019) trained a neural network to identify passing automobiles and their taillights as a whole. The first step is to use convolutional neural networks to identify and extract the following cars' outlines. After that, we extract the taillight region in the HSV color space and use histogram, color, and position correlations to find the taillight pairing.

Feng and Chen (2022) presented an image recognition and encryption algorithm that uses a multi-dimensional chaotic sequence and artificial neural networks.

Pinhe Wang et al. (2022) investigated a novel model for target detection using convolutional neural networks. In an effort to improve the speed and accuracy of high-speed scene image identification, the study's practical effects on scene picture identification are strong, and it realizes the successful combination of a multi-frame convolutional neural network with batch normalization techniques. To optimize the convolutional neural network's fundamental network architecture, one uses the L2 regularization algorithm. This, in turn, improves the algorithm's recognition accuracy, generalizability, and stability in complex environments.

Xiulai Li et al. (2018) investigated deep learning feature classification for iris-based feature Nencryption. Simulation experiments use the common iris database. Results show that the method improves iris encryption consistency and security. Using the iris as a model, researchers were able to develop an algorithm for encrypting and decrypting images using iris features. A deep learning-based algorithm for extracting iris features has been developed.

Table 1. Different Methods and Databases Used in the Literature

Sources	Encryption Technique	Methods	Database
(Alsafyani et al., 2023)	✓	DL, ML, Chaos-Based Scrambling Algorithm, Image Optimization	LFW dataset
(Zia et al., 2022)	✓	Generalised Symmetric Map, Cryptography	USC-SIPI image database
(Chen et al., 2022)	✓	Lifting Scheme and Cross-Component Permutation (CIE-LSCP)	eight plain-text images
(Liu et al., 2022)	✓	AlexNet, CNN	BOSSbase dataset
(Gao, 2022)	✓	DL, Logistic and Henon Map, Neural Network Backpropagation,	SIBI dataset
(Hua et al., 2019)	✓	IES-JPFD- Josephus Problem and Filtering technology	BSDS and CVonline image databases
(Maniyath, 2020)	✓	DL, Chaotic Map	Sipi Image Database, 2018
(Sharma et al., 2019)	✓	Steganography, Cryptography, CNN, DL, Adam optimizer	Flickr30k dataset
(Wang et al., 2019)	✗	Faster RCNN, CNN, Image Processing	BDD100K datase
(Feng & Chen, 2022)	✓	ANN, Logistic and Henon Map, PCA algorithm, DWT-DCT encryption	ORL face database
(Wang et al., 2022)	✗	CNN, L2 Regularization Algorithm, Canny edge detection	CUB-200-2011 bird dataset
(Li et al., 2018)	✓	DL	IRIS-Image Database

3. METHODOLOGY

Included in this area are more conventional studies that have confined themselves to the topic of brake light image security encryption; furthermore, the existing literature employs picture encryption based on ML techniques (Kushwaha, 2022; Kushwaha, n.d.; Kushwaha & Abirami, 2023; M.S., 2020).

3.1 Dataset Collection and Labelling

The dataset was compiled in real-time from various short-range road videos. Motorbikes, cars, trucks, buses, vans, and any other type of vehicle are all taken into account. More than 30 videos were utilized to produce 185 picture frames, which were subsequently cropped to achieve a desirable output. Convert video to still images using Python script. The process of converting videos to images is already covered by a number of Python libraries. We used image dataset, MakesenseAI tool used for labeling (Kushwaha, 2023). Braking label when back side or turn light is on and normal signal when all backside lights are turn off.

3.2 Preprocessing

Following the collection of the dataset, the Braking frame and the Normal frame proceed to normalize the frames of the cars by employing preprocessing procedures. To begin, the image should be resized to conform to a standard format. After the picture has been auto-oriented, it should be resized further and stretched to 640X640 pixels.

3.3 Encrypting Brake Light Frames

Increase the quality of the brake light frames with the assistance of the encryption method. First original images use encryption system with the help of encrypted key and converted to encrypted image. In addition, Encrypted images converted to decrypted image with the help of decrypted system. Encrypting images entails safeguarding brake light image data to prevent unauthorized access or modification while keeping brake light image quality. In order to accomplish this goal, a number of different encryption methods are utilized. By utilizing a single key for both encryption and decryption, symmetric algorithms perform both functions. Symmetric encryption doesn't immediately impair image quality but assures secrecy during transmission or storage.

3.4 Split the Dataset Into Training and Testing Dataset

By splitting the dataset in an 80:20 ratios, with 80 percent of the data being used for training and 20 percent being utilized for testing, as indicated in table II, the dataset was divided. Table II represents the 185 frames, which are divided into training 148 and testing 37 frames of the brake light detection dataset.

Table 2. Training and Testing Dataset

Dataset	Training (80%)	Testing (20%)
185 frames	148	37

3.5 Applied ML on Training dataset

Applied ANN algorithms on a testing dataset and compared with it different ML algorithms such **as** LR, RF, NB, DT, RF, KNN, SGD, SVM, ADABOOST, and GB are used for both the classification and prediction of brake lights. LR is a statistical approach that may be used to categorize brake lights into two distinct categories. Through the use of the logistic function, it does an estimation of probabilities in order to describe the connection that exists between the dependent binary variable and one or more independent variables. KNN is a non-parametric, lazy learning algorithm that classifies data points based on the majority class of brake and normal images associated with their k nearest neighbors in the feature space. KNN is the best algorithm for solving the classification and regression challenges associated with brake light detection. It assumes that things that are similar are located in close proximity to one another. When it comes to recognizing brake lights from a dataset, SVM is ML approach that may be utilized for classification or regression purposes. There is a benefit to using the SVM classifier since it is able to differentiate between the two classes (hyperplane and line) the most effectively. Bayesian probabilistic ML classification is the method that is utilized in the NB classification methodology. It is also possible to employ the DT method to address problems involving regression and classification of brake light detection. One of the most well-known and widely utilized ML techniques, SGD provide the basis for neural networks. A system or process is said to be stochastic if it is one that has a probability of occurring. An example of a tree-like model is DT, in which each node represents a choice that is dependent on input data, and the leaves reflect the final conclusion or prediction of the braking signal. The RF method is an ensemble ML methodology that is essentially constructed within a DT. The bagging method is used to generate a large number of subsets of data. This is accomplished by randomly selecting observations from the initial datasets and replacing them with new ones. These subsets are then used to construct miniature trees. For the purpose of improving accuracy and resilience, RF is an ensemble learning approach that, during training, constructs numerous decision trees and then combines the predictions of those trees. Each new forecast in GB makes up for the error that was made in the prior one. Unlike AdaBoost, the weights of the training examples are not updated; instead, each predictor is trained using the predecessor's residual errors as labels. ADABOOST is a widely used foundational ensemble ML approach based on boosting. A fundamental way of learning is utilized by both the DT and the RF.

It is finally possible to obtain, following the application of the algorithm, the projected result as either brake. If braking label, then send alert message to drivers.

3.6 Proposed Method

The proposed approach utilizes encrypted brake-light images captured by in-vehicle cameras. The ANN-based encryption scheme ensures data privacy and confidentiality without compromising the integrity of the brake-light information. To achieve this, the ANN is trained on a large dataset of brake-light images, enabling it to learn the patterns and features that distinguish brake-light activations from other background elements. During encryption, the ANN transforms the brake-light images into an encrypted format that preserves the essential information for collision detection while rendering the original data unreadable without the corresponding decryption key. The encrypted brake-light images are then transmitted to a collision avoidance system that utilizes another ANN to decrypt and interpret the brake-light signals. This ANN is trained to identify brake-light activations and estimate the distance and relative speed of the preceding vehicle. Based on the processed brake-light information, the collision avoidance system issues timely warnings and activates appropriate safety measures, such as pre-braking or evasive maneuvers, to prevent rear-end collisions.

The ANN model is used to recognize encrypted and decrypted brake light images, as shown in Figure 1. This graphic provides a schematic representation of the process. With the assistance of an encryption system and an encryption key, the initial image that was taken in its original form was transformed into an encrypted original. Using a decryption system and a key that had been decrypted, additional encrypted images of brake lights were successfully converted into decrypted images. Following this, the entire dataset was split into training and testing datasets with a ratio of 80:20. ANN model was then applied to the training dataset, and the testing dataset was used to evaluate the performance of the proposed model. A brake picture was identified by the ANN model as being present in the image.

Figure 1. Architecture of Encrypted ANN Model for Brake Light Detection

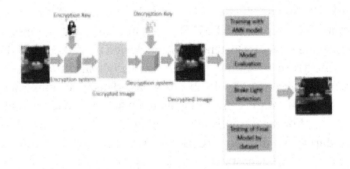

3.7 Encryption and Decryption

Images recorded by cameras facing the rear of cars would be encrypted before being analyzed by ANN. This conceals sensitive information like license plates or driver names while maintaining brake light data for rear–end collisions detection ANN for collision detection: A trained ANN would evaluate the encrypted brake light data to detect rapid braking and anticipate future crashes. After that, this information could be utilized to initiate a variety of safety interventions, such as automatic emergency braking (AEB). In order to address concerns regarding privacy, encryption is used to protect sensitive data that is collected by vehicles. The vulnerability of data to hacking and manipulation is reduced when it is encrypted. Real-time collision detection and AEB can significantly reduce rear-end collisions, saving lives and reducing injuries. Encryption is the process of encoding information such that it can't be deciphered without the right key. If the data is intercepted while being sent, this can prevent anybody from reading it. Our system work on both day and nighttime.

3.8 ANN

ANN is a model for processing messages that looks to the neuronal systems of humans (Kushwaha & Abirami, 2023). Neurons are the basic computing units of an ANN, akin to the neurons in the human brain. Each neuron takes one or more input signals, processes them, and creates an output signal. There are weights associated with the connections between neurons. The connection strength is determined by these weights. During training, the network changes these weights to discover patterns from the incoming data. The output of each neuron is determined by its activation function, which takes into account the inputs in a weighted sum. This system makes an effort to identify the brake light coming from the front vehicle by making use of an encryption and ANN algorithm in real-time.

The input layer gets the first input characteristics of the data. In the input layer, each node stands for a feature. Any number of hidden layers can exist between the input and output layer. Each node in a hidden layer performs a mathematical modification on the incoming data. The weights and biases associated with the links dictate these modifications. The ultimate outcomes are generated by the output layer. The number of nodes in the output layer varies on the kind of task.

4. RESULTS AND DISCUSSION

Because they are the most common reason for rear-end crashes on the road, rear-end collisions have developed into a significant problem that threatens both the public's health and the safety of the whole population. Injuries sustained in rear-end accidents and the passage of vehicles have a profound influence on people, families, and the hierarchical systems of society. Because of this, nations often have a deficit of three percent in their gross domestic product (GDP), which is a significant burden on their finances (Bhawani, 2023).

4.1 Brake Light Detection System

We demonstrated a real-time dataset that was developed with the intention of determining the presence of brake lights on vehicles. On the aforementioned dataset, we additionally conduct an analysis and assessment of the proposed methodology. In order to conduct the experiments, a personal computer (PC) fortified with an NVIDIA graphics processing unit (GPU), Pytorch 1.1, and Python 3.7 was operated as the experimental setting. The size of the picture in the input dataset is 64 pixels by 64 pixels. We had to create a bespoke dataset to evaluate the suggested strategy because there was no publicly accessible dataset for recognizing car brake lights. The 185 photos have "braking" and "normal" labels. Different highways with different daily and nightly traffic levels were used to collect data. Datasets that are examples of inputs are displayed in Figure 2.

Figure 3 displayed a visualization of the braking signal and the normal signal, as well as an explanation of how an ANN model is used to recognize images in order to prevent rear-end crashes. I used vast datasets to train ANN and other algorithms to anticipate rear-end collisions. To improve prediction accuracy, encryption and 10 ML algorithms are used (Bharadwaja Kumar et al., 2021; Mansoor et al., 2020; Samsudeen & Senthil Kumar, 2023). If the validation tally does not increase, the model will not train due to the constrained early stopping function.

Figure 2. Sample Input Dataset for Brake Light Detection

Figure 3. Visualization of a) Braking and b) Normal Images Detection

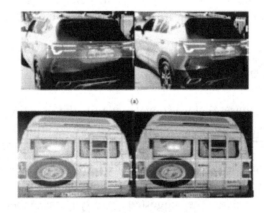

The ANN algorithm setup of parameters is shown in Table III, where we used a sigmoid function for identifying brake and normal labels. For improving the accuracy of the ANN model, we used the Adam optimizer with 100 epochs. ANN consists of input, output, and hidden layer, and finally we get two outputs: braking and normal images.

tn and fn signify true negative and false negative, while tp and fp signify true positive and false positive. Eq. (1) measures Accuracy (ACC) as the percentage of correctly recognized items (Kushwaha & Abirami, 2023):

Table 3. Setup of ANN Parameter

Parameters	Values
No. of input layer	16
Hidden layer size	(10, 3)
No. of output layer	2
Learning rates	Constant
Max number of iteration (epoch)	100
Optimizer	Adam
Activation Function	Sigmoid
Batch size	32

$$ACC = \frac{tp + tn}{tp + tn + fp + fn} \tag{1}$$

The term "precision" (P) is defined in equation (2) as the proportion of accurate observations relative to the total number of negative observations that were projected.

$$P = \frac{tp}{tp + fp} \tag{2}$$

Equation (3) is utilized to get the value of Recall (R), which is evaluated as a supplementary performance measure (Chang et al., 2020).

$$R = \frac{tp}{tp + fn} \tag{3}$$

Lastly, the F1-score is the average of P and R weighted together. Here were how the model parameters of the ML algorithm are set up: Entropy, a metric for information gain, is used to assess the splitting quality.

It is no longer possible to halt tree growth at an early stage. In order to speed up the process of finding the optimal split, I disable pre-sorting before tree splitting. The model ACC performances are displayed in Table IV as ACC, P, R, and F1-score. The differences can be attributed to shifts in the criteria for braking images categorization, the sets of images, and the total number of cases.

In table IV, shows different performance parameter of ML model. It indicates that the ACC percentage of encrypted ANN model is higher than other ML model. The ACC percentage of ANN is 93.7% . It represented the different ML model performace parameter such as ACC, P, R, f1-score. And include model as LR, ANN, DT, KNN, SGD, SVM, Adaboost, Gradient boosting, NB.

Table 4. Performance Matrices of Different Machine Learning Model

Model	ACC	P	R	F1-Score
LR	0.926	0.927	0.926	0.922
ANN	0.937	0.936	0.937	0.936
RF	0.895	0.892	0.895	0.887
DT	0.853	0.850	0.853	0.851
KNN	0.895	0.892	0.895	0.887
SGD	0.832	0.889	0.832	0.845
SVM	0.879	0.873	0.879	0.869
ADABOOST	0.889	0.884	0.889	0.884
GB	0.916	0.913	0.916	0.913
NB	0.743	0.716	0.460	0.849

Figure 4. Brake Light Detection Results for Different ML Algorithms

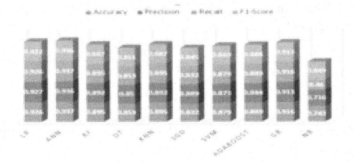

4.2 Discussion

The brake light detection was identified using several ML models. Brake light detection is one of the features that were discovered. In order to estimate the effectiveness of vehicle brake lights, the proposed model was contrasted with a number of other methods, including an ensemble approach and basic learner models like as LR, NB, DT, SVM, and KNN. Using the proposed model, we were able to identify important features, which comprised over half of the dataset's total usable characteristics. This research of work presents a proposal for an effective automatic brake light recognition system.

To begin, no ML model did not utilize available attributes as input. As part of the subsequent phase of the investigation, the most significant characteristics that were identified by the proposed model were utilized as response for all ML models. In this section, we will discuss the four most important outcomes that were observed when identifying brake lights. To begin, all ML models and ANNs performed admirably when it came to recognizing brake lights. In situations where significant characteristics are used as input, ANN achieves the highest ACC (0.937). LR attained ACC of 0.926, and GB was able to achieve 0.916. NB achieved lesser ACC as 0.743 and RF, DT, SGD, KNN, AdaBoost attain ACC as 0.895,0.853, 0.832, 0.895, 0.889 correspondingly. The ACC results of each and every ML model are displayed in Figure 5. When both brake and normal classes hold equal significance and there is no notable class imbalance, achieving a high level of ACC becomes crucial.

Figure 5. Accuracy of Different ML Models

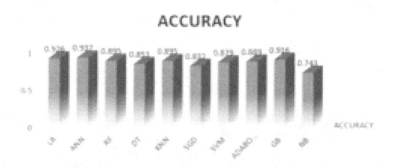

Second, as shown in Figure 6, ANN is superior to other ML models in terms of ACC. On the other hand, by utilizing crucial characteristics, ANN was able to produce better outcomes, with a precision value of 0.936. ACC rating of 0.927 was reached by the LR as a result of using all of the testing datasets as input. This score is lower than the P score of 0.936 that the ANN earned. RF of 0.892, whereas the ACC scores of the SGD, GB, and AdaBoost ensemble models are 0.889, 0.819, and 0.884, correspondingly. The Tree Ensemble model (Abirami et al., 2020) has a higher RF than the other models. However, the ACC obtains of KNN, DT, SVM, and NB were 0.892, 0.850, 0.873, and 0.716 correspondingly. It was found that the P score of NB is lower than that of other techniques. In brake light detection, for instance, where false positives can have severe repercussions, a high degree of precision is advantageous.

Figure 6. Precision of Different ML Models

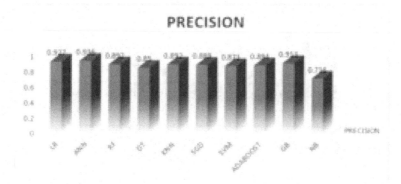

Third, using dataset, ANN obtained R (sensitivity) score of 0.937, which is the greatest R value for anticipating brake light detection. RF and KNN got identical R scores of 0.895 employing major characteristics. SGD achieved less R score with 0.832 than AdaBoost with 0.889. DT and LR attained R score as 0.853 and 0.926 respectively. NB scored lesser R score with 0.460 related with other models. Figure 7 illustrates the R value of ML models. Fourth, analyze the F1-score, which is crucial valuation metric that syndicates ACC and R scores. When the cost of missing positive cases in brake light detection is large, strong recall is critical.

Figure 7. Recall of Different ML Models

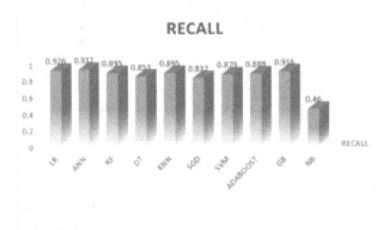

Fourth, observe the F1-score, which is crucial valuation measurement that balances ACC and memory scores. Figure 8 noted that the F1-score of ANN 0.936 is larger than that of other models. LR and GB

Figure 8. F1-Score of Different ML Models

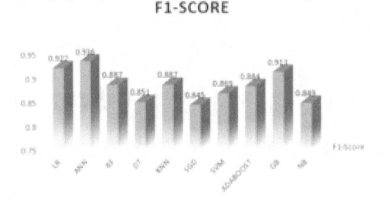

reached as 0.922 and 0.913. SGD achieve lesser F1-score as 0.845. DT, KNN, RF, SVM (M.S., 2020; Xie et al., 2021) Adaboost and NB reached F1-score as 0.851, 0.887, 0.887, 0.869, 0.884 and 0.849 correspondingly. The F1-score is especially beneficial when the class distribution is unequal or when both false positives and false negatives must be minimized. According to the results summary, models can identify important qualities that make up a subset of the original feature set when the main focus is on how well the models perform overall when it comes to recognizing car brake lights. Using key qualities as input to ML models boosts ACC, P, R, and F1-score. When combined with related attributes, the recommended technique not only boosts likelihood performance but also minimizes data collection expenses.

185 frames are included in the brake light detection system, and these frames are utilized to evaluate the brake light detection system. The brake light detection procedure is significantly improved when the critical characteristics of the braking and normal labels that were identified by the proposed model are acknowledged and taken into consideration. It is also possible to estimate the performance of the ML model after all of the characteristics and essential features have been utilized as input. The recommended model performed better than any of the other models that were used in the experiment when significant attributes were taken into consideration. The management ought to place a greater emphasis on the significant factors that have an effect on the detection of brake. In terms of ACC, R, P, and F1-score, a model that has the greatest values in these measures indicates that it is well-balanced and successful.

5. CONCLUSION

The proposed solution offers a novel way to prevent front-vehicle rear-end incidents. This paper has proposed a secure, lightweight encryption technology with ANN to protect the information in the vehicles brake light images. The method relies on an ANN that has been developed and trained using a vehicle brake light image dataset. If the ANN determines that the driver will not be able to respond quickly enough to avoid a collision, an alarm will be triggered. The research found that the proposed method might cut the frequency of rear-end crashes by as much as half. These results imply that the proposed method may be able to dramatically enhance road safety. There are several ways in which the proposed method might be enhanced. The ANN, for instance, may be taught using a more extensive collection of brake light information. As a result, the ANN would be better able to understand the driver's behavior and make reliable predictions. The suggested method may be generalized to encompass a broader range of collision scenarios, including but not limited to side impacts and frontal collisions. This would make the method more flexible, allowing it to be used in a broader range of scenarios in which road safety is being addressed. In the future, we will work with AI approaches and ML models to avoid rear-end crashes.

REFERENCES

Abirami, M. S., Vennila, B., Chilukalapalli, E. L., & Kuriyedath, R. (2020). A classification model to predict onset of smoking and drinking habits based on socio-economic and sociocultural factors. *Journal of Ambient Intelligence and Humanized Computing*, *12*(3), 4171–4179. doi:10.1007/s12652-020-01796-4

Abirami, M. S., Vennila, B., Suganthi, K., Kawatra, S., & Vaishnava, A. (2021). Detection of Choroidal Neovascularization (CNV) in Retina OCT Images Using VGG16 and DenseNet CNN. *Wireless Personal Communications*. Advance online publication. doi:10.1007/s11277-021-09086-8

Alsafyani, M., Alhomayani, F., Alsuwat, H., & Alsuwat, E. (2023). Face Image Encryption Based on Feature with Optimization Using Secure Crypto General Adversarial Neural Network and Optical Chaotic Map. *Sensors (Basel)*, 23(3), 1415–1415. doi:10.3390/s23031415 PMID:36772454

Bharadwaja Kumar, Rampavan, & Ijjina. (2021). *Deep Learning based Brake Light Detection for Two Wheelers*. doi:10.1109/ICCCNT51525.2021.9579918

Bhawani, D. (2023). Design of inception with deep convolutional neural network based fall detection and classification model. *Multimedia Tools and Applications*. Advance online publication. doi:10.1007/s11042-023-16476-6

Chang, Y., Bharadwaj, N., Edara, P., & Sun, C. (2020). Exploring Contributing Factors of Hazardous Events in Construction Zones Using Naturalistic Driving Study Data. *IEEE Transactions on Intelligent Vehicles*, 5(3), 519–527. doi:10.1109/TIV.2020.2980741

Chen, X., Gong, M., Gan, Z., Yang, L., & Chai, X. (2022). CIE-LSCP: Color image encryption scheme based on the lifting scheme and cross-component permutation. *Complex & Intelligent Systems*, 9(1), 927–950. doi:10.1007/s40747-022-00835-1 PMID:35874092

Feng, D., Haase-Schutz, C., Rosenbaum, L., Hertlein, H., Glaser, C., Timm, F., ... Dietmayer, K. (2020). Deep Multi-Modal Object Detection and Semantic Segmentation for Autonomous Driving: Datasets, Methods, and Challenges. *IEEE Transactions on Intelligent Transportation Systems*, 1–20. doi:10.1109/TITS.2020.2972974

Feng, L., & Chen, X. (2022). Image Recognition and Encryption Algorithm Based on Artificial Neural Network and Multidimensional Chaotic Sequence. *Computational Intelligence and Neuroscience*, 2022, 1–9. doi:10.1155/2022/9576184 PMID:36035834

Fu, Y., Li, C., Yu, F. R., Luan, T. H., & Zhang, Y. (2021). A Survey of Driving Safety With Sensing, Vehicular Communications, and Artificial Intelligence-Based Collision Avoidance. *IEEE Transactions on Intelligent Transportation Systems*, 1–22. doi:10.1109/TITS.2021.3083927

Gao, Y. (2022). *An Improved Image Processing Based on Deep Learning Backpropagation Technique.* . doi:10.1155/2022/5528416

Guo, F., Jiang, Z., Wang, Y., Chen, C., & Qian, Y. (2022). Dense Traffic Detection at Highway-Railroad Grade Crossings. *IEEE Transactions on Intelligent Transportation Systems*, 1–14. doi:10.1109/TITS.2022.3219923

Hadjidimitriou, N. S., Lippi, M., Dell'Amico, M., & Skiera, A. (2020). Machine Learning for Severity Classification of Accidents Involving Powered Two Wheelers. *IEEE Transactions on Intelligent Transportation Systems*, 21(10), 4308–4317. doi:10.1109/TITS.2019.2939624

Hua, Z., Xu, B., Jin, F., & Huang, H. (2019). Image Encryption Using Josephus Problem and Filtering Diffusion. *IEEE Access : Practical Innovations, Open Solutions*, 7, 8660–8674. doi:10.1109/ACCESS.2018.2890116

Karungaru, S., Dongyang, L., & Terada, K. (2021). Vehicle Detection and Type Classification Based on CNN-SVM. *International Journal of Machine Learning and Computing, 11*(4), 304–310. doi:10.18178/ijmlc.2021.11.4.1052

Kushwaha, M. (2022). Comparative Analysis on the Prediction of Road Accident Severity Using Machine Learning Algorithms. In *Micro-Electronics and Telecommunication Engineering* (pp. 269–280). Springer. doi:10.1007/978-981-16-8721-1_26

Kushwaha, M. (2023). Yolov7-based Brake Light Detection Model for Avoiding Rear-End Collisions. In *12th International Conference on Advanced Computing (ICoAC)*. IEEE. 10.1109/ICoAC59537.2023.10249731

Kushwaha, M. (n.d.). Analysis and Identifying of Important Features on Road Accidents by using Machine Learning Algorithms. 한국감성과학회 국제학술대회 *(ICES), 2021*, 110–113. Retrieved from https://kiss.kstudy.com/Detail/Ar?key=3947641

Kushwaha, M., & Abirami, M. S. (2023). Intelligent model for avoiding road accidents using artificial neural network. *International Journal of Computers, Communications & Control, 18*(5). Advance online publication. doi:10.15837/ijccc.2023.5.5317

Li, Q., Garg, S., Nie, J., Li, X., Liu, R. W., Cao, Z., & Hossain, M. S. (2021). A Highly Efficient Vehicle Taillight Detection Approach Based on Deep Learning. *IEEE Transactions on Intelligent Transportation Systems, 22*(7), 4716–4726. doi:10.1109/TITS.2020.3027421

Li, X., Jiang, Y., Chen, M., & Li, F. (2018). Research on iris image encryption based on deep learning. *EURASIP Journal on Image and Video Processing, 2018*(1). doi:10.1186/s13640-018-0358-7

Liu, L., Gao, M., Zhang, Y., & Wang, Y. (2022). Application of machine learning in intelligent encryption for digital information of real-time image text under big data. *EURASIP Journal on Wireless Communications and Networking, 2022*(1). . doi:10.1186/s13638-022-02111-9

M.S., A. (2020). Building an ensemble learning based algorithm for improving intrusion detection system. *Artificial Intelligence and Evolutionary Computations in Engineering Systems, 1056*. Retrieved from https://link.springer.com/chapter/10.1007/978-981-15-0199-9_55

Maniyath, S. R., & V, T. (2020). An efficient image encryption using deep neural network and chaotic map. *Microprocessors and Microsystems, 77*, 103134. doi:10.1016/j.micpro.2020.103134

Mansoor, U., Ratrout, N. T., Rahman, S. M., & Assi, K. (2020). Crash Severity Prediction Using Two-Layer Ensemble Machine Learning Model for Proactive Emergency Management. *IEEE Access : Practical Innovations, Open Solutions, 8*, 210750–210762. doi:10.1109/ACCESS.2020.3040165

Pu, Z., Cui, Z., Tang, J., Wang, S., & Wang, Y. (2021). Multi-Modal Traffic Speed Monitoring: A Real-Time System Based on Passive Wi-Fi and Bluetooth Sensing Technology. *IEEE Internet of Things Journal*. doi:10.1109/JIOT.2021.3136031

Samsudeen, S., & Senthil Kumar, G. (2023). FeduLPM: Federated Unsupervised Learning-Based Predictive Model for Speed Control in Customizable Automotive Variants. *IEEE Sensors Journal, 23*(13), 14700–14708. doi:10.1109/JSEN.2023.3275154

Shang, J., Guan, H., Liu, Y., Bi, H., Yang, L., & Wang, M. (2021). A novel method for vehicle headlights detection using salient region segmentation and PHOG feature. *Multimedia Tools and Applications, 80*(15), 22821–22841. doi:10.1007/s11042-020-10501-8

Sharma, K., Aggarwal, A., Singhania, T., Gupta, D., & Khanna, A. (2019). Hiding Data in Images Using Cryptography and Deep Neural Network. *Journal of Artificial Intelligence and Systems, 1*(1), 143–162. doi:10.33969/AIS.2019.11009

Shen, R., Zhen, T., & Li, Z. (2023). YOLOv5-Based Model Integrating Separable Convolutions for Detection of Wheat Head Images. *IEEE Access : Practical Innovations, Open Solutions, 11*, 12059–12074. doi:10.1109/ACCESS.2023.3241808

Silva, L. A., Leithardt, V. R. Q., Batista, V. F. L., Villarrubia González, G., & De Paz Santana, J. F. (2023). Automated Road Damage Detection Using UAV Images and Deep Learning Techniques. *IEEE Access : Practical Innovations, Open Solutions, 11*, 62918–62931. doi:10.1109/ACCESS.2023.3287770

Wang, P., Qiao, J., & Liu, N. (2022). An Improved Convolutional Neural Network-Based Scene Image Recognition Method. *Computational Intelligence and Neuroscience, 2022*(2830–2842), e3464984. . doi:10.1155/2022/3464984

Wang, X., Liu, J., Qiu, T., Mu, C., Chen, C., & Zhou, P. (2020). A Real-Time Collision Prediction Mechanism With Deep Learning for Intelligent Transportation System. *IEEE Transactions on Vehicular Technology, 69*(9), 9497–9508. doi:10.1109/TVT.2020.3003933

Wang, Z., Huo, W., Yu, P., Qi, L., Song, G., & Cao, N. (2019). Performance Evaluation of Region-Based Convolutional Neural Networks Toward Improved Vehicle Taillight Detection. *Applied Sciences (Basel, Switzerland), 9*(18), 3753–3753. doi:10.3390/app9183753

Xie, G., Shangguan, A., Fei, R., Hei, X., Ji, W., & Qian, F. (2021). Unmanned System Safety Decision-Making Support: Analysis and Assessment of Road Traffic Accidents. *IEEE/ASME Transactions on Mechatronics, 26*(2), 633–644. doi:10.1109/TMECH.2020.3043471

Yang, W., Wan, B., & Qu, X. (2020). A Forward Collision Warning System Using Driving Intention Recognition of the Front Vehicle and V2V Communication. *IEEE Access : Practical Innovations, Open Solutions, 8*, 11268–11278. doi:10.1109/ACCESS.2020.2963854

Zhang, X., Story, B., & Rajan, D. (2022). Night Time Vehicle Detection and Tracking by Fusing Vehicle Parts From Multiple Cameras. *IEEE Transactions on Intelligent Transportation Systems, 23*(7), 8136–8156. doi:10.1109/TITS.2021.3076406

Zia, U., McCartney, M., Scotney, B., Martinez, J., & Sajjad, A. (2022). A Novel Image Encryption Technique Using Multi-Coupled Map Lattice System with Generalized Symmetric Map and Adaptive Control Parameter. *SN Computer Science, 4*(1), 81. Advance online publication. doi:10.1007/s42979-022-01503-4

Chapter 9
Machine Learning Techniques to Predict the Inputs in Symmetric Encryption Algorithm

M. Sivasakthi

https://orcid.org/0000-0001-9828-8046

SRM Institute of Science and Technology, India

A. Meenakshi

SRM Institute of Science and Technology, India

ABSTRACT

Applying machine learning algorithms for encryption problems is reasonable in today's research connecting with cryptography. Using an encryption standard such as DES can give insight into how machine learning can help in breaking the encryption standards. The inspiration for this chapter is to use machine learning to reverse engineer hash functions. Hash functions are supposed to be tough to reverse one-way functions. The hash function will be learned by machine learning algorithm with a probability of more than 50%, which means the can develop their guesstimate of the reverse. This is concluded by executing the DES symmetric encryption function to generate N numerous values of DES with a set key and the machine learning algorithm is trained on a neural network to identify the first bit of the input based on the value of the function's output. Testing has ended through a new table, which was created similarly but with different inputs. The SVM runs on the new table, and it compares to the other table, and a confusion matrix is used to measure the excellence of the guesstimates.

INTRODUCTION

Our daily lives are now infinitely more accessible due to the widespread use of numerous electronic devices in the "information age." Because cryptographic algorithms can provide important insights into how cryptographic systems function internally, there has been a concern to device security (Ouladj & Guilley, 2021). Side-channel analysis is a valuable technique for identifying and resolving potential problems with improving safe cryptography systems (Cui et al., 2023).

DOI: 10.4018/979-8-3693-1642-9.ch009

A process known as encryption involves securing the document's or data's validity by employing an algorithm to jumble its contents and render them unintelligible to anybody without authorization to access them. Any kind of data, including messages and documents, can be encrypted and transformed into codes or ciphers. This is to stop unauthorized users from accessing any data, documents, or other material. By changing the data into some unintelligible code, it hides the information (Digital Guardian, n.d.). The process that entails reading the "un-readable code" is called decryption. By deciphering the encryption technique, it translates the message for the reader. The process of decrypting cipher text back into plaintext is known as decryption; symmetric encryption is employed for encrypting larger amounts of data (VTSCADA, n.d.). Data is scrambled using an algorithm during encryption to make it unreadable, and the reverse process is used during decryption to restore the data's readable state. Data is scrambled (or encrypted) using an algorithm in encryption, and the information is subsequently unlocked or decrypted using a key (Sectigostore, n.d.). The application layer is where encryption and decryption take place (Tutorialspoint, n.d.).

Encryption methods are an essential part of applications involving cryptography. Encryption provides security and protects communication channels. Encryption and decryption are tools for cybersecurity procedures, especially those related to servers and applications utilized for data or message transit. By verifying keys from the person supplying the message or data through an application or server, encryption protects the data or document being provided by transforming it into unreadable code that no one without a key can comprehend. Information is changed by data encryption so that only those with a secret key—also referred to as a password or decryption key can read it. Data that has been encrypted is called plaintext or ciphertext. You will need the decryption key in order to decrypt an encrypted message, document, or piece of data and return it to a readable format. Encryption is necessary for security-related contacts with law enforcement and the military since the data may still contain sensitive or private information. Similar to the encryption procedure, the decrypted result is the output and the document is the decryption input. It is encrypted text that cannot be deciphered, or ciphertext.

It is impossible to decode the data or determine the message's intention without a means of deciphering the ciphertext. Selecting a safe encryption technique is crucial to preventing easy data decoding. Security issues could be jeopardized in the absence of a reliable and secure encryption technique. When someone receives data or a document from the sender, they can use a private key to decrypt it and decode it. One instance would be sending a PDF document with a passcode along with an email message. To open the document, the recipient or the email message must know the passcode. Since the recipient's email address is public knowledge and should only be shared with the sender and recipient of the message, the passcode serves as an example of a private key. One frequently asked question is what the distinction is between public and private keys, as well as the kind of encryption technique to use. Both the sender and the recipient of encrypted data share a private key that is used to encrypt and decode the data. The public key is exchanged and is always kept private, while the private key is kept hidden.

Adding an additional layer of encryption using an attacker's key is the most popular method of hacking encrypted data. The private key that is used to encrypt a communication is required in order to decrypt it (Open.edu, n.d.). Numerous encryption techniques exist, each with its own unique style. The difference between symmetric and asymmetric encryption is one illustration. Asymmetric encryption employs a public key for encryption and a private key for decryption, whereas symmetric encryption uses a single key for both operations (Dataoverhaulers, n.d.).

Hashing, symmetric, and asymmetric encryption are all possible methods for protecting our data. To encrypt and decrypt data, the symmetric encryption method employs a single key. Triple Data Encryption Algorithm (TDEA), Advanced Encryption Standard (AES), and Data Encryption Standard (DES) are the most widely used symmetric algorithms.

The most widely used encryption technique available today is the DES algorithm. DES has been hacked multiple times and is no longer regarded as secure due to its widespread use and high level of awareness. For research purposes, DES is a workable but insecure encryption technique. The Data Encryption Standard, or DES, is a 56-bit symmetric encryption method. Encryption and decryption of data are carried out using the same 56-bit symmetric technique, known as DES. NIST adopted the IBM-created DES symmetric key block encryption in 1970. Sixty-eight-bit keys are used by the procedure to transform the plain text into ciphertext. By employing 48-bit keys, the Blocks Cipher Algorithm transforms 64-bit plaintext into ciphertext.

DES is a 56-bit symmetric key algorithm that encrypts a 64-bit message or piece of data using encryption keys that are 64-bit long, with every eighth bit disregarded to create a 56-bit key size. One of the most contentious parts of DES is its use of a 56-bit key. Those outside the intelligence establishment had long protested that 56-bit security was insufficient, even prior to the adoption of DES. DES has been used extensively in cryptography, although stronger encryption techniques utilize longer key lengths, which makes it more difficult to decrypt. The goal of this DES experiment was to advance future cryptography and cryber security applications. The output of a cryptographic function or method can be decrypted or decoded using a key, which is a special way to change plain text into cipher text. A machine learning technology is not a secure encryption method if it can be used to decrypt messages without the need for a key. It's like to locking the door of a house without any walls. If it were possible to foresee the output itself, a key would be meaningless.

In order to improve encryption and decryption methods, uncover potential vulnerabilities in data, and show the relationship between the input and output data produced by cryptosystems, machine learning techniques are being widely applied in cryptography (Anees, 2022).

The one-way function is reversible and therefore not secure for encryption if the machine learning method is able to estimate the input of the function without knowing the contents of the input. It is not secure if the function can be undone and the contents made visible. The definition of hash functions is one-way functions. A machine learning algorithm has the ability to decipher the contents of a document or message by guessing the secret key through the reverse engineering of a strong hashing encryption method (Armstrong, 2021).

In this paper, we propose that a supervised machine learning algorithm, SVM, can learn the probability of more than 50% of the input of a symmetric hash function, DES. This indicates that there is a greater likelihood of an attack against the input of a symmetric hash function, which is by definition supposed to be collision resistant. It should not be feasible to reverse engineer a hash function's digested message. It is possible to decipher the initial bit of encrypted data using machine learning techniques, which implies that one can use a similar approach to reverse engineer the entire communication.

BACKGROUND

It is commonly accepted that Cybersecurity refers to a collection of methods and procedures used to safeguard digital data against intrusion or attack. Given a sufficiently strong block cipher, DES can be utilized as a one-way hash function. A sufficiently big key space is a prerequisite for a block cipher to be deemed good. Brute force attacks are less effective against the larger key space. The DES algorithm may be deemed suitable for one-way function if its key space is sufficiently large. The DES algorithm converts plaintext into cipher text by applying a sequence of XOR and permutation operations. Through hashing, which can be done with DES, plaintext input is converted to a hash value. In today's commercial sector, DES is the most popular and extensively utilized encryption function (Armstrong, 2021).

Kelly Armstrong claims that most researchers simply use a guess and check or brute force attack when anticipating passwords. It's possible that these techniques will never produce an accurate estimate in a timely manner. Since most techniques only use brute force attacks, successful machine learning algorithms that can predict an encrypted document are not shown. even though robust encryption techniques—which are typically ineffective—are used (Armstrong, 2021).

In addition, the concept of creating a black box guess using a random oracle model to create an input has been thoroughly proven to yield a unique input (Mahmoody et al., 2012). This is also known as a time lock problem. Another method for deep learning password prediction from PassGAN is rule-based password guessing, also known as Markov Models. This technique trains a neural network to recognize password structures and characteristics on its own and uses this information to produce new samples with the same distribution (Hitaj et al., 2019). Effectively, this study did not concentrate on the predictability of a single correctly guessed bit of data, but rather on guessing the password as an entire string of bits.

The process of forecasting future events using data modeling is known as predictive modeling. More effort may be done to create models for more robust encryption techniques once a trend for how machine learning algorithms can forecast inputs is seen. For this kind of situation, predictive modeling works well, and utilizing machine learning to provide precise predictions is the ideal method (AWS Dashboard, n.d.). Predictive modeling mainly works with tabular data, in contrast to the more general area of machine learning, which could work with data in any type (Brownlee, 2021).

Each of the sixteen rounds of operations in DES employs a different round key and the same procedures. The DES round takes a cipher text generated by the previous round as input and outputs a cipher text that is divided into the left and right halves to be used as input for the following round. This permutation operates by shifting the positions of the bits. The 32-bit value is expanded from 32 bits to 48 bits via the mangler function, and the 48 key is then substituted into the 32-bit value (YouTube, n.d.).

The learning algorithm called Support Vector Machine is the greatest "off-the-shelf" supervised learning algorithm—many people even argue that they are the best. We must first discuss margins and the notion of separating data with a significant "gap" before we can convey the SVM story. We'll then stray into the topic of Lagrange duality by discussing the optimal margin classifier. Additionally, kernels will be discussed, providing an effective method for applying Support Vector Machines (SVMs) in very high dimensional (i.e., infinite dimensional) feature spaces (Ng & Notes, n.d.). SVM is a reasonably memory-efficient technique in the field of machine learning, according to Lipo Wang (Wang & Machines, 2005). It is also effective in high-dimensional domains. Thus, this is the option for the Symmetric Encryption Algorithm to forecast the inputs.

METHODOLOGY

The aim of this paper is to investigate how machine learning algorithms can reverse engineer hash functions, which are employed in encryption and are thought to be impervious to reverse engineering. Importing the free source library directly yields the DES algorithm. The SVM algorithm can be found in Jason Brown's eBook, Machine Learning Mastery.

Fixed-size data is encrypted using DES. Initial message fragmented into 64-bit sections. Permutation happens over divided data: the left splits to the xor function, which is then applied to the right. The right then breaks to the left and becomes expanded to the right side of 48 bits, which shrinks from dividing, and permutation happens once more, followed by the application of xor to the right side. 16 times in total for every subkey. The cipher text's right and left sides are divided into permutation and reversal. Left creation key and Right block cipher are the two components of the encryption. Binary conversion is performed on the key, and ASCII to Hex to bits DES data type conversion is performed (Exchange, n.d.). Utilizes a 56-bit key to encrypt several 64 bits. A 64-bit value is the first input. It is an eight-byte string key. Print the 0s and 1s and create a random string to get the data ready for the machine learning routine. It is unpredictable since the results are independent of the prior run, therefore it can be repeated again.

Figure 1. DES Diagram

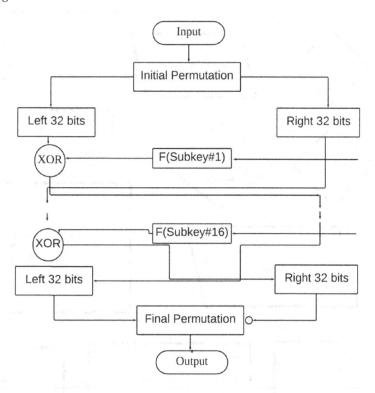

RESULT AND DISCUSSION

The flowchart is clearly shows the implementation using python. The DES encrypted text is the input for analysis using support vector classifier which in turn gives the accuracy.

The DES algorithm for implementation is:

1. Pydes from mit library permute for data permute on key permutation (Github Code Resource, n.d.; Robin David, n.d.)
2. Generate pydes string to birs data encrypted in data with key, out data

Figure 2. Flowchart of Algorithm with Code

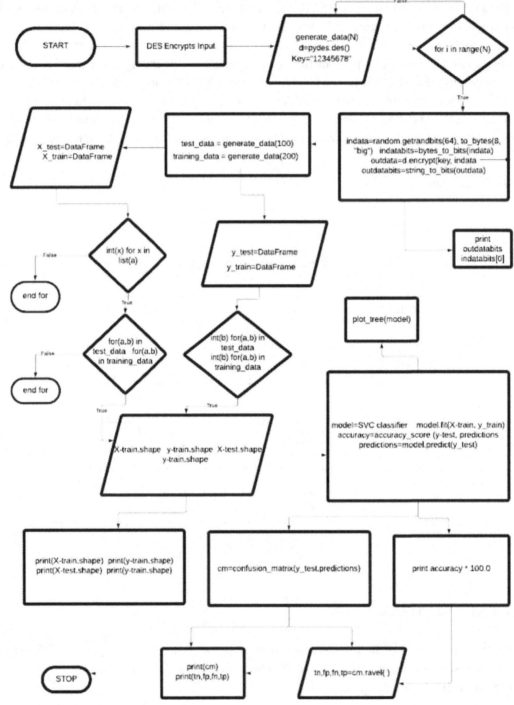

3. Next part training testing keep t as last bit of input split training x,y and testing x,y
4. Do pydes encrypt with key
5. T in data bits outdates bits
6. T' outdatabits, indatabits
7. Training and test sets known
8. Data ready for machine learning algorithm

Breaking DES would mean finding a key that maps that plaintext to that ciphertext (Speciner et al., 2002).

1. The first task is to convert 64 bits to bytes
2. T' is outdata (des encrypted) indata[0] (first bit of input)
3. T' is fed in xg
4. Each time you run it you get different xo
5. The machine learning algorithm SVM will be run each time for testing against training
6. Then confusion matrix measures the last run exp
7. The training data set is the term for the samples used to create the model.
8. The test set is used to qualify performance.

Every implementation yields a unique, unpredictable result. Data used for testing is separate from data used for training. To a list of tuples of two strings, the neural network functions as a "recognizer." The initial string is encrypted, and the subsequent one contains encrypted clear text data. Two tables contain the data. The model is fed the strings, while the test side ignores the input. The test side ignores the input and uses 200 elements to create the output, while the DES algorithm encrypts the training data, N=200, N=100, or N=300 for each test case.

Training:

('0010011001010100010001111100110011111101110011000000000000101100', '0'),

......,

('0101000010000111001100000111100011000111101010101101011111000011', '0')

Testing:

('1011001010011011101100101000010010110111111010101011011000010000', '0'),

......,

('0000100110010100001010110100101110100011100100000011000010100011', '1')

Confusion matrix from three test runs are

1) Accuracy 46.00 percent with confusion matrix:

[50 50]
[58 42]

TN 50, FP 50, FN 58, TP 42. Here the accuracy score is 46 percent. The true negatives are 50 and true positives are 42. When added together that gives a score of 46 percent. The false positive is 50 and false negatives is 58 which adds to a total of 100 percent.

2) Accuracy 53.00 percent with confusion matrix:

[63 52]
[42 43]

TN 63, FP 52, FN 42, TP 43. Here the accuracy score is 53 percent. The true negatives are 63 and true positives are 43. When added together that gives a score of 53 percent. The false positive is 52 and false negatives is 42 which make up the residual.

3) Accuracy 54.00 percent with confusion matrix:

[63 38]
[54 45]

TN 63, FP 38, FN 54, TP 45. Here the accuracy score is 54 percent. The true negatives are 63 and true positives are 45. When added together that gives a score of 54 percent. The false positive is 38 and false negatives is 54 which make up the residual.

CONCLUSION

Machine learning can be used to anticipate the input of data using encryption algorithms like DES. The first bit of encrypted data may be anticipated more accurately than 50% of the time using support vector machine learning, which is a better prediction than guesswork. Reverse engineering hash functions, which are thought to be irreversible one-way functions, can benefit from machine learning. This experiment has demonstrated that we can guess the inverse more accurately than 50% of the times, revealing that a machine learning method can reverse an encrypted message's first bit more efficiently than a guess. Although DES is a weak encryption method, this experiment has shown that it may be possible to try a more sophisticated method, like replacing DES with the stronger encryption standard AES. If we apply the same research methodology to a more complex function, like AES256, we can achieve better results than guessing the inverse with above 50% accuracy. This raises the question: How accurate could one forecast two pieces of encrypted data? Maybe even more? Alternatively, whether a machine learning algorithm can correctly predict a complete input. Or, to put it another way, how accurate could one be to forecast a single encrypted piece of data that has been encrypted using a more powerful symmetric encryption standard like AES256 or elliptic curve encryption?

REFERENCES

Anees, A. (2022). *Machine Learning and Applied Cryptography, Security and Communication networks.* Wiley.

Armstrong, K. (2021). *Applying machine learning to predict symmetric encryption algorithm inputs* [Master Thesis]. Channel Islands, California State University.

AWS Dashboard. (n.d.). https://awsacademy.instructure.com/

Brownlee. (2021). *Ensemble Learning Algorithms With Python.* Academic Press.

Cui, X., Zhang, H., Fang, X., Wang, Y., Wang, D., Fan, F., & Shu, L. (2023). A Secret Key Classification Framework of Symmetric Encryption Algorithm Based on Deep Transfer Learning. *Applied Sciences (Basel, Switzerland), 13*(21), 12025. doi:10.3390/app132112025

Dataoverhaulers. (n.d.). https://dataoverhaulers.com/can-encrypted-data-be-hacked/

Digital Guardian. (n.d.). https://digitalguardian.com/blog/what-data-encryption

Exchange, S. (n.d.). *Hash Function on Finite Fields.* https://math.stackexchange.com/questions/1347240/how-to-attack-universal-hash-functio

Github Code Resource. (n.d.). https://github.com/kongfy/DES/blob/master/Riv85.txt

Hitaj, Gasti, Ateniese, & Perez-Cruz. (2019). *PassGAN: A Deep Learning Approach for Password Guessing.* Academic Press.

Mahmoody, M., Moran, T., & Vadhan, S. (2012). Publicly Verifiable Proofs of Sequential Work. *Proceedings of the 4th Conference on Innovations in Theoretical Computer Science.*

NgA.NotesL. (n.d.). https://see.stanford.edu/materials/aimlcs229/cs229-notes3.pdf

Open.edu. (n.d.). https://www.open.edu/openlearn/science-maths-technology/computing-and-ict/systems-co

Ouladj, M., & Guilley, S. (2021). *Side-Channel Analysis of Embedded Systems: An Efficient Algorithmic Approach.* Springer. doi:10.1007/978-3-030-77222-2

Robin David. (n.d.). *GITHUB python DES.* https://github.com/RobinDavid/pydes/blob/master/LICENSE.md

Sectigostore. (n.d.). https://sectigostore.com/blog/5-differences-between-symmetric-vs-asymmetric-encrypt

Speciner, M., Perlman, R., & Kaufman, C. (2002). *Network Security: Private Communications in a Public World.* Prentice Hall PTR.

Tutorialspoint. (n.d.). https://www.tutorialspoint.com/difference-between-private-key-and-public-key

VTSCADA. (n.d.). https://www.vtscada.com/help/Content/Scripting/Tasks/proEncryptionAnddecryption.htm

Wang, L., & Machines, S. V. (2005). *Theory and Applications*. Springer.

YouTube. (n.d.). https://youtu.be/Sy0sXa73PZA

Chapter 10
Homomorphic Encryption and Machine Learning in the Encrypted Domain

Neethu Krishna
 https://orcid.org/0000-0002-6061-9193
SCMS School of Engineering and Technology, Karukutty, India

Kommisetti Murthy Raju
 https://orcid.org/0000-0002-7576-4449
Shri Vishnu Engineering College For Women, India

V. Dankan Gowda
 https://orcid.org/0000-0003-0724-0333
BMS Institute of Technology and Management, India

G. Arun
Erode Sengunthar Engineering College, India

Sampathirao Suneetha
 https://orcid.org/0009-0005-2714-6442
Andhra University College of Engineering, Andhra University, India

ABSTRACT

In cryptography, performing computations on encrypted material without first decrypting it has long been an aspiration. This is exactly what homomorphic encryption (HE) accomplishes. By allowing computation on encrypted data, the associated privacy and security of sensitive information are beyond imagination to date. This chapter delves into the vast and intricate realm of HE, its fundamental theories, and far-reaching implications for machine learning. As a result of the sensitive nature of the data on which machine learning is based, privacy and security issues often arise. In this vein, homomorphic encryption, which allows algorithms to learn from and predict encrypted data, emerges as a possible panacea. The authors thus set out in this chapter to prepare the ground for a deeper understanding of that synergy, showing how it is there but also what lies ahead.

DOI: 10.4018/979-8-3693-1642-9.ch010

1. INTRODUCTION TO HOMOMORPHIC ENCRYPTION

There exists a class of encryption, called HOMOMORPHIC Encryption (HE), that objects can be computed on directly in ciphertext. After being decrypted the results are identical to what would have been obtained if they had instead applied these operations to plain text. Because of this special property, HE becomes an effective instrument for secure data processing--sensitive information is encrypted even during computation. The principle of homomorphic HE means that the structure exists before and remains unchanged after in between encryption and computation. For instance, if you have two numbers in the clear--2 and 3 say--and wish to add them in encrypted form, HE would permit you first to transform these into ciphertexts then proceed with performing an addition operation on their respective encryptions. Decrypting the result will reveal 5, which is indeed equal to a sum of these original numbers. Historical Context and Development: The concept of Homomorphic Encryption goes back to the conception of RSA (invented in 1978) as an algorithm with homomorphic properties. But this was only for specific operations. The breakthrough came in 2009, when Craig Gentry--a student at Stanford working on his Ph.D. thesis--developed a fully homomorphic encryption scheme for the first time ever. This was a turning point, because it proved that one could perform arbitrary computations on encrypted data.

Its initial proposal for construction was lattice-based cryptography (Suryawanshi and Abhay Chaturvedi, 2022). It proposed an encryption scheme that could evaluate the circuit of its own decryption function homomorphically. This first scheme, though revolutionary, was unpractical in being too slow and complex. But it laid the groundwork for later research in that field.

Since then, HE has been a fast-developing field of research. Researchers have produced ever more effective and practical schemes. These technical breakthroughs have been brought about by the increasing importance of data privacy and security in areas from cloud computing to finance, healthcare, etc. Collaboration between cryptographers, mathematicians and computer scientists has characterized the development of HE.

Homomorphic Encryption now leads the way in search for secure data processing. In the age of big data and cloud computing, where privacy matters more than ever, this is seen as an essential technology (A. Singla, N. Sharma 2022). Later in the sections dealing with HE, we will see how this technology is not just a concept but can actually be something that people could use to radically change our handling and processing of information.

2. HOMOMORPHIC ENCRYPTION TECHNIQUES

The initial idea behind cryptography was to create a system that could guarantee safe communication between various entities. One side encrypts a message and sends it to the other, who can decode it (A. Singla, N. Sharma 2022). The idea of doing calculations on encrypted data was first proposed as a "privacy transformation" in 1978 by Rivest, Adleman, and Dertouzos. What is currently known as homomorphic encryption developed out of this idea over time. Homomorphic encryption, in a wide sense, allows us to compute on encrypted data. If a scheme has the following characteristics, we say that it is additively (or multiplicatively) homomorphic:

$$[x] \oplus [y] = [x + y] \text{ and } [x] \otimes [y] = [x \cdot y]$$

In this context, the letter [⊗] stands for the plaintext value's encryption, while the characters ⊗ and · denote the homomorphic operations of addition and multiplication carried out in the ciphertext space. If an encryption system is additively homomorphic, then encrypting data before adding it is equivalent to adding the data before encryption, to put it more simply. Figure.1 shows this idea in action. Partially Homomorphic Encryption (PHE): Partially Homomorphic Encryption schemes are specialized to allow specific types of operations on encrypted data. These schemes can perform either addition or multiplication, but not both(G. Karatas, O. Demir and O. K. Sahingoz, 2019). A prominent example is the RSA encryption, which exhibits multiplicative homomorphic properties. In PHE, if you encrypt two numbers and multiply their ciphertexts, the result, when decrypted, will be the product of the original numbers. PHE is relatively more efficient than its more advanced counterparts and forms the basis of many early applications of homomorphic encryption.

Figure 1. Concept of Homomorphic Encryption

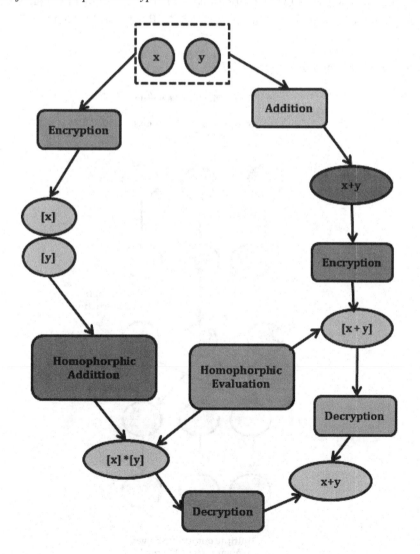

Somewhat Homomorphic Encryption (SWHE): Somewhat Homomorphic Encryption is an extension of PHE. SWHE schemes can perform a limited number of both addition and multiplication operations on ciphertexts. The limitation arises from the fact that every homomorphic operation introduces a small amount of noise into the ciphertext, and this noise accumulates with each operation(A. Sharma, K. S and M. R. Arun, 2022). Once the noise reaches a certain threshold, the ciphertext becomes too corrupted to be reliably decrypted. SWHE is a critical stepping stone towards fully homomorphic encryption, offering more flexibility than PHE while still being constrained by the noise buildup.

Supporting Single Instruction Multiple Data (SIMD) operations, Smart and Vercauteren presented a Secure Homomorphic Encryption (SHE) technique in an independent research. By using a method known as ciphertext packing, this feature enables Fully Homomorphic Encryption (FHE) to achieve parallelization. The encoding of several plaintext values into a single the ciphertext vector is an example of how SIMD instructions improve computing performance. One of the main uses of ciphertext packing is in batch calculation, which is a common feature of many FHE algorithms. In addition, it permits the reordering of plain slots within a packed ciphertext, which may result in enhanced evaluation speed. Figure 2 is a graphical representation of these ideas (M. N. Reza, and M. Islam, 2021); it shows a vector

Figure 2. Secure Homomorphic Encryption (SHE)

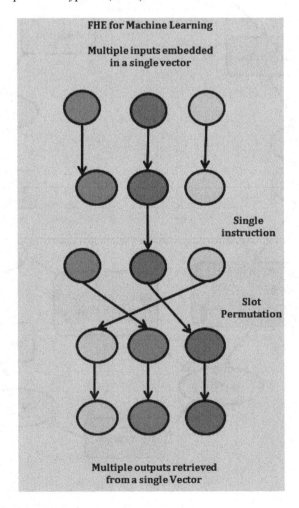

with several values within it, which may be processed with a single command and their slots may be rearranged for different uses.

At its most sophisticated, Fully Homomorphic Encryption (FHE) protects data from prying eyes. The amount of additions and multiplications that may be performed on encrypted data is limitless. The breakthrough achievement of FHE is its ability to manage and control the noise accumulation that plagues SWHE schemes(Kumar, Pullela SVVSR, & Chaturvedi, Abhay, 2023). This is accomplished by a method called bootstrapping, which serves to lower the noise level and permits continuous computation. Since its start, FHE has been a major area of research. Constant work is being done to make it more practical in terms of efficiency and computational resources.

Mathematical Foundations of Homomorphic Encryption: HE's mathematical basis lies in number theory and algebra (Kumar, R & B. Ashreetha, 2023). In fact, the essence of HE utilizes complex mathematical concepts including lattice-based cryptography; ring theory and polynomial arithmetic. These mathematical foundations allow the operations on encrypted data to be carried out in a secure and stable manner.

A simplified protocol using a single Fully Homomorphic Encryption (FHE) scheme is shown as Figure 3. Starting with the server's encryption of two critical elements, P and T; then customers down-

Figure 3. Simplified Overview of Single-Scheme FHE Protocol

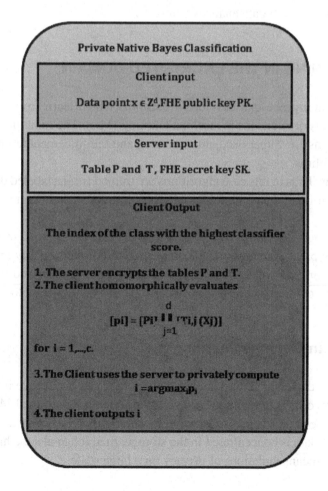

load these encrypted tables to their own computers. Next, homomorphic techniques are used on [Pi] for each class 'i', which gives an user a score. (S Tan et al., 2021) Then the client can go through a private argmax conversation with the server and find which class has pi. A series of comparisons is carried out in a linear fashion to determine this maximum value. With the goal of keeping things private, the client sends the likelihoods that follow for each class to the server in a random sequence. By comparing these probabilities with the greatest number recorded, the server determines the new maximum and delivers it back to the client via an encrypted comparison protocol. This returned value is carefully masked to ensure the client cannot infer any partial order among the values, thereby preserving the confidentiality of the process(P. H. Kumar and T. Samanta, 2022). For instance, lattice-based cryptography, which is central to many HE schemes, involves the use of multidimensional geometric lattices. Computations in these lattices are performed in a way that is easy for someone with the decryption key (who knows the structure of the lattice) but extremely difficult for anyone else. This difficulty is often based on hard mathematical problems like the shortest vector problem (SVP) or the closest vector problem (CVP), which are believed to be resistant to attacks even by quantum computers(P. Gope, O. Millwood and B. Sikdar, 2022). Qualitatively, the technique of Partially Homomorphic Encryption is simpler than Fully Homomorphic encryption. If we are to fully appreciate the potential value and limits of HE in different fields, it is necessary for us not only to know these differences but also their mathematical foundations. In this chapter, we will see how these techniques are used in machine learning. We've never seen such paradigms for privacy-preserving data analysis before now.

3. MACHINE LEARNING IN THE ENCRYPTED DOMAIN

The area of artificial intelligence that develops algorithms which learn from data, and then use this knowledge for predictions or decisions is machine learning (ML). The more data there is for learning, the better these algorithms are. Supervised, unsupervised and reinforcement learning are the three main categories of ML algorithms.

Supervised Learning: Thus in this case algorithms are trained from a labeled dataset, and understand the relationship between input data and output labels. Examples include regression and classification models.

Unsupervised Learning: Algorithms with unclassified data are used here to search for hidden patterns or internal structures. Typical examples include clustering and dimensionality reduction.

Reinforcement Learning: By interacting with a complex environment and trying to achieve given goals, algorithms learn how to make a series of decisions. It is widely employed in robotics, gaming and navigation.

Privacy Concerns in Machine Learning

For machine learning models, which must have enough data to run on, private information such as personal data or medical records is not without its privacy problems. Traditional ML works by collecting data from different sources that can be used to train models. This poses several privacy risks:

Data Breach Risk: If data is concentrated in the storage, then it can also be hacked by someone and stolen illicitly. And that means violations of privacy on a large scale.

Misuse of Data: But when third parties are involved, there is also the danger that data can be used in ways it was never originally intended.

Loss of Anonymity: However, even when the data is anonymized, strong ML sometimes gets around them to re-identify people and violate their privacy.

Homomorphic Encryption as a Solution

Homogeneous Encryption presents a hope for solving these privacy concerns. Calculations on encrypted information mean that raw data does not have to be given away when building HE ML models. Because critical information is always kept encrypted throughout the ML process, occurrences of data breaches and misuse are greatly reduced.

Training on Encrypted Data: ML models can be trained directly on encrypted data, ensuring that the underlying data remains secure and private.

Inference from Encrypted Data: ML models can make predictions on encrypted data, which is particularly useful in scenarios where the input data is sensitive.

The client may categorize her data using the owner's model in this case, but she doesn't have direct access to the model or the necessary knowledge about her data to do so. Another option for outsourcing storage and processing is to use a middleman cloud server(Kumaraswamy & Gupta, Anand Kumar, 2023). Figure 4 shows a model that exemplifies this concept. Most importantly, this approach functions

Figure 4. Displays a Categorization Model that Protects Individuals' Privacy

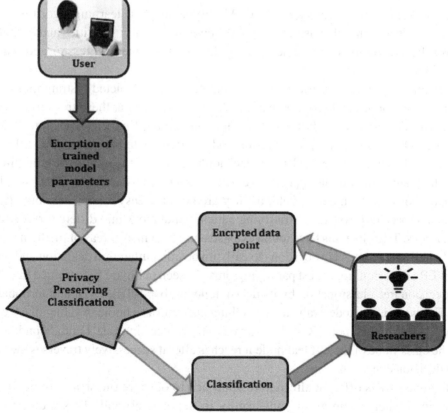

as if the client and server are not engaging in any kind of unlawful cooperation or collusion. The actual process involves many customers entrusting their encrypted data to a cloud server, which then trains a categorization algorithm. The ability to securely analyze data without sacrificing privacy makes private prediction an important use case for Fully Homomorphic Encryption (FHE) approaches. The healthcare industry is one area where this possibility has substantial practical implications(K.D.V., Gite, Pratik, Sivakumar, 2023). For instance, under the strictest confidence, doctors may use third-party, encrypted diagnostic prediction algorithms to sort patients according to their medical information.

The use of HE in machine learning, however, is not without challenges. The computational complexity of HE can lead to increased processing time and resource requirements, which we will explore in later sections. However, new opportunities for using ML in highly sensitive fields like healthcare and finance have emerged thanks to the possibility of privacy-preserving ML employing homomorphic encryption.

4. INTEGRATION OF HOMOMORPHIC ENCRYPTION WITH MACHINE LEARNING

The combination of Homomorphic Encryption (HE) with Machine Learning (ML) is a huge step forward for protecting sensitive information. Protecting data privacy is HE's top priority, which is why it allows ML algorithms to work directly on encrypted data(S. Zhu and Y. Han, 2021). This synergy not only protects sensitive information but also opens up new possibilities for securely leveraging ML in various industries.

Adapting ML Algorithms for Encrypted Data: Modifying machine learning algorithms to work with encrypted data involves a careful consideration of the computational capabilities and limitations of HE. Here, we look at how two common machine learning algorithms — linear regression and neural networks — can be adapted for this purpose.

Binary decision trees serve as an effective classification method, depicted as straightforward diagrams with internal decision nodes and terminal leaf nodes. To classify data, these trees use a succession of binary splits, with the value at the last leaf node determining the final classification (P. Pavankumar, N. K. Darwante, 2022). In this case, the decision nodes differentiate between "osteoarthritis" and "no osteoarthritis," as shown in Figure 5b. Binary decision trees are just as useful with multi-class quantitative data as they are with two-class qualitative data, as seen in this example. Their simplicity makes them a popular choice in the medical field, as they are not only easy to visualize but also align with the diagnostic approach of physicians, stratifying patient populations into different risk strata based on their characteristics. Trees like this have found extensive usage in many areas of medicine, from helping with mental health and wound care decisions to early myocardial infarction detection and predicting the probability of ER admission from chest pain symptoms. As seen in Figure 5a, a trained tree, T, is defined in a private decision tree classification by its decision nodes, $b = (b_i)1 \subseteq i \leq N$, and terminal nodes, $c = (c_i)1 \subseteq i \leq M$. Every decision node evaluates something and returns a boolean value, like 0 or 1. In order to assign a new value to data point X within T, we apply the decision tree's initial condition, b_1. After that, X gets the class value of the last leaf node it reaches after it successively traverses the branches and applies each decision condition.

Complete binary trees offer an alternative approach to obscure the structure of a tree, particularly in situations where maintaining uniformity in depth is crucial. This method involves the

Figure 5(a). The binary decision tree is depicted with distinct decision nodes, labeled as bi, and terminal leaf nodes, denoted as ci. This tree structure facilitates the classification process by guiding the data through a series of binary decisions at each node, ultimately leading to one of the leaf nodes which determine the final class. (b) In the specific context of diagnosing osteoarthritis of the knee, the decision tree is tailored for this classification task. It systematically processes patient data through its nodes, with each decision point bi contributing to the path taken in the tree, and culminates at a leaf node ci. This leaf node provides the final diagnosis, indicating whether the patient has osteoarthritis or not

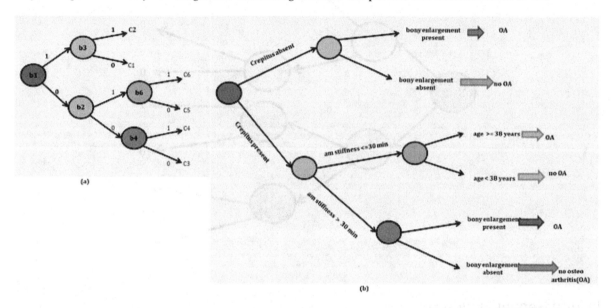

addition of "dummy" nodes, as outlined in reference. These dummy nodes are strategically placed within the tree to ensure that every branch has the same depth, creating a uniform structure (H. G. Govardhana Reddy & K. Raghavendra, 2022) . Each of these dummy nodes is programmed to give a random binary output. However, regardless of the response provided by these nodes, the path leads to the same outcome. This concept is exemplified in Figure 6, where the presence of dummy nodes in the tree can be observed, contributing to a consistent tree depth while not affecting the final result.

Linear Regression with HE

Problem Statement: To forecast a continuous outcome variable from a set of one or more predictor variables, a basic ML approach is linear regression.

Adaptation for HE: The computation in linear regression (mainly additions and multiplications) aligns well with the operations supported by HE. By encrypting the input data (predictor variables) and coefficients, linear regression can be performed on encrypted data. The encrypted output can then be decrypted to get the prediction.

Challenges: The primary challenge lies in handling the noise accumulation during the multiplication of coefficients, which requires careful management to ensure accurate results.

Figure 6. Completion of the Binary Tree

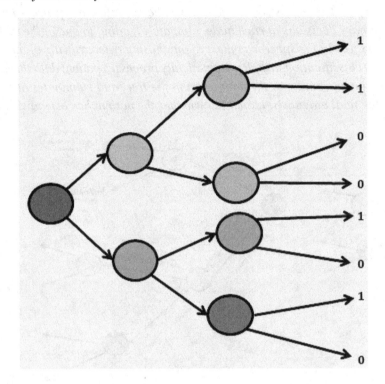

Neural Networks with HE

Problem Statement: Neural networks, particularly deep learning models, are used for complex pattern recognition tasks in various domains.

Adaptation for HE: Neural networks involve a series of linear (like weights and biases) and non-linear operations (like activation functions). To adapt neural networks for HE, one must ensure that all these operations can be performed on encrypted data(A. Musa and A. Mahmood, 2021). Techniques like polynomial approximation for non-linear functions can be employed.

Challenges: The main challenge is the computational complexity, as neural networks require a large number of operations, which can be significantly slower when performed on encrypted data.

Practical Considerations

Computational Overhead: Processing encrypted data is inherently more computationally intensive than processing plaintext. This can lead to longer training times and may require more powerful computational resources.

Precision and Scaling: Dealing with floating-point numbers in HE can be challenging. It often requires scaling them to integer values, which must be carefully managed to maintain precision.

Data Preprocessing: Preprocessing steps, like normalization, also need to be adapted to work with encrypted data.

Real-World Implications: The integration of HE with machine learning can have profound implications in areas where data privacy is crucial(N. Hussain, A. A. J. . Pazhani, and A. K. . N, 2023). For example, in healthcare, models can be trained on encrypted patient data to develop predictive models without compromising patient confidentiality. In finance, HE can enable secure risk analysis based on sensitive financial information without exposing individual data points.

As shown in Figure 7, the procedures for private classification of decision trees based on the polynomial tree follow important phases that were influenced by Bost's research. The privacy-preserving nature of these protocols ensures that the client remains in the dark about the evaluation of her data point at each node and the general layout of the tree. At the same time, the owner of the model has no idea what particulars the client's data point contains. Private comparisons between the client and server are the first step in the process(Shivashankar, and S. Mehta, 2016). At each internal judgment node of the tree, these comparisons are critical for deciding the binary output. When an input value x is compared to a predetermined threshold w at a decision node, the outcome is a binary output $b = [x > w]$. This is the conceptualization behind the evaluation. This confidential comparison is designed to keep the customer in the dark about the exact results. The server, on the other hand, deduces the comparison's outcome—but only in an encrypted manner, protected by the client's public key. Client information and the tree's structure are both protected by this method of comparison. In practice, private tree evaluation typically involves techniques like homomorphic encryption, secure multi-party computation, or the use of dummy nodes and private comparisons, as mentioned earlier. The goal is to ensure that the evalua-

Figure 7. Process of Private Tree Evaluation

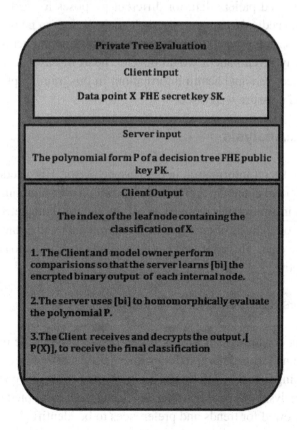

tion of data points through the decision tree occurs without revealing sensitive information, adhering to privacy regulations and ethical standards(L. R. Knudsen and J. E. Mathiassen, 2000). This approach is particularly valuable in leveraging the power of decision trees for predictive analytics while upholding the principles of data privacy and security. A blossoming new field in the quest for privacy-preserving data analysis is Homomorphic Encryption combined with machine learning (R. Beaulieu, D. Shors and J . Smith 2018). There are challenges, especially concerning computational efficiency. But the advantages in terms of data security and privacy are immense. Pushing this research further will yield ever more refined and efficient methods, making the use of HE in machine learning not only a practical option but indeed standard practice.

5. PRACTICAL APPLICATIONS AND CASE STUDIES

Applications industries for integrating Homomorphic Encryption (HE) with Machine Learning (ML), while each industry possesses unique challenges and needs in the field of data privacy. In this section, we will explore how HE is being used in different fields. There are several case studies here that illustrate just what transformative influence it has had.

Healthcare: Enhancing Patient Privacy

Application: Patient data is especially sensitive in the healthcare field. With the use of HE, healthcare providers can analyze encrypted patient data for different purposes-for instance to make predictions about disease or personalize medical treatment; yet such analysis does in no way impair patient privacy.

Case Study: Take that research project, for example, in which a neural net trained with HE was used to predict whether or not any given patient would develop heart disease. A model was trained on encrypted patient data to protect personal health information. In this training process, in addition to age, cholesterol levels and blood pressure were used.

Finance: Secure Data Analysis

Application: There's highly secret information in the finance sector. HE offers encrypted information-based safe risk evaluation, fraud detection and personal financial consultation.

Case Study: A financial institution has realized an ML model for fraud detection using HE. A model was developed on the basis of analysis of encrypted transaction data with which to differentiate normal transactions from fraudulent ones. This approach has allowed the institution to add to its security without compromising customer data.

Marketing: Privacy-Preserving Consumer Insights

Application: Understanding consumer behavior is key in marketing, but the information must be used carefully. HE enables companies to use encrypted consumer data to learn while ensuring privacy concerns.

Case Study: One marketing firm used HE to analyze encrypted consumer purchase histories, to create directed advertising. The analysis was based on data which had been encrypted to protect the consumer's right of privacy, but still allowed for trends and preferences to be identified.

Government: Secure Public Services

Application: Governments can securely handle citizen data to improve public services, or policy making and resource allocation--while still maintaining individual privacy with the help of HE.

Case Study: In a project to optimize public transportation routes, one government agency used HE. Using the information hidden within encrypted commuter data, they were able to change routes and schedules without even seeing people 'travel details.

Education: Protecting Student Data

Application: HE facilitates the systematic analysis of encrypted student data, through which schools can improve learning experiences for students and track their progress; it also helps with budget allocations. All this is done without exposing any sensitive information.

Case Study: A university that used a machine learning algorithm with HE for predicting student success rates had encrypted demographic data and academic records. This enabled tailored educational support but kept students' records in confidence.

Figure 8. Ordinary Encryption

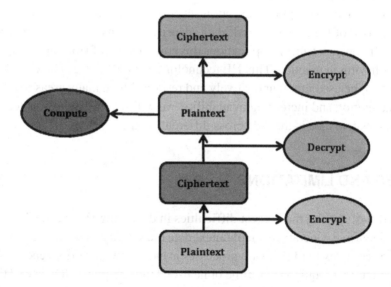

In the past few decades, data and methods have needed to be carefully guarded against theft by increasingly sophisticated technical means. The crisis becomes more serious as electronic devices fall victim to various attacks. This is a greater challenge when data has to be processed in unsecured locations. And this is where the use of homomorphic cryptosystems becomes essential. Homomorphic Encryption is an encryption method that allows complex calculations to be carried out on encrypted data, just as they would have been done with plaintext. This encryption scheme is preserved under addition, subtraction and other operations. For instance, its additive property is illustrated as $E(x + y) = E(x) + E(y)$, and its multiplicative property as $E(x * y) = E(x) * E(y)$. There's also a mixed multiplicative homomorphism,

Figure 9. Homomorphic encryption

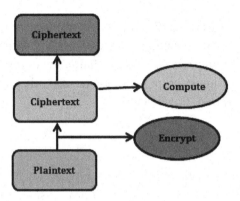

represented as E(x * y) = E(x) * y. Although this property is generally undesirable, because it may disclose the details of encrypted data, sometimes it can also be advantageous. For example, in voting protocols it supports validation of the sum of a collection of encrypted values without divulging those states. This encryption technique is particularly important in wireless sensor networks (WSN), where data flows through different nodes. In such circumstances, if a node is compromised through ordinary encryption techniques. However, if a Homomorphic encryption scheme is used (as shown in Figure 9), even if an attacker compromises one of the nodes, overall data security remains intact. These examples serve to showcase the many different and fruitful applications this combination of Homomorphic Encryption and Machine Learning is having in practice. This HE technology not only solves current privacy problems, but also helps the data to be used more innovatively and responsibly in many areas. As it becomes more popular due to its maturation and increasing availability, we will see the use of this technology expand even further in how sensitive data is treated across different fields.

6. CHALLENGES AND LIMITATIONS

Computational Overhead: Among the biggest difficulties in deploying HE for machine learning is that it's computationally intensive. Operations on plaintext data are simpler, and less resource-intensive than HE operations. As the complexity of software processes is increased, this often leads to longer processing times. In applications that require a real-time or near-real time response, however, HE's slower pace makes it impractical. For example, an operation that might take a machine learning task only seconds in plaintext could require much longer when run on encrypted data using HE.

Increased Latency: The increased latency, which is related to the computational overhead. The speed of data processing is very important in practice. But in system where timely results are important, the additional time needed for encryption, computation and decryption can prove a bottleneck. In cases such as fraud detection systems or real-time personalization engines, this latency can be very disadvantageous.

Limitations in HE Algorithms: Types and complexity of operations currently supported by HE algorithms are also limited. In fact, the practical operation of FHE schemes is also limited by a growing noise in ciphertext. Without proper management this could eventually make encrypted data too garbled to be understood. In addition, certain kinds of operations are hard to implement efficiently under encryption. Notably these include types like complex non-linear functions often used in advanced machine learning models.

Data Preprocessing and Feature Engineering: Data preprocessing and feature engineering are two difficulties in that part of the workflow. Normalization, missing value treatment or feature selection often involves direct contact with the data. Doing such operations with the data still encrypted is extremely difficult, and prevents one from using a wide variety of machine learning models that make effective use of HE.

Ongoing Research and Development

But these are the limitations of ongoing research in Homomorphic Encryption. Efforts are being made to:

Improve Efficiency: But more efficient algorithms and techniques are being developed by researchers to help reduce the computational overhead associated with HE operations.

Optimize Algorithms for Machine Learning: Special attention is being directed to designing machine-learning HE schemes that fit applications, with an emphasis on supporting a wider scope of operations and reducing noise accumulation.

Hardware Acceleration: Utilizing specialized hardware, such as GPUs or custom-made circuits can decrease the time for HE operations greatly.

Hybrid Approaches: Two privacy-preserving methods, secure multi-party computing and differential privacy combined with HE may yield the best trade-off between security, efficiency, usability.

Challenges and limitations The integration of Homomorphic Encryption with machine learning is not without difficulties, but research to date suggests a promising future. But research will persist in these obstacles, and hopefully someday we can use the newly developed HE to realize privacy-preserving machine learning. It should therefore extend its boundaries, to become increasingly employed in ever wider areas.

7. FUTURE PROSPECTS

Under growing pressure from escalating technology and data privacy problems, collaboration between Homomorphic Encryption (HE) and machine learning may have turned a corner. Looking forward, a number of significant changes are anticipated to influence this industry:

Advancements in Algorithm Efficiency: In the future we will constantly make improvements to HE algorithms, making them more efficient and scalable. The result is that much of the computational overhead and latency problems associated with HE will be eliminated, making it into a more useful tool for many machine learning applications.

Impact of Quantum Computing: Quantum computing presents both a challenge and an opportunity for HE. However, quantum computers could break most existing encryption methods. HE is thought to be virtually immune. This, then, is an ideal solution for future-proofing data security.

Increasing Data Privacy Regulations: Overseas, as more stringent data privacy regulations become law everywhere from Europe's GDPR to California's CCPA, demand for privacy-friendly technologies like HE solutions is poised to grow. Thus, the organizations will try to find a way that lets them use the data for machine learning despite these restrictions.

Collaborative Machine Learning Models: In future, collaborative machine learning models may become increasingly popular. Data from different sources can be used without having to share actual data. HE will play an important part in such models, by encrypting data even during collaborative training processes.

The Critical Role of Data Security in the Age of AI: With more and more big data collected by artificial intelligence, the protection of security and privacy have never been hotter topics. The spread of data-related technologies has raised grave worries about leaks and misappropriation of personal information, also ethical problems. The aim of HE is to use AI and big data but also at the same time protect individual privacy and ensure security of data.

Transformative Potential of Homomorphic Encryption: The impact of theirs on privacy protection is really earth shattering. Therefore, through HE, data can be used without revealing any information. It enables transnational and inter-organizational secured data analysis, but protects individual privacy.

8. CONCLUSION

The integration of HE and ML This is one method of dealing with sensitive data at a time when information is king. Some very complex interaction went on between the pairs here. HE becomes the crucial innovation. With it you can even work on encrypted data, keeping information thoroughly in the dark. This convergence touches many parts of society, from healthcare to finance and government. Sensitive information is a big issue in all these areas. On the other hand, there are obstacles specific to HE in ML. There are two main problems. One is the heavy computational overhead, the other is adapting ML algorithms to encrypted data. But research and development has allowed this field to develop rapidly. As regulations addressing data privacy start to be promulgated and the market for privacy-preserving technologies begins to emerge, it seems that HE in ML is set for a successful future. Finally, the application of Homomorphic Encryption and machine learning will be an important milestone on our way to a day when we can reap the benefits of artificial intelligence (AI) without having to sacrifice data privacy or security. Also, this joint development not only solves the problem of data protection, but also provides a platform for promoting ethical and responsible use of data under the era of artificial intelligence. In short, HE is not only a response to today's privacy problems. It will someday become an incontestable foundation on which the future of secure and humane applications of machine learning must be constructed.

REFERENCES

Gope, P., Millwood, O., & Sikdar, B. (2022). A Scalable Protocol Level Approach to Prevent Machine Learning Attacks on Physically Unclonable Function Based Authentication Mechanisms for Internet of Medical Things. *IEEE Transactions on Industrial Informatics*, *18*(3), 1971–1980. doi:10.1109/ TII.2021.3096048

Govardhana Reddy, H. G., & Raghavendra, K. (2022). Vector space modelling-based intelligent binary image encryption for secure communication. *Journal of Discrete Mathematical Sciences and Cryptography*, *25*(4), 1157–1171. doi:10.1080/09720529.2022.2075090

Gowda, V. D., Prasad, K. D. V., Gite, P., Premkumar, S., Hussain, N., & Chinamuttevi, V. S.K.D.V. (2023). A novel RF-SMOTE model to enhance the definite apprehensions for IoT security attacks. *Journal of Discrete Mathematical Sciences and Cryptography*, 26(3), 861–873. doi:10.47974/JDMSC-1766

Gowda, V. D., Sharma, A., Kumaraswamy, S., Sarma, P., Hussain, N., Dixit, S. K., & Gupta, A. K. (2023). A novel approach of unsupervised feature selection using iterative shrinking and expansion algorithm. *Journal of Interdisciplinary Mathematics*, 26(3), 519–530. doi:10.47974/JIM-1678

Hussain, A. A. J., Pazhani, & A. K., N. (2023). A Novel Method of Enhancing Security Solutions and Energy Efficiency of IoT Protocols. *IJRITCC, 11*(4S), 325–335.

Karatas, G., Demir, O., & Sahingoz, O. K. (2019). A Deep Learning Based Intrusion Detection System on GPUs. *2019 11th International Conference on Electronics, Computers and Artificial Intelligence (ECAI)*, 1-6. 10.1109/ECAI46879.2019.9042132

Knudsen, L. R., & Mathiassen, J. E. (2000). A chosen-plaintext linear attack on DES. *Proceedings of the International Workshop on Fast Software Encryption (FSE)*, 262–272.

Kumar, P. H., & Samanta, T. (2022). Deep Learning Based Optimal Traffic Classification Model for Modern Wireless Networks. *2022 IEEE 19th India Council International Conference (INDICON)*, 1-6. 10.1109/INDICON56171.2022.10039822

Kumar, R., & Ashreetha, B. (2023). Performance Analysis of Energy Efficiency and Security Solutions of Internet of Things Protocols. *IJEER, 11*(2), 442–450. doi:10.37391/ijeer.110226

Kumar & Chaturvedi. (2023). Securing networked image transmission using public-key cryptography and identity authentication. *Journal of Discrete Mathematical Sciences and Cryptography, 26*(3), 779-791. doi:10.47974/JDMSC-1754

Mali, P. S., v, D. G., Tirmare, H. A., Suryawanshi, V. A., & Chaturvedi, A. (2022). Novel Predictive Control and Monitoring System based on IoT for Evaluating Industrial Safety Measures. *IJEER, 10*(4), 1050–1057. doi:10.37391/ijeer.100448

Musa, A., & Mahmood, A. (2021). Client-side Cryptography Based Security for Cloud Computing System. *2021 International Conference on Artificial Intelligence and Smart Systems (ICAIS)*, 594-600. 10.1109/ICAIS50930.2021.9395890

Pavankumar, P., & Darwante, N. K. (2022). Performance Monitoring and Dynamic Scaling Algorithm for Queue Based Internet of Things. *2022 International Conference on Innovative Computing, Intelligent Communication and Smart Electrical Systems (ICSES)*, 1-7. 10.1109/ICSES55317.2022.9914108

Reza, M. N., & Islam, M. (2021). Evaluation of Machine Learning Algorithms using Feature Selection Methods for Network Intrusion Detection Systems. *2021 5th International Conference on Electrical Information and Communication Technology (EICT)*, 1-6. 10.1109/EICT54103.2021.9733679

Sharma & Arun. (2022). Priority Queueing Model-Based IoT Middleware for Load Balancing. *2022 6th International Conference on Intelligent Computing and Control Systems (ICICCS)*, 425-430. 10.1109/ICICCS53718.2022.9788218

Shivashankar & Mehta. (2016). MANET topology for disaster management using wireless sensor network. *International Conference on Communication and Signal Processing, ICCSP 2016*, 736–740. . doi:10.1109/ICCSP.2016.7754242

Singla, A., & Sharma, N. (2022). IoT Group Key Management using Incremental Gaussian Mixture Model. *2022 3rd International Conference on Electronics and Sustainable Communication Systems (ICESC)*, 469-474. 10.1109/ICESC54411.2022.9885644

Tan, S., Knott, B., & Wu, D. J. (2021). CryptGPU: Fast Privacy-Preserving Machine Learning on the GPU. *2021 IEEE Symposium on Security and Privacy (SP)*, 1021-1038. 10.1109/SP40001.2021.00098

Zhu, S., & Han, Y. (2021, August). Generative trapdoors for public key cryptography based on automatic entropy optimization. *China Communications*, *18*(8), 35–46. doi:10.23919/JCC.2021.08.003

Chapter 11

An Effective Combination of Pattern Recognition and Encryption Scheme for Biometric Authentication Systems

Vijayalakshmi G. V. Mahesh

(iD) https://orcid.org/0000-0002-1917-7506

BMS Institute of Technology and Management, India

ABSTRACT

Authentication based on biometric technology is largely preferred in providing access control to the systems. This technology has gained wider attention due to the rise in data generation and the need of data security. The authentication depends upon the physiological traits of human such as face, finger-print, hand geometry, iris scan, retinal scan, and voice. Depending upon the level of security required, a single trait or multiple traits could be utilized. The key features or patterns extracted from the biometric data play a significant role during authentication process that involves pattern recognition. That is, the patterns that exist in the database are matched with the patterns provided during log on. The access is provided based on complete match. Though biometry-based authentication systems provide an effective way of accessing the system, still it is affected by attacks that try to get unauthorized entry into the system. Thus, this chapter focuses on working with the methodologies that provide additional security to the biometric authentication system by utilizing encryption algorithm.

1. INTRODUCTION

The process of authentication is significant related to any system's security as it verifies the user before providing access to the system. Authentication is a part of three step procedure for obtaining access to a resource or system ie., identification, authentication and authorization. Authentication falls into the following types:

DOI: 10.4018/979-8-3693-1642-9.ch011

(i) Knowledge based or password based authentication: this is the most frequently used method for gaining access. But passwords are reused by the users, they are easy to guess and break. The user accounts here are vulnerable to brute force and phishing attacks.

(ii) Two factor authentication: Most commonly known as 2FA. This method is improved version of the knowledge based method as the user has to provide an additional authentication feature apart from the password. The additional feature can be rather like One time password which is shared to the user through email or SMS. The 2FA is more secured as the attacker needs additional information along with login credentials to break in to the system but there is also a possibility of SMS and email breach.

(iii) Single sign on authentication: Here identity provider is used by the user to have an account and the user is verified by identity provider. User with single set of credentials can access multi resources. The benefit of the method lies in reduction of the credentials a user needs to remember. With this method, the attackers can gain access to the systems if identity provider is data breached.

(iv) Token based authentication: In this method user uses token that verifies the identity of the user. Token based authentication relies on physical token such as physical devices: Smart card, Smart key, Smart phone and Computer system or web token to gain access to a system. Tokens need to be kept track of if otherwise leads to locking of the user accounts.

(v) Certificate based authentication: In this authentication method, digital certificates which are the electronic documents with important details generated from public key cryptography are distributed by the certificate authority to identify the users before gaining access to the systems. They are resistant to phishing attacks, also are expensive and time consuming to establish.

(vi) Biometric authentication: In this method, a person's unique physical and behavioral traits that include: face, voice, iris/retina, palm, gait, voice, finger print, shape of ears, facial thermograms and physiological signals are used to gain access to the system. Unlike other methods it is easier to deploy, need not remember and recall and difficult to hack.

Though biometric authentication is proved to be more secure as the physical and behavioral traits of a person are distinct but still is affected by attacks such as spoofing where the attacker masquerades as the authenticated user. With the development of secure cryptographic algorithms one can provide privacy protection to the biometric template. Thus during enrolment, the biometric trait is encrypted to form encrypted-biometric template, further features/patterns are derived from the encrypted template and stored. During verification process, user presents the biometry to the system where the features or the patterns are compared with that of the stored patterns to find the match and thus grant the access while the non-match will result in the discard of the input trait. The chapter presents and discusses about the encryption of the biometric data for authentication in a pattern recognition(PR) approach.

The next section (section 2) presents a review of the literature survey on biometric authentication. Then it is followed by methodology section (section 3) that describes the overall framework and giving details about the biometric data used, encryption scheme, the feature extraction and selection methods. This section The performance metrics used for the evaluation are also presented here. The results and discussion is presented in section 4. The conclusion of the chapter is provided in section 5.

2. RELATED WORK

Numerous research works have been carried on biometric data for authentication under several domains. A comprehensive review on the importance and challenging aspects of design and implementation of authentication system using biometric traits is provided by (Nita, S. L., Mihailescu, M. I., and Pau, V., 2018).

A design of biometric authentication system based on the multiple biometric characteristics of finger print, palm print and iris is presented by (Patil, S. D et al., 2022). The work used discrete cosine and Langranges's interpolation transformations with the mentioned biometric data. The simulation results showed an exceptional average genuine acceptance rate(GAR) of 95.42% and false rejection rate (FRR) of 4.57% indicating secured authentication system where the privacy of the biometric data is preserved.

The literature review identifies the deployment of biometric authentication for several domains such as healthcare, forensics, web applications, e-commerce etc., Securing Internet of Things(IoT) where all the digital devices are connected and information exchange happens is very important. Biometric authentication has proved to provide secure communication in IoT using iris trait (Meena, G and Choudhary, S. 2019). Further biometric authentication is also used to secure Internet of Medical things. (Hamidi, H, 2019) presented a novel means of applying biometrics for smart healthcare to improve the capacity of access and reducing the complexity making it easy to establish and use. (Makrushin, A et al., 2021) discussed about the common requirements on synthetic fingerprint images for biometric authentication and forensic applications. (Scheidat, T., Kalbitz, M., and Vielhauer, C, 2017) have worked on sensing forensic traces of handwriting. The researchers suggest a new method for forensic trace analysis in order to compare the forensic recognition performance using equal error rates obtained from biometric sensors and forensic 2D/3D sensors in parallel. Tongue prints were used as biometric traits for verifying the identity of the users by (Jeddy, N., Radhika, T., and Nithya, S, 2017). The authors evaluated the tongue prints and its variations in male and female population to prove that the tongue prints are unique and cannot be forged.

(Penteado, B. E., and Marana, A. N,2009) developed a system with video data for biometric authentication for e learning applications. Here facial images were captured continuously by a web camera to have a natural interaction between the users online. (Klonovs, J., Petersen, C. K., Olesen, H., and Hammershoj, A, 2013) has come up with system of using Electroencephalogram(EEG) integrated with facial recognition with mobile phones for authenticating the users to gain access. A study was conducted by (Ogbanufe, O., and Kim, D. J,2018). to understand the perceptions, beliefs and concerns of an individual in using biometric traits as compared to credit cards for making electronic payments. A systematic survey on using multiple biometric traits for authentication and enhancing the security levels in cloud computing is provided by(David, B,2023). Social media is one of the greatest concern in terms of security where majority of the population connect and exchange information. As compared to the traditional methods biometric authentication can create safe and trusted social networks with biometric authentication (Chang, H. B., and Schroeter, K. G,2010). A combination of multimodal biometrics: facial image & fingerprints and cryptographic technology was found to be applied for border control applications (Kwon, T., & Moon, H,2008).

The review was further continued to identify the use of different biometric traits for authentication such as EEG(Ingale, M et al., 2020), fingerprint(Hemalatha, S,2020) (Ali, S et al., 2020), facial image(Zulfiqar, M et al., 2019), Electrocardiogram(ECG) (Al Alkeem, 2019) (Kim, S. K et al,2019), Inner-Knuckle-

Print (IKP)(Viswanathan, M et al., 2020), combination of fingerprint and palmprint (Sengar, S. S et al., 2020), voice (Singh, N et al.,2018), retina(Mazumdar, J. B., and Nirmala, S. R, 2018), combination of facial image and voice (Zhang, X et al., 2020), gait (Tao, S, 2018), integration of facial image and gait (Kumar, A et al., 2023) etc.,

Through various research works conducted and presented, the significance of using biometric traits was realized. In parallel it was also identified that the biometric authentication process is vulnerable to spoofing attacks (Abusham, E et al., 2023). The encryption methods are the ideal solution to counter spoofing attack. This chapter presents an effective solution by combining the idea of pattern recognition with encryption scheme applied to a biometric authentication system.

3. METHODOLOGY

The methodology of implementing encryption process on the biometric data to achieve enhanced security of a system is displayed in Figure 1. The methodology is based on the pattern recognition framework

Figure 1. Methodology of the proposed biometric authentication system

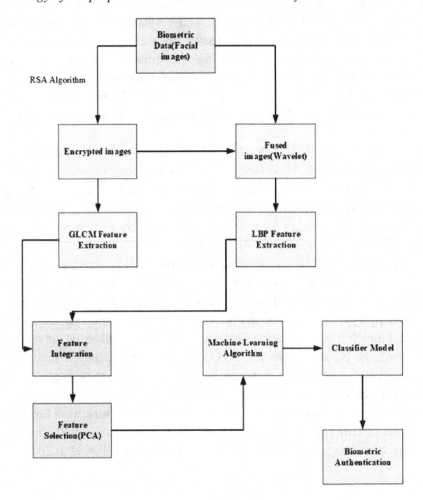

where the encrypted biometric data is provided to the machine learning algorithm to create a classifier model and the model is used to predict the validity of the user to gain the access to the system.

3.1 Elements of Pattern Recognition Framework

The elements of a pattern recognition framework include: Data acquisition, preprocessing, feature extraction, training and learning (Machine learning algorithm) and classification. The elements are to be selected prudently for least classification errors. The requirements of a pattern recognition system are

(i)　The acquired data should be of good quality support derivation of adequate and distinguishable features or attributes. The data can be image, voice, text, sound, video etc.,

(ii)　Preprocessing conditions the data and the method has to be selected based on the requirement. If the input data is image, then the preprocessing could be image filtering, image enhancement, noise removal, segmentation etc.,

(iii)　Feature extraction is the crucial step in pattern recognition as the features represent the key characteristics of the data. Features of the data belonging to the same class must be similar while the features should be different for the data belonging to other classes. Choice of the features are dependent on the type of the data and application for which the pattern recognition system is designed. The success of the PR system depends on the quality of features derived or extracted. The features need to be reliable, robust, discriminative, non-redundant and independent.

(iv)　Training and learning step trains the machine learning algorithm providing examples and class labels. This phase involves assigning the class labels to the data and partitioning the data into training set and testing set. The machine learning algorithm is selected and is provided the labeled data from the training set for training which finally results in a creation of classifier model. Later the classifier model classifies an unseen sample provided to it from the test set in to one of the classes.

The detailed methodology of the work done is presented in the following subsections,

3.2 Biometric Data

The work considered facial image as the biometric data obtained from the Texas 3D Face Recognition Database (Gupta, S et al., 2010). The Texas 3D Face Recognition Database has 1,149 pairs of color and range facial images of 118 persons that have been preprocessed, pose normalized, and captured with a stereo camera. The images have a resolution of 751×501 pixels. For every person, there are between one and eighty-nine images. The images in the database represent a variety of ethnic groups and have differing lighting and expressions. Figures 2.a and 2.b respectively, display representative images (color and range) from the database. The person with one or two facial images were not given considered for the work presented. For the experiment, out of 1,149 image pairs, 963 color images from 18 individuals were chosen where the number of images of a person varied from 4 to 89. These 963 images were split in the ratio of 3:2 for training and testing. Thus the training set has 578 images and the testing set is formed with 385 images.

The images from both the training and testing sets were resized and converted to gray scale as a preprocessing. The preprocessed images were further carried to move through all the steps of pattern recognition framework.

Figure 2. Sample Color(a) and Range(b) Facial Images From the Database

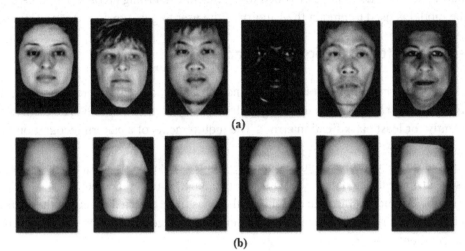

3.3 Image Encryption

As specified earlier image encryption is much essential for securing the biometric data used for authentication. For encrypting the facial images RSA (Gong, L et al.,2019) an asymmetric key cryptographic algorithm was considered. The asymmetric key or public key cryptographic algorithm works on two keys: public key and private key. The private key is kept private to the user while the public key is shared. The strength of this algorithm lies in its difficulty of factorizing the large integer. The large is the product of two large prime number. The private key of the user would be compromised if the attacker succeeds in factorizing the large integer but it could be overcome by selecting a key with larger size. The structure of the RSA algorithm which involves key generation and encryption/decryption is presented here

RSA Algorithm

Key generation	
Select two large prime numbers p and q	$p \neq q$
Calculate n	$n = p \times q$
Calculate Euler's totient function, $\phi(n)$	$\phi(n) = (p-1) \times (q-1)$
Select integer e	$\gcd(\phi(n), e) = 1; 1 < e < \phi(n)$
Calculate d	$d \equiv e^{-1} \bmod \phi(n)$
Public key generated Private key generated	$Pu = \{e, n\}$ $Pr = \{d, n\}$
Encryption	
Message(Plain text), M	$M < n$
Encrypted message(Cipher text), C	$C = M^e \bmod n$
Decryption	
Cipher text, C	
Message, M	$M = C^d \bmod n$

The preprocessed images I(x,y) are passed through the RSA algorithm to obtain the encrypted facial image I_e(x,y). The encryption of every image is carried out pixel by pixel i.e., a window of size 1 x 1 slides through the preprocessed image covering all the rows and columns to generate encrypted pixel for every slide. Next the original images(preprocessed) are fused with the encrypted images to make the attacker confused. This step results in generating the fused image I_f(x,y),

I_f(x,y) = I(x,y) fusion I_e(x,y)

3.4 Image Fusion

Image fusion results in a composite image that integrates the information of the individual images into one that is more informative with better quality. Fusion can be applied to images at different levels such as pixel level, feature level and decision level and the images can be fused in transform or in spatial domain (Kaur, H et al., 2021). Fusion is also specific to domains of application like it could be multi modal, multi view, multi spectral, multi focus, multi resolution or multi temporal (Kaur, H et al., 2021). A survey on the available and practiced methods finds Wavelet transform to be more efficient and successful (Ashwanth, B., and Swamy, K. V,2020). The wavelet transform works by decomposing the images to be fused into various high and low frequency bands, later fusing the wavelet coefficients based on definite rules. For the work considered Daubechies wavelet (Thomas, E et al.,2014) was used as the basis for the reasons such as: it possesses symmetry, completely capable of reconstruction and is non redundant.

The Daubechies wavelet ψ(t) is

$$\psi(t) = 2\sum_{m} (-1)^m \, \overline{a}_{1-m} \, \varphi(2t - m) \tag{1}$$

ψ(t) and $\varphi(t)$ has the range (-M, M+1)

$\varphi(t)$ is the scaling function in the L^2(R) multiresolution analysis given by

$$\varphi(t) = 2\sum_{l} a_l \varphi(2t - l) \tag{2}$$

where a_l are the coefficients that can be both real values and complex valued and $\sum_{l} a_l = 1$

To start with the fusion process, the images I(x,y) and I_e(x,y) are decomposed at several levels. Here for the work on image authentication, the images are decomposed to 2 levels to obtain the wavelet coefficients and the coefficients are later combined using mean fusion rule. Daubechies wavelet preserves multilevel edge information, it provides phase information that is immune to distortions in contrast and noise

Figure 3. Result of the Fusion process: (a) Actual Image, (b) Encrypted Image, and (c) Fusion of Actual and Encrypted Image

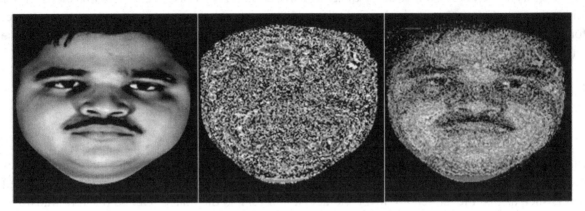

3.5 Feature Extraction

Features play a significant role in pattern recognition systems as they are the key parameters to represent the data in a meaningful form. The quality of the features determines the performance of the system. Features to be derived vary according to the nature of the data and the objective of the pattern recognition system. The work presented uses facial images for authenticating a system. For a system to be more secured, the facial images or the biometric data are encrypted using RSA algorithm at first level and the encrypted images are fused with original images to get fused images at the second level. The result of the encryption and fusion process indicates that the images provide texture information (Figure 2). Thus texture features are extracted from the images of both the levels, that is statistical texture features based on Gray level co-occurrence matrix(GLCM) are derived from encrypted images $I_e(x,y)$ and texture features based on Local binary pattern(LBP) are derived from fused images $I_f(x,y)$. Later they are concatenated to obtain the integrated texture features that carry significant information and can specifically authenticate the system,

3.5.1 GLCM Feature Extraction

GLCM (Haralick, R.M et al., 1973), a second order statistical analysis method works on the relationship between a pair of pixels in an image. It describes the texture of an image by finding the frequency of occurrence of a pair of pixels with definite value in a specific direction(Θ) and distance(d) and then deriving the statistical features from the matrix. GLCM has been used many of the image processing applications under different domains. GLCM based features proved to provide better accuracy for crop classification (] Iqbal, N et al., 2021). The statistical features derived from GLCM were utilized in healthcare to improve the performance of the system, (Mall, P. K et al., 2019) worked on musculoskeletal radiographs and classified them into fracture and no fracture category, (Aggarwal, A. K,2022). and (Hussain, L et al.,2022) reported a promising accuracy of the framework that classified the MRI images based on tumor detection. Further they were utilized to classify the surfaces resulted after the machining process (Prasad, G et al., 2023) that provided an accuracy of 95.3%. They were found to be significant in analyzing vibration signals to detect the faults (Pouyap, M et al., 2021). Several works utilized the combination of GLCM features with other descriptors to improve the data representation. (Gustian, D. A et al., 2019) combined GLCM features with PCA to classify torso fabrics. (Yang, G et al., 2022) integrated GLCM and Gabor features to analyze the flame images for monitoring the boiler combustions in boiler industries.

Here POI Indicates Pixel of Interest

Figure 4. GLCM with four directions and distance d=1

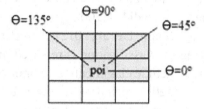

In the work presented, for all the encrypted images $I_e(x,y)$, GLCMs, $G(m, n)$ are framed considering four directions$[\Theta]= [0°, 45°, 90°, 135°]$ and four distances $[(0\ d); (-d\ d); (-d\ 0)\ (-d\ -d)]_{d=1,2,3,4}$. GLCM computation in all four directions and $d=1$ is presented in Figure 4. Thus for every image sixteen GLCMs are obtained and from every GLCM four statistical features contrast, correlation, homogeneity and energy are computed

$$\text{Contrast} = \sum_{m=0}^{N-1}\sum_{n=0}^{N-1}\left(m-n\right)^2 \tag{3}$$

$$\text{Correlation} = \sum_{m=0}^{N-1}\sum_{n=0}^{N-1}\frac{\left(m-\mu_m\right)\left(n-\mu_n\right)}{\sqrt{\sigma_m\ \sigma_n}} \tag{4}$$

$$\text{Homogenity} = \sum_{m=0}^{N-1}\sum_{n=0}^{N-1}\frac{G\left(m,n\right)}{1+\left(m-n\right)^2}$$

$$\text{Energy} = \sqrt{\sum_{m=0}^{N-1}\sum_{n=0}^{N-1}G\left(m,n\right)^2}$$

Here $\mu_m, \mu_n, \sigma_m, \sigma_n$ are the mean and standard deviation respectively and NxN is the size of the matrix.

Later the four features extracted from all the sixteen GLCMs were combined to form a single GLCM statistical feature vector $G_{lcm}SF = \left[Contrast_i, \ Correlation_i, \ Homogenity_i, \ Energy_i \right]_{i=1}^{16}$.

3.5.2 LBP Feature Extraction

LBP is a texture descriptor that captures localized statistical patterns from the images. These type of features are significant in identifying the minutest variations in the spatial distribution of the images by detecting corners, edges, lines and leveled regions. LBP is prevalent in most of the application due to its high discriminating ability and low computational complexity. A tutorial on LBP and its applications towards facial image analysis is found in (Hadid, A,2008). A survey on LBP texture features as applied to image classification is presented by (Nanni, L et al., 2012). A work on modified LBP termed as center symmetric LBP used for object category classification is reported in (Heikkilä, M et al., 2009). LBP has testified in many applications that include classification of brain tumor in to: Glioma, Meningioma and pituitary types (Kaplan, K et al., 2020) which proved to provide an accuracy of 95.56%. LBP has also found its use in data hiding to overcome steganographic attacks (Sahu, M et al.,2022). The feature was also explored to use in weather detection systems (Khan, M. N et al., 2021). (Yuan, H et al., 2023) used multiscale LBP for fault diagnosis in driving gear. LBP was combined with fuzzy color for content based image retrieval system (Zulkurnain, N. F et al., 2022). Further its efficacy was verified in forensic analysis by (Agarwal, S., and Jung, K. H,2023). The feature was put to use in detecting the defects on the fabric surfaces for quality assessment (Pourkaramdel, Z et al., 2022). Research work on integration of GLCM and LBP based features had found to provide favorable results in (Barburiceanu, S et al., 2021).

LBP features are extracted from the fused facial images $I_f(x,y)$. As LBP involves extracting localized features, the images are divided into blocks or windows of size 3x3. Each block is processed serially to extract the texture features. For every block, the extraction involves

Figure 5. Illustration of first and second step of LBP generation

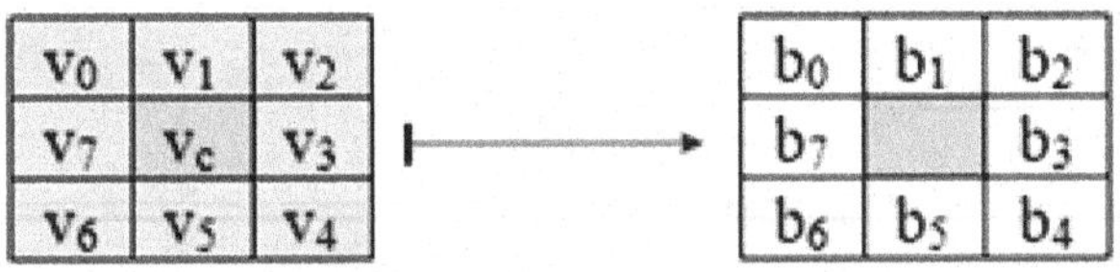

(i)   Identifying the center pixel with its intensity value

(ii)   The intensities of the center pixel and the surrounding pixels are compared to generate a binary vector B

$B=[s(v_0 - v_c), \ s(v_1 - v_c), \ s(v_2 - v_c), \ s(v_3 - v_c), \ s(v_4 - v_c), \ s(v_5 - v_c), \ s(v_6 - v_c), \ s(v_7 - v_c)]$

$B=[b_0, \ b_1, \ b_2, \ b_3, \ b_4, \ b_5, \ b_6, \ b_7]$, here b_j is the binary value = 1 or 0

where s(v) is defined as $s\left(v \right) = \begin{cases} 1, v < 0 \\ 0, v \geq 0 \end{cases}$

(iii) Compute the LBP of the center pixel using the binary set B

$$LBP\left(v_c\right) = \sum_{j=1}^{7} b_j 2^j \tag{7}$$

(iv) The steps from (i) till (iii) are repeated for all the blocks of the image to obtain the LBP map of the fused image.

(v) Finally the texture feature is obtained from the histogram of the LBP map, LBP_{hist}

After extracting the GLCM statistical feature vector $G_{lcm}SF$ from encrypted facial images and LBP features LBP_{hist} from the fused images, the features are concatenated to form the integrated texture features $IT_{ex}F = [G_{lcm}SF: LBP_{hist}]$.

3.5.3 Feature Selection

From the texture features extracted only a subset of features that are pertinent are selected removing the redundant features. Several methods are available for feature selection such as wrapper methods, embedded methods and filter methods. The most widely used feature selection method with dimensionality reduction is Principal Component Analysis(PCA) (Song, F., Guo, Z., & Mei, D. (2010), (Omuya, E. O., Okeyo, G. O., & Kimwele, M. W. (2021). The feature matrix $[F_x]$ is created using the final feature vector ITexF = [GlcmSF: LBPhist] for all the images in the dataset. The columns of $[F_x]$ are the texture features and the rows are number of samples or the images. The most relevant features are selected from this feature matrix using PCA. The process includes calculating the covariance matrix first of PCA using $[F_x]$ and find the Eigen values and Eigen vectors of the matrix. The Eigen values are arranged in the descending order and the first M largest Eigen values are noted. Later the columns of $[F_x]$ (texture features) that correspond to the first M largest Eigen values are selected to form the subset of $[F_x]$ '$[F_{xs}]$' that correspond to new feature matrix with reduced number of features. These features are further provided to the machine learning algorithm to create a classifier model and the model is used to predict the validity of the user to gain the access to the system.

3.6 Classification and Evaluation

The texture features are input to the machine learning algorithms (Bishop, C. M., & Nasrabadi, N. M. (2006) k Nearest Neighbor(kNN), Support vector machine(SVM), Naive Bayesian(NB), Linear discriminant analysis, Quadratic discriminant analysis(QDA) for learning, training and classifier model creation. The model is tested and evaluated to assess the performance of the system. The performance is evaluated based on the performance metrics: Accuracy, Recall, Precision, F1 score, Kappa value and Matthew's correlation coefficient(MCC) computed (Mahesh, V. G., Raj, A. N. J., & Nersisson, R,2022) using the entries of the contingency or confusion matrix(CM). CM is a 2x2 matrix that provides the classification summary in terms of true positive(TP), true negative(TN), false positive(FP) and false negative.

Figure 6. Contingency table or confusion matrix

		Actual class	
		True	False
Predicted class	True	**True Positive**	**False Positive**
	False	**False Negative**	**True Negative**

	Correct classifications
	Misclassifications

The performance measures are as computed

$$Accuracy = \frac{(TP + TN)}{(TP + TN + FP + FN)} \qquad (8)$$

$$Precision = \frac{TP}{(TP + FP)} \qquad (9)$$

$$Recall = \frac{TP}{(TP + FN)} \qquad (10)$$

$$MCC = \frac{(TP \times TN) - (FP \times FN)}{(Y)}$$

where

$$Y = \sqrt{((TP + FP) \times (TP + FN) \times (TN + FP) \times (TN + FN))} \qquad (11)$$

$$F1score = \frac{(2 \times Precision \times Recall)}{(Precision + Recall)} \qquad (12)$$

$$Kappa = \frac{(Po - Pe)}{(1 - Pe)}$$

where

$$P_o = Accuracy \text{ and } Pe = \frac{\left((TP + FN) \times (TP + FP) + (FP + TN) \times (FN + TN)\right)}{(TP + TN + FP + FN)} \tag{13}$$

4. RESULTS AND DISCUSSION

The objective of the proposed work is the encryption of the biometric data for authentication in a pattern recognition(PR) approach. The detailed implementation of the proposed methodology is illustrated in Figure 7. The biometric data considered for the experiment was facial images from Texas 3D face recognition dataset that has both RGB and range/depth images. The simulation was carried on 963 RGB images. These 963 of images were split in the ratio of 3:2 for training and testing. Thus the training set has 578 images and the testing set is formed with 385 images. Initially the images of both data sets training and testing were converted to grayscale and resized as a preprocessing step. Next the images were encrypted using the RSA algorithm and then the encrypted images were fused with actual images for increasing the security.

Figure 7. Implementation of the Proposed Methodology

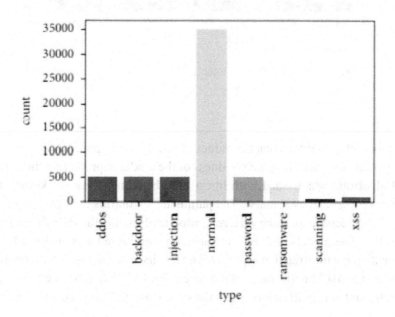

Now the two sets of images Encrypted and fused from both the training and testing datasets were provided to feature extraction and selection process as explained in section 3.5. The resulted feature matrices $[F_{xs\_tr}]$ and $[F_{xs\_te}]$ were provided for training and testing respectively. The feature set $[F_{xs\_tr}]$ was labelled with class categories and the labelled matrix was provided to k Nearest Neighbor(kNN), Support vector machine(SVM), Naive Bayesian(NB), Linear discriminant analysis, Quadratic discriminant analysis(QDA) machine learning algorithms for learning, training and building the classifier models. During this process the learnable parameters were varied to reduce the training error.

In case of kNN classifier, the number of nearest neighbors were varied from 2 to 6 keeping the Euclidean distance metric. Once the kNN model was built, it was testing using $[F_{xs\_te}]$. The results of the test were evaluated for its performance for all the nearest neighbor values using the metrics calculated using the equations from (8) to (13). The performance metrics obtained after the evaluation is displayed in Figure 8.

Figure 8. Performance Metrics Computed for kNN Model

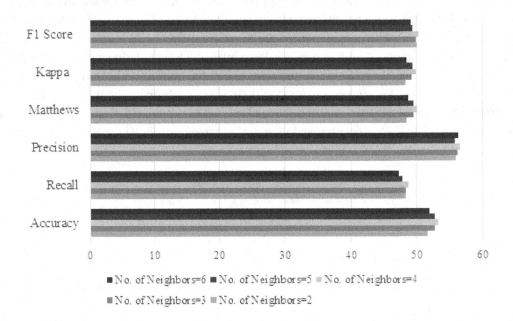

From the evaluation, it can be seen that the values of accuracy and precision metrics are high as compared to the other parameters indicating the goodness of the model in predicting the categories correctly.

Further, SVM algorithm was trained with linear and rbf kernels. For rbf kernel, the hyperparameters C and gamma were set and later tuned. The parameter C controls the error while gamma provides curvature weight of the decision boundary. Here C was fixed to one, the default value and gamma was varied from 0.1 to 0.7. The models with all the variation were tested and evaluated. The performance metrics of the evaluation are illustrated in Figure 9. The results indicated the variation in the metrics with gamma shifting from 0.1 to 0.3 but the metrics remained almost constant for the later variation. Thus the gamma value after 0.3 did not significantly affect the performance. The performance of the SVM model

Figure 9. Performance Metrics Computed for SVM Models

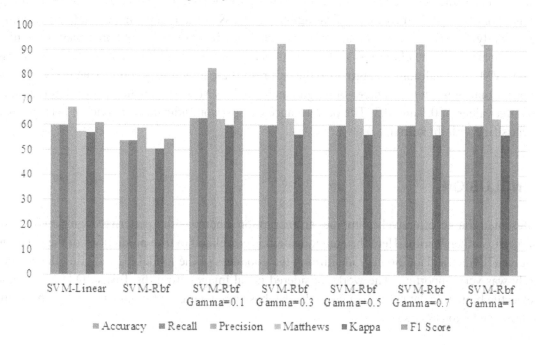

indicated a higher F1 score and much higher precision of 92.58% with gamma=0.3. As F1score is the harmonic mean of Precision and Recall, a higher value of it points towards better quality classification.

Later, the NB, LDA and QDA algorithms were trained with labeled training data set. For training SVD solver is set for LDA and the regularization parameter of QDA is tuned to regularize the covariance estimates. The performance of NB, LDA and QDA models is depicted in Figure 10. These classi-

Figure 10. Performance Metrics Computed for NB, LDA, and QDA Classifier Models

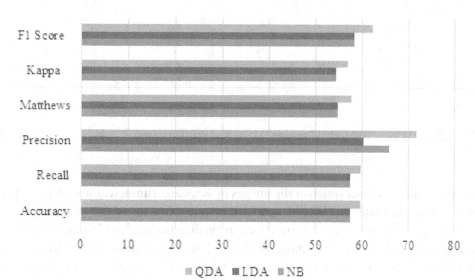

fier models also turned out be good in terms of better F1 score and Precision. As noticed from Figure 8, NB and QDA has performed well indicating the goodness of the models in precisely classifying the classes. Finally, a performance comparison of all the classifiers are made and presented in Figure 11. For the comparison all the classifiers with the obtained performance metrics are considered. In case of kNN and SVM, the conditions that provided the best results are took into account. That is kNN provided better performance when the number of neighbors=4 and SVM worked better with rbf kernel and for the Gamma values of 0.1 and 0.3. The performance comparison indicates exceptional performance of SVM classifier with rbf kernel.

5. CONCLUSION

This presented chapter effectively combines an encryption scheme with a pattern recognition framework for biometric authentication. Here the authentication is correlated to true predictions of the class labels of the given biometric data. So here identifying the goodness of the model in predicting the categories correctly was very important. The work considered facial images from the Texas 3D face recognition dataset as the biometric data. The images in the database has a variety of ethnic groups and have differing lighting and expressions.

Figure 11. Performance Comparison of All the Classifiers

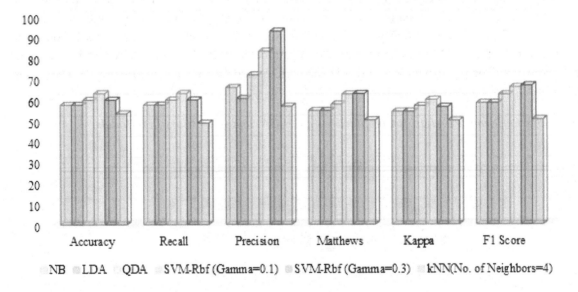

The experiment involved encryption of the images by RSA algorithm, fusion of actual and encrypted images using Debauchees wavelet, GLCM and LBP texture extraction from the encrypted and fused images, concatenation of features and feature selection, feeding the selected features to kNN, SVM, NB, LDA and QDA machine learning algorithms for classifier model creation and finally evaluation of the models. The models were evaluated with the performance metrics Accuracy, precision, recall, MCC, kappa and F1 score. As compared to all the metrics the precision was high in case of all models and of those SVM with rbf kernel was outstanding. This indicates that encryption of images incorporated within the pattern recognition framework was significant in providing better biometric authentication to get access to the systems.

REFERENCES

Abusham, E., Ibrahim, B., Zia, K., & Rehman, M. (2023). Facial image encryption for secure face recognition system. *Electronics (Basel)*, *12*(3), 774. doi:10.3390/electronics12030774

Agarwal, S., & Jung, K. H. (2023). Forensic analysis and detection using polycolor model binary pattern for colorized images. *Multimedia Tools and Applications*, 1–20. doi:10.1007/s11042-023-16675-1

Aggarwal, A. K. (2022). Learning texture features from glcm for classification of brain tumor mri images using random forest classifier. *Transactions on Signal Processing*, *18*, 60–63. doi:10.37394/232014.2022.18.8

Al Alkeem, E., Kim, S. K., Yeun, C. Y., Zemerly, M. J., Poon, K. F., Gianini, G., & Yoo, P. D. (2019). An enhanced electrocardiogram biometric authentication system using machine learning. *IEEE Access : Practical Innovations, Open Solutions*, *7*, 123069–123075. doi:10.1109/ACCESS.2019.2937357

Ali, S. S., Baghel, V. S., Ganapathi, I. I., & Prakash, S. (2020). Robust biometric authentication system with a secure user template. *Image and Vision Computing*, *104*, 104004. doi:10.1016/j.imavis.2020.104004

Ashwanth, B., & Swamy, K. V. (2020, March). Medical image fusion using transform techniques. In *2020 5th International conference on devices, circuits and systems (ICDCS)* (pp. 303-306). IEEE. 10.1109/ICDCS48716.2020.243604

Barburiceanu, S., Terebes, R., & Meza, S. (2021). 3D texture feature extraction and classification using GLCM and LBP-based descriptors. *Applied Sciences (Basel, Switzerland)*, *11*(5), 2332. doi:10.3390/app11052332

Bishop, C. M., & Nasrabadi, N. M. (2006). *Pattern recognition and machine learning* (Vol. 4). New York: Springer.

Chang, H. B., & Schroeter, K. G. (2010, January). Creating safe and trusted social networks with biometric user authentication. In *International Conference on Ethics and Policy of Biometrics* (pp. 89-95). Springer Berlin Heidelberg. 10.1007/978-3-642-12595-9_12

David, B. (2023, April). An Analytical Survey on Multi-Biometric Authentication System for Enhancing the Security Levels in Cloud Computing. In *2023 Eighth International Conference on Science Technology Engineering and Mathematics (ICONSTEM)* (pp. 1-6). IEEE.

Gong, L., Qiu, K., Deng, C., & Zhou, N. (2019). An optical image compression and encryption scheme based on compressive sensing and RSA algorithm. *Optics and Lasers in Engineering*, *121*, 169–180. doi:10.1016/j.optlaseng.2019.03.006

Gupta, S., Castleman, K. R., Markey, M. K., & Bovik, A. C. (2010). Texas 3D Face Recognition Database. *2010 IEEE Southwest Symposium on Image Analysis & Interpretation (SSIAI)*, 97–100. http://live. ece.utexas.edu/research/texas3dfr/index.htm

Gustian, D. A., Rohmah, N. L., Shidik, G. F., Fanani, A. Z., & Pramunendar, R. A. (2019, September). Classification of troso fabric using SVM-RBF multi-class method with GLCM and PCA feature extraction. In *2019 International Seminar on Application for Technology of Information and Communication (iSemantic)* (pp. 7-11). IEEE. 10.1109/ISEMANTIC.2019.8884329

Hadid, A. (2008). *The Local Binary Pattern Approach and its Applications to Face Analysis. 2008 First Workshops on Image Processing Theory.* Tools and Applications. doi:10.1109/IPTA.2008.4743795

Hamidi, H. (2019). An approach to develop the smart health using Internet of Things and authentication based on biometric technology. *Future Generation Computer Systems*, *91*, 434–449. doi:10.1016/j. future.2018.09.024

Haralick, R. M., Dinstein, I., & Shanmugam, K. (1973). *Textural features for image classification.* Trans. Syst. Man Cybern. doi:10.1109/TSMC.1973.4309314

Heikkilä, M., Pietikäinen, M., & Schmid, C. (2009). Description of interest regions with local binary patterns. *Pattern Recognition*, *42*(3), 425–436. doi:10.1016/j.patcog.2008.08.014

Hemalatha, S. (2020, February). A systematic review on Fingerprint based Biometric Authentication System. In *2020 International Conference on Emerging Trends in Information Technology and Engineering (ic-ETITE)* (pp. 1-4). IEEE. 10.1109/ic-ETITE47903.2020.342

Hussain, L., Malibari, A. A., Alzahrani, J. S., Alamgeer, M., Obayya, M., Al-Wesabi, F. N., Mohsen, H., & Hamza, M. A. (2022). Bayesian dynamic profiling and optimization of important ranked energy from gray level co-occurrence (GLCM) features for empirical analysis of brain MRI. *Scientific Reports*, *12*(1), 15389. doi:10.1038/s41598-022-19563-0 PMID:36100621

Ingale, M., Cordeiro, R., Thentu, S., Park, Y., & Karimian, N. (2020). Ecg biometric authentication: A comparative analysis. *IEEE Access : Practical Innovations, Open Solutions*, *8*, 117853–117866. doi:10.1109/ACCESS.2020.3004464

Iqbal, N., Mumtaz, R., Shafi, U., & Zaidi, S. M. H. (2021). Gray level co-occurrence matrix (GLCM) texture based crop classification using low altitude remote sensing platforms. PeerJ Comp. *Sci.*, *7*, e536. PMID:34141878

Jeddy, N., Radhika, T., & Nithya, S. (2017). Tongue prints in biometric authentication: A pilot study. *Journal of Oral and Maxillofacial Pathology : JOMFP*, *21*(1), 176. doi:10.4103/jomfp.JOMFP_185_15 PMID:28479712

Kaplan, K., Kaya, Y., Kuncan, M., & Ertunç, H. M. (2020). Brain tumor classification using modified local binary patterns (LBP) feature extraction methods. *Medical Hypotheses*, *139*, 109696. doi:10.1016/j. mehy.2020.109696 PMID:32234609

Kaur, H., Koundal, D., & Kadyan, V. (2021). Image fusion techniques: A survey. *Archives of Computational Methods in Engineering*, *28*(7), 4425–4447. doi:10.1007/s11831-021-09540-7 PMID:33519179

Khan, M. N., Das, A., Ahmed, M. M., & Wulff, S. S. (2021). Multilevel weather detection based on images: A machine learning approach with histogram of oriented gradient and local binary pattern-based features. *Journal of Intelligent Transport Systems*, *25*(5), 513–532. doi:10.1080/15472450.2021.1944860

Kim, S. K., Yeun, C. Y., Damiani, E., & Lo, N. W. (2019). A machine learning framework for biometric authentication using electrocardiogram. *IEEE Access : Practical Innovations, Open Solutions*, *7*, 94858–94868. doi:10.1109/ACCESS.2019.2927079

Klonovs, J., Petersen, C. K., Olesen, H., & Hammershoj, A. (2013). ID proof on the go: Development of a mobile EEG-based biometric authentication system. *IEEE Vehicular Technology Magazine*, *8*(1), 81–89. doi:10.1109/MVT.2012.2234056

Kumar, A., Jain, S., & Kumar, M. (2023). Face and gait biometrics authentication system based on simplified deep neural networks. *International Journal of Information Technology : an Official Journal of Bharati Vidyapeeth's Institute of Computer Applications and Management*, *15*(2), 1005–1014. doi:10.1007/s41870-022-01087-5

Kwon, T., & Moon, H. (2008). Biometric authentication for border control applications. *IEEE Transactions on Knowledge and Data Engineering*, *20*(8), 1091–1096. doi:10.1109/TKDE.2007.190716

Mahesh, V. G., Raj, A. N. J., & Nersisson, R. (2022). Implementation of Machine Learning-Aided Speech Analysis for Speaker Accent Identification Applied to Audio Forensics. In *Aiding Forensic Investigation Through Deep Learning and Machine Learning Frameworks* (pp. 174–194). IGI Global. doi:10.4018/978-1-6684-4558-7.ch008

Makrushin, A., Kauba, C., Kirchgasser, S., Seidlitz, S., Kraetzer, C., Uhl, A., & Dittmann, J. (2021, June). General requirements on synthetic fingerprint images for biometric authentication and forensic investigations. In *Proceedings of the 2021 ACM Workshop on Information Hiding and Multimedia Security* (pp. 93-104). 10.1145/3437880.3460410

Mall, P. K., Singh, P. K., & Yadav, D. (2019, December). GLCM based feature extraction and medical X-RAY image classification using machine learning techniques. In *2019 IEEE Conference on Information and Communication Technology* (pp. 1-6). IEEE. 10.1109/CICT48419.2019.9066263

Mazumdar, J. B., & Nirmala, S. R. (2018). Retina based biometric authentication system: A review. *International Journal of Advanced Research in Computer Science*, *9*(1). Advance online publication. doi:10.26483/ijarcs.v9i1.5322

Meena, G., & Choudhary, S. (2019). Biometric authentication in internet of things: A conceptual view. *Journal of Statistics and Management Systems*, *22*(4), 643–652. doi:10.1080/09720510.2019.1609722

Nanni, L., Lumini, A., & Brahnam, S. (2012). Survey on LBP based texture descriptors for image classification. *Expert Systems with Applications*, *39*(3), 3634–3641. doi:10.1016/j.eswa.2011.09.054

Nita, S. L., Mihailescu, M. I., & Pau, V. C. (2018). Security and cryptographic challenges for authentication based on biometrics data. *Cryptography*, *2*(4), 39. doi:10.3390/cryptography2040039

Ogbanufe, O., & Kim, D. J. (2018). Comparing fingerprint-based biometrics authentication versus traditional authentication methods for e-payment. *Decision Support Systems*, *106*, 1–14. doi:10.1016/j.dss.2017.11.003

Omuya, E. O., Okeyo, G. O., & Kimwele, M. W. (2021). Feature selection for classification using principal component analysis and information gain. *Expert Systems with Applications*, *174*, 114765. doi:10.1016/j.eswa.2021.114765

Patil, S. D., Raut, R., Jhaveri, R. H., Ahanger, T. A., Dhade, P. V., Kathole, A. B., & Vhatkar, K. N. (2022). Robust authentication system with privacy preservation of biometrics. *Security and Communication Networks*, *2022*, 2022. doi:10.1155/2022/7857975

Penteado, B. E., & Marana, A. N. (2009). A video-based biometric authentication for e-Learning web applications. *Enterprise Information Systems: 11th International Conference, ICEIS 2009, Milan, Italy, May 6-10, 2009. Proceedings*, *11*, 770–779.

Pourkaramdel, Z., Fekri-Ershad, S., & Nanni, L. (2022). Fabric defect detection based on completed local quartet patterns and majority decision algorithm. *Expert Systems with Applications*, *198*, 116827. doi:10.1016/j.eswa.2022.116827

Pouyap, M., Bitjoka, L., Mfoumou, E., & Toko, D. (2021). Improved Bearing Fault Diagnosis by Feature Extraction Based on GLCM, Fusion of Selection Methods, and Multiclass-Naïve Bayes Classification. *Journal of Signal and Information Processing*, *12*(4), 71–85. doi:10.4236/jsip.2021.124004

Prasad, G., Gaddale, V. S., Kamath, R. C., Shekaranaik, V. J., & Pai, S. P. (2023). A Study of Dimensionality Reduction in GLCM Feature-Based Classification of Machined Surface Images. *Arabian Journal for Science and Engineering*, 1–23.

Sahu, M., Padhy, N., Gantayat, S. S., & Sahu, A. K. (2022). Local binary pattern-based reversible data hiding. *CAAI Transactions on Intelligence Technology*, *7*(4), 695–709. doi:10.1049/cit2.12130

Scheidat, T., Kalbitz, M., & Vielhauer, C. (2017). Biometric authentication based on 2D/3D sensing of forensic handwriting traces. *IET Biometrics*, *6*(4), 316–324. doi:10.1049/iet-bmt.2016.0127

Sengar, S. S., Hariharan, U., & Rajkumar, K. (2020, March). Multimodal biometric authentication system using deep learning method. In *2020 International Conference on Emerging Smart Computing and Informatics (ESCI)* (pp. 309-312). IEEE. 10.1109/ESCI48226.2020.9167512

Singh, N., Agrawal, A., & Khan, R. A. (2018). Voice biometric: A technology for voice based authentication. *Advanced Science, Engineering and Medicine*, *10*(7-8), 754–759. doi:10.1166/asem.2018.2219

Song, F., Guo, Z., & Mei, D. (2010, November). Feature selection using principal component analysis. In *2010 international conference on system science, engineering design and manufacturing informatization* (Vol. 1, pp. 27-30). IEEE.

Tao, S., Zhang, X., Cai, H., Lv, Z., Hu, C., & Xie, H. (2018). Gait based biometric personal authentication by using MEMS inertial sensors. *Journal of Ambient Intelligence and Humanized Computing*, *9*(5), 1705–1712. doi:10.1007/s12652-018-0880-6

Thomas, E., Nair, P. B., John, S. N., & Dominic, M. (2014, July). Image fusion using Daubechies complex wavelet transform and lifting wavelet transform: a multiresolution approach. In *2014 Annual International Conference on Emerging Research Areas: Magnetics, Machines and Drives (AICERA/iCMMD)* (pp. 1-5). IEEE. 10.1109/AICERA.2014.6908205

Viswanathan, M., Loganathan, G. B., & Srinivasan, S. (2020, September). IKP based biometric authentication using artificial neural network. In AIP Conference Proceedings (Vol. 2271, No. 1). AIP Publishing. doi:10.1063/5.0025229

Yang, G., He, Y., Li, X., Liu, H., & Lan, T. (2022). Gabor-glcm-based texture feature extraction using flame image to predict the o2 content and no x. *ACS Omega*, 7(5), 3889–3899. doi:10.1021/acsomega.1c03397 PMID:35155886

Yuan, H., Lei, Z., You, X., Dong, Z., Zhang, H., Zhang, C., Zhao, Y., & Liu, J. (2023). Fault diagnosis of driving gear in rack and pinion drives based on multi-scale local binary pattern extraction and sparse representation. *Measurement Science & Technology*, 34(5), 055017. doi:10.1088/1361-6501/acbab4

Zhang, X., Cheng, D., Jia, P., Dai, Y., & Xu, X. (2020). An efficient android-based multimodal biometric authentication system with face and voice. *IEEE Access : Practical Innovations, Open Solutions*, 8, 102757–102772. doi:10.1109/ACCESS.2020.2999115

Zulfiqar, M., Syed, F., Khan, M. J., & Khurshid, K. (2019, July). Deep face recognition for biometric authentication. In *2019 international conference on electrical, communication, and computer engineering (ICECCE)* (pp. 1-6). IEEE.

Zulkurnain, N. F., Azhar, M. A., & Mallik, M. A. (2022, February). Content-Based Image Retrieval System Using Fuzzy Colour and Local Binary Pattern with Apache Lucene. In *Proceedings of Second International Conference on Advances in Computer Engineering and Communication Systems: ICACECS 2021* (pp. 13-20). Singapore: Springer Nature Singapore. 10.1007/978-981-16-7389-4_2

212

Chapter 12
Enhancing Crypto Ransomware Detection Through Network Analysis and Machine Learning

S. Metilda Florence
SRM Institute of Science and Technology, India

Shreya Sinha
SRM Institute of Science and Technology, India

Akshay Raghava
SRM Institute of Science and Technology, India

Kavya Pasagada
SRM Institute of Science and Technology, India

M. J. Yadhu Krishna
SRM Institute of Science and Technology, India

Tanuja Kharol
SRM Institute of Science and Technology, India

ABSTRACT

Crypto ransomware presents an ever-growing menace as it encrypts victim data and demands a ransom for decryption. The increasing frequency of ransomware attacks underscores the need for advanced detection techniques. A machine learning classification model is proposed to identify ransomware families. These models utilize specific network traffic features, with a particular emphasis on analyzing the user datagram protocol (UDP) and internet control message protocol (ICMP). Importantly, this approach incorporates feature selection to enhance efficiency without compromising accuracy, resulting in reduced memory usage and faster processing times. The proposed experiment utilizes various machine learning algorithms, including decision trees and random forest, to create highly accurate models for classifying ransomware families. Furthermore, the experiment combined network traffic analysis with other sophisticated methods such as behavioral analysis and honeypot deployment to effectively scale crypto ransomware detection.

DOI: 10.4018/979-8-3693-1642-9.ch012

1. INTRODUCTION

Crypto ransomware is a malware software encrypting files, demanding payment in cryptocurrency for decryption. It spreads through phishing, exploiting vulnerabilities. Attackers prefer crypto for anonymity. Prevention involves updates, cybersecurity measures, backups, and user education. Incident response plans aid recovery from these increasingly sophisticated cyber threats.

Crypto ransomware typically relies on traditional communication protocols such as HTTP or HTTPS(Krzysztof Cabaj, Marcin Gregorczyk, and Wojciech Mazurczyk, 2018) for command and control (C2) communication, rather than UDP or ICMP. However, cyber threats evolve, and attackers may experiment with different protocols. A study conducted by (May Almousa, Janet Osawere, and Mohd Anwar, 2021) leveraged analysis of TCP packets to detect Crypto ransomware. TCP serves as a fundamental protocol in network communication; however, its application in the context of Crypto ransomware detection comes with inherent limitations. One significant challenge lies in the prevalence of encrypted traffic, a common tactic employed by modern ransomware variants. Encryption serves to secure communications, rendering the inspection of packet content a formidable task for detection mechanisms. As a result, identifying malicious behavior within encrypted TCP packets becomes increasingly challenging.

Moreover, ransomware developers often exploit the dynamic nature of TCP communication. Techniques like port-hopping, wherein the ransomware rapidly switches between different network ports, hence posing difficulties for TCP-based detection systems. The ability of these mechanisms to adapt to rapidly changing communication patterns and port numbers becomes a critical consideration in countering the evasion tactics of sophisticated ransomware variants.

Employing strong network security, monitoring, and regular updates helps mitigate risks associated with potential variations in ransomware tactics. Attackers might leverage UDP for specific purposes such as command and control communications or data exfiltration, but it's not as prevalent as TCP.

Attackers might misuse ICMP for certain functionalities due to its presence in many networks and the possibility of bypassing some firewall rules.

1.1 Contributions to This Work

This chapter is organized into several sections to provide a comprehensive understanding of the proposed architecture for enhancing crypto ransomware detection through the integration of unconventional network protocols and machine learning algorithms. The structured approach ensures clarity and facilitates a step-by-step exploration of the research methodology and findings.

The first section of the paper delineates the foundational stages of the proposed architecture. This involves the meticulous collection of crypto ransomware network traffic data, an essential step in building a robust dataset for analysis. The chosen network protocols, UDP and ICMP, serve as the focal point for feature extraction and selection, aiming to capture distinctive patterns indicative of malicious activity. By isolating relevant packet fields, the research establishes a framework for effective data processing and subsequent utilization in machine learning algorithms.

The subsequent section delves into the intricacies of feature extraction and selection, elucidating the rationale behind choosing specific fields from UDP and ICMP packets. This process is fundamental in distilling pertinent information from the vast array of network traffic data, facilitating the identification of unique characteristics associated with crypto ransomware. The rationale behind the selection of features is expounded upon, providing insight into the considerations that guided this critical aspect of the research.

Following this, the paper transitions into a detailed exploration of the machine learning algorithms employed in the proposed architecture. Notably, the inclusion of algorithms such as the gradient boosting algorithm and decision tree signifies a deliberate choice to leverage diverse methodologies for enhanced accuracy and robustness. A comprehensive discussion on the implementation and customization of these algorithms within the context of crypto ransomware detection enriches the understanding of their role in the overall architecture.

A pivotal section of the paper focuses on the practical application of the proposed model. Here, the gathered data on malicious network traffic serves as the foundation for training and validating the machine learning models. This step aligns the research with the overarching goal of detecting various ransomware families, emphasizing the real-world relevance of the proposed architecture.

Section II Describes the Proposed Architecture, Section III Describes the Implementation, Section IV Describes the Results obtained, Section V concludes the paper and Section VI consists of references used in the paper.

2. RELATED WORK

In June 2019, Lake City, Florida, found itself ambushed in the grips of a formidable cybersecurity menace, a meticulously orchestrated crypto ransomware attack. The assault commenced with a seemingly innocuous phishing email that served as the gateway for the infiltrators. Employing a combination of Emotet and TrickBot malware, the attackers exploited vulnerabilities to navigate the city's digital infrastructure. The climax of their offensive was marked by the deployment of the notorious Ryuk crypto ransomware, a pernicious variant known for its sophisticated encryption techniques.

Once Ryuk took hold, its insidious algorithms swiftly encrypted critical files and systems across Lake City's network, rendering them inaccessible and held hostage by cryptographic shackles. The malicious actors behind the attack, shrouded in anonymity, left behind a digital ransom note. In the stark language of the note, a demand echoed: a substantial ransom payment in Bitcoin, with a clear ultimatum — pay promptly or face irrevocable loss of essential data.

The repercussions were profound, resonating through the heart of Lake City's operations. Vital services, including email systems and the online utility payment infrastructure, were thrust into disarray. The city faced an excruciating dilemma, a modern-day ransom conundrum: whether to succumb to the demands of the cybercriminals and expedite the recovery process, or to withstand the onslaught and explore alternative avenues for system restoration.

In a strategic decision fraught with complexities, Lake City chose to meet the ransom demand. The cryptocurrency transaction facilitated the acquisition of a decryption key from the perpetrators. Yet, the aftermath was far from a swift resolution. The road to recovery was paved with intricate challenges, underscoring the intricate nature of combating crypto ransomware.

The incident triggered a cascade of investigations, involving not only local authorities but also federal agencies such as the FBI. Attribution in the realm of crypto ransomware attacks is notoriously elusive, with the digital footprints often leading through a labyrinth of virtual obfuscation. Despite the collaborative efforts to unearth the malefactors, their identities remained shrouded in the digital shadows.

The Lake City crypto ransomware attack serves as a poignant reminder of the relentless evolution of cyber threats and the critical importance of proactive cybersecurity measures. It illuminated the imperative for organizations to fortify their defenses against phishing attempts, bolster incident response capabilities, and contemplate the ethical and strategic implications of acceding to ransom demands. As cities and institutions navigate the digital landscape, the specter of crypto ransomware looms large, underscoring the ever-present need for vigilance and resilience in the face of evolving cyber threats.

Figure 1. Number of Ransomware Attacks in Recent Years

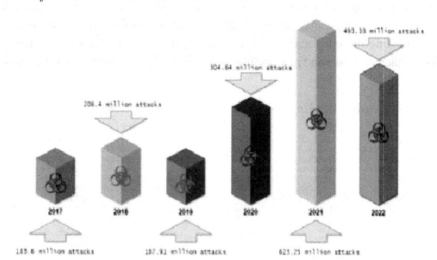

3. METHODOLOGY

3.1 Concept of Crypto Ransomware

Crypto ransomware operates like a digital intruder, slipping into a user's computer with the sole purpose of encrypting all files or, in more severe cases, the entire system. This encryption process is similar to locking the files in a virtual vault that can only be accessed with a specific key. The attackers behind this malicious software demand a ransom, typically in cryptocurrency, as payment in exchange for providing the decryption key or tool necessary to unlock the files (D Udhaya Mugil, S Metilda Florence, 2022). The use of cryptocurrency adds a layer of anonymity for the attackers, making it difficult to trace their identities.

The hallmark of this ransomware is its utilization of robust encryption algorithms, such as Advanced Encryption Standard (AES) or Rivest–Shamir–Adleman (RSA), transforming valuable files into inaccessible entities. This creates a distressing hostage situation for the victim, who is left without access to their important data

To communicate their demands and intensify the pressure on the victim, the attackers employ a ransom note. This note is typically delivered through anonymous networks (Hamdan Ahmed, S Metilda Florence, Ashlesh Upganlawar, 2022), obscuring the identity of the perpetrators. The note outlines payment instructions and imposes a deadline, heightening the urgency and fear of permanent data loss. The demand for payment in cryptocurrency further contributes to the covert nature of the transaction.

It's essential to highlight that even if victims choose to pay the ransom, there is no assurance of successful data recovery. The attackers may not uphold their end of the bargain, leaving victims at risk of losing both their data and the ransom payment. Additionally, paying the ransom does not guarantee immunity from future attacks, as the initial vulnerabilities exploited by the ransomware may persist.

Crypto ransomware commonly spreads through deceptive tactics, including phishing emails and the exploitation of system vulnerabilities. This underscores the importance of preventive measures, such as regular data backups and robust cybersecurity practices. The figure (Figure 2) illustrates the step-by-step activities of Crypto ransomware, emphasizing the need for awareness and proactive cybersecurity measures to foil potential attacks and safeguard against the significant consequences of data loss and system compromise. In essence, understanding the intricacies of Crypto ransomware is crucial for individuals and organizations alike to fortify their defenses and respond effectively to mitigate the impact of such insidious attacks.

Figure 2. Crypto Ransomware Working Model

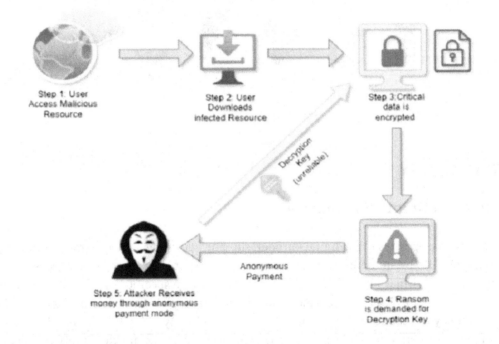

3.2 Working of Crypto Ransomware

Ransomware, malicious software, typically follows a well-defined sequence of events during its insidious attack on computer systems. The initial stage involves infiltration, often achieved through delivering deceptive emails containing malicious attachments or links and exploiting vulnerabilities in software or operating systems. Once activated, the ransomware executes its damaging payload, employing robust encryption algorithms to lock a wide array of files on the victim's system, rendering them inaccessible. The encryption process is a critical component of the attack, strategically targeting various file types to maximize the impact on the victim (Toshima Singh Rajput, 2017). Subsequently, a ransom note is prominently displayed, outlining the attackers' demands for payment, usually in cryptocurrency, in exchange for the decryption key needed to unlock the compromised files.

Communication is another side of this malicious process, with the ransomware establishing contact with a command and control server controlled by the attackers. This communication channel may serve various purposes, including transmitting information about the compromised system or receiving instructions from the offender. If the victim succumbs to the pressure and chooses to pay the ransom, a risky undertaking without guarantees, they may be given a decryption key. However, the ethical and practical concerns associated with funding criminal activities make this option highly discouraged within the cybersecurity community.

Following the resolution, or lack thereof, of the ransom negotiation, the victim is left with the Demanding task of post-infection cleanup. This involves removing the ransomware from the system to prevent further damage and potential reinfection. Additionally, organizations and individuals are strongly advised to implement comprehensive cybersecurity measures to fortify their defenses against such attacks. These measures may include regular data backups, timely software updates to patch known vulnerabilities, and ongoing employee training to enhance awareness and resilience against social engineering tactics. By adopting a proactive and multi-testing approach to cybersecurity, individuals and organizations can mitigate the risk of falling victim to ransomware and safeguard their digital assets.

Figure 3. Proposed Model

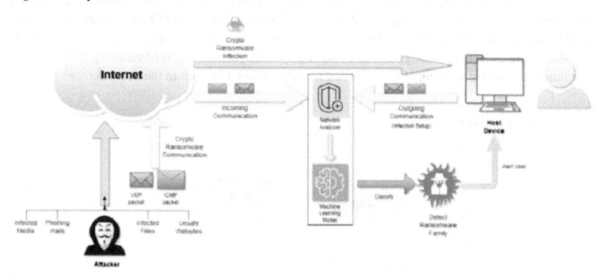

3.3 Proposed Model

In the proposed model, a series of modules work collaboratively to establish a comprehensive defense against Crypto ransomware. The process begins with an attacker uploading malicious content, such as infected media, phishing emails, or compromised websites, to the internet. When a user downloads these corrupted files, their device becomes susceptible to Crypto ransomware infection. Subsequently, the infected device initiates communication with the attacker, potentially utilizing UDP and ICMP packets during the infection setup phase.

Upon the initiation of the infection setup, a Network Analyzer module comes into play. This component is responsible for capturing and analyzing all packet data related to the ongoing communication between the infected device and the attacker. The Network Analyzer serves as a crucial surveillance mechanism, closely monitoring the intricacies of network traffic during the infection process.

The captured packet data is then relayed to a continuously running Machine Learning model (Greg Cusack, Oliver Michel, and Eric Keller, 2018). This model serves as the core intelligence hub, employing sophisticated algorithms to scrutinize the network for any signs of malicious activity. Leveraging its learning capabilities, the Machine Learning model becomes adept at recognizing patterns associated with Crypto ransomware infections.

In the event of the Machine Learning model detecting malicious activity in either incoming or outgoing communication, it swiftly takes action. The model not only identifies the presence of Crypto ransomware but goes a step further by classifying the specific family of the ransomware involved (Omar MK Alhawi, James Baldwin, and Ali Dehghantanha, 2018). This nuanced classification capability enhances the system's ability to tailor its response measures effectively.

The system, upon classification of the Crypto ransomware family, promptly alerts the overall security infrastructure. This alert triggers a series of preventive measures aimed at mitigating the impact of the infection. These preventive actions may include isolating the infected device, terminating malicious communication channels, and initiating recovery processes to restore compromised data.

By integrating the Network Analyzer and Machine Learning model into the proposed architecture, the system gains a proactive and adaptive defense mechanism against Crypto Ransomware threats. The continuous monitoring, analysis, and classification of network activity enable the system to swiftly detect, classify, and respond to emerging threats, bolstering overall cybersecurity resilience.

Figure 4 shows the working of the proposed model and its interaction in the network.

Figure 4. Machine Learning Models

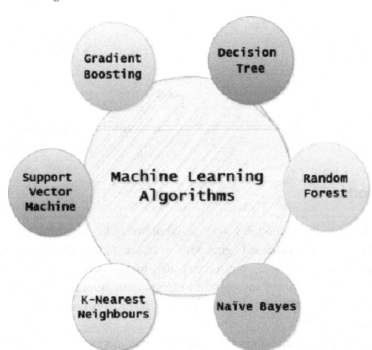

3.4 Benefits of Analyzing UDP and ICMP Over Other Protocols

The strategic use of UDP and ICMP in the detection of crypto ransomware is a noteworthy approach, capitalizing on the distinctive characteristics of these protocols to identify potentially malicious activities. UDP, as a connectionless protocol, offers swift communication between devices without the establishment of a formal connection. This characteristic makes it well-suited for detecting the rapid propagation often associated with crypto ransomware. The speed and efficiency of UDP can be leveraged to identify patterns of fast and widespread communication, which are indicative of the aggressive nature of ransomware as it seeks to encrypt files across a network swiftly.

Similarly, ICMP, primarily known for its role in network diagnostics, becomes a valuable tool for anomaly detection in the context of crypto ransomware. Anomalous patterns in ICMP traffic may signify efforts to establish or control malicious connections. ICMP packets are typically used for tasks such as network error reporting or testing the reachability of a host. Deviations from the expected patterns of ICMP traffic can be indicative of abnormal and potentially malicious behavior. Monitoring ICMP traffic becomes a crucial aspect of detecting irregular activities related to the deployment or communication of crypto ransomware within a network.

Furthermore, both UDP and ICMP can play a pivotal role in detecting potential data exfiltration, a common tactic employed by ransomware. Signature-based detection methods can be applied to these protocols, allowing for the identification of known patterns associated with ransomware activities. This involves comparing the network traffic against a database of predefined signatures that match characteristics of known ransomware strains. By doing so, security systems can promptly recognize and respond to suspicious activities associated with data exfiltration attempts.

The combined monitoring of UDP and ICMP adds a layer of depth to the overall cybersecurity strategy. By integrating these protocols into the detection mechanisms, organizations enhance their ability to identify and mitigate the threats posed by crypto ransomware. This proactive approach involves not only identifying the rapid spread of ransomware but also detecting deviations in network behavior and recognizing established patterns of data exfiltration. This comprehensive strategy contributes to a more resilient and responsive cybersecurity posture in the face of evolving ransomware threats.

3.5 Machine Learning Algorithms

The Proposed model leverages Machine learning algorithms (Omar MK Alhawi, James Baldwin, and Ali Dehghantanha, 2018) to classify the Crypto Ransomware Families. An Efficient and robust algorithm must be selected to train the machine learning model to classify rapidly and in real time, Else the model wouldn't be effective in real life scenarios. Therefore, Six machine learning algorithms has been found suitable for the scenario. Figure 4. Shows all the machine learning algorithms considered for the research.

A Study conducted by (May Almousa, Janet Osawere, and Mohd Anwar, 2021) revealed Decision tree Algorithm and Random forest algorithm performed the best compared to others in a similar scenario involving network analysis using machine learning.

The Decision Tree algorithm stands out as a robust and versatile tool within the domain of supervised learning, showcasing proficiency in handling both classification and regression tasks. Its operational methodology involves recursive partitioning, where datasets are systematically divided into subsets based on the most influential attributes identified at each node. This iterative process leads to the creation of a tree-like structure resembling a flowchart, where internal nodes represent attribute tests, branches signify the outcomes of these tests, and leaf nodes carry class labels. The Decision Tree algorithm's interpretability and ease of visualization make it an attractive choice for understanding and explaining the decision-making process within a model.

Complementing the Decision Tree, the Random Forest algorithm takes a collaborative approach to enhance predictive accuracy and mitigate overfitting. Embracing the concept of ensemble learning, Random Forest leverages the strengths of multiple decision trees. Each tree is constructed independently, introducing a level of diversity in the learning process. During predictions, the algorithm aggregates results from these individual trees, offering a more robust and accurate overall prediction. This ensemble approach proves particularly effective in handling complex problems and contributes to elevating the performance of the machine learning model.

One key advantage of these algorithms lies in their efficiency and high accuracy when compared to other methods. The Decision Tree's interpretability and Random Forest's ability to address overfitting make them well-suited for a range of applications. In the proposed architecture, these algorithms are selected to train the machine learning model, emphasizing their capability to provide accurate predictions while maintaining transparency in the decision-making process. Their combined strengths contribute to the overall effectiveness of the model, positioning it as a reliable and interpretable solution for the intended application.

3.6 Data Privacy and Security

The architecture acknowledges the importance of protecting user privacy by mentioning the potential use of UDP and ICMP protocols for communication. Anonymizing personally identifiable information in network packet data helps adhere to privacy principles and prevents the exposure of identifiable details.

Strict access controls are proposed to limit access to critical components such as the machine learning model and network analyzer. This ensures that only authorized individuals have the privilege to interact with and retrieve sensitive information, enhancing overall system security.

The proposal subtly suggests the need for adherence to data protection regulations, indirectly acknowledging the relevance of compliance. By referencing the utilization of machine learning for classification, it aligns with the privacy-by-design principles, underscoring the significance of meeting legal requirements, including those delineated in regulations such as GDPR.

The inclusion of machine learning algorithms, specifically Decision Tree and Random Forest, highlights a commitment to regularly assessing and enhancing system security. Additionally, the acknowledgment of potential repeat attacks underscores the importance of having a robust incident response plan to mitigate and learn from security incidents.

The elements mentioned suggest a proactive approach to data privacy and security. Organizations implementing such a system should further articulate and document these measures, ensuring transparency and building trust with users regarding the protection of their sensitive information.

3.7 Implementation

In this section, the experiment stages are demonstrated. The research unfolds in three key stages. The first involves collecting diverse crypto ransomware network traffic data, ensuring representation across various ransomware families. The second stage focuses on extracting and selecting features from UDP and ICMP packet fields, including preprocessing steps for data quality. In the final phase, machine learning methods, such as the gradient boosting algorithm and decision tree, are employed to build classification models that label different crypto ransomware families.

The paper highlights the significance of the collected dataset, detailing its sources and addressing any challenges in obtaining comprehensive data. Feature extraction and selection processes are explained, emphasizing the chosen packet fields and preprocessing steps. The machine learning phase is characterized by insights into algorithm choices, customization, interpretability, and validation metrics. Comparative analyses with existing methods and considerations for scalability and adaptability add depth to the proposed architecture.

In essence, the research offers a concise yet comprehensive overview of a systematic approach to enhancing crypto ransomware detection, bridging data collection, feature extraction, and machine learning applications.

Figure 5 demonstrates the workflow of the experiment: data collection and extraction, data preprocessing, and machine learning.

Figure 5. Workflow of the Experiment

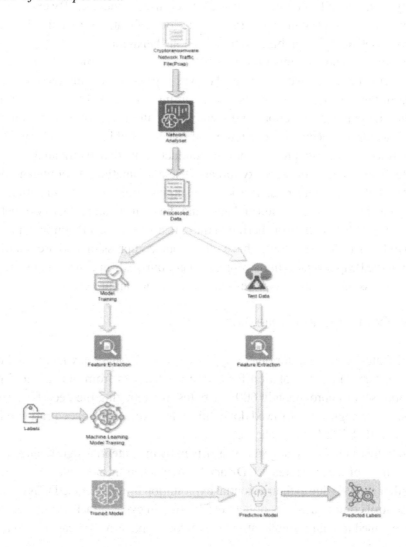

3.7.1 Data Collection

Samples of network traffic packets captured in Pcap (Packet Capture) network traffic. This data was compressed into a zip file in Pcap format. These Pcap files serve as repositories of information, containing detailed records of individual packets transmitted across a network.

Pcap files contain a multitude of features that provide a comprehensive view of network communication. Among these features, the source and destination IP addresses play a crucial role in identifying the participants in a communication session. These addresses are fundamental for tracking the origin and destination of network traffic, aiding in the identification of communicating devices and potential sources of malicious activity.

Another set of vital features revolves around protocol information. Pcap files capture details about the protocols employed in network communication, offering insights into the nature of the traffic. This information allows analysts to discern whether the communication involves common protocols such as HTTP, TCP, UDP, or more specialized ones, providing context for further investigation.

Port numbers constitute another essential feature within Pcap files. Analyzing port-related features assists in identifying the specific communication channels used by devices. By examining port numbers, analysts can gain a deeper understanding of the services or applications associated with network traffic, helping to pinpoint potential vulnerabilities or anomalous behavior.

Packet timestamps provide a temporal dimension to network communication analysis. Timestamp features offer information about when each packet was captured, enabling the reconstruction of timelines and aiding in the correlation of events during an investigation. This temporal context is crucial for understanding the sequence of actions and identifying patterns or irregularities in network activity.

These various features collectively contribute to the richness of information embedded in Pcap files, empowering analysts and security professionals to conduct in-depth network analysis, detect anomalies, and respond effectively to potential security threats. The combination of source and destination IP addresses, protocol details, port numbers, and packet timestamps forms a robust foundation for understanding the intricacies of network communication and ensuring the security and integrity of networked systems.

To facilitate storage, distribution, or sharing of these Pcap datasets, it is common practice to compress them into archive formats. These samples have undergone compression and are bundled into a zip file while maintaining the Pcap format. This compression not only aids in conserving storage space but also streamlines the process of disseminating these network traffic captures.

3.7.2 Feature Extraction and Collection

In the process of feature extraction for our study, we employed Tshark, a widely-used network protocol analyzer. Tshark offered a robust solution for extracting features from the captured network packets, providing an initial set of approximately 600 attributes. Recognizing the need for a more targeted and refined analysis, we strategically narrowed down this extensive list by concentrating on specific categories associated with IP, UDP, ICMP, Ethernet, and Frame attributes.

The decision to focus on these categories was driven by the potential significance of certain network protocols in the context of security threats. UDP and ICMP packets, in particular, were identified as crucial elements for further analysis due to their potential exploitation by attackers. UDP is often associated with command and control communications or data exfiltration in cyber-attacks. By filtering and examining UDP packets, we aimed to gain insights into any anomalous patterns indicative of malicious activities.

Simultaneously, ICMP packets were selected for scrutiny due to their known role in potential firewall rule bypassing. ICMP, being a fundamental part of network diagnostics, is commonly permitted through firewalls. Attackers might leverage ICMP for covert communications, attempting to evade detection by exploiting its prevalence in various networks. Hence, our dataset extraction specifically filtered and focused on UDP and ICMP packets to hone in on potential threat vectors associated with these protocols.

This meticulous feature extraction process allowed us to distill the dataset to a more manageable and relevant set of attributes. By concentrating on IP, UDP, ICMP, Ethernet, and Frame categories, we aimed to uncover patterns that could be indicative of malicious intent. This approach ensured that our analysis was not only comprehensive but also tailored to the specific network behaviors that are often exploited in cyber threats. The utilization of Tshark, coupled with the strategic narrowing down of features, forms a critical foundation for the subsequent stages of our experimental design.

3.7.3 Data Preprocessing

Data preprocessing is a critical step in preparing a dataset for analysis, ensuring that it is organized and suitable for the intended purposes. In the case of the mentioned dataset, a structured and formatted approach was employed to handle missing values and enhance data quality.

Approximately 40% of the dataset contained missing values, which could potentially impact the accuracy and reliability of subsequent analyses. To address this, a systematic removal of these missing values was carried out, effectively eliminating data points where information was absent. This elimination process aimed to streamline the dataset and mitigate the impact of missing values on the overall analysis.

However, recognizing the potential loss of valuable information due to outright removal, an interpolation technique was adopted to handle the missing values. Interpolation involves estimating and substituting missing data points based on known values in the dataset. This method is particularly useful when dealing with sequential or time-series data, where maintaining the temporal order of observations is crucial.

The interpolation process enhances the dataset's completeness by filling in the missing values with estimated data points, thus preserving the temporal structure and continuity of the information. By relying on known values and their relationships, interpolation contributes to a more holistic dataset that is conducive to accurate analyses and meaningful insights.

In summary, the data preprocessing phase involved a dual strategy of removing a portion of the missing values and employing interpolation to impute the remaining gaps. This meticulous approach aimed to strike a balance between data quality and the preservation of valuable information, setting the stage for robust and reliable analyses of the dataset.

3.7.4 Model Training

In the process of model training, Feature Extraction plays a pivotal role in transforming the raw data, specifically the processed Pcap file, into a structured and informative format. Features, in the context of network packets, represent measurable properties or characteristics that serve as input for the machine learning model (Asaf Shabtai, Robert Moskovitch, Yuval Elovici, and Chanan Glezer, 2009). These features are crucial as they encapsulate the essential information necessary for the model to discern patterns and make predictions.

Feature Extraction can involve various techniques such as dimensionality reduction, transformation, or selection. These techniques are employed to highlight the most important aspects of the data, ensuring that the model is fed with relevant and impactful information. Dimensionality reduction, for example, simplifies the dataset by reducing the number of features, making it more manageable for the model to process while retaining the most critical information.

Simultaneously, the concept of labels is integral to supervised learning, a paradigm where the model is trained using labeled data. Labels represent the known outputs or outcomes associated with the input data, serving as the ground truth or the correct answers that the model endeavors to learn and predict. In the context of a Ransomware classification task, labels assign a specific class or category to each set of features, indicating whether the network traffic is associated with ransomware or not.

The machine learning model is then trained using these labeled data. During training, the model learns to recognize patterns and associations between the features and their corresponding labels. The iterative nature of this process involves adjusting the model's parameters until a satisfactory level of accuracy or performance is achieved. This iterative training allows the model to generalize its learning from the labeled data to make predictions on new, unseen data, enhancing its ability to accurately classify network traffic and detect potential ransomware activity.

In summary, model training begins with Feature Extraction, which transforms raw data into meaningful features. These features, along with labeled data representing ground truth information, are used to train the machine learning model iteratively until it achieves a desired level of accuracy and proficiency in predicting outcomes, providing a powerful tool for detecting ransomware in network traffic.

3.7.5 Model Testing

Testing a machine learning model is a crucial step to evaluate its performance and assess how well it can generalize to new, unseen data.(Yun-Chun Chen, Yu-Jhe Li, Aragorn Tseng, and Tsungnan Lin, 2017) The test data used for evaluation constitutes a subset of the overall dataset, and notably, it has not been utilized during the training phase of the model. This separation ensures an unbiased assessment of the model's capabilities, simulating real-world scenarios where the model encounters previously unseen packet data.

Test data typically consists of input features, or feature vectors, but lacks the associated labels. These feature vectors represent the numerical representations derived from the features or properties of the UDP and ICMP packets, embodying the critical information the model learned during training. The absence of labels in the test data mimics the real-world scenario where the model needs to predict outcomes based solely on its training.

Feature vectors encapsulate the essential characteristics of the data and serve as the input for the trained model during the testing phase. The machine learning model, having learned patterns and associations during training, is now confronted with these new, unseen feature vectors. The goal is to evaluate the model's accuracy and efficiency in making predictions about the nature of network traffic, specifically identifying potential instances of ransomware based on its training.

Testing the machine learning model involves feeding the feature vectors into the model, and its predictions are then compared against the actual, unseen outcomes. The accuracy of the model is assessed by measuring how well it aligns with the ground truth, providing insights into its generalization capabilities. Efficient and accurate prediction on the test data indicates that the model has successfully learned to recognize patterns and associations, and it can effectively apply this knowledge to novel data instances.

In essence, the model testing phase is a critical checkpoint in the development and deployment of machine learning solutions. It validates the model's ability to generalize beyond the training data, ensuring that it can make reliable predictions in real-world situations where it encounters previously unseen network traffic packets.

4. RESULTS AND DISCUSSION

The proposed project is aimed at the detection of crypto ransomware using UDP and ICMP. The theoretical approach showcases promising insights into the potential effectiveness of leveraging UDP and ICMP protocols for the early detection of crypto-ransomware activities. Through a carefully designed experimental setup, it is observed that distinct patterns in network traffic associated with crypto ransomware behavior.

4.1 Crypto Ransomware Families Classified

The proposed model, following an early analysis, has demonstrated its capability to classify several Crypto Ransomware Families. Among the identified families, CryptoLocker stands out as a notorious ransomware type known for encrypting user files and demanding cryptocurrency as ransom for a decryption key. CryptoLocker has been a significant threat, causing disruptions and financial losses for individuals and organizations alike. Its modus operandi involves encrypting files on the victim's system, rendering them inaccessible until a ransom is paid, highlighting the urgent need for robust cybersecurity measures.

Another prominent family identified by the model is TeslaCrypt, which gained notoriety for its prevalence on Windows systems. TeslaCrypt, like many ransomware variants, encrypts files on the infected device. However, its impact diminished over time following the release of a master decryption key. This instance showcases the dynamic nature of the ransomware landscape, where external interventions can significantly impact the effectiveness of these malicious campaigns.

Petya represents another classification by the proposed model, and it distinguishes itself by encrypting entire hard drives rather than individual files. This approach renders systems inoperable until a ransom is paid, surpassing the conventional strategy of mere file encryption. Petya's ability to immobilize entire systems underscores the evolving tactics employed by ransomware actors to maximize the impact of their attacks.

CryptoWall and Cerber, both targeting Windows systems, are also recognized by the model. These ransomware families are characterized by their demand for cryptocurrency in exchange for file decryption. Cerber, in particular, is known for employing advanced tactics, showcasing the continuous evolution and sophistication of ransomware campaigns. The identification of these families by the proposed model emphasizes the need for a comprehensive defense strategy against the diverse range of ransomware threats.

Lastly, the model has flagged WastedLocker, a ransomware variant that focuses on data encryption. The inclusion of WastedLocker in the analysis signifies the model's ability to adapt to emerging threats and its proactive stance in identifying and categorizing evolving ransomware variants. WastedLocker's specialization in data encryption underscores the varying objectives and techniques employed by ransomware actors, demanding continuous vigilance and innovation in cybersecurity practices.

In summary, the early analysis conducted by the proposed model has successfully classified several prominent Crypto ransomware Families, each with its distinct characteristics and modus operandi. This recognition is instrumental in developing targeted and effective countermeasures to mitigate the impact of ransomware threats on cybersecurity.

Table 1. Exhibits Crypto ransomware Families classified by the proposed Model.

Table 1. Crypto ransomware families classified by the proposed model

S.NO	Family Name	Family Description
1	Crypto-Locker	Employs 2048-bit RSA encryption
2	Teslacrypt	Doesn't encrypt files more than 268 Mb
3	Petya	Targets Windows Operating System
4	CryptoWall	Variant of Crypto-Locker
5	WatsedLocker	Targets big corporations
6	Cerber	Utilizes Ransomware as a Service Model

4.2 Traffic Features

The process of feature extraction is a critical step in distilling meaningful information from raw data, particularly in the context of analyzing captured network packets. The initial phase involved the use of Tshark, a powerful network protocol analyzer, to extract features from the packets. This extraction process yielded an initial set of approximately 600 attributes, providing a comprehensive but potentially overwhelming array of information.

To enhance the efficiency and relevance of the experiment, a focused approach was adopted, narrowing down the features to specific categories associated with network protocols. The selected categories included IP, UDP, ICMP, Ethernet, and Frame. Each of these categories represents fundamental aspects of network communication, and by honing in on them, the experiment aimed to capture the most relevant and impactful features for further analysis.

The proposed methodology leveraged the Recursive Feature Elimination (RFE) method to refine the feature set further. RFE is a technique that systematically removes less important features, iteratively refining the set to include only the most salient attributes. This step is crucial for simplifying the dataset and focusing on the features that contribute significantly to the experiment's objectives, thereby enhancing the model's interpretability and efficiency.

Table 2. serves as a visual representation of the refined traffic features relevant to the experiment. This compilation encapsulates the distilled set of attributes derived from the initial 600, showcasing the specific features chosen for their significance in the context of the scenario under investigation. The table provides a concise overview of the selected features, offering a reference point for researchers and analysts to understand and interpret the critical elements considered in the subsequent stages of the experiment.

In summary, the feature extraction process initiated with Tshark, encompassing a broad spectrum of attributes from the captured network packets. The subsequent focus on specific protocol categories and the implementation of the Recursive Feature Elimination method allowed for a refined and relevant feature set. Table 2 serves as a visual summary of the chosen traffic features, laying the groundwork for a more targeted and efficient analysis of the network data within the proposed experiment.

4.3 Machine Learning Algorithm

Based on the Test Data Analysis, Decision tree algorithm and Random Forest algorithm performed the best with 99% accuracy followed by Naïve Bayes with 97%. Figure 6. Illustrates the performance of all the machine learning algorithms considered for testing.

Table 2. Traffic features selected for the proposed model

S.NO	Features	Description
1.	Udp.srcport	Source port Address
2.	Udp.dstport	Destination port Address
3.	Ip.src	Source IP Address
4.	Ip.dst	Destination IP Address
5.	Frame_len	Frame Length
6.	Ip_len	Length of IP Frame
7.	Udp_len	Length of UDP payload
8.	Eth.Addr.oui	Address OUI
9.	Eth.Source.oui	Source OUI
10.	Icmp.code	Info on the type of ICMP packet
11.	Icmp.type	Info on the type of ICMP packet
12.	Class	Names of Ransomware Families

Figure 6. Machine Learning Algorithm Accuracy for the Proposed Model

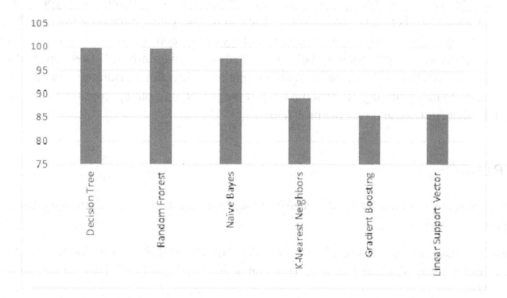

5. CONCLUSION

In conclusion, the early stages of our project have illuminated a promising pathway towards advancing crypto ransomware detection methodologies. The decision to explore unconventional network protocols, such as UDP and ICMP, has provided a unique vantage point that could prove instrumental in fortifying our defenses against cyber threats. The potential benefits of this approach lie not only in the identification but also in the proactive mitigation of crypto ransomware, potentially averting substantial damage before it occurs.

As we look ahead, the imperative lies in the thorough validation and refinement of our algorithms through rigorous testing. The dynamic nature of cyber threats necessitates real-world integration, allowing us to assess the adaptability and effectiveness of our system in diverse scenarios. This iterative process of testing, refinement, and integration will be instrumental in ensuring the robustness and reliability of our detection mechanisms.

The broader implications of our work extend beyond the confines of our project, holding the promise of contributing significantly to the field of cybersecurity. In an era where the digital landscape is constantly evolving, defenders require innovative tools to keep pace with the ever-adapting tactics of malicious actors. The insights gained from our research could furnish defenders with invaluable resources, empowering them to stay ahead of emerging threats and fortify digital ecosystems against the pervasive menace of crypto ransomware.

Detecting crypto ransomware presents a complex challenge within network security, and the use of specific protocols like UDP and ICMP introduces both advantages and disadvantages to the detection process. UDP, known for its speed and simplicity, lacks the reliability mechanisms crucial for confirming successful data transmission, making it less suitable for scenarios where data integrity is paramount. Its vulnerability to packet spoofing and the absence of robust error handling may result in a compromised detection system. Similarly, ICMP, designed for network management and diagnostics, is susceptible to flood attacks and has a limited payload capacity. The potential for false positives due to the widespread use of ICMP for various network purposes further complicates its application in crypto ransomware detection. Additionally, both UDP and ICMP traffic can be encrypted, bypassing traditional detection methods. A holistic crypto ransomware detection strategy should consider these limitations and employ multifaceted approaches, incorporating behavioral analysis, signature-based detection, and anomaly detection to enhance overall effectiveness in identifying and mitigating ransomware threats.

In essence, the initial findings underscore not just the potential of our approach but also the responsibility to further cultivate and validate its efficacy.

REFERENCES

Ahmed, Florence, & Upganlawar. (2022). *A Novel Model to gain Internet Anonymity using Elastic Cloud Computing*. Academic Press.

Almousa, M., Osawere, J., & Anwar, M. (2021). Identification of Ransomware families by Analyzing Network Traffic Using Machine Learning Techniques. *International Conference on transdisciplinary AI (TransAI)*.

Almousa, M., Osawere, J., & Anwar, M. (2021). Identification of Ransomware families by Analyzing Network Traffic Using Machine Learning Techniques. *2021 Third International Conference on Transdisciplinary AI (TransAI)*, 19-24. 10.1109/TransAI51903.2021.00012

Cabaj, K., Gawkowski, P., Grochowski, K., & Osojca, D. (2015). Network activity analysis of crypto wall ransomware. *Przegląd Elektrotechniczny*, *91*(11), 201–204.

Cabaj, K., Gregorczyk, M., & Mazurczyk, W. (2018). Software-defined networking-based crypto ransomware detection using HTTP traffic characteristics. *Computers & Electrical Engineering*, *66*, 353–368. doi:10.1016/j.compeleceng.2017.10.012

Chen, Li, Tseng, & Lin. (2017). Deep learning for malicious flow detection. *2017 IEEE 28th Annual International Symposium on Personal, Indoor, and Mobile Radio Communications (PIMRC)*, 1–7.

Chesti, I. A., Humayun, M., Sama, N. U., & Jhanjhi, N. (2020). Evolution, Mitigation, and Prevention of Ransomware. *2020 2nd International Conference on Computer and Information Sciences (ICCIS)*, 1-6. 10.1109/ICCIS49240.2020.9257708

Cusack, G., Michel, O., & Keller, E. (2018). Machine learning-based detection of ransomware using sdn. *Proceedings of the 2018 ACM International Workshop on Security in Software Defined Networks & Network Function Virtualization*, 1–6. 10.1145/3180465.3180467

Lee, S.-J., Shim, H.-Y., Lee, Y.-R., Park, T.-R., Park, S.-H., & Lee, I.-G. (2021). Study on Systematic Ransomware Detection Techniques. *2021 23rd International Conference on Advanced Communication Technology (ICACT)*, 297-301. 10.23919/ICACT51234.2021.9370472

Omar, M. K. (2018). Leveraging machine learning techniques for windows ransomware network traffic detection. In *Cyber threat intelligence* (pp. 93–106). Springer.

Shabtai, Moskovitch, Elovici, & Glezer. (2009). Detection of malicious code by applying machine learning classifiers on static features: A state-of-the-art survey. *Information Security Technical Report, 14*(1), 16–29.

Singh, T. (2017). Evolving threat agents: Ransomware and their variants. *International Journal of Computer Applications, 164*(7), 28–34. doi:10.5120/ijca2017913666

Udhaya Mugil & Metilda Florence. (2022). *Efficient Sensitive File Encryption Strategy with Access Control and Integrity Auditing*. Academic Press.

Urooj, U., Maarof, M. A. B., & Al-rimy, B. A. S. (2021). A proposed Adaptive Pre-Encryption Crypto-Ransomware Early Detection Model. *2021 3rd International Cyber Resilience Conference (CRC), Langkawi Island, Malaysia*, 1-6. 10.1109/CRC50527.2021.9392548

Venkatesh, J., Vetriselvi, V., Parthasarathi, R., Subrahmanya, G., & Rao, V. R. K. (2018). Identification and isolation of crypto ransomware using honeypot. *2018 Fourteenth International Conference on Information Processing (ICINPRO)*, 1-6. 10.1109/ICINPRO43533.2018.9096875

KEY TERMS AND DEFINITIONS

Behavioural Analysis: Behavioural analysis is the examination and study of individuals' actions, responses, and patterns of behavior to gain insights into their motives, intentions, and characteristics. This analysis is often used in various fields, including psychology, cybersecurity, and finance, to understand and predict human or system behavior based on observed patterns.

Crypto Ransomware: Crypto ransomware is a form of malicious software that encrypts a user's files, rendering them unusable. In exchange for the decryption key, attackers demand a ransom, often in cryptocurrency.

Machine Learning: Machine learning is a field of artificial intelligence that involves the development of algorithms and models that enable computers to learn and make predictions or decisions without being explicitly programmed, by leveraging patterns and insights from data.

Network Analysis: Network analysis is the study of relationships and interactions within a system or network to understand its structure, behavior, and patterns of connections.

Ransomware Families: Ransomware families are distinct groups or types of ransomware characterized by specific traits, techniques, and code similarities. Each family represents a category of malicious software designed to encrypt files or systems, demanding a ransom for their release. Examples include WannaCry, Ryuk, and Sodinokibi. Each family may have unique features and methods of propagation, making it identifiable and distinguishable from other ransomware variants.

Chapter 13
A Survey of Innovative Machine Learning Approaches in Smart City Applications

M. Saranya

School of Computing, SRM Institute of Science and Technology, Kattankulathur, Chennai, India

B. Amutha

Computing, SRM Institute of Science and Technology, Kattankulathur, Chennai, India

ABSTRACT

Smart cities are emerging as a response to the growing need for urban housing, with the goal of improving residents' quality of life through the integration of innovative machine learning technology. For these "smart cities" to work, massive amounts of data need to be collected and analyzed for insights. However, due to the various and noisy nature of the data generated, only a small portion of the enormous smart city data that is collected is actually used. The capacity to process massive amounts of noisy, inaccurate data is a hallmark of artificial intelligence and state-of-the-art machine learning. There are numerous significant everyday uses for it, including healthcare, pollution prevention, efficient transportation, improved energy management, and security. Plus, this chapter presents the ideas and evaluations of numerous innovative machine learning algorithms for their particular applications.

1. INTRODUCTION

Innovation and technology are the backbone of a "Smart City," which aims to better the lives of its citizens and the globe at large. Focusing on individuals and their needs, it aims to encourage participation and welcome everyone. Our mission is to create sustainable, resilient, and habitable ecosystems so that communities can flourish. The primary focus of smart cities is on addressing complex urban problems, (Ahmed et al., 2021) particularly those pertaining to society, the economy, and the environment. In order to achieve this goal, we must adopt a more holistic approach to city administration and think creatively about how to handle challenges. The current trend in computer programming toward capabilities similar

DOI: 10.4018/979-8-3693-1642-9.ch013

to human intelligence in domains such as vision, speech recognition, and language processing is referred to as "artificial intelligence" (AI). The objective of AI is to train computers to think more intelligently and solve problems independently, without the need for programming or human oversight. One of the several potential benefits of artificial intelligence is more efficient and precise decision-making across various organizations. Moreover, AI Cugurullo, 2020, has the potential to transform city planning by facilitating the creation of "Smart Cities" that are more efficient, environmentally friendly, and visually beautiful. This is achieved by providing new tools for studying, modeling, and simulating urban processes.

One day, AI might revolutionize urban planning by helping researchers come up with new ways to analyze and model complex urban systems. Traditional urban planning is notoriously inefficient and prone to bad decision-making due to its reliance on static models and data shortages. On the other hand, a more collaborative, data-driven, and adaptable method of city planning is becoming possible with the advent of AI. Data monitoring and analysis is a crucial component of AI in urban planning. Sensors, IoT devices, social media, and government databases all produce massive amounts of data, which machine learning algorithms can efficiently sort through. Public safety, energy consumption, transportation, waste management, and citizen behavior are just a few of the many aspects of city life that this data covers. Artificial intelligence (AI) integration and analysis of this data Yücel et al., 2022can detect trends, patterns, and issues with the city's operation, revealing crucial insights. Urban planners greatly benefit from artificial intelligence's ability to optimize resource utilization and provide suggestions. Machine learning techniques and data analysis allow artificial intelligence systems to identify inefficiencies and propose solutions. Artificial intelligence paves the way for efficient urban systems, better citizen experiences, and personalized services. Systems driven by artificial intelligence (AI) can examine data on citizens' preferences and actions to propose events, activities, and restaurants based on their unique likes. The different smart city applications displayed in Figure 1In addition to boosting engagement and satisfaction among city dwellers, this contributes to the development of a vibrant urban culture. As seen in Table 1, there are several parts to the smart city system.

Figure 1. Smart City Applications

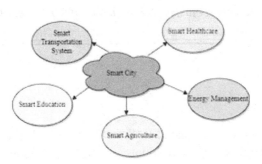

2. BACKGROUND AND MOTIVATION

The main objective of this research is to examine how machine learning technologies have contributed to the development of smart cities. Cities are confronted with enormous challenges in effectively managing their resources and enhancing the quality of life for residents as a result of the growing population.

Table 1. Components of Smart City Infrastructure

Components	Infrastructure
Advanced Transportation	Implementing intelligent transportation systems, such as traffic management, smart parking, and public transit systems with real-time data to reduce congestion and pollution.
Energy Management	Using smart grids, renewable energy sources, and efficient energy distribution systems to optimize energy consumption and reduce waste.
Public Safety	Utilizing sensors, cameras, and data analytics to enhance public safety through improved emergency response systems, surveillance, and predictive policing.
Waste Management	Implementing IoT devices for waste collection and recycling, optimizing routes, and reducing environmental impact.
Digital Connectivity	Establishing robust communication networks and high-speed internet access for residents, businesses, and municipal services.
Urban Planning	Utilizing data analytics and modeling for better city planning, including infrastructure development, land use, and zoning decisions.
Water Management	Deploying smart systems for monitoring water quality, reducing leaks, and optimizing water distribution.
Governance and Citizen Engagement	Leveraging technology for citizen participation, feedback mechanisms, and transparent governance through digital platforms and apps.

In order to tackle these issues, smart technologies are being used more and more by cities to gather and analyze massive amounts of data in real-time. City planners, traffic engineers, and resource allocators can all benefit from the insights provided by machine learning algorithms (Ullah et al., 2023)that study this data. Machine learning has many applications in city living, and this paper looks at a few of them, including transportation, energy management, and public safety.

In a perfect world, a smart city would do double duty by improving residents' quality of life and their economy. The public can benefit from a suite of integrated services while the infrastructure incurs less expense thanks to this. The imminent population expansion in metropolitan regions will necessitate more efficient use of infrastructure and assets, making this an increasingly essential factor. Smart city (Su, 2011) software and services will make these improvements possible, which will improve the quality of life for citizens. Smart city upgrades not only save money for citizens and governments, but they also improve the utilization of existing infrastructure, leading to the creation of new revenue streams and operational savings. A smart city is one that optimizes city functions, boosts economic growth, and enhances people's quality of life through the use of smart technologies and data analysis. What matters more than the sheer amount of technology is how it is utilized. Integration of IoT, (*IoT Devices Installed Base Worldwide 2015-2025 | Statista*, 2022) machine learning, and automation into smart city technology has numerous possible applications. To illustrate the point, smart parking allows drivers to do things like find available spaces and pay for them digitally using their smartphones.

Smart traffic management also includes optimizing traffic lights and monitoring traffic patterns, and smart city infrastructure can even control ride-sharing services. Automatically turning off lights when no one is around is only one of many energy-saving and environmentally beneficial features of smart cities. Smart grid technologies can improve electricity supply, operations, maintenance, and planning. Smart city projects can assist with environmental concerns such as air pollution and climate change in many ways. For instance, there are garbage cans that are internet-connected and fleet management systems. Smart cities enable not only services but also safety measures, such as the monitoring of crime hotspots or the use of sensors to give early warning of natural disasters such as hurricanes, floods, landslides, or prolonged droughts. In addition, smart buildings can offer real-time feedback and monitoring of construction health, which helps to identify essential repairs early on. While the system's sensors can identify major infrastructure problems like water pipe leaks, users can also report smaller issues like potholes. Smart city technologies can also improve energy usage, industry, and urban farming. Smart cities are able to provide integrated solutions to their citizens since they are able to connect different services. The success of a smart city depends on the collaboration of the public and private sectors to create and maintain a data-driven environment, which falls outside the jurisdiction of local governments.

In many real-world contexts, data classification tasks such as disease diagnosis, activity recognition, anomaly detection, text classification, face recognition, electricity consumption prediction, and finding available parking slots are assisted by Support Vector Machine (Kousis & Tjortjis, 2021), one of the most famous supervised learning models. The ant colony (Xu et al., 2022) technique has also found widespread application in the processing of data from smart cities. Classic ant colony algorithms have mostly dealt with one-to-one scenarios, therefore many-to-one scenarios have unfortunately gotten less attention in their research. Smart city applications heavily rely on artificial neural networks. Collectively, ANNs offer a strong foundation for modeling that can manage complex datasets. Recent applications of ANNs include forecasting, regression, and curve-fitting. Neural networks, or ANNs (Band et al., 2022), rely on transfer functions to generate output values. Artificial neural networks (ANNs) are great for handling large datasets since they are simple, cheap, and efficient.

3. PROPOSED METHODOLOGY

3.1. Smart Transportation System

Pollution from vehicle emissions, traffic, and the value of public transit for the poor and the elderly are just a few of the transportation problems that public-private partnerships, a common component of smart mobility, can help alleviate. Some smart transportation solutions have been around for a while; for instance, public transportation smart cards, electronic toll collection, bike sharing, dynamic pricing for vehicles entering the city, and real-time arrival data from the city's transportation department. The smart Transportation system shown in Fig.2. However, an intelligent transportation system cannot be created by combining numerous separate technologies. It calls for a well-thought-out plan and the coordinated use of numerous intelligent technologies. Cities can accomplish more with less thanks to smart mobility, which helps with resource allocation and helps cut down on wasteful energy and material spending.

3.1.1. Vehicles Accidents

Accidents involving vehicles, inflexible traffic grids, bad weather, increasing populations, and inadequate infrastructure are only a few of the numerous causes of traffic congestion. Before the driver is even aware that anything horrible is about to happen, connected cars equipped with sensors can prevent accidents from happening.

Figure 2. Smart Transportation System

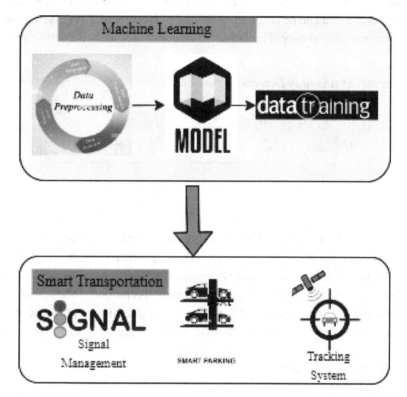

3.1.2. Traffic Control

In the past, traffic lights would change according to set schedules, regardless of any unanticipated events. Although traffic signal timing windows can vary during the day (for instance, during rush hour on a busy roadway), they seldom alter according to the actual traffic flow. In the very few large cities where such data may be used to adjust traffic light timings, it is often done by hand. Connected to real-time data on traffic flows, smart traffic lights that use AI and machine learning to adjust intersection lights depending on thousands of variables are the future of traffic management.

3.1.3. Updates on Accidents and Road Conditions as They Happen

Just like traffic, road conditions can cause delays in travel plans. Citizen reporting is a common source for the real-time traffic updates made available by map programs for cellphones. By investing in vehicle-to-infrastructure (V2I) and vehicle-to-vehicle (V2V) technologies, public-private partnerships can improve this data and make it possible for every car to automatically submit information, preventing traffic jams before they happen.

3.1.4. Anomaly Detection

A system built on cloud computing and the Machine Learning (can efficiently identify traffic incidents, claim Liang et al. (Liang, 2015). The SVM technique, which was created via the Ant Colony technique

(ACA), can be used to identify a traffic calamity. The use of ACA for the SVM parameter range determines the level of precision that can be attained. One kind of Internet of Things sensor utilized in vehicle control is the magneto resistive sensor. The Basic Structure of Anomaly detection shown in Fig.3.

Figure 3. Basic Diagram of Anomaly Detection

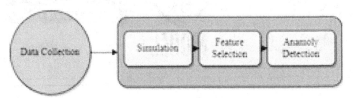

Car behavior, especially how it responds to various road conditions, is monitored by sensor modules. These modules include ones that measure variations in the magnetic field of the road. The trajectory of the vehicle can be ascertained by using information from two different sensors as well as noise from objects and collisions. ("Research Anthology on Machine Learning Techniques, Methods, and Applications," 2022) For testing, we use real-time data, and for training, we use historical traffic data. To generate a decision plan, the algorithm splits the classes "traffic accident" and "no traffic accident."

3.2. Smart Healthcare System

Machine learning (ML) has recently played a pivotal role in improving healthcare and simplifying patient data. Thanks to machine learning, (*Smart City Technologies: Transformation of Cities*, n.d.) doctors can now better track patient records, see patterns in health care, and suggest therapies. The Smart Healthcare Shown in Fig.4. By utilizing machine learning, healthcare providers can enhance their decision-making abilities and mitigate medical risks. Machine learning's implementation in the business world is in its infancy, but the health care sector is very solid, so there are lots of chances to specialize in this area and build a career in machine learning. Gathering patient data is essential for machine learning in healthcare. Machine learning algorithms may find patterns in datasets using data sorting and categorization systems and tools, which can help doctors, detect new diseases and forecast how well treatments will

Figure 4. Smart Healthcare System

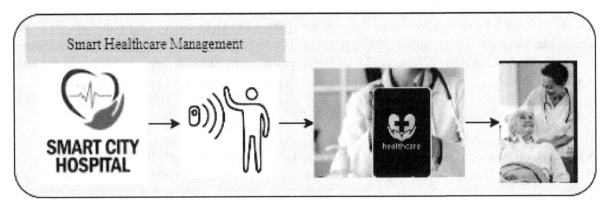

work. Data collected from patients in a single healthcare facility is enormous compared to data collected from entire states or countries.

An intriguing possibility to customize health care, increase the accuracy of diagnoses, and discover new solutions to long-standing problems is presented by machine learning, which is made possible by the exponential growth of technology. By teaching computers to draw conclusions and make predictions, machine learning has the potential to improve community health in ways that would be impossible for health care personnel to achieve on their own. Better patient outcomes and new medical insights are the end goals of machine learning. It paves the door for the use of predictive algorithms to verify the validity of doctors' thinking and choices. Take the hypothetical situation where a patient is given a certain prescription by a doctor. So, if machine learning can identify a patient with a comparable medical history who had a positive outcome from the identical treatment, it can validate this treatment plan.

3.2.1. Machine Learning in Smart Healthcare System

The primary applications of machine learning in healthcare currently include the automation of administrative tasks like patient records, the discovery of patterns in massive amounts of clinical data, and the development of tools to aid doctors in their work. Some applications of machine learning in healthcare include as follows.

3.2.2. Neural Network

A branch of machine learning, neural networks attempt to replicate the way the human brain's neural networks work. These networks go by a variety of names, including artificial neural networks (ANNs) and simulated neural networks (SNNs). Utilizing ANNs ("A Committee of Neural Networks for Traffic Sign Classification," 2011) in the healthcare industry can result in computer-generated diagnoses that closely resemble those made by humans. The capacity of an ANN to learn from massive datasets is known as deep learning, and it is based on ANNs. One use of deep learning in healthcare is the analysis of magnetic resonance imaging (MRI) and other medical images for the purpose of anomaly detection. The doctor's work is still essential, but this helps them do their jobs better by allowing them to make a diagnosis and begin treating patients faster.

3.2.3. Natural Language Processing

One subfield of machine learning, natural language processing focuses on teaching computers to read, comprehend, and produce written and spoken English. To interact and converse with the computer using natural language processing. Extracting information from doctors' notes is one way that natural language processing is being used in healthcare.

3.2.4. Robotic Automation

As a subfield of machine learning, robotic process automation tries to do mundane but necessary jobs, such data input, in the same way that a human would. To automate these operations, medical organizations and hospitals utilize machine learning. This can allow doctors and hospital administrators more time for what really matters: providing excellent care to patients.

3.2.5. Data Fusion Techniques

Machine Learning aims to create a system that facilitates the networking and integration of offline and online objects. IoT uses a huge number of wireless sensor devices to create a plethora of heterogeneous, multi-sourced, sparse, and large datasets. A common first step in streamlining data flow and minimizing data dimensions and size is data fusion. The unprocessed data is then analyzed to extract useful information that can be applied to improve Internet of Things services and offer intelligent services. IoT data fusion has been the subject of many studies, many of which expressly address security and privacy; nonetheless, there is still a dearth of comprehensive research and discussion of this topic in relation to many IoT application domains in the literature. Data Fusion on a Smart Healthcare shown in Fig.5

Figure 5. Hierarchical Data Fusion on a Smart Healthcare

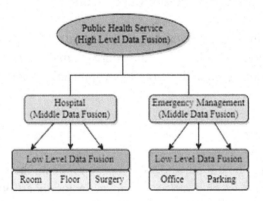

"Data fusion" is the process of combining data from several sources to create intelligent data that may be used for decision-making. Data correctness and consistency are the primary goals of data fusion (Wikipedia contributors, 2023). While high-level data fusion focuses on decision-making, low-level data fusion combines raw data to produce quality data.

3.3. Smart Energy Management

Smart cities are increasingly turning to machine learning (ML), a relatively new technique, to better control their energy use. A frequent objective of artificial intelligence and machine learning initiatives is to increase the efficiency of smart city power systems by utilizing renewable energy sources and cutting-edge technologies like vehicle-to-grid (V2G) (*Advanced Analytics for Optimizing Energy Management in Smart Cities*, n.d.) and other energy storage solutions.

One important field that makes use of sophisticated analytics is the creation and optimization of smart grid technologies. Smart grids use sophisticated sensor and communication networks to gather and analyze data on power generation, distribution, and use in real time (*Advanced Analytics for Optimizing Energy Management in Smart Cities*, n.d.-b). By using this data, the city may reduce the need for expensive and environmentally harmful fossil fuel power plants by managing its electricity distribution and usage more effectively. Specifically, distribution network management, demand-side management, and load forecasting can all profit from AI and ML algorithms. They are also used to identify and isolate defects and forecast when power system equipment may break. One popular technique for load forecasting is to use artificial neural networks (ANNs), which are reliable and accurate—especially when working with complex and non-linear systems. AI and ML systems can assist better predict and control the possible effects of distributed energy resources (Dzobo & Sun, 2020) on the electrical grid. Figure 6 depicts the Smart Energy Management system. By estimating the output of solar panels and wind turbines using machine learning (ML) methods such as support vector machines (SVM), random forests, gradient boosting machines, and deep neural networks (DNN), the grid operator may better balance supply and demand. With AI algorithms like ANN, the operator may anticipate future energy requirements and identify patterns in energy usage, so proactively managing the grid (Maheswari et al., 2020) and preventing disruptions.

Figure 6. Smart Energy Management

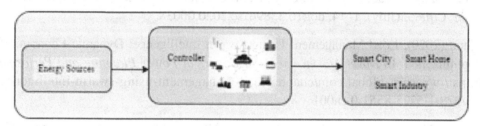

4. FUTURE SCOPE

The success of smart cities depends on Machine learning algorithms, so make them better and more efficient. As a result, work must be done to improve machine learning algorithms so they can process massive volumes of data with ease and deliver reliable insights and predictions. One potential consequence of smart cities' increasing connectivity is the potential exposure of individuals' private data. Hence, while developing and implementing Machine Learning in [15] smart cities, privacy and security must be prioritized. The use of secure data encryption and the restriction of access to authorized personnel can accomplish this. Local governments and communities must be actively involved in the development and implementation of machine learning for smart cities for it to be successful. In this way, the community's unique worries and wants can be better addressed by the technology. Anyone who isn't an expert in the field may struggle to make sense of machine learning technologies. Consequently, it is critical to design intuitive interfaces that facilitate the access and comprehension of data produced by Machine learning algorithms by both city authorities and citizens Smart cities can benefit from machine learning technology by better allocating resources and cutting down on waste. It is critical, however, to use the technology in a sustainable manner that limits its negative effects on the environment. To do this, smart city infrastructure should be designed to be energy efficient and renewable energy sources should be utilized. There may be serious moral and societal ramifications to using machine learning technologies. Hence, before implementing Machine learning in smart cities, it's crucial to think about the moral consequences and make sure everyone benefits from the technology. The development and implementation processes can be made more open and inclusive to accomplish this goal.

5. CONCLUSION

Using a machine learning system, smart city services are provided. Among the services offered are energy motilities, smart transportation, and smart healthcare. A positive outcome for the critical matter can be achieved by selecting appropriate machine learning technologies. Researchers should look at various forms of collaboration to answer the numerous unanswered concerns surrounding smart city-based algorithmic research in the future. The machine learning algorithm has the ability to facilitate more development and implementation, and it also has the ability to ensure its success.

REFERENCES

Cugurullo, F. (2020). Urban Artificial Intelligence: From Automation to Autonomy in the Smart City. *Front. Sustain. Cities*, 2(July), 1–14. doi:10.3389/frsc.2020.00038

Dzobo & Sun. (2020). Load Management Using Swarm Intelligence: Dynamic Economic Emission Dispatch Optimization. In *Novel Advancements in Electrical Power Planning and Performance*. IGI Global. https://www.igi-global.com/chapter/load-management-using-swarm-intelligence/234781 doi:10.4018/978-1-5225-8551-0.ch001

Khan, Arshad, & Mohsin. (n.d.). Population Growth and Its Impact on Urban Expansion: A Case Study of Bahawalpur, Pakistan. *Univers. J. Geosci., 2*.

Kousis, A., & Tjortjis, C. (2021). Data Mining Algorithms for Smart Cities: A Bibliometric Analysis. *Algorithms, 14*(8), 242. doi:10.3390/a14080242

Liang, G. J. (2015). Automatic Traffic Accident Detection Based on the Internet of Things and Support Vector Machine. *International Journal of Smart Home*, 9(4), 97–106. doi:10.14257/ijsh.2015.9.4.10

Maheswari, M., & Gunasekharan, S. (n.d.). Sumadeepthi Veeraganti. *Energy Management*.

Novel Advancements in Electrical Power Planning and Performance. (2020). IGI Global. doi:10.4018/978-1-5225-8551-0.ch008

Shahab, S. (2022). When Smart Cities Get Smarter via Machine Learning: An In-Depth Literature Review. *IEEE Access : Practical Innovations, Open Solutions*.

Statista. (2021). *Internet of Things (IoT) connected devices installed base worldwide from 2015 to 2025 (in billions)*. https://www.statista.com/statistics/471264/iot-number-of-connecteddevices-worldwide/

Su, K., Li, J., & Fu, H. (2011, September). Smart city and the applications. In *2011 international conference on electronics, communications and control (ICECC)* (pp. 1028-1031). IEEE.

Technologies, S. C. (2011). Advancing Healthcare Systems. In *The 2011 International Joint Conference on Neural Networks*. IEEE. https://en.wikipedia.org/wiki/Data_fusion

Teguh Wahyono. (2022). *Machine Learning Applications for Anomaly Detection*. Research Anthology on Machine Learning Techniques, Methods, and Applications.

Xu, K., Wu, J., Huang, T., & Liang, L. (2022). An Improvement of a Mapping Method Based on Ant Colony Algorithm Applied to Smart Cities. *Applied Sciences (Basel, Switzerland)*, *12*(22), 11814. doi:10.3390/app122211814

Yucel, M., & Bekdaş, G. (2023). Review and Applications of Machine Learning and Artificial Intelligence in Engineering: Overview for Machine Learning and AI. *Complex & Intelligent Systems*.

Chapter 14
Securing the IoT System of Smart Cities by Interactive Layered Neuro–Fuzzy Inference Network Classifier With Asymmetric Cryptography

B. Prakash

Computing Technologies, School of Computing, SRM Institute of Science and Technology, India

A. Saranya

School of Computing, SRM Institute of Science and Technology, India

P. Saravanan

Computing Technologies, School of Computing, SRM Institute of Science and Technology, India

P. Kirubanantham

Computing Technologies, School of Computing, SRM Institute of Science and Technology, India

V. Bibin Christopher

Computing Technologies, School of Computing, SRM Institute of Science and Technology, India

ABSTRACT

Smart environments (SE) aim to improve daily comfort in the form of the internet of things (IoT). It starts many everyday services due to its stable and easy-to-use operations. Any real-world SE based on IoT architecture prioritises privacy and security. Internet of things systems are vulnerable to security flaws, affecting SE applications. To identify attacks on IoT smart cities, an IDS based on an iterative layered neuro-fuzzy inference network (ILNFIN) is presented. Initially the TON-IoT dataset was preprocessed, and the sparse wrapper head selection approach isolates attack-related features. The Iterative stacking neuro-fuzzy inference network classifies attacked data from the normal data. The asymmetric prime chaotic Rivest Shamir Adleman technique ensures the secure transmission of non-attacked data. To show the effectiveness of the suggested secure data transfer techniques, the authors compare their experimental results to existing approaches.

DOI: 10.4018/979-8-3693-1642-9.ch014

1. INTRODUCTION

The Internet of Things (IoT) has gained significant popularity in several regions worldwide in recent times. The projected number of Internet of Things (IoT) devices by 2030 is predicted to reach 125 billion, with the current number of linked devices already surpassing 27 billion this year. Smart city apps facilitate the connection between many IoT devices and tangible items in the real world, resulting in a substantial influence on urban life. Administering IoT networks in the future will be a significant challenge due to the vast quantity of IoT devices spanning many technologies and protocols, including Wired/Wireless, Satellite/Cellular, Bluetooth/Wi-Fi, and more. As a result, the personal information of citizens is in danger owing to significant cyber security concerns and weaknesses that might be taken advantage of. Irrespective of the user or administrator's awareness, these cyber threats may gain entry to Internet of Things devices. Consequently, smart city applications are susceptible to two primary hazards. Detecting zero-day attacks in a smart city's cloud data centre poses an initial hurdle due to the diverse range of IoT protocols and the potential for large-scale attacks to be concealed inside IoT devices. By using a sophisticated method for detecting cyber-attacks, it is possible to identify IoT malware assaults in advance, hence preventing their impact on a smart city via the IoT networks. At now, Internet of Things (IoT) sensors are gathering the whole of the data that is being sent via the large volume of data currently being processed on cloud servers by the majority of the sensors currently in operation. Conventional intrusion detection systems (IDS) are unsuitable for devices with restricted resources and capabilities (Haseeb et al., 2020; Kolivand et al., 2021; Saba, 2020; Saba, Sadad, Rehman et al, 2021; Yar et al., 2021).

1.1 The internet of things (IoT)

Devices are linked to the internet via the Internet of Things in order to exchange information via authorised protocols. Consequently, all information may be retrieved at any given moment and from any place. Microscopic sensors integrated into common objects provide the fundamental infrastructure of an Internet of Things (IoT) network. IoT devices are capable of intercommunication without the need for human intervention. Figure 1 depicts the potential applications of IoT in several domains such as health monitoring, intelligent settings, residential automation, urban infrastructure, and wearable technology.

Smart cities use IoT-enabled technology communications to optimise operational efficiency, enhance the quality of services offered, and improve the overall quality of life for residents (Al-Hamar et al., 2021; Rehman Khan et al., 2022). With the increasing use of Internet of Things (IoT) technology, there is a rising number of expressed concerns. The issue of IoT security is of utmost importance and requires immediate attention, along with several other concerns. Massive cloud servers are connected to sensors.

Smart cities are vulnerable to attacks due to the presence of Internet of Things (IoT) devices. IoT devices may be accessed from any location via untrusted networks, such as the internet. In other words, the Internet of Things (IoT) is susceptible to a diverse range of risks. Figure 1 illustrates the many components of the Internet of Things.

1.2 The Smart City

"The smart city's technology, population, and infrastructure are all vital aspects of a city. Cities may be characterized as digital cities, omnipresent cities, or even as smart communities depending on their degree of functionality. Smart cities are those that have high levels of emphasis and operational effi-

Figure 1. Components of IoT

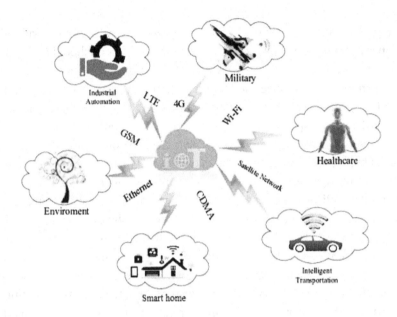

ciency in the three areas listed above. Increasing human population is a major problem for governments across the world. There must be no scarcity of resources, and the supply must be maintained to keep up with demand. Additional criteria include a concern for the environment and a desire to save as many resources as possible.

Efforts are made to maintain security standards and regulate traffic congestion on highways using more controlled methods. Numerous Information and Communication Technologies (ICTs) are used in urban development plans in order to enhance quality of life. A healthy and positive connection between government and citizens is fostered through the use of Information and Communication Technology (ICT) in urban services (British Standards Institute 2014). The integration of ICT with urban development has resulted in the creation of intelligent cities.

Smart cities' individual dwellings would be included in the automation system. In a home automation system, many appliances and electrical loads react to human-created stimuli. An android smartphone or a PC may access a single localhost server (Abubakar & Pranggono, 2017; Ajaeiya et al., 2017; Al-Hamar et al., 2021; Rahul et al., 2018).

An example of a smart home is shown in Figure 2, illustrates just a few instances of IoT's influence on residential, domestic, and commercial settings include home and office products, smart power management systems and floor and building optimization software.

1.3 Intrusion Detection System

The Internet of Things (IoT) breaks down the barrier between the digital and physical world. Despite this, its inevitable expansion in the global economy is challenged by a lack of adequate security management. Physical equipment security, network security, sensor security, and data transmission security all need management. As a result of this, researchers must automate IoT security management operations in order

Figure 2: A Smart Home in a Smart City With Intelligent Devices
(Source: Adapted from chase: White paper 2014)

(<u>Source :</u> **Adapted from chase: White paper 2014**)

to detect unlawful access and take essential steps at any time. A company's requirements should guide the design of an IoT security management architecture. There are three components of the IoT Security Management System (IoTSMS), which are: the IoT reference model, the Layered functional architecture, and the Security Management information base (Abubakar & Pranggono, 2017).

Correct Intrusion Detection Systems (IDS) can safeguard data against unauthorised access, tampering, and dissemination. It is important to notify clients in advance when their software and technologies are nearing expiration and need updating. This will ensure that they are aware of the necessity to safeguard IoT devices and systems (Kapitonov et al., 2017; Li et al., 2019). Periodic password resets may be used to deter users from using the same password for an extended duration. To ensure the system's security from physical and cryptographic threats, it is essential that only important functions be accessible remotely. IDS equipment are used to monitor IoT networks and provide defence against intruders or attackers, as seen in Figure 3.

When confronted with attacks such as the ones mentioned before, an Intrusion Detection System is a valuable asset to possess. It is often regarded as a supplementary security measure used when other security approaches, such as encryption or Access Control (AC), fail to detect potential threats. The Intrusion Detection System (IDS) has the capability to identify abnormal patterns of activity that suggest the ongoing occurrence of the attacks. Mistreatment-based detection approaches use predetermined patterns of harmful exploits to identify intrusions. An intrusion detection system (IDS) that does not take into account the problems of communication overhead and traffic analysis is thus not as desirable as other IDS options. Probing attacks, DoS attacks, U2R attacks, and R2L attacks are all instances of data connections that may be classified into two categories: standard or invasive.

Figure 3. An Intrusion Detection System (IDS) Model

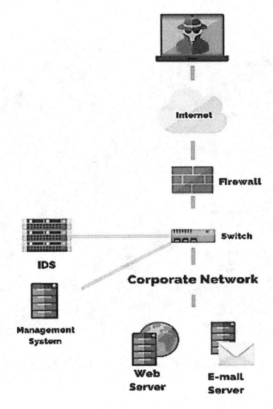

1.4 Attack Detection

Presently, the predominant emphasis of research lies on Network Intrusion Detection Systems (NIDS). The classification method may use the retrieved unique features as an input. It involves the aggregation and prediction performance of many machine learning or deep learning algorithms. Emerging risks often emerge due to the operation of IoT devices within an embedded and interconnected environment. Moreover, due to the constant lack of supervision, IoT devices are susceptible to unauthorised intrusion by malevolent individuals. Given that IoT devices are often linked to cellular networks (Saba, Sadad, Rehman et al, 2021), it is possible for eavesdropping to intercept confidential information stored on the contact platform. In addition to these security challenges, IoT devices are unable to maintain complex security measures owing to their constrained energy and processing capabilities. In order to enhance the security of IoT applications against cyber-attacks, it is necessary to implement an additional layer of protection inside IoT networks. AI-based solutions have lately acquired legitimacy as a prevalent framework for detecting network assaults, particularly in IoT networks. It is important to record and examine data from IoT sensors and network traffic in order to identify and understand typical trends. When an individual's conduct diverges from the norm, it indicates irregular behaviour. These methodologies have also been shown to forecast upcoming dangers, creating a collection of IoT interfaces and network security standards. Therefore, in this study, the Iterative Stacked Neuro-Fuzzy Inference network was used to identify assaults.

1.5 Secured Data Transmission in IoT

The security of IoT has always been a significant apprehension, ever since the inception of the Internet of Things, ranking it as one of the top five security threats in 2015. To effectively address IoT security problems and fully harness the many benefits of IoT for global expansion, it is essential to adopt a collaborative approach to security when building efficient and appropriate solutions. Given the increasing prevalence of the Internet of Things (IoT), it is crucial to acknowledge that IoT security cannot be simplified into a simple option between being safe or insecure. Alternatively, it is more prudent to consider the security of Internet of Things in relation to a spectrum of potential weaknesses in devices. With the expansion of the Internet of Things, the potential vulnerabilities that might be exploited are also increasing.

A major security concern in IoT devices is the disclosure of sensitive information, which can lead to a breach of traditional security measures. If users lack confidence in the security of their connected devices, such as smart TVs, phones, and home appliances, and fear that their information may be misused or compromised, it will result in a loss of trust and reluctance to adopt IoT technology worldwide. Due to the interconnected and diverse nature of IoT devices, security breaches can occur when malicious individuals gain access to these devices and intercept, eavesdrop on, or modify confidential information. The majority of the paper focuses on a security model that utilises a cryptographic approach to address the issue of data confidentiality loss in the Internet of Things. The security of confidential information and data is ensured by using the technique of encryption to safeguard it from unauthorised access by hackers. Cryptography is the scientific discipline concerned with devising cyphers to encrypt communications and information in a way that ensures only the intended receivers can decipher and comprehend it. All Internet of Things (IoT) devices are categorised as sensors due to their ability to gather data from their environment and transmit it to a central server located at home. The security model discussed before may be divided into the following two sections: IoT devices possess inherent hardware limitations, including restricted memory, limitations on battery power, and limited computational capabilities. Consequently, they are not efficient in executing computationally intensive and intricate encryption algorithms during the data transmission phase between the sensor node and the authentication/home server.

During the data transmission phase between home servers and cloud services, secure encryption methods like Advanced Encryption Standard (AES) and Data Encryption Standard (DES) are used. The current research aims to solve the worry of data confidentiality in the Internet of Things (IoT) by using enhanced two-level security measures. Optimal security in smart settings is attained by the simultaneous implementation of cryptography and threat detection methods. Utilising an encryption method may attract malicious individuals to decipher sensitive information that is encoded in a textual format (cyphers), given that they possess sufficient time or computational resources. This is the rationale behind this proposal. The inherent incapacity of cryptography to conceal confidential information from malicious users or adversaries is undeniably evident. In order to guarantee the secure and reliable transfer of data in the Internet of Things (IoT), it is advisable to include an intrusion detection system into the existing cryptographic technology. Therefore, the inclusion of the asymmetric prime chaotic Rivest Shamir Adleman technique provides an extra layer of security to the work.

Hence the overall main contributions of this research are detailed as follows:

(a) A deep-learning based approach with current databases is employed to categorize the attacks
(b) A cryptographic asymmetric prime chaotic Rivest Shamir Adleman technique is introduced for the network's approved users to get the data securely

(c)   A basis for incorporating IDS into an cryptographic method for the IoT-based system as an application is proposed.

2. RELATED WORKS

Multiple publications are examining the feasibility of using conventional machine learning methods for the purpose of detecting distributed denial of service attacks. In Yasin et al. (2010), a detailed and systematic approach is presented for identifying DDoS attacks using the same architecture. The system employs Artificial Intelligence methodologies such as Random Forest and XGBoost classification approaches to detect and predict the many forms of DDoS assaults. Additionally, it formulates a defensive plan to mitigate the risk of DDoS assaults being magnified on the smart grid. The research suggests using an information-centric design technique known as iCAD to mitigate DoS/DDoS assaults on the smart grid (Haseeb et al., 2022).

A hybrid detection system is being developed to identify potentially hostile behaviours in the Cyber layer of a standard power grid, such as DDoS and FDI. Quantum technology is a globally encompassing discipline, characterised by a substantial body of literature. An inquiry into the first quantum encounters of optimisation, modelling, communication, and machine learning (Zhao et al., 2019). The present literature encompasses research on quality control in smart grids. To accommodate researchers with diverse scientific backgrounds, including those without a physics background, a web-based tool is available in QS. This tool aims to assist in the application of QSVM to various real-world classification difficulties. This is due to the need for highly qualified and talented individuals in the age of quality control (Haseeb et al., 2019).

Many individuals believe that cryptography is associated with clandestine operatives who transmit information using enigmatic symbols that are incomprehensible to both the sender and the receiver. As a result, many people are frequently oblivious of the profound influence that cryptography has on the world and their everyday existence. Cryptography is classified as a subfield within the domains of computer science and mathematics (Haseeb, Ud Din, Almogren et al, 2021). The cryptosystem might be either symmetric or asymmetric. Therefore, an alternative term for asymmetric cryptosystems is public key cryptosystem. The absence of adequate security measures for those seeking to safeguard their data or communications related to secret key transfers has always been a problem within asymmetric cryptographic systems. The problem is remedied by using public key cryptosystems, which use cryptographic algorithms such as the aforementioned DES and the far more robust RSA, to produce both the secret key and the private key (Abdulaziz et al., 2020).

The public secret comprises a cryptographic key to an encrypted database and the sum of the two fundamental integers. At that point, Ron Rivest devised a straightforward algorithm that may have facilitated the exploitation of the private key and the decryption of communications by another individual. The plaintext would be converted into a decrypted text by using the equation that includes the large product (Abbasi et al., 2018). Finally, Ron Rivest provided the decryption key, which could only be decoded by using the first two integer numbers. This was achieved by using a technique devised by Euclid, the eminent mathematician (Abbasi et al., 2019).

The key management was controlled using a comprehensive delegation approach based on Hierarchical Attribute-Based Encryption. Subsequently, the cloud server's processing burden is alleviated by the use of signature construction and partial decryption techniques. However, the degree of data secrecy is not taken into account. Implemented a cutting-edge security framework that integrates proxy signature and proxy re-encryption to enable dynamic sharing of safety groups. This architectural implementation enhances the security of cloud servers by safeguarding the data from potential attackers (Deepika & Poonam, 2017). The group leader grants the privilege of group administration to the selected group using the proxy signature mechanism. Subsequently, using cloud servers, the group is engaged in negotiations and the group key pairs are refreshed. Proxy re-encryption enhances security while reducing calculation time, but it does not provide enough confidentiality (Shashi et al., 2015). IoT networks have distinct security difficulties compared to traditional computer systems for several reasons. To begin with, IoT systems exhibit a high degree of complexity in terms of processors, platforms, communication techniques, and protocols. Furthermore, in order to link physical entities, IoT systems use a combination of Internet-connected modules and control devices. Furthermore, the boundaries of IoT schemes are not firmly fixed and often change as a result of the adaptability of people and computers. Furthermore, individuals may face physical risks due to the presence of IoT constructions or their components. Furthermore, the scarcity of resources renders the integration of sophisticated security approaches and applications unfeasible on IoT devices. Due to the rapid growth of IoT-based computers, these networks are susceptible to privacy and security breaches (Kolivand et al., 2021; Rehman Khan et al., 2022).

Various tools and apps have been developed to address network assaults by using machine-learning and deep-learning approaches to identify irregularities in the IoT environment. Various cutting-edge approaches for categorising these abnormalities utilising machine learning methodologies in the IoT framework have been documented in the literature. However, a small number of individuals have used deep learning techniques for the same purpose. Deep learning techniques have shown their superiority in pattern recognition, making them the most advanced way for detecting and classifying inputs in an Internet of Things (IoT) system as either true or false. There are four primary forms of intrusion detection attacks: signature-based approaches, specification-based methods, anomaly-based tactics, and mixed strategies (Saba, 2020). Signature-based methods start by searching for correlations between a collection of network data and a functional database. If the scanned data matches the signature record, it will be deemed unlawful. It is advantageous to accurately ascertain the specific sort of assault. This project requires little labour and has limited demand. They promote the practice of predefining rules and thresholds for machine administrators. The same regulations will be adhered to. IDS is capable of identifying the present condition of both the system and the network. Once the threshold is surpassed or the rules are breached, the Intrusion Detection System (IDS) will promptly identify an anomalous condition and respond accordingly (Rehman Khan et al., 2022).

Anomaly-based strategies seek to discern between abnormal and normal events. The primary benefit of using this approach is the ability to identify possibly novel incursions. Nevertheless, it is susceptible to false positives, which is its only drawback. Presently, researchers are examining machine learning techniques in order to enhance the benefits of anomaly-based intrusion detection approaches. Machine learning algorithms may analyse ongoing activity and compare it to established patterns of infiltration in order to detect prospective assaults utilising anomaly-based intrusion detection approaches. A hybrid method involves the use of various recognition techniques within a single scheme. This technique would eradicate the existing constraints of a solitary mechanism and enhance the general robustness of the IoT approach. The fully formed IDS, however, would be very voluminous and intricate. The method will increase in complexity, necessitating a greater amount of cash. Furthermore, the process of intrusion detection may be both time-consuming and costly, mostly owing to the involvement of several protocols (Al-Hamar et al., 2021). Rahul et al. (2018) devised an intrusion detection system (IDS) based on anomalies, which operates on conventional networks. The model is trained and evaluated using the KD-DCup99 dataset. The suggested method has a commendable accuracy rate of 95% and is highly recommended for adoption. Nevertheless, the researchers use the KDDCup99 dataset, which is characterised by its lack of uniform data and limited number of unique entries, hence posing difficulties in obtaining dependable conclusions.

Ajaeiya et al. (2017) proposed the usage of anomaly-based Intrusion Detection Systems (IDS) that only rely on network functioning. The R-tree approach demonstrates superior performance compared to other machine learning models, with a true positive rate of 99.5 percent and a false-positive rate of 0.001 percent. Their findings demonstrated the efficacy of mathematical methods such as Random Forest. Conversely, their dataset does not provoke any doubts about its authenticity. Abubakar and Pranggono (2017) introduced a tool for identification that is compatible with Software-Defined Networking (SDN). Their identification system consisted of two types of identification methods: a signature-based identification and an anomaly-based identification. Both methods were trained and evaluated using the NSLKDD dataset. The detection accuracy exceeds 97.4%. However, intrusions identified just by anomaly detection cannot be differentiated from those detected using signature detection.

A protocol was proposed by Kapitonov et al. (2017) that utilises blockchain technology to enable peer-to-peer communication in linked networks. The protocol guarantees the security of the communication mechanism and handles fluctuations in operational conditions. Presently, academics are investigating the transformation of blockchain into a multiagent system.

Li et al. (2019) proposed an improved technique for collecting characteristics from IoT data in order to identify Intrusion Detection Systems (IDS) for smart cities. This approach uses deep migrating learning. According to them, their approach aims to make up for the absence of a suitable training set. In addition, they said that their methodology achieved superior detection rates at high levels of performance compared to traditional techniques, while also substantially reducing clustering time.

Yar et al. (2021) proposed a novel intrusion prevention strategy tailored for IoT systems that have constrained resources. Consequently, intrusion prevention is off for both IoT devices and the edge router. IoT devices serve as IDS nodes for the purpose of examining network traffic. The host router node only receives unprocessed packets containing sensitive information. Al-Hamar et al. (2021) introduced a three-layer IDS design to address the issue of real-time destructive behaviour in household IoT devices. The protective layers within this architecture establish intrusion detection for IoT systems by analysing their typical or anomalous behaviour.

2.1. Risks in the Internet of Things (IoT)

IoT refers to a diverse collection of sensing devices that link to each other over the Internet (Saba, Haseeb, Shah et al, 2021). The threads related to IoT are distinct from traditional networks due to their constrained processing capacity and memory. In addition, IoT devices make use of unsecured wireless communication protocols such as 802.15.4, LoRa, ZigBee, and 802.11ac. In addition, IoT devices suffer from the absence of standardised operating systems, varying formats, and application-specific capabilities, making it challenging to establish a uniform security protocol (Elhoseny et al., 2021). These deficiencies give rise to a multitude of security and privacy risks.

Furthermore, the interconnected Internet of Things (IoT) gadgets often come from different vendors, necessitating a dependable solution to serve as a bridge (Abbasi et al., 2018). Multiple research studies have emphasised the problem of software upgrades for billions of Internet of Things (IoT) devices

(Abbasi et al., 2019). Hence, it is crucial to identify and address potential risks and difficulties linked to IoT-based systems when developing and executing security protocols for IoT devices. The Internet Engineering Task Force (IETF) has acknowledged many risks to the Internet of Things (IoT), including man-in-the-middle (MiTM) attacks, Denial of Service (DoS) assaults, firmware replacement with malicious code, privacy concerns, and eavesdropping attacks (Islam et al., 2021).

The fundamental concepts of security and privacy revolve on the network's availability, the confidentiality of data, and the integrity of data. Unauthorised access to data may lead to a violation of availability, confidentiality, or integrity. Hence, the issue of privacy danger pertains to the safeguarding of data privacy, while security strands impact data integrity and network availability. Figure 1 depicts several privacy and security risks linked to Internet of Things (IoT) devices.

2.2. Security Threats

2.2.1. Denial of Service (DoS)

A Denial of Service (DoS) attack is a prevalent and fundamental method of exploiting security vulnerabilities that may be used to target an Internet of Things (IoT) device. The low-security characteristics found in many IoT devices make DoS attacks a favoured technique among attackers. A Denial of Service (DoS) assault occurs when malicious actors gain control to make a device unavailable.

Figure 4. Privacy and Security of IoT Threats

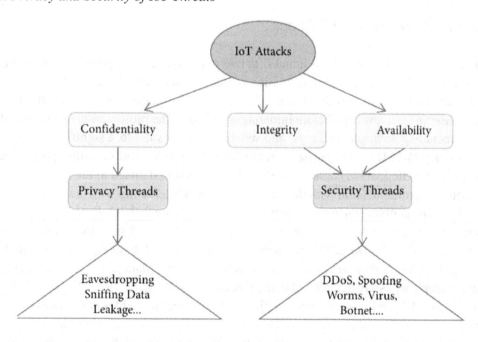

The primary objective of a Denial of Service (DoS) assault is to disrupt the functioning of a network by inundating it with unauthorised requests. The more sophisticated variant of the DOS is known as Distributed Denial of Service (DDoS), when several assaults are directed on a single target (Haseeb, Ahmad, Awan et al, 2021). Various types of DDoS assaults are used, although they all have a common purpose. The most prevalent sort of attack in an IoT network is a Botnet attack (Yasin et al., 2010).

2.2.2. Man-in-the-Middle (MiTM) Attack

These attack methodologies are considered antiquated in the realm of cybersecurity (Haseeb et al., 2022). Sybil attacks, message tampering, and spoofing may all be categorised as Man-in-the-Middle (MiTM) attacks. IP spoofing, DNS spoofing, ARP spoofing, and HTTPS spoofing are prevalent forms of spoofing attacks.

2.2.3. Malicious Software

Malicious software is sometimes referred to as malware. It may be found in several forms such as trojan horse, worm, spyware, virus, malvertising, or rootkit (Zhao et al., 2019). Healthcare gadgets, vehicle sensors, and smart home items are among the instances that have been affected by malware.

2.3. Risks to Privacy

The users and their data stored in IoT devices are vulnerable to inference attacks, sniffing, and deanonymization.

2.3.1. Man-in-the-Middle (MiTM) Attack

There are two distinct forms of MITM attacks: active and passive. The passive Man-in-the-Middle (MiTM) attacks covertly intercept the transmission of data between two devices. This assault does not alter the data but just breaches privacy. Upon gaining access to a device, an unauthorised individual might quietly observe for a few days before initiating an assault. The proliferation of Internet of Things (IoT) gadgets, including smartphones, toys, and wristwatches, has led to a significant rise in passive Man-in-the-Middle (MiTM) attacks, namely in the form of sniffing and eavesdropping. In addition, active Man-in-the-Middle (MiTM) assaults are capable of causing damage to the data. For instance, a client will establish communication with the server, potentially interacting with the Man-in-the-Middle (MiTM) attacker, who is impersonating the server, as seen in Figure 2. 2.3.2. Data Privacy. The subject matter encompasses issues such as data leakage (Haseeb et al., 2019), identity theft, data manipulation, and reidentification (Haseeb, Ud Din, Almogren et al, 2021). Data tampering refers to the deliberate modification of data, and it may be classified as an active breach of data privacy. Data leaking and re-identification exemplify passive assaults on data privacy.

In summary, an IoT-based system lacks complete security since it enables individuals to effortlessly access their data. However, it creates an unsafe environment that allows attackers to get access to any network section. Figure 3 illustrates many methods by which IoT-based systems might be compromised, presenting various types of dangers. Hence, it is important for users to possess knowledge of these security vulnerabilities in order to safeguard themselves from cyber assaults. Diverse strategies are used to mitigate cyber risks. Recently, a method based on artificial intelligence has been used to categorise network traffic in a big configuration.

Figure 5. Example of MiTM Attack

3. RESEARCH GAP

This chapter explores the implementation of intrusion detection systems in a cloud computing environment, using a range of methodologies including signature-based, anomaly-based, host-based, network-based, hypervisor-based, distributed, and machine learning-based systems. The research gaps and constraints of an intrusion detection system based on cloud computing are as follows:

- The standard Intrusion Detection System (IDS) is not suitable for identifying suspicious or malicious activity in the cloud environment. The efficacy of conventional intrusion detection systems in mitigating and managing substantial hostile assaults in the context of the dispersed nature of cloud computing infrastructures.
- All virtual computers use conventional techniques to detect network intrusion. However, the majority of the jobs become laborious and monotonous.
- Virtual machines launched by individuals may execute attacks that are susceptible to host handling. To enhance network security, a sophisticated network attack detection system is implemented by diverting the individual intrusion detection system of each virtual machine via a host.
- Anomaly and signature-based intrusion detection methods do not provide effective and resilient outcomes. The anomaly-based intrusion detection system exhibited a significant percentage of false positives in cases when signature-based intrusion detection systems were unable to identify unknown threats. The intrusion detection system is effectively impl
- emented by the cloud service provider due to the dispersed, scalable, and dynamic nature of the cloud architecture.

   In the context of intrusion detection, the majority of studies need a longer duration to carry out the procedure.

- Increased data transport expenses pose a significant challenge in cloud computing. Researchers seldom focus on these domains in order to mitigate network vulnerabilities.

4. PROPOSED SYSTEM

Data protection is one of most prominent problems in IoT environment. As a result, in this research work, an appropriate intrusion detection approach was proposed. The intruder detection technique of the suggested method is depicted in Figure 6.

Figure 6. Suggested Architecture for Secure Data Transmission

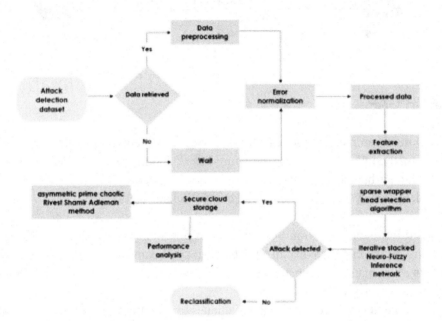

4.1 Dataset

TON-IoT is a revised and enhanced iteration of KDD99. Furthermore, the KDD 99 dataset has redundancy, making it suitable for addressing and resolving them. This dataset may also be used to detect intrusions in the big data of the smart city. Typically, it demonstrates 24 distinct forms of assaults, categorised into four classes: Remote to Local (R2L), Denial of Service (DoS), User to Root (U2R), and probing attack.

4.2 Preprocessing

The normalisation approach may be used to forecast the errors of a dynamical system. Data records are used in this process to calculate values. The stages of this approach are computed using mathematical calculations, resulting in a "forward" process. The model and data may be represented as

$$H_{k+1} = \phi_k H_k + B_k u_k + w_k$$
$$y_k = H_k Y_k + v_k$$

(1)

The internal state of the system is denoted by H, whereas u is the input, and y is the observed output. When v is the measurement error and w is the process error. The matrix of transitions is, while the matrix of measurements is H.

The filter generates the prior estimates during the time update phase, namely the state estimate $\bar{H}$ and the state covariance matrix $\bar{P}$.

$$\bar{H}_k = \phi_{k-1} H_{k-1} + B_{k-1} u_{k-1}$$

$$\bar{P}_k = \phi_{k-1} P_{k-1} \phi_{k-1}^T + Q_{k-1} \tag{2}$$

Next, the phase measure update is conducted to determine the posterior estimate x and P. The equations may be expressed in the following manner.

$$K_k = \bar{P}_k H_k^T \left(H_k \bar{P}_k H_k^T + R_k \right)^{-1}$$

$$H_k = K_k \left(y_k - H_k H_k \right) \tag{3}$$

$$P_k = \left(I - K_k H_k \right) \bar{P}_k$$

During this particular step, the estimate that has been smoothed $\hat{H}_k^s$ and $\hat{P}_k^s$ as,

$$C_k = P_k \phi_k \bar{P}_{k+1}^{-1}$$

$$\hat{H}_k^s = x_k + C_k \left(\hat{H}_{k+1}^s - H_{k+1} \right) \tag{4}$$

$$\hat{P}_k^s = P_k + C_k \left(\hat{P}_{k+1}^s - \bar{P}_{k+1} \right) C_k^T$$

The use of the suggested smoothing procedure has clearly led to a decrease in the presence of disturbances in the filtered data.

4.3 Feature Extraction

In the context of a suggested method for selecting a sparse wrapper head, a vector $\bar{v}$ is constructed, which contains N high-dimensional points $z_1, z_2, \cdots z_n$. The Euclidean distances between any two points z_i and z_j inside the vector $\bar{v}$ are calculated to determine a conditional probability P_(j|i). The conditional probability functions as a metric of similarity between the point z_i and the point z_j. The conditional probability $P_{j|i}$ represents the likelihood of point z_i selecting z_j as its neighbour, given that the probability density of the characteristics follows a normal distribution (Gaussian) centred at z_i. Hence, the conditional probability experiences an augmentation when taking into account adjacent data points, but for data points that are far, $P_{j|i}$ becomes almost insignificant. The conditional probability $P_{j|i}$ may be represented mathematically as follows:

$$p_{j|i} = \frac{\exp\left(-z_i - z_{j2} / 2\sigma_i^2\right)}{\sum_{k \neq i} \exp\left(-z_i - z_j^2 / 2\sigma_i^2\right)} \tag{5}$$

where σ_i is the mean of the Gaussian distribution centred at the position x_i. The likelihood of a point being next to itself is 0, since the approach primarily aims to depict pairwise similarities $P_{i|i} = 0$.

A conditional probability, $q_{j|i}$ may be derived to characterise the similarities between the map feature points y_i and y_j, which are the low-dimensional analogues of the high-dimensional z_i and z_j, respectively.

$$q_{j|i} = \frac{\exp\left(-z_i - z_{j2}\right)}{\sum_{k \neq i} \exp\left(-z_i - z_j^2\right)} \tag{6}$$

Since this method is solely interested in simulating pairwise similarities, the conditional probability $q_{i|i}$ is similarly zero ($q_{i|i} = 0$).

In order to obtain a low-dimensional representation of the data that minimises the discrepancies between $p_{j|i}$ and $q_{j|i}$, the dimensionality reduction mapping is performed. The gradient descent technique is used frequently in sparse wrapper to achieve this for a certain cost function C, such that:

$$C = \sum_i KL\left(P_i \| Q_i\right) = \sum_i \sum_j p_{j|i} \log \frac{p_{i|i}}{q_{i|i}} \tag{7}$$

The Kullback-Leibler divergence function of $P_i \| Q_i$ is denoted by $KL\left(P_i \| Q_i\right)$. The Kullback-Leibler divergence, denoted as $KL\left(P_i \| Q_i\right)$, is the distance between two discrete probability distributions P_i and Q_i, and it is defined as,

$$KL\left(P_i \| Q_i\right) = -\sum_{x \in X} P_i(z) \log\left(\frac{Q_i(z)}{P_i(z)}\right) \tag{8}$$

The expectation of the logarithmic difference between P_i and Q_i is given by Equation (9) above. Any random continuous variable x in P_i and Q_i may be treated in the same way.

$$KL\left(P_i \parallel Q_i\right) = \int_{-\infty}^{\infty} p_{\not{j}i}\left(z\right)\log\left(\frac{p_{\not{j}i}\left(z\right)}{q_{\not{j}i}\left(z\right)}\right)dz \tag{9}$$

where $p_{j|i}$ and $q_{j|i}$ are the distributions of likelihoods of P_i and Q_i.

The Kullback-Leibler divergence function may be rewritten as when P_i and Q_i are evaluated over continuous sets X and P.

$$KL\left(P_i \parallel Q_i\right) = \int_z \log\left(\frac{dP_i}{dQ_i}\right)dP_i \tag{10}$$

where $\frac{dP_i}{dQ_i}$ in (7) is a derivative of Radon and Nikolayevich Nikodym of P_i with respect to Q_i.

By using the chain rule for factorization, we can rewrite (10) as:

$$KL\left(P_i \parallel Q_i\right) = \int_X \log\left(\frac{dP_i}{dQ_i}\right)\frac{dP_i}{dQ_i}dQ_i \tag{11}$$

It is commonly agreed that the entropy of P_i with respect to Q_i is given by the preceding equation.

If we have two absolutely continuous probability densities $p_{j|i}$ and $q_{j|i}$ such that $p_{j|i} = \frac{dP_i}{d\mu}$ and $q_{j|i} = \frac{dQ_i}{d\mu}$, then the Kullback-Leibler divergence from Q_i to P_i is given by for every measure on the set z.

$$KL\left(P_i \parallel Q_i\right) = \int_z \log\left(\frac{p_{j|i}}{q_{j|i}}\right)d\mu \tag{12}$$

To minimise the cost function in equation (13), a recursive gradient descent process is used using the following form:

$$\frac{\delta C}{\delta y_i} = 2\sum_j\left(p_{j|i} - q_{j|i} + p_{i|j} - q_{i|j}\right)\left(z_i - z_j\right) \tag{13}$$

z_i and z_j are located at different coordinates on a map.

To continuously update the coordinates of the map at each iteration, the factorised gradient is combined with an exponentially declining sum of previous gradients. This update is governed by the provided formula.

$$z^t = z^{(t-1)} + \beta \frac{\delta C}{\delta y_i} + \alpha \left(t \right) \left(z^{(t-1)} - z^{(t-2)} \right) \tag{14}$$

where z^t represents the gradient value at iteration t is denoted as β, the learning rate is represented by α, and α(t) Momentum is a significant element that is added to the gradient to improve the detection of local minima.

It is important to emphasise that the computational cost of Non-Negative Matrix Factorization is O(N^2). However, the use of the cost function for selecting a sparse wrapper head is limited since it increases quadratically as the number of objects N increases. Hence, it is only appropriate for datasets that consist of a limited number of input items, usually ranging from a few thousand. As datasets get larger, it is expected that the learning process would slow down, while the memory requirements will rise.

4.4 Attack Detection

In this section for attack detection Iterative stacked Neuro-Fuzzy Inference network was, we detail the mathematical formulation for the proposed method. Let the confidence scores for C number of classes given by base learner i are $\left(P_1^i, P_2^i, P_3^i, \ldots, P_C^i \right)$, here $i = 1, 2, 3$. At first, we accumulate all the confidence scores obtained from each of the base learners. As $\left(P_1^i, P_2^i, P_3^i, \ldots, P_C^i \right)$ represent probabilities, essentially it will follow Eq. (15).

$$\sum_{k=1}^{C} P_k^i = 1, \forall i = 1, 2, 3 \tag{15}$$

Let $\left(R_1^{i_1}, R_2^{i_1}, R_3^{i_1}, \ldots, R_C^{i_1} \right)$ and $\left(R_1^{i_2}, R_2^{i_2}, R_3^{i_2}, \ldots, R_C^{i_2} \right)$ are fuzzy ranks generated by using the two non-linear functions.

The fuzzy ranks are calculated by Eqs.15.

$$R_k^{i_1} = 1 - \tanh \left[\frac{\left(P_k^i - 1 \right)^2}{2} \right]$$

$$R_k^{i_2} = 1 - \exp \left(-\frac{\left(P_k^i - 1 \right)^2}{2} \right) \tag{16}$$

The domain of definition for the functions calculating non-linear rankings will be $[0,1]$ as $P_k^i \epsilon [0,1]$.

Equation (16) provides a reward for a classification. If x approaches 1, then the value of Eq. (16) increases i.e., the amount of reward increases. Conversely for Eq. (17), when we calculate deviation from 1, i.e., if x approaches 0, the deviation will be more.

Let $\left(RS_1^i, RS_2^i, RS_3^i, \ldots, RS_C^i \right)$ be the fused rank scores, where RS_k^i is given by Eq. (16).

$$RS_k^i = R_1^{i_1} \times R_1^{i_2} \tag{17}$$

1. $\exp\left(-\dfrac{(x-1)^2}{2}\right)$ The function is concave downward across its domain of definition, which is [0,1], for this research. Given the worry over the negative aspect of this function, it may be concluded that it is concave upward. Due to its negative slope inside the range of 0 to 1, the output rank score will attempt to go closer to 1.

2. $\tanh\left(\dfrac{(x-1)^2}{2}\right)$ The function is convex in its domain of definition [0,1] for this research. Given the worry about the negative aspect of this function, it will exhibit concavity in a downward direction. Due to its upward slope inside the interval [0,1], the output rank score will tend to go closer to 0.

The rank score is calculated by multiplying the reward and deviation for a certain confidence level acquired from a base learner. Since the range of Equation (17) is less than the range of Equation (16), the behaviour of the product will be determined by Equation (17). A smaller divergence derived from the confidence score corresponds to a lower rank score. Ultimately, the only factor that has to be considered when computing the fused scores is the rank scores. The RS_k^i represents the confidence level towards a certain class, which is determined by multiplying the fuzzy rankings provided by two distinct kinds of functions.

Now the fused score tuple is $\left(DS_1, DS_2, DS_3, \ldots, DS_C\right)$, where DS_k is given by Eq. (18).

$$DS_k = \sum_{i=1}^{L} RS_k^i, \forall k = 1, 2, \ldots, C \tag{18}$$

The fused score is the ultimate score associated with each assault class. Next, we choose the class with the lowest fused score and designate it as the victor using Equation (6). The computational complexity of the fusion technique is determined by the number of classes, and may be expressed as O (number of classes).

$$\text{class}\left(I\right) = \min_{\forall k} DS_k \tag{19}$$

By analysing the plot of the product of two rank generating functions, it becomes evident that the final rank falls as the confidence (probability) score increases. This observation serves as evidence of the validity of the analysis.

4.5 Secure Data Transmission

The asymmetric prime chaotic Rivest Shamir Adleman method algorithm can be used for both key exchange and digital signatures. Although employed with numbers using hundreds of digits, the mathematics behind asymmetric prime chaotic Rivest Shamir Adleman method is relatively straight-forward.

To create an asymmetric prime chaotic Rivest Shamir Adleman method public and private key pair, the following steps can be used:

i.   Choose two prime numbers, p and q. From these numbers you can calculate the modulus, $n = AB$

ii. Choose a third integer, e, that is coprime with (i.e. it has no common factors with) the product. $(A-1)(-1)$, the number e is the public exponent.

iii. Calculate an integer d from the quotient $\dfrac{(ed-1)}{(A-1)(B-1)}$. The number d is the private exponent.

iv. The public key consists of a numerical pair represented as (n,e). While these numbers are widely accessible, it is almost impossible to calculate the value of d using n and e if A and B are sufficiently big.

v.   To encrypt a message, M, with the public key, creates the cipher-text, C, using the equation: $C = M^e \mathrm{Mod}\, n$

vi. The receiver then decrypts the cipher-text with the private key using the equation: $M = C^d \mathrm{Mod}\, n$

The equation is Block Size = (2 * Key Size) -1 (1) The values derived from the equation are used to partition the file into segments of varying key sizes. Due to the key size, the block size varies, resulting in the generation of blocks with varying sizes for files of the same size.

5. RESULTS AND DISCUSSIONS

The efficacy of the suggested approach was assessed using tables and graphical representations, using the following measures.

Figure 7. Simulated Output

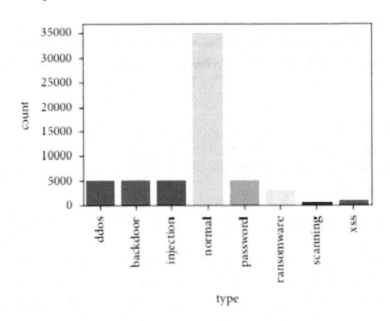

The comprehensive results of the assault detection simulation are shown in figure 7. The effectiveness of the suggested approach is measured by calculating several performance measures, including Accuracy, Sensitivity, and F-Measure.

Accuracy

The Accuracy A_i depends on the number of intrusions that are classified correctly and is evaluated by the formula

$$Ai = TP+TN+FP+FN/ TP+TN \qquad (20)$$

where FN-False Negative, FP-False Positive, TN-True Negative and TP-True Positive,

Sensitivity

Sensitivity quantifies the accuracy of accurately identifying affirmative cases, and is formally defined as

$$S_n = \frac{TP}{TP + TN} \qquad (21)$$

F-Measure

F-measure is obtained by combining precision and recall.

$$F - Score = \frac{2 * prevision * recall}{precision + recall} \qquad (22)$$

The sector compares the performances of the suggested classifier, which detects projected attacks on IoT exploitation, with the prevailing Support Vector Machine (SVM), ANN, and Deep Learning Neural Network (DLNN). The comparison is done separately based on sensitivity, accuracy, and F-Measures, and the results are presented in Tables 1 to 4.

Table 1. Performance Comparison of Proposed and Existing Techniques in Terms of Sensitivity

Number of Iterations	SVM (Kim & Park, 2003)	ANN (Hodo et al., 2016)	DLNN (Abdulaziz et al., 2020)	Proposed
20	83.870	87.650	88.120	**90.3400**
40	85.550	88.90	89.40	**92.230**
60	89.1200	92.6	93.20	**95.80**
80	90.77	94.800	95.340	**97.40**
100	91.600	95.90	93.80	**98.970"**

Figure 8. Sensitivity Analysis

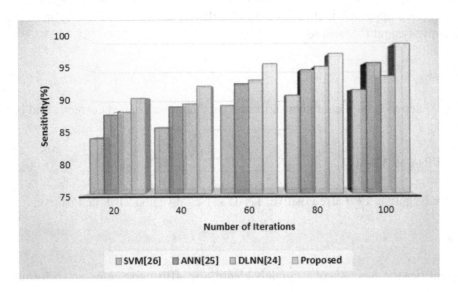

Table 2. Performance Comparison of Proposed MANFIS and Existing Techniques in Terms of Accuracy

Number of Iterations	SVM (Kim & Park, 2003)	ANN (Hodo et al., 2016)	DLNN (Abdulaziz et al., 2020)	Proposed
20	84.120	88.1200	89.30	**92.120**
40	86.230	89.870	90.340	**93.450**
60	88.340	92.830	93.230	**95.620**
80	89.130	94.760	95.380	**97.230**
100	91.120	92.340	94.430	**99.230**

Figure 9. Accuracy Analysis

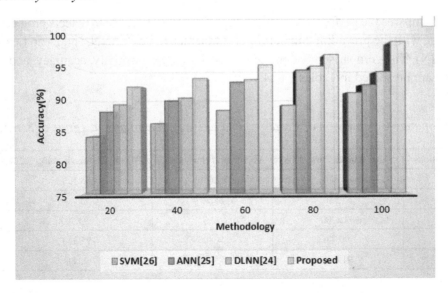

Table 3. Performance Comparison of Proposed and Existing Techniques in Terms of F-Measure

Number of Iterations	SVM (Kim & Park, 2003)	ANN (Hodo et al., 2016)	DLNN (Abdulaziz et al., 2020)	Proposed
20	86.120	89.580	90.840	**92.760**
40	87.440	91.730	92.450	**94.560**
60	90.850	93.460	94.560	**96.420**
80	91.870	95.5600	96.4800	**97.7200**
100	93.120	97.120	97.88	**99.3800**

Figure 10. F Measure Analysis

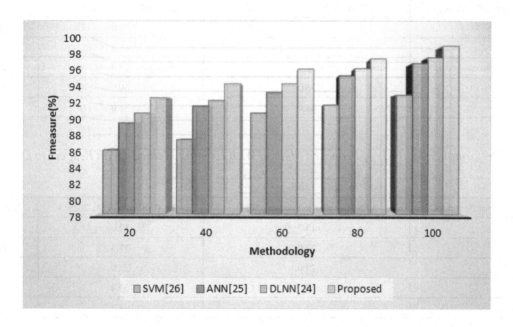

Tables 1 to 4 provide a performance comparison between the recommended classifier and established approaches such as SVM, ANN, and DLNN. The comparison is based on 20 to 100 iterations. The classifiers are evaluated based on parameters such as f-measure, sensitivity, and accuracy. The suggested classifier achieves a sensitivity of 90.34%, accuracy of 92.12%, and F-measure of 92.76% after approximately 20 iterations. In comparison, the traditional SVM, ANN, and DLNN techniques offer sensitivities of 83.87%, 87.65%, and 88.12%, accuracies of 84.12%, 88.12%, and 89.3%, and F-measures of 86.12%, 89.58%, and 90.84%, respectively. Similarly, after conducting 100 iterations, the conventional SVM, ANN, and DLNN methods achieved sensitivity rates of 91.6%, 95.9%, and 93.8% respectively. They also achieved accuracy rates of 91.12%, 92.34%, and 94.43% respectively, as well as f-measure rates of 93.12%, 97.12%, and 97.88% respectively. In contrast, the proposed classifier achieved a sensitivity rate of 98.97%, an accuracy rate of 99.23%, and an f-measure rate of 99.38%. Similarly, for the remaining iterations such as 40, 60, and 80, the recommended classifier achieves the highest values of sensitivity, accuracy, and F-measure when compared to SVM, ANN, and DLNN. Thus, it is shown that the proposed classifier outperforms other alternatives.

Performance Analysis of Asymmetric Prime Chaotic Rivest Shamir Adleman Method

In this, the presented technique exploited in secure data transmission and the existing Advanced Encryption Standard (AES) and Elliptical Curve Cryptography (ECC) techniques are compared with respect to Encryption Time (ET), Decryption Time (DT), and security level which is shown in Tables 5 to 7.

Table 5. Performance Analysis of Proposed Method With Existing Methods With Respect to Encryption Time

Number of Iterations	AES (Deepika & Poonam, 2017)	ECC (Shashi et al., 2015)	Proposed
20	14.0	10.0	5.4
40	22.0	18.0	7.0
60	28.0	23.0	12.0
80	36.0	30.0	18.0
100	44.0	38.0	20.0

Table 6. Performance Analysis of Proposed Method With Existing Methods With Respect to Decryption Time

Number of Iterations	AES (Deepika & Poonam, 2017)	ECC (Shashi et al., 2015)	Proposed
20	13.5	12.0	4.8
40	22.0	17.5	8.0
60	29.0	22.0	12.5
80	38.0	31.4	17.5
100	45.8	38.2	20.0

Table 7. Performance Analysis of Proposed Method With Existing Methods With Respect to Security Level

Techniques	Security LEVEL (%)
AES (Deepika & Poonam, 2017)	90
ECC (Shashi et al., 2015)	93
Proposed	97.4

Tables 5 to 6 compare the recommended asymmetric prime chaotic Rivest Shamir Adleman technique with the classic AES and ECC methods in terms of security level, Decryption Time (DT), and Encryption Time (ET). The ET and DT are evaluated according to the range of iterations, often between 20 and 100. The asymmetric prime chaotic Rivest Shamir Adleman technique takes around 5.4 seconds to encrypt and 4.8 seconds to decode the data for roughly 20 rounds. In comparison, the classic AES and ECC methods need 14 and 10 seconds, respectively, to encode the data, and 13.5 and 12 seconds, respectively, to decode the data. For 100 rounds, the asymmetric prime chaotic Rivest Shamir Adleman method requires 20 seconds for both encryption and decryption. In contrast, typical AES and ECC approaches take 44 and 38 seconds respectively for encryption, and 45.8 and 38.2 seconds respectively for decryption. The residual iterations (40, 60, and 80) of the asymmetric prime chaotic Rivest Shamir Adleman technique exhibit reduced DT and ET, as seen in Table 5 and Table 6, respectively. The security level of several approaches is shown in Table 7. The asymmetric prime chaotic Rivest Shamir Adleman technique provides the highest degree of security at 97.4%. In comparison, the AES and ECC methods give security levels of 90% and 96% respectively, which are lower than the asymmetric prime chaotic Rivest Shamir Adleman method as seen in Figure 11. Based on the analysis, it can be deduced that the asymmetric prime chaotic Rivest Shamir Adleman technique is the most effective for securely sending data.

Figurer 11. Security Analysis

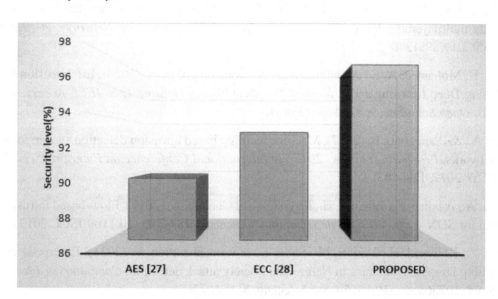

As of from the result obtained the suggested methodology outperforms well over data security when compared to other existing mechanisms in use".

6. CONCLUSION

Presently, several cybersecurity measures are in place to uphold the security and privacy of IoT networks. Therefore, this study has introduced an artificial intelligence (AI) model for detecting intrusions in Internet of Things (IoT) networks. The model utilises TON-IoT datasets and aims to make a valuable contribution in this field. The suggested approach monitors traffic inside the IoT-based system and predicts potential intrusions using integrated artificial intelligence. The proposed model attained an accuracy of 99.7% on average by using a recommended classifier. Further endeavours are necessary to establish a smart city that is completely equipped with Internet of Things (IoT) sensors for the purpose of secure and substantial monitoring of all potential risks. It is imperative to develop and construct robust security and privacy protocols for IoT devices, since they are essential components of any network. As part of our future study, we want to combine the seven datasets from the TON-IoT dataset using different deep learning models.

REFERENCES

Abbasi, R., Luo, B., Rehman, G., Hassan, H., Iqbal, M. S., & Xu, L. (2018). A new multilevel reversible bit-planes data hiding technique based on histogram shifting of efficient compressed domain. *Vietnam Journal of Computer Science*, *5*(2), 185–196. doi:10.1007/s40595-018-0114-z

Abbasi, R., Xu, L., Amin, F., & Luo, B. (2019). Efficient lossless compression based reversible data hiding using multilayered n-bit localization. *Security and Communication Networks*, *2019*, 8981240. doi:10.1155/2019/8981240

Abdulaziz, F., Mohamed, A. E., Abdelghani, D., & Mohammed, A. A. (2020). IoT Intrusion Detection System Using Deep Learning and Enhanced Transient Search Optimization. *IEEE Access : Practical Innovations, Open Solutions*, *9*, 123448–123464.

Abubakar, A., & Pranggono, B. (2017). Machine learning based intrusion detection system for software defined networks. *Proceedings of the - 2017 7th International Conference on Emerging Security Technologies, EST 2017,* 138–143.

Ajaeiya, G. A., Adalian, N., Elhajj, I. H., Kayssi, A., & Chehab, A. (2017). Flow-based intrusion detection system for SDN. *Proc. - IEEE Symp. Comput. Commun.*, 787–793. 10.1109/ISCC.2017.8024623

Al-Hamar, Y., Kolivand, H., Tajdini, M., Saba, T., & Ramachandran, V. (2021). Enterprise credential spear-phishing Discrete Dynamics in Nature and Society attack detection. *Computers & Electrical Engineering*, *94*, 107363. doi:10.1016/j.compeleceng.2021.107363

Deepika, K., & Poonam, D. (2017). Secure Data Transmission using AES in IoT. *International Journal of Application or Innovation in Engineering & Management*, *6*(6), 283–289.

Elhoseny, M., Haseeb, K., Shah, A. A., Ahmad, I., Jan, Z., & Alghamdi, M. I. (2021). IoT solution for AI-enabled PRIVACYPREServing with big data transferring: An application for healthcare using blockchain. *Energies*, *14*(17), 5364. doi:10.3390/en14175364

Haseeb, K., Ahmad, I., Awan, I. I., Lloret, J., & Bosch, I. (2021). A machine learning SDN-enabled big data model for IoMT systems. *Electronics (Basel)*, *10*(18), 2228. doi:10.3390/electronics10182228

Haseeb, K., Islam, N., Almogren, A., & Ud Din, I. (2019). Intrusion prevention framework for secure routing in WSN-based mobile Internet of, ings. *IEEE Access : Practical Innovations, Open Solutions*, *7*, 185496–185505. doi:10.1109/ACCESS.2019.2960633

Haseeb, K., Islam, N., Javed, Y., & Tariq, U. (2020). A lightweight secure and energy-efficient fog-based routing protocol for constraint sensors network. *Energies*, *14*(1), 89. doi:10.3390/en14010089

Haseeb, K., Jan, Z., Alzahrani, F. A., & Jeon, G. (2022). A secure mobile wireless sensor networks based protocol for smart data gathering with cloud. *Computers & Electrical Engineering, 97*, 107584. doi:10.1016/j.compeleceng.2021.107584

Haseeb, K., Ud Din, I., Almogren, A., Ahmed, I., & Guizani, M. (2021). Intelligent and secure edge-enabled computing model for sustainable cities using green internet of things. *Sustainable Cities and Society, 68*, 102779. doi:10.1016/j.scs.2021.102779

Hodo, E., Bellekens, X., Hamilton, A., Dubouilh, P.-L., Iorkyase, E., & Tachtatzis, C. (2016). Threat analysis of IoT networks using artificial neural network intrusion detection system. *2016 International Symposium on Networks, Computers and Communications (ISNCC)*, 1-6. 10.1109/ISNCC.2016.7746067

Islam, N., Altamimi, M., Haseeb, K., & Siraj, M. (2021). Secure and sustainable predictive framework for IoT-based multimedia services using machine learning. *Sustainability (Basel), 13*(23), 13128. doi:10.3390/su132313128

Kapitonov, A., Lonshakov, S., Krupenkin, A., & Berman, I. (2017). Blockchain-based protocol of autonomous business activity for multi-agent systems consisting of UAVs. *Proceedings of the 2017 Workshop on Research, Education and Development of Unmanned Aerial Systems, RED-UAS 2017*, 84–89. 10.1109/RED-UAS.2017.8101648

Kim, D. S., & Park, J. S. (2003). Network-Based Intrusion Detection with Support Vector Machines. Information Networking, Lecture Notes in Computer Science, 2662. doi:10.1007/978-3-540-45235-5_73

Kolivand, H., Rahim, M. S., Sunar, M. S., Fata, A. Z. A., & Wren, C. (2021). An integration of enhanced social force and crowd control models for high-density crowd simulation. *Neural Computing & Applications, 33*(11), 6095–6117. doi:10.1007/s00521-020-05385-6

Li, D., Deng, L., Lee, M., & Wang, H. (2019). IoT data feature extraction and intrusion detection system for smart cities based on deep migration learning. *International Journal of Information Management, 49*, 533–545. doi:10.1016/j.ijinfomgt.2019.04.006

Rahul, V. K., Vinayakumar, R., Soman, K., & Poornachandran, P. (2018). Evaluating shallow and deep neural networks for network intrusion detection systems in cyber security. *Proceedings of the 2018 9th Int. Conf. Comput. Commun. Netw. Technol. ICCCNT.*

Rehman Khan, A., Saba, T., Sadad, T., & Hong, S. (2022). Cloudbased framework for COVID-19 detection through feature fusion with bootstrap aggregated extreme learning machine. *Discrete Dynamics in Nature and Society, 2022*, 1–7. doi:10.1155/2022/3111200

Saba, T. (2020). Intrusion detection in smart city hospitals using ensemble classifiers. In *Proceedings of the 13th International Conference on the Developments on eSystems Engineering (DeSE2020).* IEEE. 10.1109/DeSE51703.2020.9450247

Saba, T., Haseeb, K., Shah, A. A., Rehman, A., Tariq, U., & Mehmood, Z. (2021). A machine-learning-based approach for autonomous IoT security. *IT Professional, 23*(3), 69–75. doi:10.1109/MITP.2020.3031358

Saba, T., Sadad, T., Rehman, A., Mehmood, Z., & Javaid, Q. (2021). Intrusion detection system through advance machine learning for the internet of things networks. *IT Professional*, *23*(2), 58–64. doi:10.1109/MITP.2020.2992710

Shashi, K. S., Anurag, S. T., & Gaurav, K. T. (2015). Secure Medical Data Transmission by using ECC with Mutual Authentication in WSNs. *Elsevier Procedia Computer Science*, *70*, 455–461.

Yar, H., Hussain, T., Khan, Z. A., Koundal, D., Lee, M. Y., & Baik, S. W. (2021). Vision sensor-based real-time fire detection in resource-constrained IoT environments. *Computational Intelligence and Neuroscience*, *2021*, 1–15. doi:10.1155/2021/5195508 PMID:34970311

Yasin, M., Cheema, A. R., & Kausar, F. (2010). Analysis of Internet Download Manager for collection of digital forensic artefacts. *Digital Investigation*, *7*(1-2), 90–94. doi:10.1016/j.diin.2010.08.005

Zhao, Ikram, Asghar, Kaafar, Chaabane, & Ilakarathna. (2019). A decade of mal-activity reporting: a retrospective analysis of internet malicious activity blacklists. *Proceedings of the AsiaCCS - 2019 ACM Asia Conference on Computer and Communications Security,* 193–205.

Compilation of References

Abbasinezhad-Mood, D., & Nikooghadam, M. (2018). An anonymous ecc-based self-certified key distribution scheme for the smart grid. *IEEE Transactions on Industrial Electronics*, *65*(10), 7996–8004. doi:10.1109/TIE.2018.2807383

Abbasi, R., Luo, B., Rehman, G., Hassan, H., Iqbal, M. S., & Xu, L. (2018). A new multilevel reversible bit-planes data hiding technique based on histogram shifting of efficient compressed domain. *Vietnam Journal of Computer Science*, *5*(2), 185–196. doi:10.1007/s40595-018-0114-z

Abbasi, R., Xu, L., Amin, F., & Luo, B. (2019). Efficient lossless compression based reversible data hiding using multilayered n-bit localization. *Security and Communication Networks*, *2019*, 8981240. doi:10.1155/2019/8981240

Abdulaziz, F., Mohamed, A. E., Abdelghani, D., & Mohammed, A. A. (2020). IoT Intrusion Detection System Using Deep Learning and Enhanced Transient Search Optimization. *IEEE Access : Practical Innovations, Open Solutions*, *9*, 123448–123464.

Abirami, M. S., Vennila, B., Chilukalapalli, E. L., & Kuriyedath, R. (2020). A classification model to predict onset of smoking and drinking habits based on socio-economic and sociocultural factors. *Journal of Ambient Intelligence and Humanized Computing*, *12*(3), 4171–4179. doi:10.1007/s12652-020-01796-4

Abirami, M. S., Vennila, B., Suganthi, K., Kawatra, S., & Vaishnava, A. (2021). Detection of Choroidal Neovascularization (CNV) in Retina OCT Images Using VGG16 and DenseNet CNN. *Wireless Personal Communications*. Advance online publication. doi:10.1007/s11277-021-09086-8

Abubakar, A., & Pranggono, B. (2017). Machine learning based intrusion detection system for software defined networks. *Proceedings of the - 2017 7th International Conference on Emerging Security Technologies, EST 2017*, 138–143.

Abusham, E., Ibrahim, B., Zia, K., & Rehman, M. (2023). Facial image encryption for secure face recognition system. *Electronics (Basel)*, *12*(3), 774. doi:10.3390/electronics12030774

Agarwal, S., & Jung, K. H. (2023). Forensic analysis and detection using polycolor model binary pattern for colorized images. *Multimedia Tools and Applications*, 1–20. doi:10.1007/s11042-023-16675-1

Aggarwal, A. K. (2022). Learning texture features from glcm for classification of brain tumor mri images using random forest classifier. *Transactions on Signal Processing*, *18*, 60–63. doi:10.37394/232014.2022.18.8

Ahmad, S., & Mirvaziri, H. (2019). Performance improvement of intrusion detection system using neural networks and particle swarm optimization algorithms. *International Journal of Information Technology : an Official Journal of Bharati Vidyapeeth's Institute of Computer Applications and Management*, *12*, 849–860.

Ahmed, Florence, & Upganlawar. (2022). *A Novel Model to gain Internet Anonymity using Elastic Cloud Computing*. Academic Press.

Ajaeiya, G. A., Adalian, N., Elhajj, I. H., Kayssi, A., & Chehab, A. (2017). Flow-based intrusion detection system for SDN. *Proc. - IEEE Symp. Comput. Commun.*, 787–793. 10.1109/ISCC.2017.8024623

Al Alkeem, E., Kim, S. K., Yeun, C. Y., Zemerly, M. J., Poon, K. F., Gianini, G., & Yoo, P. D. (2019). An enhanced electrocardiogram biometric authentication system using machine learning. *IEEE Access : Practical Innovations, Open Solutions*, 7, 123069–123075. doi:10.1109/ACCESS.2019.2937357

Al-Hamar, Y., Kolivand, H., Tajdini, M., Saba, T., & Ramachandran, V. (2021). Enterprise credential spear-phishing Discrete Dynamics in Nature and Society attack detection. *Computers & Electrical Engineering*, 94, 107363. doi:10.1016/j.compeleceng.2021.107363

Ali, E. S., Hasan, M. K., Hassan, R., Saeed, R. A., Hassan, M. B., Islam, S., Nafi, N. S., & Bevinakoppa, S. (2021). Machine Learning Technologies for Secure Vehicular Communication in Internet of Vehicles: Recent Advances and Applications. Security and Communication Networks, (1), 1-23.

Ali, S. S., Baghel, V. S., Ganapathi, I. I., & Prakash, S. (2020). Robust biometric authentication system with a secure user template. *Image and Vision Computing*, 104, 104004. doi:10.1016/j.imavis.2020.104004

Almousa, M., Osawere, J., & Anwar, M. (2021). Identification of Ransomware families by Analyzing Network Traffic Using Machine Learning Techniques. *International Conference on transdisciplinary AI (TransAI)*.

Almousa, M., Osawere, J., & Anwar, M. (2021). Identification of Ransomware families by Analyzing Network Traffic Using Machine Learning Techniques. *2021 Third International Conference on Transdisciplinary AI (TransAI)*, 19-24. 10.1109/TransAI51903.2021.00012

Al-Rawe, Y. H. A., & Naimi, S. (2023). Project construction risk estimation in iraq based on delphi, RII, spearman's rank correlation coefficient (DRS) using machine learning. *International Journal of Intelligent Systems and Applications in Engineering*, 11(5s), 335–342. www.scopus.com

Alroobaea, R., Arul, R., Rubaiee, S., Alharithi, F. S., Tariq, U., & Fan, X. (2022). AI-assisted bio-inspired algorithm for secure IoT communication networks. *Cluster Computing*, 25(3), 1805–1816. doi:10.1007/s10586-021-03520-z

Alsadhan, A. A., & Alani, M. M. A. (2018). Detecting ndp distributed denial of service attacks using machine learning algorithm based on flow-based representation. *Developments in eSystems Engineering (DeSE), 2018 Eleventh International Conference on.* 10.1109/DeSE.2018.00028

Alsafyani, M., Alhomayani, F., Alsuwat, H., & Alsuwat, E. (2023). Face Image Encryption Based on Feature with Optimization Using Secure Crypto General Adversarial Neural Network and Optical Chaotic Map. *Sensors (Basel)*, 23(3), 1415–1415. doi:10.3390/s23031415 PMID:36772454

Alshammari, R., & Zincir-Heywood, A. N. (2009). Machine learning based encrypted traffic classification: Identifying ssh and skype. *Computational Intelligence for Security and Defense Applications, 2009. IEEE Symposium on CISDA 2009*, 1–8.

Amritha, Jo, & Kim. (2014). Application of ntru cryptographic algorithm for scada security. In *2014 11th international conference on information technology: new generations* (pp. 341–346). IEEE.

Anees, A. (2022). *Machine Learning and Applied Cryptography, Security and Communication networks*. Wiley.

Anees, A., Hussain, I., Khokhar, U. M., Ahmed, F., & Shaukat, S. (2022). Machine learning and applied cryptography. *Security and Communication Networks*, 2022, 1–3. doi:10.1155/2022/9797604

Anilkumar, C., Lenka, S., Neelima, N., & v e, S. (2024). A secure method of communication through BB84 protocol in Quantum Key Distribution. *Scalable Computing: Practice and Experience*, 25(1), 21–33. doi:10.12694/scpe.v25i1.2152

Armstrong, K. (2021). *Applying machine learning to predict symmetric encryption algorithm inputs* [Master Thesis]. Channel Islands, California State University.

Ashwanth, B., & Swamy, K. V. (2020, March). Medical image fusion using transform techniques. In *2020 5th International conference on devices, circuits and systems (ICDCS)* (pp. 303-306). IEEE. 10.1109/ICDCS48716.2020.243604

AthalyeA.EngstromL.IlyasA.KwokK. (2018). *Synthesizing robust adversarial examples.* arXiv:1707.07397v3

Auernhammer, K., Kolagari, R. T., & Zoppelt, M. (2019). Attacks on Machine Learning: Lurking Danger for Accountability. *Conf. of AAAI Workshop on Artificial Intelligence Safety.*

AWS Dashboard. (n.d.). https://awsacademy.instructure.com/

Bagdasaryan, E., Veit, A., Hua, Y., Estrin, D., & Shmatikov, V. (2018). *How to backdoor federated learning.* arXiv preprint arXiv:1807.00459.

Bailey, M., Oberheide, J., Andersen, J., Mao, Z. M., Jahanian, F., & Nazario, J. (2007). Automated classification and analysis of internet malware. In *International Workshop on Recent Advances in Intrusion Detection.* Springer. 10.1007/978-3-540-74320-0_10

Banafa, A. (2023). Quantum Computing trends. *Introduction to Quantum Computing, 31–35,* 31–35. Advance online publication. doi:10.1201/9781003440239-8

Banerjee, S., & Mondal, A. C. (2023). An intelligent approach to reducing plant disease and enhancing productivity using machine learning. *International Journal on Recent and Innovation Trends in Computing and Communication, 11*(3), 250–262. doi:10.17762/ijritcc.v11i3.6344

Barburiceanu, S., Terebes, R., & Meza, S. (2021). 3D texture feature extraction and classification using GLCM and LBP-based descriptors. *Applied Sciences (Basel, Switzerland), 11*(5), 2332. doi:10.3390/app11052332

Barnett, S. (2009). *Quantum cryptography.* Quantum Information. doi:10.1093/oso/9780198527626.003.0006

Basu, S., Karuppiah, M., Nasipuri, M., Halder, A. K., & Radhakrishnan, N. (2019). Bio-inspired cryptosystem with DNA cryptography and neural networks. *Journal of Systems Architecture, 94,* 24–31. doi:10.1016/j.sysarc.2019.02.005

Bharadwaja Kumar, Rampavan, & Ijjina. (2021). *Deep Learning based Brake Light Detection for Two Wheelers.* doi:10.1109/ICCCNT51525.2021.9579918

Bhattacharyya, D. K., & Kalita, J. K. (2013). *Network anomaly detection: A machine learning perspective.* Chapman and Hall/CRC. doi:10.1201/b15088

Bhawani, D. (2023). Design of inception with deep convolutional neural network based fall detection and classification model. *Multimedia Tools and Applications.* Advance online publication. doi:10.1007/s11042-023-16476-6

Bhushan, S. (2022). Quantum cryptography. *Holistic Approach to Quantum Cryptography in Cyber Security,* 193–206. doi:10.1201/9781003296034-11

Bibak, K., & Ritchie, R. (2021). Quantum key distribution with prf (hash, nonce) achieves everlasting security. *Quantum Information Processing, 20*(7), 228. doi:10.1007/s11128-021-03164-3

Biggio, B., Corona, I., Maiorca, D., Nelson, B., Šrndić, N., Laskov, P., Giacinto, G., & Roli, F. (2023). Evasion attacks against machine learning at test time. *ECMLPKDD'13: Proceedings of the 2013th European Conference on Machine Learning and A Survey on Security Threats to Machine Learning Systems at Different Stages of its Pipeline,* 15, 387–402.

Bilge, L., Kirda, E., Krügel, C., & Balduzzi, M. (2011). EXPOSURE: Finding Malicious Domains Using Passive DNS Analysis. *Network and Distributed System Security Symposium.*

Bishop, C. M., & Nasrabadi, N. M. (2006). *Pattern recognition and machine learning* (Vol. 4). New York: Springer.

Blum, A. (2007). Machine learning theory. Carnegie Melon University, School of Computer Science.

Bonawitz, K., Ivanov, V., Kreuter, B., Marcedone, A., McMahan, H. B., Patel, S., Ramage, D., Segal, A., & Seth, K. (2017). Practical secure aggregation for privacy-preserving machine learning. *Proceedings of the 2017 ACM SIGSAC Conference on Computer and Communications Security,* 1175– 1191. 10.1145/3133956.3133982

Borges, P., Sousa, B., Ferreira, L., Saghezchi, F. B., Mantas, G., Ribeiro, J., & Simoes, P. (2017). Towards a Hybrid Intrusion Detection System for Android-based PPDR terminals. In *Proceedings of the 2017 IFIP/IEEE Symposium on Integrated Network and Service Management (IM).* IEEE. 10.23919/INM.2017.7987434

Brassard, G., & Crépeau, C. (n.d.). Quantum cryptography. Encyclopedia of Cryptography and Security, 495–500. doi:10.1007/0-387-23483-7_338

Brownlee. (2021). *Ensemble Learning Algorithms With Python.* Academic Press.

Brown, M., & Davis, R. (2020). Efficient Secure Multi-Party Computation for Collaborative Genomic Analysis. *Journal of Bioinformatics and Computational Biology,* 18(3), 235–257.

Bykovsky, A. Y., & Kompanets, I. N. (2018). Quantum cryptography and combined schemes of Quantum Cryptography Communication Networks. *Quantum Electronics,* 48(9), 777–801. doi:10.1070/QEL16732

Cabaj, K., Gawkowski, P., Grochowski, K., & Osojca, D. (2015). Network activity analysis of crypto wall ransomware. *Przegląd Elektrotechniczny,* 91(11), 201–204.

Cabaj, K., Gregorczyk, M., & Mazurczyk, W. (2018). Software-defined networking-based crypto ransomware detection using HTTP traffic characteristics. *Computers & Electrical Engineering,* 66, 353–368. doi:10.1016/j.compeleceng.2017.10.012

Canali, D., Robertson, W., Kirda, E., Kruegel, C., & Vigna, G. (2011). A Large-Scale Analysis of the Security of Embedded Firmwares. *Proceedings of the 18th Annual Network and Distributed System Security Symposium.*

Chang, H. B., & Schroeter, K. G. (2010, January). Creating safe and trusted social networks with biometric user authentication. In *International Conference on Ethics and Policy of Biometrics* (pp. 89-95). Springer Berlin Heidelberg. 10.1007/978-3-642-12595-9_12

Chang, Y., Bharadwaj, N., Edara, P., & Sun, C. (2020). Exploring Contributing Factors of Hazardous Events in Construction Zones Using Naturalistic Driving Study Data. *IEEE Transactions on Intelligent Vehicles,* 5(3), 519–527. doi:10.1109/TIV.2020.2980741

Chaofei, T. (2020). An Efficient Intrusion Detection Method Based on LightGBM and Autoencoder. *Semantic Scholar, Symmetry,* 12(1458), 1-16.

Chen, Li, Tseng, & Lin. (2017). Deep learning for malicious flow detection. *2017 IEEE 28th Annual International Symposium on Personal, Indoor, and Mobile Radio Communications (PIMRC),* 1–7.

Chen, Liu, Li, & Lu. (2017). *Targeted Backdoor Attacks on Deep Learning Systems Using Data Poisoning.* arXiv:1712.05526 v1 [cs.CR]

Chen, B., & Chandran, V. (2007, December). Biometric based cryptographic key generation from faces. In *9th Biennial Conference of the Australian Pattern Recognition Society on Digital Image Computing Techniques and Applications (DICTA 2007)* (pp. 394-401). IEEE. 10.1109/DICTA.2007.4426824

Chen, J. H., Ma, S. F., & Wu, Y. (2021). International carbon financial market prediction using particle swarm optimization and support vector machine. *Journal of Ambient Intelligence and Humanized Computing, 2021*, 1–15.

Chen, L. (2018). Privacy-Preserving Data Analytics using Secure Multi-Party Computation: A Survey. *ACM Computing Surveys, 51*(3), 1–35. doi:10.1145/3190507

Chen, R. Y., Pan, B., & Lin, X. D. (2016). Chinese stock index futures price fluctuation analysis and prediction based on complementary ensemble empirical mode decomposition. *Mathematical Problems in Engineering, 2016*, 1–13. doi:10.1155/2016/3791504

Chen, X., Gong, M., Gan, Z., Yang, L., & Chai, X. (2022). CIE-LSCP: Color image encryption scheme based on the lifting scheme and cross-component permutation. *Complex & Intelligent Systems, 9*(1), 927–950. doi:10.1007/s40747-022-00835-1 PMID:35874092

Chen, Z. (2022). Secure Multi-Party Computation for Collaborative Fraud Detection: A Systematic Review. *Journal of Financial Crime, 29*(2), 345–367.

Chesti, I. A., Humayun, M., Sama, N. U., & Jhanjhi, N. (2020). Evolution, Mitigation, and Prevention of Ransomware. *2020 2nd International Conference on Computer and Information Sciences (ICCIS)*, 1-6. 10.1109/ICCIS49240.2020.9257708

Chindiyababy, Jayaraman, R., & Kumar, M. (2022). Quantum cryptography and Quantum Key Distribution. *Holistic Approach to Quantum Cryptography in Cyber Security*, 179–192. doi:10.1201/9781003296034-10

Chung-Jui, T., Chuang, L.-Y., Jun-Yang, C., & Yang, C.-H. (2007). Feature selection using PSO-SVM. *IAENG International Journal of Computer Science, 33*.

Ciesla, R. (2020). Quantum cryptography. *Encryption for Organizations and Individuals*, 227–234. doi:10.1007/978-1-4842-6056-2_11

Cong, Y.-Q., Guan, T., Cui, J., & Cheng, X. (2022). LGBM: An Intrusion Detection Scheme for Resource-Constrained End Devices in Internet of Things. *Security and Communication Networks, 2022*, 1–12. doi:10.1155/2022/1761655

Cova, M., Kruegel, C., & Vigna, G. (2010, April). Detection and analysis of drive-by-download attacks and malicious JavaScript code. In *Proceedings of the 19th international conference on World wide web* (pp. 281-290). ACM. 10.1145/1772690.1772720

Cugurullo, F. (2020). Urban Artificial Intelligence: From Automation to Autonomy in the Smart City. *Front. Sustain. Cities, 2*(July), 1–14. doi:10.3389/frsc.2020.00038

Cui, X., Zhang, H., Fang, X., Wang, Y., Wang, D., Fan, F., & Shu, L. (2023). A Secret Key Classification Framework of Symmetric Encryption Algorithm Based on Deep Transfer Learning. *Applied Sciences (Basel, Switzerland), 13*(21), 12025. doi:10.3390/app132112025

Cusack, G., Michel, O., & Keller, E. (2018). Machine learning-based detection of ransomware using sdn. *Proceedings of the 2018 ACM International Workshop on Security in Software Defined Networks & Network Function Virtualization*, 1–6. 10.1145/3180465.3180467

Dalvi, Domingos, Mausam, & Sanghai. (2004). Adversarial Classification. *Proceedings Of The Tenth ACM SIGKDD International Conference On Knowledge Discovery And Data Mining*, 99–108.

Dang, H., Huang, Y., & Chang, E. C. (2017). Evading classifiers by morphing in the dark. *CCS '17: Proceedings of the 2017 ACM SIGSAC Conference on Computer and Communications Security*, 119–133. 10.1145/3133956.3133978

Dataoverhaulers. (n.d.). https://dataoverhaulers.com/can-encrypted-data-be-hacked/

David, B. (2023, April). An Analytical Survey on Multi-Biometric Authentication System for Enhancing the Security Levels in Cloud Computing. In *2023 Eighth International Conference on Science Technology Engineering and Mathematics (ICONSTEM)* (pp. 1-6). IEEE.

Deepika, K., & Poonam, D. (2017). Secure Data Transmission using AES in IoT. *International Journal of Application or Innovation in Engineering & Management*, *6*(6), 283–289.

Devan, P., & Khare, N. (2020). An efficient XGBoost-DNN-based classification model for network intrusion detection system. *Neural Computing & Applications*, *32*(16), 16. doi:10.1007/s00521-020-04708-x

Digital Guardian. (n.d.). https://digitalguardian.com/blog/what-data-encryption

Dwork, C., & Roth, A. (2014). The algorithmic foundations of differential privacy. Foundations and Trends® in Theoretical Computer Science, 9(3-4), 211–407.

Dzobo & Sun. (2020). Load Management Using Swarm Intelligence: Dynamic Economic Emission Dispatch Optimization. In *Novel Advancements in Electrical Power Planning and Performance*. IGI Global. https://www.igi-global.com/chapter/load-management-using-swarm-intelligence/234781 doi:10.4018/978-1-5225-8551-0.ch001

Ekert, A. (2005). Quantum cryptography. *Optical Science and Engineering*, 1–15. doi:10.1201/9781420026603.ch1

El Kamel, Eddabbah, Lmoumen, & Touahni. (2020). A Smart Agent Design for Cyber Security Based on Honeypot and Machine Learning. *Hindawi Security and Communication Networks*, 1-9.

Elhoseny, M., Haseeb, K., Shah, A. A., Ahmad, I., Jan, Z., & Alghamdi, M. I. (2021). IoT solution for AI-enabled PRIVACYPREServing with big data transferring: An application for healthcare using blockchain. *Energies*, *14*(17), 5364. doi:10.3390/en14175364

Esmaeili, M., Goki, S. H., Masjidi, B. H. K., Sameh, M., Gharagozlou, H., & Mohammed, A. S. (2022). ML-DDoSnet: IoT Intrusion Detection Based on Denial-of-Service Attacks Using Machine Learning Methods and NSL-KDD. *Wireless Communications and Mobile Computing*, *2022*, 1–16. doi:10.1155/2022/8481452

Exchange, S. (n.d.). *Hash Function on Finite Fields*. https://math.stackexchange.com/questions/1347240/how-to-attack-universal-hash-functio

Feng, D., Haase-Schutz, C., Rosenbaum, L., Hertlein, H., Glaser, C., Timm, F., ... Dietmayer, K. (2020). Deep Multi-Modal Object Detection and Semantic Segmentation for Autonomous Driving: Datasets, Methods, and Challenges. *IEEE Transactions on Intelligent Transportation Systems*, 1–20. doi:10.1109/TITS.2020.2972974

Feng, L., & Chen, X. (2022). Image Recognition and Encryption Algorithm Based on Artificial Neural Network and Multidimensional Chaotic Sequence. *Computational Intelligence and Neuroscience*, *2022*, 1–9. doi:10.1155/2022/9576184 PMID:36035834

Fu, Y., Li, C., Yu, F. R., Luan, T. H., & Zhang, Y. (2021). A Survey of Driving Safety With Sensing, Vehicular Communications, and Artificial Intelligence-Based Collision Avoidance. *IEEE Transactions on Intelligent Transportation Systems*, 1–22. doi:10.1109/TITS.2021.3083927

Gala, Y., Vanjari, N., Doshi, D., & Radhanpurwala, I. (2023). AI based Techniques for Network-based Intrusion Detection System: A Review. *2023 10th International Conference on Computing for Sustainable Global Development (INDIACom)*, 1544-1551.

Gao, Y. (2022). *An Improved Image Processing Based on Deep Learning Backpropagation Technique.* . doi:10.1155/2022/5528416

Gautam, S., Henry, A., Zuhair, M., Rashid, M., Javed, A. R., & Maddikunta, P. K. R. (2022). A Composite Approach of Intrusion Detection Systems: Hybrid RNN and Correlation-Based Feature Optimization. *Electronics (Basel)*, *11*(21), 3529. doi:10.3390/electronics11213529

Github Code Resource. (n.d.). https://github.com/kongfy/DES/blob/master/Riv85.txt

Gong, L., Qiu, K., Deng, C., & Zhou, N. (2019). An optical image compression and encryption scheme based on compressive sensing and RSA algorithm. *Optics and Lasers in Engineering*, *121*, 169–180. doi:10.1016/j.optlaseng.2019.03.006

González, G. G., Casas, P., & Fernández, A. (2023, July). Fake it till you Detect it: Continual Anomaly Detection in Multivariate Time-Series using Generative AI. In *2023 IEEE European Symposium on Security and Privacy Workshops (EuroS&PW)* (pp. 558-566). IEEE. 10.1109/EuroSPW59978.2023.00068

Gope, P., Millwood, O., & Sikdar, B. (2022). A Scalable Protocol Level Approach to Prevent Machine Learning Attacks on Physically Unclonable Function Based Authentication Mechanisms for Internet of Medical Things. *IEEE Transactions on Industrial Informatics*, *18*(3), 1971–1980. doi:10.1109/TII.2021.3096048

Govardhana Reddy, H. G., & Raghavendra, K. (2022). Vector space modelling-based intelligent binary image encryption for secure communication. *Journal of Discrete Mathematical Sciences and Cryptography*, *25*(4), 1157–1171. doi:10.1080/09720529.2022.2075090

Gowda, V. D., Prasad, K. D. V., Gite, P., Premkumar, S., Hussain, N., & Chinamuttevi, V. S.K.D.V. (2023). A novel RF-SMOTE model to enhance the definite apprehensions for IoT security attacks. *Journal of Discrete Mathematical Sciences and Cryptography*, *26*(3), 861–873. doi:10.47974/JDMSC-1766

Grier, C., Ballard, L., Caballero, J., Chachra, N., Dietrich, C. J., Levchenko, K., Mavrommatis, P., McCoy, D., Nappa, A., Pitsillidis, A., Provos, N., Rafique, M. Z., Rajab, M. A., Rossow, C., Thomas, K., Paxson, V., Savage, S., & Voelker, G. M. (2012). Manufacturing compromise: the emergence of exploit-as-a-service. *Proceedings of the 2012 ACM conference on Computer and communications security*. 10.1145/2382196.2382283

Grosse, K., Papernot, N., Manoharan, P., Backes, M., & McDaniel, P. (2017). Adversarial examples for malware detection. In *ESORICS* (pp. 62–67). Computer Security – ESORICS.

Guo, F., Jiang, Z., Wang, Y., Chen, C., & Qian, Y. (2022). Dense Traffic Detection at Highway-Railroad Grade Crossings. *IEEE Transactions on Intelligent Transportation Systems*, 1–14. doi:10.1109/TITS.2022.3219923

Gupta, S., Castleman, K. R., Markey, M. K., & Bovik, A. C. (2010). Texas 3D Face Recognition Database. *2010 IEEE Southwest Symposium on Image Analysis & Interpretation (SSIAI)*, 97–100. http://live.ece.utexas.edu/research/texas3dfr/index.htm

Gustian, D. A., Rohmah, N. L., Shidik, G. F., Fanani, A. Z., & Pramunendar, R. A. (2019, September). Classification of troso fabric using SVM-RBF multi-class method with GLCM and PCA feature extraction. In *2019 International Seminar on Application for Technology of Information and Communication (iSemantic)* (pp. 7-11). IEEE. 10.1109/ISEMANTIC.2019.8884329

Hadid, A. (2008). *The Local Binary Pattern Approach and its Applications to Face Analysis. 2008 First Workshops on Image Processing Theory*. Tools and Applications. doi:10.1109/IPTA.2008.4743795

Hadjidimitriou, N. S., Lippi, M., Dell'Amico, M., & Skiera, A. (2020). Machine Learning for Severity Classification of Accidents Involving Powered Two Wheelers. *IEEE Transactions on Intelligent Transportation Systems*, *21*(10), 4308–4317. doi:10.1109/TITS.2019.2939624

Hamidi, H. (2019). An approach to develop the smart health using Internet of Things and authentication based on biometric technology. *Future Generation Computer Systems*, *91*, 434–449. doi:10.1016/j.future.2018.09.024

Hanieh, A., Richard, M. K., Wanchat, T., & Kenneth, A. L. (2019). A swarm intelligence-based approach to anomaly detection of dynamic systems. *Swarm and Evolutionary Computation*, *44*, 806–827. doi:10.1016/j.swevo.2018.09.003

Hao, F., Anderson, R., & Daugman, J. (2006). Combining crypto with biometrics effectively. *IEEE Transactions on Computers*, *55*(9), 1081–1088. doi:10.1109/TC.2006.138

Hao, F., & Chan, C. W. (2002). Private key generation from on-line handwritten signatures. *Information Management & Computer Security*, *10*(4), 159–164. doi:10.1108/09685220210436949

Haralick, R. M., Dinstein, I., & Shanmugam, K. (1973). *Textural features for image classification*. Trans. Syst. Man Cybern. doi:10.1109/TSMC.1973.4309314

Haseeb, K., Ahmad, I., Awan, I. I., Lloret, J., & Bosch, I. (2021). A machine learning SDN-enabled big data model for IoMT systems. *Electronics (Basel)*, *10*(18), 2228. doi:10.3390/electronics10182228

Haseeb, K., Islam, N., Almogren, A., & Ud Din, I. (2019). Intrusion prevention framework for secure routing in WSN-based mobile Internet of, ings. *IEEE Access : Practical Innovations, Open Solutions*, *7*, 185496–185505. doi:10.1109/ACCESS.2019.2960633

Haseeb, K., Islam, N., Javed, Y., & Tariq, U. (2020). A lightweight secure and energy-efficient fog-based routing protocol for constraint sensors network. *Energies*, *14*(1), 89. doi:10.3390/en14010089

Haseeb, K., Jan, Z., Alzahrani, F. A., & Jeon, G. (2022). A secure mobile wireless sensor networks based protocol for smart data gathering with cloud. *Computers & Electrical Engineering*, *97*, 107584. doi:10.1016/j.compeleceng.2021.107584

Haseeb, K., Ud Din, I., Almogren, A., Ahmed, I., & Guizani, M. (2021). Intelligent and secure edge-enabled computing model for sustainable cities using green internet of things. *Sustainable Cities and Society*, *68*, 102779. doi:10.1016/j.scs.2021.102779

Heikkilä, M., Pietikäinen, M., & Schmid, C. (2009). Description of interest regions with local binary patterns. *Pattern Recognition*, *42*(3), 425–436. doi:10.1016/j.patcog.2008.08.014

Hemalatha, S. (2020, February). A systematic review on Fingerprint based Biometric Authentication System. In *2020 International Conference on Emerging Trends in Information Technology and Engineering (ic-ETITE)* (pp. 1-4). IEEE. 10.1109/ic-ETITE47903.2020.342

Hitaj, Gasti, Ateniese, & Perez-Cruz. (2019). *PassGAN: A Deep Learning Approach for Password Guessing*. Academic Press.

Hodo, E., Bellekens, X., Hamilton, A., Dubouilh, P.-L., Iorkyase, E., & Tachtatzis, C. (2016). Threat analysis of IoT networks using artificial neural network intrusion detection system. *2016 International Symposium on Networks, Computers and Communications (ISNCC)*, 1-6. 10.1109/ISNCC.2016.7746067

Holz, T., Gorecki, C., Rieck, K., & Freiling, F. C. (2009). Measuring and Detecting Fast-Flux Service Networks. *Proceedings of the 14th European Conference on Research in Computer Security*.

Huang, Y. (2021). Privacy-Preserving Collaborative Natural Language Processing using Secure Multi-Party Computation. *Journal of Artificial Intelligence Research*, *70*, 965–988.

Hua, Z., Xu, B., Jin, F., & Huang, H. (2019). Image Encryption Using Josephus Problem and Filtering Diffusion. *IEEE Access : Practical Innovations, Open Solutions*, *7*, 8660–8674. doi:10.1109/ACCESS.2018.2890116

Hussain, A. A. J., Pazhani, & A. K., N. (2023). A Novel Method of Enhancing Security Solutions and Energy Efficiency of IoT Protocols. *IJRITCC, 11*(4), 325–335.

Hussain, A. A. J., Pazhani, & A. K., N. (2023). A Novel Method of Enhancing Security Solutions and Energy Efficiency of IoT Protocols. *IJRITCC, 11*(4S), 325–335.

Hussain, Pazhani, & A. K. (2023). A Novel Method of Enhancing Security Solutions and Energy Efficiency of IoT Protocols. *IJRITCC, 11*(4), 325–335.

Hussain, L., Malibari, A. A., Alzahrani, J. S., Alamgeer, M., Obayya, M., Al-Wesabi, F. N., Mohsen, H., & Hamza, M. A. (2022). Bayesian dynamic profiling and optimization of important ranked energy from gray level co-occurrence (GLCM) features for empirical analysis of brain MRI. *Scientific Reports, 12*(1), 15389. doi:10.1038/s41598-022-19563-0 PMID:36100621

Incode. (2022, December 12). *The Future of Biometrics Technology: An Overview by Industry.* Retrieved from https://incode.com/blog/future-of-biometrics/

Ingale, M., Cordeiro, R., Thentu, S., Park, Y., & Karimian, N. (2020). Ecg biometric authentication: A comparative analysis. *IEEE Access : Practical Innovations, Open Solutions, 8*, 117853–117866. doi:10.1109/ACCESS.2020.3004464

Iqbal, N., Mumtaz, R., Shafi, U., & Zaidi, S. M. H. (2021). Gray level co-occurrence matrix (GLCM) texture based crop classification using low altitude remote sensing platforms. PeerJ Comp. *Sci., 7*, e536. PMID:34141878

Islam, N., Altamimi, M., Haseeb, K., & Siraj, M. (2021). Secure and sustainable predictive framework for IoT-based multimedia services using machine learning. *Sustainability (Basel), 13*(23), 13128. doi:10.3390/su132313128

Jeddy, N., Radhika, T., & Nithya, S. (2017). Tongue prints in biometric authentication: A pilot study. *Journal of Oral and Maxillofacial Pathology : JOMFP, 21*(1), 176. doi:10.4103/jomfp.JOMFP_185_15 PMID:28479712

Jia-Lun & Lo. (2015). Secure anonymous key distribution scheme for smart grid. *IEEE Transactions on Smart Grid, 7*(2), 906–914.

Joshi, N., Sheth, T., Shah, V., Gupta, J., & Mujawar, S. (2022). A Detailed Evaluation of SQL Injection Attacks, Detection and Prevention Techniques. *2022 5th International Conference on Advances in Science and Technology (ICAST),* 352-357. 10.1109/ICAST55766.2022.10039662

Kandhro, I. A., Alanazi, S. M., Ali, F., Kehar, A., Fatima, K., Uddin, M., & Karuppayah, S. (2023). Detection of Real-Time Malicious Intrusions and Attacks in IoT Empowered Cybersecurity Infrastructures. *IEEE Access : Practical Innovations, Open Solutions, 11*, 9136–9148. doi:10.1109/ACCESS.2023.3238664

Kapitonov, A., Lonshakov, S., Krupenkin, A., & Berman, I. (2017). Blockchain-based protocol of autonomous business activity for multi-agent systems consisting of UAVs. *Proceedings of the 2017 Workshop on Research, Education and Development of Unmanned Aerial Systems, RED-UAS 2017,* 84–89. 10.1109/RED-UAS.2017.8101648

Kaplan, K., Kaya, Y., Kuncan, M., & Ertunç, H. M. (2020). Brain tumor classification using modified local binary patterns (LBP) feature extraction methods. *Medical Hypotheses, 139*, 109696. doi:10.1016/j.mehy.2020.109696 PMID:32234609

Karatas, G., Demir, O., & Sahingoz, O. K. (2019). A Deep Learning Based Intrusion Detection System on GPUs. *2019 11th International Conference on Electronics, Computers and Artificial Intelligence (ECAI),* 1-6. 10.1109/ECAI46879.2019.9042132

Karungaru, S., Dongyang, L., & Terada, K. (2021). Vehicle Detection and Type Classification Based on CNN-SVM. *International Journal of Machine Learning and Computing, 11*(4), 304–310. doi:10.18178/ijmlc.2021.11.4.1052

Kaur, H., Koundal, D., & Kadyan, V. (2021). Image fusion techniques: A survey. *Archives of Computational Methods in Engineering, 28*(7), 4425–4447. doi:10.1007/s11831-021-09540-7 PMID:33519179

Khan, Arshad, & Mohsin. (n.d.). Population Growth and Its Impact on Urban Expansion: A Case Study of Bahawalpur, Pakistan. *Univers. J. Geosci., 2.*

Khan, H., Alam, M., Al-Kuwari, S., & Faheem, Y. (2021). Offensive AI: Unification of Email Generation Through GPT-2 Model With A Game-Theoretic Approach For Spear-Phishing Attacks. Competitive Advantage in the Digital Economy (CADE 2021), 178 – 184. doi:10.1049/icp.2021.2422

Khan, M. N., Das, A., Ahmed, M. M., & Wulff, S. S. (2021). Multilevel weather detection based on images: A machine learning approach with histogram of oriented gradient and local binary pattern-based features. *Journal of Intelligent Transport Systems, 25*(5), 513–532. doi:10.1080/15472450.2021.1944860

Kim, D. S., & Park, J. S. (2003). Network-Based Intrusion Detection with Support Vector Machines. Information Networking, Lecture Notes in Computer Science, 2662. doi:10.1007/978-3-540-45235-5_73

Kim, S. K., Yeun, C. Y., Damiani, E., & Lo, N. W. (2019). A machine learning framework for biometric authentication using electrocardiogram. *IEEE Access : Practical Innovations, Open Solutions, 7,* 94858–94868. doi:10.1109/ACCESS.2019.2927079

Klein, E., Mislovaty, R., Kanter, I., Ruttor, A., & Kinzel, W. (2005). Synchronization of neural networks by mutual learning and its application to cryptography. *Advances in Neural Information Processing Systems,* 689–696.

Klonovs, J., Petersen, C. K., Olesen, H., & Hammershoj, A. (2013). ID proof on the go: Development of a mobile EEG-based biometric authentication system. *IEEE Vehicular Technology Magazine, 8*(1), 81–89. doi:10.1109/MVT.2012.2234056

Knudsen, L. R., & Mathiassen, J. E. (2000). A chosen-plaintext linear attack on DES. *Proceedings of the International Workshop on Fast Software Encryption (FSE),* 262–272.

Kolivand, H., Rahim, M. S., Sunar, M. S., Fata, A. Z. A., & Wren, C. (2021). An integration of enhanced social force and crowd control models for high-density crowd simulation. *Neural Computing & Applications, 33*(11), 6095–6117. doi:10.1007/s00521-020-05385-6

Kousis, A., & Tjortjis, C. (2021). Data Mining Algorithms for Smart Cities: A Bibliometric Analysis. *Algorithms, 14*(8), 242. doi:10.3390/a14080242

Kruegel, C., Vigna, G., & Robertson, W. (2005, August). A multi-model approach to the detection of web-based attacks. *Computer Networks, 48*(5), 717–738. doi:10.1016/j.comnet.2005.01.009

Kumar & Chaturvedi. (2023). Securing networked image transmission using public-key cryptography and identity authentication. *Journal of Discrete Mathematical Sciences and Cryptography, 26*(3), 779-791. doi:10.47974/JDMSC-1754

Kumar, P. H., & Samanta, T. (2022). Deep Learning Based Optimal Traffic Classification Model for Modern Wireless Networks. *2022 IEEE 19th India Council International Conference (INDICON),* 1-6. 10.1109/INDICON56171.2022.10039822

Kumar, A., Jain, S., & Kumar, M. (2023). Face and gait biometrics authentication system based on simplified deep neural networks. *International Journal of Information Technology : an Official Journal of Bharati Vidyapeeth's Institute of Computer Applications and Management, 15*(2), 1005–1014. doi:10.1007/s41870-022-01087-5

Kumar, A., & Kumar, A. (2008, March). A palmprint-based cryptosystem using double encryption. In *Biometric technology for human identification V* (Vol. 6944, pp. 115–123). SPIE. doi:10.1117/12.778833

Kumar, R., & Ashreetha, B. (2023). Performance Analysis of Energy Efficiency and Security Solutions of Internet of Things Protocols. *IJEER, 11*(2), 442–450. doi:10.37391/ijeer.110226

Kushwaha, M. (n.d.). Analysis and Identifying of Important Features on Road Accidents by using Machine Learning Algorithms. 한국감성과학회 국제학술대회 *(ICES), 2021*, 110–113. Retrieved from https://kiss.kstudy.com/Detail/Ar?key=3947641

Kushwaha, M. (2022). Comparative Analysis on the Prediction of Road Accident Severity Using Machine Learning Algorithms. In *Micro-Electronics and Telecommunication Engineering* (pp. 269–280). Springer. doi:10.1007/978-981-16-8721-1_26

Kushwaha, M. (2023). Yolov7-based Brake Light Detection Model for Avoiding Rear-End Collisions. In *12th International Conference on Advanced Computing (ICoAC)*. IEEE. 10.1109/ICoAC59537.2023.10249731

Kushwaha, M., & Abirami, M. S. (2023). Intelligent model for avoiding road accidents using artificial neural network. *International Journal of Computers, Communications & Control, 18*(5). Advance online publication. doi:10.15837/ijccc.2023.5.5317

Kwon, T., & Moon, H. (2008). Biometric authentication for border control applications. *IEEE Transactions on Knowledge and Data Engineering, 20*(8), 1091–1096. doi:10.1109/TKDE.2007.190716

Lee, S.-J., Shim, H.-Y., Lee, Y.-R., Park, T.-R., Park, S.-H., & Lee, I.-G. (2021). Study on Systematic Ransomware Detection Techniques. *2021 23rd International Conference on Advanced Communication Technology (ICACT)*, 297-301. 10.23919/ICACT51234.2021.9370472

Lee, C., Sohn, I., & Lee, W. (2022). Eavesdropping detection in bb84 quantum key distribution protocols. *IEEE Transactions on Network and Service Management, 19*(3), 2689–2701. doi:10.1109/TNSM.2022.3165202

Lee, H., & Wang, S. (2021). Secure Multi-Party Computation for Collaborative Machine Learning: Challenges and Solutions. *IEEE Transactions on Knowledge and Data Engineering, 33*(8), 1234–1256.

Li, H., Wang, Y., Xie, X., Yang, L., Wang, S., & Wan, R. (2020). Light can hack your face! Black-box backdoor attack on face recognition systems. *arXiv preprint arXiv:2009.06996.*

Li, P., Qiang, W. & Christopher, J. B. (2007). McRank: Learning to rank using multiple classification and gradient boosting. Advances in Neural Information Processing Systems, 20.

Li, X., Jiang, Y., Chen, M., & Li, F. (2018). Research on iris image encryption based on deep learning. *EURASIP Journal on Image and Video Processing, 2018*(1). doi:10.1186/s13640-018-0358-7

Liang, Y., Wu, J., & Wang, W. (2019). ACM Product Marketing Prediction Based on XGboost and LightGBM Algorithm. Association for Computing Machinery.

Liang, G. J. (2015). Automatic Traffic Accident Detection Based on the Internet of Things and Support Vector Machine. *International Journal of Smart Home, 9*(4), 97–106. doi:10.14257/ijsh.2015.9.4.10

Li, D., Deng, L., Lee, M., & Wang, H. (2019). IoT data feature extraction and intrusion detection system for smart cities based on deep migration learning. *International Journal of Information Management, 49*, 533–545. doi:10.1016/j.ijinfomgt.2019.04.006

Li, Q., Garg, S., Nie, J., Li, X., Liu, R. W., Cao, Z., & Hossain, M. S. (2021). A Highly Efficient Vehicle Taillight Detection Approach Based on Deep Learning. *IEEE Transactions on Intelligent Transportation Systems, 22*(7), 4716–4726. doi:10.1109/TITS.2020.3027421

Liu, L., Gao, M., Zhang, Y., & Wang, Y. (2022). Application of machine learning in intelligent encryption for digital information of real-time image text under big data. *EURASIP Journal on Wireless Communications and Networking,* *2022*(1). . doi:10.1186/s13638-022-02111-9

Liu, X. (2022). Secure Multi-Party Computation for Collaborative Financial Analysis: A Systematic Review. *Journal of Financial Data Science, 2*(1), 45–68.

Lowd & Meek. (2005). Good word attacks on statistical spam filters. In CEAS-2005, Palo Alto, CA.

Lu, Du, Li, Chen, & Wang. (2020). Android Malware Detection Based on a Hybrid Deep Learning Model. *Security and Communication Networks,* 1–11.

M.S., A. (2020). Building an ensemble learning based algorithm for improving intrusion detection system. *Artificial Intelligence and Evolutionary Computations in Engineering Systems, 1056.* Retrieved from https://link.springer.com/chapter/10.1007/978-981-15-0199-9_55

Machado, F. P. (2003). *Communication and memory efficient parallel decision tree construction.* Academic Press.

Mahesh, V. G., Raj, A. N. J., & Nersisson, R. (2022). Implementation of Machine Learning-Aided Speech Analysis for Speaker Accent Identification Applied to Audio Forensics. In *Aiding Forensic Investigation Through Deep Learning and Machine Learning Frameworks* (pp. 174–194). IGI Global. doi:10.4018/978-1-6684-4558-7.ch008

Maheswari, M., & Gunasekharan, S. (n.d.). Sumadeepthi Veeraganti. *Energy Management.*

Mahmoody, M., Moran, T., & Vadhan, S. (2012). Publicly Verifiable Proofs of Sequential Work. *Proceedings of the 4th Conference on Innovations in Theoretical Computer Science.*

Makrushin, A., Kauba, C., Kirchgasser, S., Seidlitz, S., Kraetzer, C., Uhl, A., & Dittmann, J. (2021, June). General requirements on synthetic fingerprint images for biometric authentication and forensic investigations. In *Proceedings of the 2021 ACM Workshop on Information Hiding and Multimedia Security* (pp. 93-104). 10.1145/3437880.3460410

Ma, L., Cheng, S., & Shi, Y. (2021). Enhancing learning efficiency of brain storm optimization via orthogonal learning design. *IEEE Transactions on Systems, Man, and Cybernetics. Systems, 51*(11), 6723–6742. doi:10.1109/TSMC.2020.2963943

Ma, L., Huang, M., Yang, S., Wang, R., & Wang, X. (2021). An adaptive localized decision variable analysis approach to large-scale multi-objective and many-objective optimization. *IEEE Transactions on Cybernetics, 52*(7), 6684–6696. doi:10.1109/TCYB.2020.3041212 PMID:33476273

Mall, P. K., Singh, P. K., & Yadav, D. (2019, December). GLCM based feature extraction and medical X-RAY image classification using machine learning techniques. In *2019 IEEE Conference on Information and Communication Technology* (pp. 1-6). IEEE. 10.1109/CICT48419.2019.9066263

Maniyath, S. R., & V, T. (2020). An efficient image encryption using deep neural network and chaotic map. *Microprocessors and Microsystems, 77,* 103134. doi:10.1016/j.micpro.2020.103134

Mansoor, U., Ratrout, N. T., Rahman, S. M., & Assi, K. (2020). Crash Severity Prediction Using Two-Layer Ensemble Machine Learning Model for Proactive Emergency Management. *IEEE Access : Practical Innovations, Open Solutions, 8,* 210750–210762. doi:10.1109/ACCESS.2020.3040165

Mazumdar, J. B., & Nirmala, S. R. (2018). Retina based biometric authentication system: A review. *International Journal of Advanced Research in Computer Science, 9*(1). Advance online publication. doi:10.26483/ijarcs.v9i1.5322

Meena, G., & Choudhary, S. (2019). Biometric authentication in internet of things: A conceptual view. *Journal of Statistics and Management Systems, 22*(4), 643–652. doi:10.1080/09720510.2019.1609722

Memos, V. A., & Psannis, K. E. (2020). AI-Powered Honeypots for Enhanced IoT Botnet Detection. *2020 3rd World Symposium on Communication Engineering (WSCE), Thessaloniki, Greece*, 64-68. 10.1109/WSCE51339.2020.9275581

miniOrange. (n.d.). *What is Authentication? Different Types of Authentication.* Retrieved from https://blog.miniorange.com/different-types-of-authentication-methods-for-security/

Mohamed, K. S. (2020). New trends in cryptography: Quantum, blockchain, lightweight, chaotic, and DNA cryptography. *New Frontiers in Cryptography*, 65–87. doi:10.1007/978-3-030-58996-7_4

Mohamed, S. A., Alsaif, O. I., & Saleh, I. A. (2022). Intrusion Detection Network Attacks Based on Whale Optimization Algorithm. *Ingénierie Des Systèmes D Information, 27*(3), 441–446. doi:10.18280/isi.270310

Mohassel, P., & Zhang, Y. (2017). Secureml: A system for scalable privacy-preserving machine learning. *2017 38th IEEE Symposium on Security and Privacy (SP)*, 19–38. 10.1109/SP.2017.12

Monrose, F., Reiter, M. K., & Wetzel, S. (1999, November). Password hardening based on keystroke dynamics. In *Proceedings of the 6th ACM Conference on Computer and Communications Security* (pp. 73-82). ACM.

Mourad, A., Tout, H., Wahab, O. A., Otrok, H., & Dbouk, T. (2020). Ad-hoc Vehicular Fog Enabling Cooperative Low-Latency Intrusion Detection. *IEEE Internet of Things Journal*, 1–1. doi:10.1109/JIOT.2020.3008488

Mthunzi, S. N., Benkhelifa, E., Bosakowski, T., & Hariri, S. (2019). A bio-inspired approach to cyber security. *Machine Learning for Computer and Cyber Security: Principle, Algorithms, and Practices*, 75.

Muhammed, S., Gianni, A. D. C., & Muddassar, F. (2011). Swarm intelligence based routing protocol for wireless sensor networks: Survey and future directions'. *Information Sciences, 181*(20), 4597–4624. doi:10.1016/j.ins.2010.07.005

Musa, A., & Mahmood, A. (2021). Client-side Cryptography Based Security for Cloud Computing System. *2021 International Conference on Artificial Intelligence and Smart Systems (ICAIS)*, 594-600. 10.1109/ICAIS50930.2021.9395890

Nadiya El, K., Mohamed, E., Youssef, L., & Raja, T. (2020). A Smart Agent Design for Cyber Security Based on Honeypot and Machine Learning. *Security and Communication Networks, 2020*, 1–9.

Nanni, L., Lumini, A., & Brahnam, S. (2012). Survey on LBP based texture descriptors for image classification. *Expert Systems with Applications, 39*(3), 3634–3641. doi:10.1016/j.eswa.2011.09.054

Neetesh & Grijalva. (2016). Dynamic secrets and secret keys based scheme for securing last mile smart grid wireless communication. *IEEE Transactions on Industrial Informatics, 13*(3), 1482–1491.

NgA.NotesL. (n.d.). https://see.stanford.edu/materials/aimlcs229/cs229-notes3.pdf

Nitaj, A., & Rachidi, T. (2023). Applications of neural network-based AI in cryptography. *Cryptography, 7*(3), 39. doi:10.3390/cryptography7030039

Nita, S. L., Mihailescu, M. I., & Pau, V. C. (2018). Security and cryptographic challenges for authentication based on biometrics data. *Cryptography, 2*(4), 39. doi:10.3390/cryptography2040039

Novel Advancements in Electrical Power Planning and Performance. (2020). IGI Global. doi:10.4018/978-1-5225-8551-0.ch008

O'Connell-Rodwell, C. E. (2007). Keeping an "ear" to the ground: Seismic communication in elephants. *Physiology (Bethesda, MD), 22*(4), 287–294. doi:10.1152/physiol.00008.2007 PMID:17699882

Odelu, V., Das, A. K., Wazid, M., & Conti, M. (2016). Provably secure authenticated key agreement scheme for smart grid. *IEEE Transactions on Smart Grid, 9*(3), 1900–1910. doi:10.1109/TSG.2016.2602282

Ogbanufe, O., & Kim, D. J. (2018). Comparing fingerprint-based biometrics authentication versus traditional authentication methods for e-payment. *Decision Support Systems*, *106*, 1–14. doi:10.1016/j.dss.2017.11.003

Ohrimenko, O., Schuster, F., Fournet, C., Mehta, A., Nowozin, S., Vaswani, K., & Costa, M. (2016). Oblivious multiparty machine learning on trusted processors. *USENIX Security Symposium*, 619–636.

Omar, M. K. (2018). Leveraging machine learning techniques for windows ransomware network traffic detection. In *Cyber threat intelligence* (pp. 93–106). Springer.

Omuya, E. O., Okeyo, G. O., & Kimwele, M. W. (2021). Feature selection for classification using principal component analysis and information gain. *Expert Systems with Applications*, *174*, 114765. doi:10.1016/j.eswa.2021.114765

Open.edu. (n.d.). https://www.open.edu/openlearn/science-maths-technology/computing-and-ict/systems-co

Ouladj, M., & Guilley, S. (2021). *Side-Channel Analysis of Embedded Systems: An Efficient Algorithmic Approach*. Springer. doi:10.1007/978-3-030-77222-2

Papernot, N., McDaniel, P., Sinha, A., & Wellman, M. (2016). *Towards the science of security and privacy in machine learning*. arXiv preprint arXiv:1611.03814.

Patil, S. D., Raut, R., Jhaveri, R. H., Ahanger, T. A., Dhade, P. V., Kathole, A. B., & Vhatkar, K. N. (2022). Robust authentication system with privacy preservation of biometrics. *Security and Communication Networks*, *2022*, 2022. doi:10.1155/2022/7857975

Pavankumar, P., & Darwante, N. K. (2022). Performance Monitoring and Dynamic Scaling Algorithm for Queue Based Internet of Things. *2022 International Conference on Innovative Computing, Intelligent Communication and Smart Electrical Systems (ICSES)*, 1-7. 10.1109/ICSES55317.2022.9914108

Pearce, H., Tan, B., Ahmad, B., Karri, R., & Dolan-Gavitt, B. (2023). Examining Zero-Shot Vulnerability Repair with Large Language Models. In *Proceedings - 44th IEEE Symposium on Security and Privacy, SP 2023* (pp. 2339-2356). Institute of Electrical and Electronics Engineers Inc. 10.1109/SP46215.2023.10179324

Penteado, B. E., & Marana, A. N. (2009). A video-based biometric authentication for e-Learning web applications. *Enterprise Information Systems: 11th International Conference, ICEIS 2009, Milan, Italy, May 6-10, 2009. Proceedings*, *11*, 770–779.

Petr Gallus. (2023). *Generative Neural Networks as a Tool for Web Applications Penetration Testing*. Institute of Electrical and Electronic Engineers.

Pourkaramdel, Z., Fekri-Ershad, S., & Nanni, L. (2022). Fabric defect detection based on completed local quartet patterns and majority decision algorithm. *Expert Systems with Applications*, *198*, 116827. doi:10.1016/j.eswa.2022.116827

Pouyap, M., Bitjoka, L., Mfoumou, E., & Toko, D. (2021). Improved Bearing Fault Diagnosis by Feature Extraction Based on GLCM, Fusion of Selection Methods, and Multiclass-Naïve Bayes Classification. *Journal of Signal and Information Processing*, *12*(4), 71–85. doi:10.4236/jsip.2021.124004

Prasad, S. G., Sharmila, V. C., & Badrinarayanan, M. K. (2023). Role of Artificial Intelligence based Chat Generative Pre-trained Transformer (ChatGPT) in Cyber Security. *2023 2nd International Conference on Applied Artificial Intelligence and Computing (ICAAIC)*, 107-114. 10.1109/ICAAIC56838.2023.10141395

Prasad, G., Gaddale, V. S., Kamath, R. C., Shekaranaik, V. J., & Pai, S. P. (2023). A Study of Dimensionality Reduction in GLCM Feature-Based Classification of Machined Surface Images. *Arabian Journal for Science and Engineering*, 1–23.

Pu, Z., Cui, Z., Tang, J., Wang, S., & Wang, Y. (2021). Multi-Modal Traffic Speed Monitoring: A Real-Time System Based on Passive Wi-Fi and Bluetooth Sensing Technology. *IEEE Internet of Things Journal*. doi:10.1109/JIOT.2021.3136031

Rahman, S. A., Tout, H., Talhi, C., & Mourad, A. (2020). Internet of Things intrusion Detection: Centralized, On-Device, or Federated Learning? *IEEE Network*, *34*(6), 310–317. doi:10.1109/MNET.011.2000286

Rahul, V. K., Vinayakumar, R., Soman, K., & Poornachandran, P. (2018). Evaluating shallow and deep neural networks for network intrusion detection systems in cyber security. *Proceedings of the 2018 9th Int. Conf. Comput. Commun. Netw. Technol. ICCCNT*.

Raymer, M. G. (2017). *Application: Quantum computing*. Quantum Physics. doi:10.1093/wentk/9780190250720.003.0010

Rehman Khan, A., Saba, T., Sadad, T., & Hong, S. (2022). Cloudbased framework for COVID-19 detection through feature fusion with bootstrap aggregated extreme learning machine. *Discrete Dynamics in Nature and Society*, *2022*, 1–7. doi:10.1155/2022/3111200

Reza, M. N., & Islam, M. (2021). Evaluation of Machine Learning Algorithms using Feature Selection Methods for Network Intrusion Detection Systems. *2021 5th International Conference on Electrical Information and Communication Technology (EICT)*, 1-6. 10.1109/EICT54103.2021.9733679

Ristè, da Silva, Ryan, Cross, Córcoles, Smolin, Gambetta, Chow, & Johnson. (2017). Demonstration of quantum advantage in machine learning. *NPJ Quantum Information, 3*(1), 16.

Rivest, R. L. (1991, November). Cryptography and machine learning. In *International Conference on the Theory and Application of Cryptology* (pp. 427-439). Springer Berlin Heidelberg.

Robin David. (n.d.). *GITHUB python DES*. https://github.com/RobinDavid/pydes/blob/master/LICENSE.md

Rongfeng, Z., Jiayong, L., Weina, N., Liang, L., Kai, L., & Shan, L. (2020). Preprocessing Method for Encrypted Traffic Based on Semisupervised Clustering. *Security and Communication Networks*, *2020*, 1–13.

Rosen-Zvi, M., Klein, E., Kanter, I., & Kinzel, W. (2002). Mutual learning in a tree parity machine and its application to cryptography. *Physical Review. E, 66*(6), 066135.

Saba, T. (2020). Intrusion detection in smart city hospitals using ensemble classifiers. In *Proceedings of the 13th International Conference on the Developments on eSystems Engineering (DeSE2020)*. IEEE. 10.1109/DeSE51703.2020.9450247

Saba, T., Haseeb, K., Shah, A. A., Rehman, A., Tariq, U., & Mehmood, Z. (2021). A machine-learning-based approach for autonomous IoT security. *IT Professional*, *23*(3), 69–75. doi:10.1109/MITP.2020.3031358

Saba, T., Sadad, T., Rehman, A., Mehmood, Z., & Javaid, Q. (2021). Intrusion detection system through advance machine learning for the internet of things networks. *IT Professional*, *23*(2), 58–64. doi:10.1109/MITP.2020.2992710

Sahil, G., Kuljeet, K., Shalini, B., Gagangeet, S. A., Graham, M., Neeraj, K., Albert, Y. Z., & Rajiv, R. (2020). En-ABC: An ensemble artificial bee colony based anomaly detection scheme for cloud environment. *Journal of Parallel and Distributed Computing*, *135*, 219–233. doi:10.1016/j.jpdc.2019.09.013

Sahu, M., Padhy, N., Gantayat, S. S., & Sahu, A. K. (2022). Local binary pattern-based reversible data hiding. *CAAI Transactions on Intelligence Technology*, *7*(4), 695–709. doi:10.1049/cit2.12130

Samsudeen, S., & Senthil Kumar, G. (2023). FeduLPM: Federated Unsupervised Learning-Based Predictive Model for Speed Control in Customizable Automotive Variants. *IEEE Sensors Journal*, *23*(13), 14700–14708. doi:10.1109/JSEN.2023.3275154

Sasaki, Y. (2012). Quantum computing and number theory. *Quantum Information and Quantum Computing*. doi:10.1142/9789814425223_0005

Scheidat, T., Kalbitz, M., & Vielhauer, C. (2017). Biometric authentication based on 2D/3D sensing of forensic hand-writing traces. *IET Biometrics*, *6*(4), 316–324. doi:10.1049/iet-bmt.2016.0127

Sectigostore. (n.d.). https://sectigostore.com/blog/5-differences-between-symmetric-vs-asymmetric-encrypt

Sengar, S. S., Hariharan, U., & Rajkumar, K. (2020, March). Multimodal biometric authentication system using deep learning method. In *2020 International Conference on Emerging Smart Computing and Informatics (ESCI)* (pp. 309-312). IEEE. 10.1109/ESCI48226.2020.9167512

Shabtai, Moskovitch, Elovici, & Glezer. (2009). Detection of malicious code by applying machine learning classifiers on static features: A state-of-the-art survey. *Information Security Technical Report, 14*(1), 16–29.

Shahab, S. (2022). When Smart Cities Get Smarter via Machine Learning: An In-Depth Literature Review. *IEEE Access : Practical Innovations, Open Solutions*.

Shang, J., Guan, H., Liu, Y., Bi, H., Yang, L., & Wang, M. (2021). A novel method for vehicle headlights detection using salient region segmentation and PHOG feature. *Multimedia Tools and Applications*, *80*(15), 22821–22841. doi:10.1007/s11042-020-10501-8

Sharma & Arun. (2022). Priority Queueing Model-Based IoT Middleware for Load Balancing. *2022 6th International Conference on Intelligent Computing and Control Systems (ICICCS)*, 425-430. 10.1109/ICICCS53718.2022.9788218

Sharma, A. (2023). A novel approach of unsupervised feature selection using iterative shrinking and expansion algorithm. *Journal of Interdisciplinary Mathematics*, *26*(3), 519–530. doi:10.47974/JIM-1678

Sharma, A., & Singh, B. (2020). AE-LGBM: Sequence-based novel approach to detect interacting protein pairs via ensemble of autoencoder and LightGBM. *Computers in Biology and Medicine*, *103964*, 103964. Advance online publication. doi:10.1016/j.compbiomed.2020.103964 PMID:32911276

Sharma, K., Aggarwal, A., Singhania, T., Gupta, D., & Khanna, A. (2019). Hiding Data in Images Using Cryptography and Deep Neural Network. *Journal of Artificial Intelligence and Systems*, *1*(1), 143–162. doi:10.33969/AIS.2019.11009

Sharma, P., Austin, D., & Liu, H. (2019). Attacks on Machine Learning: Adversarial Examples in Connected and Autonomous Vehicles. *IEEE International Symposium on Technologies for Homeland Security (HST)*.

Shashi, K. S., Anurag, S. T., & Gaurav, K. T. (2015). Secure Medical Data Transmission by using ECC with Mutual Authentication in WSNs. *Elsevier Procedia Computer Science*, *70*, 455–461.

Sheng, Y.-B., & Zhou, L. (2017). Distributed secure quantum machine learning. *Science Bulletin*, *62*(14), 1025–1029. doi:10.1016/j.scib.2017.06.007 PMID:36659494

Shen, R., Zhen, T., & Li, Z. (2023). YOLOv5-Based Model Integrating Separable Convolutions for Detection of Wheat Head Images. *IEEE Access : Practical Innovations, Open Solutions*, *11*, 12059–12074. doi:10.1109/ACCESS.2023.3241808

Shivashankar & Mehta. (2016). MANET topology for disaster management using wireless sensor network. *International Conference on Communication and Signal Processing, ICCSP 2016*, 736–740. . doi:10.1109/ICCSP.2016.7754242

Silva, L. A., Leithardt, V. R. Q., Batista, V. F. L., Villarrubia González, G., & De Paz Santana, J. F. (2023). Automated Road Damage Detection Using UAV Images and Deep Learning Techniques. *IEEE Access : Practical Innovations, Open Solutions*, *11*, 62918–62931. doi:10.1109/ACCESS.2023.3287770

Singh, N., Agrawal, A., & Khan, R. A. (2018). Voice biometric: A technology for voice based authentication. *Advanced Science, Engineering and Medicine, 10*(7-8), 754–759. doi:10.1166/asem.2018.2219

Singh, T. (2017). Evolving threat agents: Ransomware and their variants. *International Journal of Computer Applications, 164*(7), 28–34. doi:10.5120/ijca2017913666

Singla, A., & Sharma, N. (2022). IoT Group Key Management using Incremental Gaussian Mixture Model. *2022 3rd International Conference on Electronics and Sustainable Communication Systems (ICESC),* 469-474. 10.1109/IC-ESC54411.2022.9885644

Smith, J., & Johnson, A. (2019). Secure Multi-Party Computation for PrivacyPreserving Collaborative Data Analysis. *Journal of Privacy and Security, 15*(2), 123–145.

Song, F., Guo, Z., & Mei, D. (2010, November). Feature selection using principal component analysis. In *2010 international conference on system science, engineering design and manufacturing informatization* (Vol. 1, pp. 27-30). IEEE.

Song, D., Brumley, D., Yin, H., Caballero, J., Jager, I., & Kang, M. G. (2008). BitBlaze: A New Approach to Computer Security via Binary Analysis. *Proceedings of the 4th International Conference on Information Systems Security.* 10.1007/978-3-540-89862-7_1

Speciner, M., Perlman, R., & Kaufman, C. (2002). *Network Security: Private Communications in a Public World.* Prentice Hall PTR.

Srinivasan, S., & Deepalakshmi, P. (2021). Malware Multi Perspective Analytics with Auto Deduction in Cybersecurity. *2021 Fifth International Conference on I-SMAC (IoT in Social, Mobile, Analytics and Cloud) (I-SMAC),* 1627-1630. 10.1109/I-SMAC52330.2021.9640803

Statista. (2021). *Internet of Things (IoT) connected devices installed base worldwide from 2015 to 2025 (in billions).* https://www.statista.com/statistics/471264/iot-number-of-connecteddevices-worldwide/

Su, K., Li, J., & Fu, H. (2011, September). Smart city and the applications. In *2011 international conference on electronics, communications and control (ICECC)* (pp. 1028-1031). IEEE.

Suryawanshi, V. A., & Chaturvedi, A. (2022). Novel Predictive Control and Monitoring System based on IoT for Evaluating Industrial Safety Measures. *IJEER, 10*(4), 1050–1057. doi:10.37391/ijeer.100448

Tan, S., Knott, B., & Wu, D. J. (2021). CryptGPU: Fast Privacy-Preserving Machine Learning on the GPU. *2021 IEEE Symposium on Security and Privacy (SP),* 1021-1038. 10.1109/SP40001.2021.00098

Tan, Z., Zhang, H., Hu, P., & Gao, R. (2021). Distributed Outsourced Privacy-Preserving Gradient Descent Methods among Multiple Parties. *Hindawi Security and Communication Networks,* 1–16.

Tao, S., Zhang, X., Cai, H., Lv, Z., Hu, C., & Xie, H. (2018). Gait based biometric personal authentication by using MEMS inertial sensors. *Journal of Ambient Intelligence and Humanized Computing, 9*(5), 1705–1712. doi:10.1007/s12652-018-0880-6

Technologies, S. C. (2011). Advancing Healthcare Systems. In *The 2011 International Joint Conference on Neural Networks.* IEEE. https://en.wikipedia.org/wiki/Data_fusion

Teguh Wahyono. (2022). *Machine Learning Applications for Anomaly Detection.* Research Anthology on Machine Learning Techniques, Methods, and Applications.

Theepa Sri, S., & Rama, A. (2023). Efficient Intrusion Detection System Using Convolutional Long Short Term Memory Network. doi:10.1109/CSITSS60515.2023.10334106

Thomas, E., Nair, P. B., John, S. N., & Dominic, M. (2014, July). Image fusion using Daubechies complex wavelet transform and lifting wavelet transform: a multiresolution approach. In *2014 Annual International Conference on Emerging Research Areas: Magnetics, Machines and Drives (AICERA/iCMMD)* (pp. 1-5). IEEE. 10.1109/AICERA.2014.6908205

Tutorialspoint. (n.d.). https://www.tutorialspoint.com/difference-between-private-key-and-public-key

Udhaya Mugil & Metilda Florence. (2022). *Efficient Sensitive File Encryption Strategy with Access Control and Integrity Auditing.* Academic Press.

Ullah, A., Wang, J., Anwar, M. S., Ahmad, U., Saeed, U., & Fei, Z. (2019). Facial expression recognition of nonlinear facial variations using deep locality de-expression residue learning in the wild. *Electronics (Basel)*, *8*(12), 1487.

Uludag, U., Pankanti, S., & Jain, A. K. (2005, July). Fuzzy vault for fingerprints. In *International Conference on Audio- and Video-Based Biometric Person Authentication* (pp. 310-319). Springer Berlin Heidelberg. 10.1007/11527923_32

Uma Maheswari, S., & Arunesh, K. (2020). Unsupervised Binary BAT algorithm based Network Intrusion Detection System using enhanced multiple classifiers. *2020 International Conference on Smart Electronics and Communication (ICOSEC).* 10.1109/ICOSEC49089.2020.9215453

Urooj, U., Maarof, M. A. B., & Al-rimy, B. A. S. (2021). A proposed Adaptive Pre-Encryption Crypto-Ransomware Early Detection Model. *2021 3rd International Cyber Resilience Conference (CRC), Langkawi Island, Malaysia*, 1-6. 10.1109/CRC50527.2021.9392548

V. Srividya, B., & Sasi, S. (2021). An emphasis on quantum cryptography and quantum key distribution. *Cryptography - Recent Advances and Future Developments.* doi:10.5772/intechopen.95383

Vasilchenko, A. (2024, January 23). *AI Biometric Authentication for Enterprise Security.* Retrieved from https://mobidev. biz/blog/ai-biometrics-technology-authentication-verification-security

Venkatesh, J., Vetriselvi, V., Parthasarathi, R., Subrahmanya, G., & Rao, V. R. K. (2018). Identification and isolation of crypto ransomware using honeypot. *2018 Fourteenth International Conference on Information Processing (ICINPRO)*, 1-6. 10.1109/ICINPRO43533.2018.9096875

Viswanathan, M., Loganathan, G. B., & Srinivasan, S. (2020, September). IKP based biometric authentication using artificial neural network. In AIP Conference Proceedings (Vol. 2271, No. 1). AIP Publishing. doi:10.1063/5.0025229

VTSCADA. (n.d.). https://www.vtscada.com/help/Content/Scripting/Tasks/proEncryptionAnddecryption.htm

Vyas, T., Prajapati, P., & Gadhwal, S. (2015). A survey and evaluation of supervised machine learning techniques for spam e-mail filtering. In *Proceedings of the 2015 IEEE international conference on electrical, computer and communication technologies (ICECCT).* IEEE.

Wang, P., Qiao, J., & Liu, N. (2022). An Improved Convolutional Neural Network-Based Scene Image Recognition Method. *Computational Intelligence and Neuroscience, 2022*(2830–2842), e3464984. . doi:10.1155/2022/3464984

Wang. (2021). A new hybrid forecasting model based on SW-LSTM and wavelet packet decomposition: A case study of oil futures prices. *Computational Intelligence and Neuroscience, 2021*, 1–22. PMID:34335724

Wang, L., & Machines, S. V. (2005). *Theory and Applications.* Springer.

Wang, X., Liu, J., Qiu, T., Mu, C., Chen, C., & Zhou, P. (2020). A Real-Time Collision Prediction Mechanism With Deep Learning for Intelligent Transportation System. *IEEE Transactions on Vehicular Technology, 69*(9), 9497–9508. doi:10.1109/TVT.2020.3003933

Wang, Z., Huo, W., Yu, P., Qi, L., Song, G., & Cao, N. (2019). Performance Evaluation of Region-Based Convolutional Neural Networks Toward Improved Vehicle Taillight Detection. *Applied Sciences (Basel, Switzerland), 9*(18), 3753–3753. doi:10.3390/app9183753

Wu, H. (2024). Feature-Weighted Naive Bayesian Classifier for Wireless Network Intrusion Detection. *Security and Communication Networks, 2024*, 1–13. doi:10.1155/2024/7065482

Xiang, W., Shen, G., Yibin, G., Shiyu, Z., Yonghui, D., & Daqing, W. (2022). A Combined Prediction Model for Hog Futures Prices Based on WOA-LightGBM-CEEMDAN. *Complexity, 22*, 1–15.

Xie, G., Shangguan, A., Fei, R., Hei, X., Ji, W., & Qian, F. (2021). Unmanned System Safety Decision-Making Support: Analysis and Assessment of Road Traffic Accidents. *IEEE/ASME Transactions on Mechatronics, 26*(2), 633–644. doi:10.1109/TMECH.2020.3043471

Xu, K., Wu, J., Huang, T., & Liang, L. (2022). An Improvement of a Mapping Method Based on Ant Colony Algorithm Applied to Smart Cities. *Applied Sciences (Basel, Switzerland), 12*(22), 11814. doi:10.3390/app122211814

Xu, W., Qi, Y., & Evans, D. (2016). Automatically Evading Classifiers: A Case Study on PDF Malware Classifiers. *Conference of Network and Distributed System Security Symposium*, 1–15. 10.14722/ndss.2016.23115

Yang, C. (2020). Privacy-Preserving Collaborative Social Network Analysis using Secure Multi-Party Computation. *Social Network Analysis and Mining, 10*(1), 1–22.

Yang, G., He, Y., Li, X., Liu, H., & Lan, T. (2022). Gabor-glcm-based texture feature extraction using flame image to predict the o2 content and no x. *ACS Omega, 7*(5), 3889–3899. doi:10.1021/acsomega.1c03397 PMID:35155886

Yang, W., Wan, B., & Qu, X. (2020). A Forward Collision Warning System Using Driving Intention Recognition of the Front Vehicle and V2V Communication. *IEEE Access : Practical Innovations, Open Solutions, 8*, 11268–11278. doi:10.1109/ACCESS.2020.2963854

Yan, S., Haowei, L., Xu, P., & Dan, L. (2022). A Method of Intrusion Detection Based on WOA-XGBoost Algorithm. *Discrete Dynamics in Nature and Society, 22*, 1–9. doi:10.1155/2022/7771216

Yar, H., Hussain, T., Khan, Z. A., Koundal, D., Lee, M. Y., & Baik, S. W. (2021). Vision sensor-based real-time fire detection in resource-constrained IoT environments. *Computational Intelligence and Neuroscience, 2021*, 1–15. doi:10.1155/2021/5195508 PMID:34970311

Yasin, M., Cheema, A. R., & Kausar, F. (2010). Analysis of Internet Download Manager for collection of digital forensic artefacts. *Digital Investigation, 7*(1-2), 90–94. doi:10.1016/j.diin.2010.08.005

Yonghong, Wang, & Cui. (2013). Secure communication mechanism for smart distribution network integrated with subcarrier multiplexed quantum key distribution. *Power Syst. Technol., 11*, 36.

YouTube. (n.d.). https://youtu.be/Sy0sXa73PZA

Yuan, H., Lei, Z., You, X., Dong, Z., Zhang, H., Zhang, C., Zhao, Y., & Liu, J. (2023). Fault diagnosis of driving gear in rack and pinion drives based on multi-scale local binary pattern extraction and sparse representation. *Measurement Science & Technology, 34*(5), 055017. doi:10.1088/1361-6501/acbab4

Yucel, M., & Bekdaş, G. (2023). Review and Applications of Machine Learning and Artificial Intelligence in Engineering: Overview for Machine Learning and AI. *Complex & Intelligent Systems*.

Zhang, J., Nazir, S., Huang, A., & Alharbi, A. (2020). Multicriteria Decision and Machine Learning Algorithms for Component Security Evaluation: Library-Based Overview. *Hindawi Security and Communication Networks*, (September), 1–14.

Zhang, W., & Zhang, L. (2020). Secure Multi-Party Computation for Collaborative Internet of Things Data Analysis. *IEEE Internet of Things Journal*, *7*(5), 3789–3807.

Zhang, X., Cheng, D., Jia, P., Dai, Y., & Xu, X. (2020). An efficient android-based multimodal biometric authentication system with face and voice. *IEEE Access : Practical Innovations, Open Solutions*, *8*, 102757–102772. doi:10.1109/ACCESS.2020.2999115

Zhang, X., Story, B., & Rajan, D. (2022). Night Time Vehicle Detection and Tracking by Fusing Vehicle Parts From Multiple Cameras. *IEEE Transactions on Intelligent Transportation Systems*, *23*(7), 8136–8156. doi:10.1109/TITS.2021.3076406

Zhang, Y. L., & Hamori, S. (2020). Forecasting crude oil market crashes using machine learning technologies. *Energies, 13*, 10.

Zhang, Y., Sharif, M., Chen, H., & Lee, W. (2010). Side-Channel Leaks in Web Applications: a Reality Today, a Challenge Tomorrow. *Proceedings of the 17th ACM Conference on Computer and Communications Security.*

Zhao, Ikram, Asghar, Kaafar, Chaabane, & Ilakarathna. (2019). A decade of mal-activity reporting: a retrospective analysis of internet malicious activity blacklists. *Proceedings of the AsiaCCS - 2019 ACM Asia Conference on Computer and Communications Security, 193–205.*

Zhao, B., Liu, B., Wu, C., Yu, W., & Su, J. (2016). A novel ntt-based authentication scheme for 10-ghz quantum key distribution systems. *IEEE Transactions on Industrial Electronics*, *63*(8), 5101–5108.

Zhao, R., Yin, J., Zhi, X., & Gui, G. (2021). An Efficient Intrusion Detection Method Based on Dynamic Autoencoder. *IEEE Wireless Communications Letters*, *10*(8), 1707–1711. doi:10.1109/LWC.2021.3077946

Zhou, J., Lu, L., Lei, Y., & Chen, X. (2014). Research on improving security of protection for power system secondary system by quantum key technology. *Power Syst. Technol*, *38*(6), 1518–1522.

Zhou, Y., Qin, R., Xu, H., Sadiq, S., & Yu, Y. (2018). A Data Quality Control Method for Seafloor Observatories: The Application of Observed Time Series Data in the East China Sea. *Sensors (Basel)*, *18*(8), 2628. doi:10.3390/s18082628 PMID:30103440

Zhu, S., & Han, Y. (2021, August). Generative trapdoors for public key cryptography based on automatic entropy optimization. *China Communications*, *18*(8), 35–46. doi:10.23919/JCC.2021.08.003

Zia, U., McCartney, M., Scotney, B., Martinez, J., & Sajjad, A. (2022). A Novel Image Encryption Technique Using Multi-Coupled Map Lattice System with Generalized Symmetric Map and Adaptive Control Parameter. *SN Computer Science*, *4*(1), 81. Advance online publication. doi:10.1007/s42979-022-01503-4

Zulfiqar, M., Syed, F., Khan, M. J., & Khurshid, K. (2019, July). Deep face recognition for biometric authentication. In *2019 international conference on electrical, communication, and computer engineering (ICECCE)* (pp. 1-6). IEEE.

Zulkurnain, N. F., Azhar, M. A., & Mallik, M. A. (2022, February). Content-Based Image Retrieval System Using Fuzzy Colour and Local Binary Pattern with Apache Lucene. In *Proceedings of Second International Conference on Advances in Computer Engineering and Communication Systems: ICACECS 2021* (pp. 13-20). Singapore: Springer Nature Singapore. 10.1007/978-981-16-7389-4_2

About the Contributors

Vijayalakshmi G V Mahesh received her BE in Electronics and Communication Engineering from Bangalore University, India in 1999, and M.Tech in Digital Communication and Networking from Visvesvaraya Technological University in 2005 and the Ph.D. degree from the Vellore Institute of Technology, Vellore, India. Currently she is working as an Associate Professor at BMS Institute of Technology and Management, Bangalore, India. She has been in academics for over 19 years and has published her research in various reputed journals and conferences. Her research interests include Machine Learning, Image Processing, Pattern Recognition and Deep learning, Affective computing. She has Memberships in Professional Bodies such as ISTE and IEI.

P. Visalakshi is an Associate Professor at SRM Institute of Science and Technology based in Dist, Tamil Nadu.

R. Uma is working as Associate Professor in the Department of Computer Science and Engineering, Sri Sairam Engineering College, Chennai, India. with 23 years of teaching experience for undergraduate and post graduate students in Computer Science Department. She has a Doctorate degree in Computer Science and Engineering from Anna University Chennai, India. She also completed her Master Degree in Computer Science and Engineering from College of Engineering Guindy, Anna University, India and Bachelor Degree from university of Madras. She has published her papers over 14 International Journals. She is a member of CSI, IACSIT and life member of ISTE. Her current research interest includes Information Retrieval, Data Mining, Deep learning and Machine learning .

* * *

Meenakshi A. is working as an Assistant Professor in Computer Science and Applications at SRM Institute of Science and Technology, Vadapalani Campus, Chennai, India for more than 24 years. She obtained her Bachelor's degree in Mathematics from University of Madras, Chennai, India, Master's degree in Computer Applications, M.Phil in Computer Science from Bharathidasan University, Tricky, India. M.S in Computer Science and Engineering and Doctorate in Computer Science and Engineering at S.R.M University. Her specialization includes Distributed Computing, Clous computing, Machine Learning and Deep Learning. She published more than 10 papers in Q1 and Q2 journals. She is a member in CSI, ACM transactions.

A. Arokiaraj Jovith is working as Assistant Professor in the Department of Networking and Communications and Supporting Faculty in the Internal Quality Assurance Cell (IQAC) at SRM Institute of Science and Technology, Kattankulathur, Chennai, India. He has published 2 books and 2 Book chapters, 6 patents and over 30 articles in Peer-reviewed Indexed Journals. His Research areas are Wireless Sensor Networks, IoT, Deep Learning and Network security.

G. Arun, a highly accomplished individual in the field of Computer Science and Engineering, is a dedicated academician and researcher with a rich and diverse professional journey. He is not only a distinguished educator but also a prolific researcher. He has published numerous papers and actively participates in conferences, showcasing his commitment to advancing the field of Computer Science and Engineering.

Prakash B. has completed his Ph.D from Anna University, Chennai in the year 2019. Prakash is currently working as Assistant Professor in the Department of Computing Technology in SRM Institute of Science and Technology, Kattangulathur, Chennai. His Research Interest includes Wireless Networks, Optimization Algorithms and Machine Learning. He has published more than 20 papers in National and International Journals and also has 3 patents out of which one is granted. He has more than 15 years of experience in Professional Teaching for young Engineering Students. He has attended many National and International conferences and presented papers. He has organized various National Level Technical Symposiums and Conferences and He is a Life member of ISTE.

Vetriselvi D. is a Research Scholar pursuing studies in the Department of Computing Technologies at the School of Computing, SRM Institute of Science and Technology, Kattankulathur, Chennai, India. Her research domain is Deep Learning.

Joohi Garg is working as an Assistant Professor in the Department of Electronics and Communication Engineering, Mody University of Science and Technology (MUST), Lakshmangarh (Sikar), Rajasthan, India. She received her B.Tech in Electronics and Communication Engineering from ACEIT, Jaipur, India (2011) and M.Tech in 2013 from Mody Institute of Technology and Science, Rajasthan, India. She completed her Ph.D. from Malaviya National Institute of Technology (MNIT), Jaipur, in 2023. She has contributed efforts as a Chair to the RFID Student Branch Chapter, MNIT, Jaipur, since 2020. She was Chair of the Women in Engineering (WIE) Committee in InCAP 2021, Jaipur, India. She also received an appreciation certificate as a reviewer at the 1st IEEE International Conference Microwave, Antennas, and Propagation Conference MAPCON- 2022, held in Bengaluru, India, and IEEE- MAC 2023, held in MNNIT Allahabad, etc. Her research interests include FSS, Metamaterials, Absorbers, Rasorbers, Conformal Antenna and their applications.

Shaifali Garg, Associate Professor, Amity Business School, Amity University, Madhya Pradesh (Gwalior), has 14 years of experience in area of Human Resource management. Earlier she was working with a GLA University, Mathura and associated with Galgotias Educational Institute, Greater Noida, so far she got 11 papers published in Scopus indexed journal and presented research papers in various National and International Conferences and also published papers in renowned UGC Care journals. Teaching students effectively and innovative ways is her strength. She believe in work out for mutual support and cooperation in building the students path of success.

Dankan Gowda V. is currently working as an Assistant Professor in the Department of Electronics and Communication Engineering at BMS Institute of Technology and Management in Bangalore. Previously, he worked as a Research Fellow at ADA DRDO and as a Software Engineer at Robert Bosch. With a total experience of 14 years, including teaching and industry, Dr. Gowda has made significant contributions to both academia and research. He has published over 60 research papers in renowned international journals and conferences. In recognition of his innovative work, Dr. Gowda has been granted six patents, including four from Indian authorities and two international patents. His research interests primarily lie in the fields of IoT and Signal Processing, where he has conducted workshops and handled industry projects. Dr. Gowda is passionate about teaching and strives to create an engaging and effective learning environment for his students. He consistently seeks opportunities to enhance his knowledge and stay updated with the latest advancements in his field.

Venkata J. is an Assistant Professor in SRM Institute of Science and Technology, Chennai has been serving in Education Profession for the past 13+ years. Earlier he was working as a Lecturer in RDB College, Papanasam for about 4 Years. Currently he carries out Research in Mobile Computing with Neural Networks. He has guided more than 50 Students in completing their UG and PG Graduation Projects.

Manoj Kushwaha is currently working as an Assistant Professor in SRM Institute of Science and Technology, Chennai, India. He is pursuing his PhD in SRM Institute of Science and Technology, Chennai, India. He completed his M.Tech. from Vel Tech University, Chennai, India and B.Tech. Computer Science Engineering from Vel Tech University, Chennai, India in the year 2020 and 2016 respectively. He has 2 years of industrial exposure in information technology. His research interests include Machine Learning, Deep Learning, and Artificial Intelligence. He is an excellent learner and knowledge sharer.

Sivasakthi M. is an educationist. He has received B.Sc and M.Sc in Computer Science from Periyar University, Salem, Tamil Nadu, India in 2004 and 2006 respectively, M. Phil in Computer Science from University of Madras, Chennai, in 2007, and he obtained Ph. D in Computer Science - Engineering Education from National Institute of Technical Teachers Training and Research (Ministry of HRD, Govt. of INDIA) affiliated to University of Madras in 2013. He is qualified UGC-NET conducted by NTA, Govt. of India. He is working as Assistant Professor in the College of Science and Humanities, SRM Institute of Science and Technology, Vadapalani City Campus, Chennai, since 2017. He has a decade of experience in the ground of teaching. He has received 'Discipline Star' certificate from NPTEL-SWAYAM. He has obtained topper in Database Management System and Programming in Java, gold in 'Joy of Computing using python', Silver in 'Learning Analytics Tools', and elite in 'Data Science for Engineers', 'Python for Data Science' and in Machine Learning Certificate course conducted by IIT-NPTEL. He is International Java Programmer Certified by Sun Micro System in 2008. His research is concerned with the pedagogical aspects of computer programming, Computing education and Machine Learning. He has contributed his research publications through 11 Journal publications, 13 Conference proceedings. He is life member in professional bodies such as Indian Society for Technical Education Computer Society of India and Annual member in Computer Science Teachers Association and Indian Science Congress.

Abirami M. S. is currently working as an Associate Professor in the Department of Computational Intelligence, SRM Institute of Science and Technology, Chennai, India. She received the Ph.D. degree in Kidney segmentation from abdominal CT images and finding its abnormalities from Bharathiar

University, Coimbatore, India. She received the M.Tech. degree in Computer Science and Engineering from SRM Institute of Science and Technology, Chennai. She received the undergraduate degree from Bharathidasan University, Tamilnadu, India. She has authored or co-authored over 30 research papers in reputed journals/conferences. She has published 6 patents and 1 patent granted. She has organized 5 national research training programmes in SRM IST and showing interest to be a part of various training programmes. Her research interests include Computer Vision, Machine Learning, Deep Learning, Medical Image Processing, Pattern Recognition, Internet of Things and Distributed Computing. She is a member of Institution of Engineers (India), Indian Society for Technical Education.

K. D. V. Prasad works as a Faculty of Research at Symbiosis Institute of Business Management, Hyderabad; Symbiosis International (Deemed University), Pune, India. Dr. Prasad holds a Master's in Computer Applications and a Master's in Software Systems from BITS, Pilani; MBA (Human Resources), IGNOU, New Delhi. Dr. Prasad possesses a Ph.D. in Business Management (Kanpur University), and PhD in Business Administration (RTM Nagpur University. He is AIMA-Certified Management Teacher and Fellow, World HR Board, Carlton Advanced Management Institute, USA; Fellowship of the Management and Business Research Council (FMBRC) by Open Association Research Society, Delaware, USA Dr. Prasad Published over 100 articles in Scopus/WoS indexed journals and 3 books.

Jayashree R., PhD, is an assistant professor at the College of Science and Humanities, SRM Institute of Science and Technology, Kattankulathur, Chennai, India. She has served as coordinator for conducting various events in the National Level Symposium and Workshops organized by SRM IST. She has published many papers in International and National Journals. She is a reviewer in Scopus and Web of Science Indexed journals: IEEE Access, IEEE Transactions on Computational Social systems and The Journal of SuperComputers. She won a Gold Medal for a paper entitled "A splay tree based approach for a recommending system in ranking a community driven question-answering website", which was presented under Faculty category for Research Day 2019. She is an Editorial board member of the journal "American Journal of Education and Information Technology". Her area of interests includes Machine Learning and Deep learning.

V. Srivatsan is currently studying under Sri Sairam Engineering college. Professionalizes in Cyber Security and Game Development Domains, also in some other domains such as AR/VR, networking, Web and App development. Published few obscure tools for bruteforce in deep web blog and grey hat hacking, as well as production of few game titles.

R. Thenmozhi is working as Associate Professor in the Department of Computing Technologies and Supporting Faculty in the Internal Quality Assurance Cell (IQAC) at SRM Institute of Science and Technology, Kattankulathur, Chennai, India. She has published 1 book and 3 Book chapters, 7 patents and over 25 articles in Peer- reviewed Indexed Journals. Her Research areas are Vehicular Adhoc Network, Machine Learning, Deep Learning and Network security.

Index

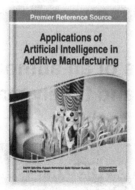

  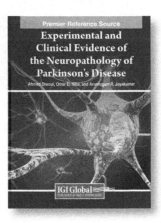 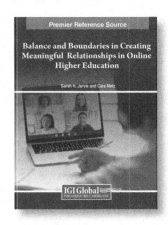

Submit an Open Access Book Proposal

Have Your Work Fully & Freely Available Worldwide After Publication

Seeking the Following Book Classification Types:

Authored & Edited Monographs • Casebooks • Encyclopedias • Handbooks of Research

Gold, Platinum, & Retrospective OA Opportunities to Choose From

Easily Track Your Work in Our Advanced Manuscript Submission System With **Rapid Turnaround Times**

Double-Blind Peer Review by Notable Editorial Boards (*Committee on Publication Ethics* (COPE) Certified)

Publications Adhere to All **Current OA Mandates & Compliances**

Affordable APCs *(Often 50% Lower Than the Industry Average)* Including Robust Editorial Service Provisions

Direct Connections with **Prominent Research Funders** & OA Regulatory Groups

Institution Level OA Agreements Available (Recommend or Contact Your Librarian for Details)

Join a **Diverse Community of 150,000+ Researchers Worldwide** Publishing With IGI Global

Content Spread Widely to Leading Repositories (AGOSR, ResearchGate, CORE, & More)

Retrospective Open Access Publishing

You Can Unlock Your Recently Published Work, Including Full Book & Individual Chapter Content to Enjoy All the Benefits of Open Access Publishing

Learn More

Printed in the United States
by Baker & Taylor Publisher Services